THE BRAIN DRAIN AND TAXATION

Theory and Empirical Analysis

THE BRAIN DRAIN AND TAXATION

II

Theory and Empirical Analysis

Edited by

JAGDISH N. BHAGWATI

Massachusetts Institute of Technology

1976

NORTH-HOLLAND PUBLISHING COMPANY
AMSTERDAM · NEW YORK · OXFORD

Library of Congress Catalog Card Number: 75–45070

ISBN North-Holland 0 7204–0428 2
ISBN American Elsevier 0 444–11076 3

Publishers:

NORTH-HOLLAND PUBLISHING COMPANY—AMSTERDAM · NEW YORK · OXFORD

Sole distributors for the U.S.A. and Canada:

AMERICAN ELSEVIER PUBLISHING COMPANY, INC.
52 VANDERBILT AVENUE, NEW YORK, N.Y. 10017

Library of Congress Cataloging in Publication Data
Main entry under title:

The Brain drain and taxation.

(The Brain drain ; 2)
Papers on the Bellagio Conference on the Brain Drain and Income Taxation, held Feb. 15-19, 1975.
Includes index.
1. Brain drain--Taxation--Congresses. I. Bhagwati, Jagdish N., 1934-   II. Bellagio Conference on the Brain Drain and Income Taxation, 1975. III. Series.
JV6487.B72   336.2'78   75-45070
ISBN 0-444-11076-3 (American Elsevier Pub.)

PRINTED IN THE NETHERLANDS

FOR

Anuradha Kristina

The royalties from this volume are being donated to UNICEF.

PREFACE

This volume of papers on the brain drain has grown out of the proceedings of the Bellagio Conference on The Brain Drain and Income Taxation, held at the Villa Serbelloni, February 15–19, 1975, with the aid of a generous grant from the Rockefeller Foundation and disbursed under the auspices of the Institute for World Order.

The immediate motivating force behind the conference was the intention to explore, from several different points of view, a proposal I advanced in 1972 in the *Daedalus*, and then developed further from an empirical standpoint in 1973 in *World Development* and from a theoretical angle in 1974 in the *Journal of Development Economics*, to levy a surtax on the incomes of professional immigrants from the less developed countries (LDCs) into the DCs. This 'link' proposal would raise funds which, in a preferred version, could be routed to the United Nations for disbursement in LDCs for their developmental programmes.

In consequence, the majority of the papers which appear in this volume address themselves, in some fashion, to the consequences of imposing such a surtax, instead of merely working out theoretical models and econometric estimates of the brain drain process per se. From the viewpoint of the professional economist, this is an added bonus as none of the earlier analyses of the brain drain had formally integrated their theoretical modelling with this kind (or, for that matter, any kind) of policy intervention.

To enhance the utility of the volume to potential graduate students in international economics, development and planning, and the economics of education, as also to researchers in these areas of theory and policy, each major section includes a fairly complete review-cum-synthesis of the major contributions in the area plus the papers at the conference. Where these are not provided, I have added shorter notes which place the paper(s) into perspective. Hence the volume is designed to be far more than just a standard printing of conference proceedings.

All the theoretical and econometric papers in this volume were published in a special symposium issue of the *Journal of Development Economics* (vol. 2, no. 3). Furthermore, the Bhagwati–Hamada paper (now in a revised and augmented version) and the Tobin paper were also published earlier in the same *Journal* (vol. 1, no. 1). Thanks are due to the editors of the *Journal* for permission to reprint these papers. It should also be mentioned that the economic and legal papers directly and *exclusively* addressed to the Bhagwati tax proposal have been published partially in another special symposium, in *World Development*, October 1975, and are being fully published, with substantial introduction and summary, as a companion volume to this one, by North-Holland; the volume is edited by Martin Partington and myself, and is entitled *Taxing the Brain Drain: A Proposal*.

Finally, I thank Grace Clark of the Institute for World Order, and Katherine Laperche Eisenhaure for their secretarial help throughout this project. Carlos Rodriguez, Koichi Hamada and Asim Dasgupta also assisted me generously with their ideas and comments on the numerous papers; and indeed all the Bellagio Conference participants, including Robert E.B. Lucas, Dharm Ghai, George Psacharopoulos, Carlos Diaz Alejandro, Rachel McCulloch and Peter Balacs, provided valuable input which led to substantial improvements in many of the papers. And, it is not merely a courtesy but also a great pleasure to thank Dr. and Mrs. William Olson of the Villa Serbelloni, without whose gracious hospitality and keen interest in the outcome of the conference, our task would have been much more difficult. Thanks must also be extended to the I.B.R.D., and especially to Ernest Stern and Timothy King, for contributing to the costs of the Bellagio conference the travel costs of one of the participants.

Jagdish N. Bhagwati
Cambridge, June 1975

CONTENTS

Part V – Alternative types of skilled migration

PART I

INTRODUCTION

CHAPTER 1

THE INTERNATIONAL BRAIN DRAIN AND TAXATION

A survey of the issues*

Jagdish N. BHAGWATI

Massachusetts Institute of Technology, Cambridge, MA 02139, U.S.A.

1. Introduction

The international emigration of skilled people from the less developed countries (LDCs), to the developed countries (DCs), has become a matter for concern at LDC levels for a number of years. In fact, as is often the case, this question was to become particularly topical when some of the DCs themselves (e.g., Britain) became concerned about their own loss of skilled manpower to other DCs (e.g., the United States). The issue has characteristically reached international forums, with an outpouring of resolutions and reports from a number of agencies of the United Nations.[1]

At the same time, the matching output of academic writings[2] on the subject, largely stemming from the countries of immigration, has been surprisingly in the *other* direction: the complaints of the LDCs find little echo, and if anything an irritated response of the 'you do not understand the issues involved' variety,

---

*This paper was prepared for the Conference on Brain Drain and Income Taxation, in Bellagio, Italy, February 15–19, 1975, to introduce many of the major issues to be discussed at the Conference.

[1]Thus, note the following: UN General Assembly Resolution 3017 (XXVII) on the outflow of trained personnel from LDCs to DCs; Resolution 1573 (L) of the Economic and Social Council of the UN (ECOSOC); and Conference Resolution 39(III) and Resolution I (II) of the Intergovernmental Group on the Transfer of Technology at UNCTAD. In addition to these, and other, intergovernmental resolutions, there have been numerous studies and reports by multilateral and governmental agencies, of which the following may be noted: (i) a number by UNITAR, published as Research Reports and occasionally presented by the Secretary-General to The Economic and Social Council; a major ongoing study, under the direction of William Glaser at Columbia University, of the international movement of students and professionals from LDCs, focusing mainly on motivational patterns from a sociological, as distinct from economic, standpoint; (ii) reports by UNESCO (SC/W5/57 of 29 February 1968 and 17C/58 of 10 October 1972); (iii) ongoing studies by UNCTAD, Centre for Development Planning, Projections and Policies (CDPPP) and WHO, which is currently conducting a major analysis of the international movement of physicians and nurses (HMD/73.5).

[2]The adjective 'academic' is deliberately used as many DC governmental reports take a more concerned viewpoint. A good example is the recent U.S. House (1974) report on the subject.

so that one might well infer that the concern of several LDCs and UN agencies is neatly balanced by the (possible) complacency of the academics.

Before I discuss the substantive issues involved in this debate, it is worth noting that the discrepancy between academic opinion and public policymaking is not entirely novel to economists with a historical feel for their subject. In fact, economists have only to remind themsevles that Keynesian economics, the greatest professional advance of the present century in their subject, was anticipated by the policies of deficit spending precisely directed at reducing unemployment. So perhaps a little humility, and a more persistent attempt at discovering the possible realities lurking behind the concerns of the LDCs, may well repay handsome dividends. And the impatience of some of us with the LDCs, as exemplified beautifully by the following characteristic quote from my good friend Harry Johnson (1972) in another context, may well be the complacent and erroneous attitude to start from:

> It is in fact very unfortunate, in my judgement, that the less developed countries have chosen, and particularly that UNCTAD has chosen, to put so much weight on the link proposal as the way ahead in development assistance, and to support that proposal with obsolete arguments derived from the 1930s. ... But I can understand that countries that are thirty years behind the advanced countries technologically find it most comfortable to be thirty years behind them intellectually as well, and to select their approved advisers and spokesmen accordingly – though one might have expected the concept of 'leapfrogging' to be as applicable to intellectual as to industrial development.

The present survey of the issues raised by the international brain drain is undertaken keeping this historical perspective in mind, and focuses the analysis especially on the issues pertinent to the problem of devising taxes related to the brain drain: a focus that follows from the subject matter of this conference.

2. Flows and consequences

The main outlines of the gross flows of skilled manpower from the LDCs to the DCs are well known by now: and the readers can find the necessary statistics for the U.S., U.K. and Canada in the papers for this conference by Bhagwati and Dellalfar (1975), Balacs and Gordon (1975), and DeVoretz and Maki (1975), respectively.[3] These three countries of immigration seem to

---

[3]These three papers are addressed to making revenue estimates if a surtax, as I proposed in 1972, were levied on the incomes of professional immigrants into DCs in these DCs of immigration. These papers will appear in Bhagwati and Partington (1976). Additional information can be obtained also from the contributions of Lucas and Reubens at the conference, and printed in this volume. Also, the reader may consult two further sources: Friedman (1973) and U.S. House (1974).

provide over 75 percent of the flows by countries of destination, so that the trends in their immigration flows are generally good approximations to the trends in overall immigration flows from LDCs to DCs.[4]

2.1. Data problems

It is unfortunate that the data on immigration of skilled manpower are quite inadequate for a number of analytical purposes, though perhaps no more than several statistics which economists are perforce thrown back on using for their quantitative analysis (a point requiring some sense of perspective by us qua economists).[5] The major difficulties are clearly the following:

(1) The data on immigration, when systematically available, almost always relate to gross flows and do not include information on reverse migrations. Such reverse migrations may well be of the order of up to a quarter of the gross flows at any point of time, if one may generalize from a very limited number of surveys (such as that cited in the Balacs–Gordon paper on the UK); and to-and-fro migrations of the same people have been attested to, not merely by casual empiricism, but also by more systematic studies, such as that conducted recently on Swedish skilled migrants by Friborg.[6]

(2) When it comes to skilled migrants, again the category of immigration used in the United States studies, for example, fails to include those skilled immigrants who come under the categories of 'relatives' or 'refugees'. A female Harvard Ph.D. in economics from an LDC, working at a professorial level, can thus marry an M.I.T. Professor of Economics and enter as an immigrant 'relative' and not be registered in the data that the Bhagwati–Dellalfar study utilizes, for example.

(3) One does not have any systematic estimates of illegal immigration: a phenomenon that is of some importance in the U.S. and, by available accounts, does not exclude the PTK (Professional, Technical and Kindred) categories altogether.

(4) The data on immigration, in the principal countries of immigration, do not generally give information on the educational level of the immigrants, or on the transitional path by which they have arrived from the LDC of origin to the DC of destination. At times, as for Canada, the data are available in the requisite detail only by country of last residence rather than by country of

---

[4]The European Economic Community and Australia are two other destinations for LDC immigrants which should not be ignored in a comprehensive analysis. See Reubens (1975) for details on the former.

[5]Thus, for example, economists continually use the GNP figures which are, for the vast majority of countries, far less than perfect; and recently, income distribution estimates, which are even more remote from what we seek to know, have been used for several influential analyses of developmental strategies in LDCs.

[6]Grubel, in his paper at this conference, cites this unpublished study.

origin or nationality. Sophisticated analysis of the flow levels and patterns, along some of the lines to be suggested below, is thus handicapped and made dependent on indirect evidence and guesstimates.

(5) Finally, as will be evident to the reader from comparing the Bhagwati–Dellalfar, Balacs–Gordon and DeVoretz–Maki papers, it is not yet possible to use a standard set of definitions for classifying immigrants into different categories such as PTK immigrants, so that the analysis of cross-country patterns of immigration by such categories is again handicapped.

The list of such difficulties can be multiplied: but the reader will get an excellent, and fuller, sense of the problems faced by the statistical analyst of skilled migration flows from the Balacs–Gordon paper for the conference. We therefore proceed immediately to discuss the trends and patterns in skilled migrations from LDCs to DCs.

2.2. Trends and patterns

Despite the enormous statistical difficulties detailed above, certain trends and patterns in the gross immigration of PTK-type manpower from LDCs into the major DCs during the last decade have become manifest. These must be noted, though we will also have occasion to raise questions about the endurability of these trends and patterns.

The major change in the last decade, and more, has of course been the general loosening up of the earlier racist quotas on immigration in nearly all countries of immigration. This has also been accompanied by an overall shift in preference for 'higher-level' manpower, with explicit acknowledgements to that effect by the government of the DCs.[7]

The major acts of legislation, reducing or eliminating racial elements and promoting quality immigration, were passed in the U.S. in 1965, in Australia in 1958 and 1966, in Canada in 1967 and in the United Kingdom in 1962 and 1965.[8]

The result was to cause a great spurt in the absolute and relative (to total PTK immigration) immigration of PTK manpower from LDCs into the United States, though this is not quite manifest in the same degree in the data available for the U.K. and Canada. For the U.S., since 1965, the share of LDCs in PTK

---

[7]Thus: 'Secretary of State Dean Rusk exposed the American view this way: 'We are in the international market of brains'; while Canada's Jean Marchand, Minister of Manpower and Immigration, explained his country's view: 'The high cost of training professional and skilled people – engineers, doctors, skilled technicians, etc. – is a measure of the benefit derived upon [their] arrival in Canada. Other countries are in competition with us for immigrants.' Cf. U.S. House (1974, p. 36). Much useful information on postwar trends in migration is neatly stated in chapter III of this report.

[8]For additional information on the U.K. and on Canada, see the papers by Balacs–Gordon (1975) and DeVoretz–Maki (1975), respectively, at this conference.

immigration had gone from 37.4 percent to 71.3 percent by 1970 whereas the share of PTK in total immigration (from all sources) had increased by more than 200 percent.[9]

A similar expansion was noted after the 1962 act in the U.K. but the trend after 1965 has been somewhat erratic, with the flows of PTK-type manpower fluctuating possibly inversely to the domestic employment situation; though no time-series analysis of the data on gross PTK immigration flows is yet available.[10]

As for Canada, the conclusions of DeVoretz and Maki are that the data on immigration before and after the 1967 act show that: '... immigration from LDCs has become an increasing proportion of total immigration destined to the labour force since 1967. A similar, but less dramatic trend exists for professionals . . .. However, professionals as a percentage of total immigrants destined to the labour force, either for total immigration or immigration from LDCs, displays a *downtrend* in recent years. Further, total migrants destined to the labour force has declined every year since 1967, as has the total number of professionals immigrating to Canada. The net effect of these two competing forces is that the number of professionals migrating to Canada from LDCs in 1972 is not much greater than it was in 1965, and is substantially lower than it was in the late 1960s.'[11] To what extent the Canadian decline in the *ratio* of LDC to total professional immigration since 1966 is attributable to the greater availability of the U.S. for PTK immigration since 1965 is not easy to determine. In fact, since the immigration levels are restricted by overall quotas in any case, one might speculate that the facilitated entry into the U.S. has siphoned off the more-talented, potential PTK immigrants to the U.S. and left the Canadians to handle the less-talented LDC applicants, thus reducing the number they choose to admit (given the weights assigned to talent/qualifications and given the fact that prior job availability must be certified before becoming an applicant for immigration).

Clearly, a comprehensive, time-series econometric analysis of PTK immigration flows into the U.S., U.K., and Canada will have to consider *both* that there is as much a possibility of 'brain drain diversion' among them (and possibly Australia, in the English-speaking world of immigrants) as of 'brain drain creation' into them as a group, *and* that the immigration is not free but subject to overall and specific quotas. Unfortunately, while Lucas' paper for this conference does manage to exploit imaginatively the data on labour certification of potential immigrants into the U.S. and thus recognizes explicitly the quota-restricted nature of the labour market in this area, and Balacs–Gordon do discuss the interrelationship of the PTK immigration flows from LDCs into the U.S. and the U.K., we do not yet have the necessary statistics to undertake a satisfactory

---

[9]Fuller details are given in Friedman (1973). Also consult U.S. House (1974, ch. III).

[10]For informed speculations, including on the impact of the U.S. act of 1965 on reemigration of LDC origin PTK immigrants in the U.K. to the U.S., see the Balacs–Gordon paper.

[11]See DeVoretz and Maki (1975, p. 6 and table 2).

econometric analysis using all the English-speaking destination countries simultaneously, as suggested above.

But that the trends of overall PTK immigration from LDCs in the shape of increased and continuing, large ratios in total PTK immigration during the 1960s are likely to persist seems plausible for the simple reason that, as indicated in the later Krugman–Bhagwati conference survey of the decision to migrate, the economic motivation to migrate *is* indicated by several studies to be quite powerful and there is little reason to suppose that the disparities in relative wages (or present discounted values) in LDCs and DCs will narrow significantly *on the average*. All this is, of course, on the assumption that DCs will maintain relatively nonracist and generous quotas for PTK immigration: a situation that may well undergo reversal if deflationary trends in the OECD countries persist. One also should not rule out, though it is currently difficult to assess, the impact of the substantial redistribution of wealth to the OPEC countries, implied by the oil price increases. For LDCs such as Indonesia, Nigeria and Iran, the resulting acceleration of their investments, job opportunities and wage-hikes must imply a greater restraint in emigration of their PTK manpower in several categories. For OPEC countries with low literacy and still lower endowments of PTK skills, such as Libya, Saudi Arabia, Kuwait and Abu Dhabi, the result must be a substantial attraction of external PTK manpower to these areas. Whether this will divert LDC professionals from the DCs, or attract more LDC professionals directly out of LDCs, or result in indirectly attracting more LDC professionals into DCs as the DCs themselves send more professionals to these OPEC countries, or a convex combination of these possibilities, must only be a matter of guesswork. I should imagine, however, that thanks to all these possibilities plus the economic difficulties created by the oil price increases in several non-OPEC LDCs, the net result could well be to *increase* the outflow of PTK manpower, on the average, from the non-OPEC LDCs in the coming decade.[12]

Whether the observed flows are 'large' or 'small' and whether their impact on the LDCs in particular is sufficiently adverse (if at all) to warrant policy intervention, are of course matters that have attracted much of the current debate and will be addressed, along with the analysis of proposals to tax immigrants, at this conference.

It is sufficient, however, to note at this stage that there can be no meaningful assessment of these gains and losses independent of the analytical framework

---

[12]While the preceding remarks relate to PTK totals from LDCs, there is indeed a substantial breakdown available on flows by individual LDCs and by categories of PTK occupations; for such detailed discussion, see U.S. House (1974), Friedman (1973), and the Balacs–Gordon paper on the U.K. for the conference. Note also that there is some evidence for the U.S., U.K., France and Australia that the rate of nonreturn among foreign graduate students in these countries may run as high as a fifth of the total number of students, so that the pool of 'non-immigrants' which includes students, exchange visitors, etc., at any point of time could provide some clue to the number of immigrants at some future date in a lagged analysis.

used to estimate them; there are no facts without theories, as it were. The distinction that is often made between 'brain drain' and 'surplus overflow' or 'safety valve', the latter indicating that unemployed engineers or doctors leaving their LDC for a DC are a source of relief, rather than an economic loss, to the LDC in question is a good illustration of how different theories can yield different answers. The Adams–Watanabe–Baldwin thesis that it does not hurt the Philippines if a doctor driving a taxicab (because of too many doctors) in Manila leaves for New York is predicated on the assumption that the doctor's private and social marginal product are zero. But, as the Bhagwati–Hamada (1974) model[13] demonstrates, in a sticky-wage model, there could still be a loss because the doctor's departure raises the expected return on training to be a doctor by reducing unemployment, by also allowing the New York returns to be reflected in the expected wage, and also by raising the actual returns to practicing doctors by reducing the pressure of unemployment on cutting the returns in a straightforward neoclassical manner. Similarly, the Hamada–Bhagwati (1975) paper for this conference[14] formalizes the notion that if the doctor driving the taxicab in Manila does not have the option of migrating at some stage to New York, he will eventually decide to stop wasting his training and will migrate into the hinterland, taking his services to the smaller towns and earning a substantially greater return to his medical investments than driving a taxicab would enable him to. What the option to leave for New York does is to frustrate this slow but sure capitalist process by which even the Philippines would be able to move in the direction of the Maoist objective of taking doctors away from the large cities. The theoretical papers at this conference bring out the critical nature of the conceptualization of the LDC realities in assessing, therefore, the costs to LDCs of their loss of PTK manpower to the DCs. In doing so, they both stand on the earlier theoretical work in different, more neoclassical, moulds and simultaneously modify the presuppositions and preconceptions derived from it.[15]

I proceed now to discussing the alternative concepts that are worthy of development in an analysis of high-level migration flows from LDCs to DCs.

3. Alternative concepts related to skilled migration

From the viewpoint of LDCs, and LDC-oriented international agencies such as the UNCTAD, one can think of four alternative concepts related to the flows of skilled manpower from LDCs to DCs:

(1) The losses (or gains) to LDCs (excluding the emigrants) from the emigration;

---

[13]This paper is reprinted, with a new appendix, in this volume.
[14]This paper is included in this volume.
[15]These and earlier theoretical analyses of the welfare effects of the brain drain are reviewed in the Bhagwati–Rodriguez (1975) paper in this volume.

(2) The gains (or losses) to DCs (excluding the immigrants) from the immigration;
(3) The gains (or losses) to the emigrants;
(4) The imputed capital flows implicit in skilled emigration.

   Each of these four concepts is of importance, as we will presently argue, in providing some form of rationale and corresponding tax base for some form of taxation whose proceeds could be utilized for developmental assistance to individual LDCs of emigration or to LDCs as a generalized group. Here we develop these rationales explicitly; a discussion of how these four concepts may be measured in practice, and the associated conceptual and measurement difficulties, is deferred until a later section.

(1) *The losses to LDCs* (excluding the emigrants) from the skilled emigration should be of interest because they could conceivably constitute the tax rationale and base for a tax levied (i) on the emigrants to compensate the LDC of origin *or* (ii) on the emigrants to constitute generalized tax revenue for spending via multilateral donor agencies such as UNDP on LDCs in the aggregate *or* (iii) on the DCs of destination. The tax could be located on the emigrants on the argument that it is their emigration (which is both desirable to permit under individualistic ethics and human-rights principles *and*, almost certainly, accompanied by improvement in material comforts to the emigrants in transiting from LDCs to DCs) which is the proximate source of these losses and hence it would be fair to consider the emigrants as a tax source for compensation to the LDCs. The argument for treating the losses to LDCs as a source of (*generalized*) taxation in DCs of destination would, however, have to be based, for fairness, on some notion such as that the immigration is not free but restricted for national advantage and hence there is a prima facie case that the DCs benefit from the immigration of skilled manpower; if so, one could fairly assess a tax on DCs, who improve their welfare through permitting such skilled immigration, by relating it to the losses on the LDCs that such migration entails.

(2) *The gains to DCs* (excluding the immigrants) from the skilled immigration from LDCs should be equally of interest because such an estimate could constitute the tax rationale and base for a tax levied on DCs of destination for *either* spending via multilateral agencies on development of the LDCs *or* for bilateral transmission to the LDCs of origin alone. The rationale for either would be that it is fair to tax the DCs that benefit from skilled immigration from LDCs which are clearly far less affluent – to create funds for disbursement on desirable developmental objectives in the LDCs. Alternatively, where the LDCs can be regarded as having suffered losses from the emigration of their skilled manpower, a la the preceding subsection, one could argue that it is fair that the more prosperous DCs benefiting from the migration compensate the

LDCs losing from the migration, and that such tax be related to the benefits accruing from the immigration to the DCs.

(3) *The gains to the emigrants* from the LDCs to the DCs, on the other hand, are of interest in providing a rationale and base for a tax levied on the emigrants themselves. Such a rationale could be argued as follows: it would be fair to ask the emigrants, who register an improvement in their economic wellbeing by migrating from the LDCs to the DCs, to make a contribution to developing the LDCs; this would be tantamount to extending the notion of a progressive tax, normally applied among residents of one nation, to the group constituted by emigrants from the LDCs together with LDCs themselves. Again, depending on whether this group is restricted to individual LDCs or extended to the aggregate of LDCs – a political reality evidenced in international bargaining – the tax proceeds could be earmarked for bilateral or multilateral developmental spending.

(4) *The imputed capital flows* implicit in skilled migration from the LDCs to the DCs, however, constitute a very different concept from the notions of gains and losses that we have just outlined. Indeed, the difference corresponds precisely to that between normal capital (e.g., portfolio) flows and their welfare effects on host and origin countries. Whereas, however, the usual capital flows are explicit and readily measured, the *imputation* of capital flows implied by the migration of skilled people across national boundaries creates a number of difficulties, raising the question as to the desirability of such a computation. This desirability would appear to be essentially one of a political-economy nature. The international posture of LDCs towards DCs until OPEC's success has been aptly described by Lipton as one of 'confrontation by moral suasion'. It is clear that LDCs seek generally to demonstrate that the flows of capital, assistance, etc. from the DCs to the LDCs fall short of what appears to be reasonable, and even mutually-agreed-upon targets, whereas DCs generally seek to minimize their own obligations and maximize the ostensible magnitude of their contributions. In this international economic order, built almost cynically upon maximal LDC pressures and minimal DC responses, it is a favourite game for the DCs to compute their contributions of capital to LDCs by adding together private capital flows and official assistance of varying content in terms of grant-equivalence. It is well known, of course, that this aggregate of nominal capital flows is excellent for cosmetics; and, regardless of the real worth of these different types of flows, the overall figures in nominal terms possess good value in persuading people into considering the actual DC contributions to be very much more substantial than they are. LDCs have countered this by breaking down capital flow targets into aid and private flow targets with UNCTAD II at New Delhi. An alternative, and equally useful, procedure would be to compute the imputed, 'reverse' flow of capital implied in the outflow of skilled

personnel to DCs; and UNCTAD could well produce a net balance sheet of capital flows between LDCs and DCs that would include not merely the traditional, financial flows but also the imputed flows. There is little doubt that, given the brain drain, such a balance sheet would register a significantly reduced, *net* outflow of 'capital' to the LDCs from the DCs: making it possible to register more moral suasion, and more effectively perhaps, to increase further the capital flows from the DCs to the LDCs.

How should we measure these four aspects of the flow of skilled manpower to the DCs? And what precise kinds of taxes (i.e., Soviet-style exit taxes prior to emigration, Bhagwati-style surtax on incomes subsequent to immigration, etc.) can we relate to them? Moreover, on what criteria may one rank these alternative taxes and which should we prefer as the tax form to be adopted by the world community? We turn to these questions in turn.

4. Measurement of the four alternative concepts

Since the three measures of gains and losses are both amenable to familiar analysis and related to one another, we begin with the analysis of the fourth measure; the imputed capital flows implicit in skilled emigration. The following analysis is deliberately aimed at the essential questions that are pertinent to the matter: for, as will be evident, the issues raised require the adoption among nations of mutually-agreed-upon conventions and our analysis can only underline the nature of the problems that will have to be faced.

4.1. Imputed flows of capital

The measurement of imputed capital flows implied by skilled migration raises problems which are both conceptual and statistical. The 'minimum' set of difficulties is illustrated by considering the simplistic case of once-and-for-all skilled migration from LDCs to DCs. To that, we next add the complexities that arise from the possibility of 'reverse' migration of the emigrants; a phenomenon that is certainly important and cannot be ignored.

4.1.1. Case I: Once-and-for-all migration. There are several possible measures which one may distinguish, most having some parallel in standard capital-theoretic analysis, for evaluating the imputed capital flows in skilled migration.

(1) HC_e: historic cost (as of time of emigration) in LDC of emigration. In this measure, we compute the direct and indirect costs of education to acquire the skills embodied in the emigrant as of the time of emigration. These costs would naturally be at 'local' currency prices and would presumably be translated at some parity to convert them into 'standard dollar' values. With exchange rates changing as the education is acquired, and with multiple effective exchange

rates applying in many LDCs (quite aside from the usual conceptual problems afflicting conversion even at unified and unchanged parities), the least complicated convention to adopt would seem to be to convert at the average parity prevailing in the year of emigration.

(2) HC_i: Equivalent historic cost (as of time of immigration) in DC of immigration. In this measure, we would compute the direct and indirect cost of education that would have had to be incurred in the country of *immigration* to produce an equivalent, skilled person available at the time of immigration. Given the normal excess of educational costs, both direct and indirect, in DCs over LDCs, we could confidently expect that $HC_i > HC_e$.

(3) PDV_e^{PMP}: Present discounted value in LDC of emigration, taking the private marginal product of the emigrant. In this measure, we take the present discounted value of the skilled emigrant, as it would emerge in a capital market, from bidding so as to exploit the services of this 'asset'. From the point of view of prospective employees in a decentralized system, the relevant parameters in the calculation are clearly the familiar discount rate, the time-span over which the emigrant would be producing the services, and the estimated private marginal product of the emigrant over this time-span.

(4) PDV_e^{wage}: Present discounted value in LDC of emigration, taking the wage of the emigrant. This measure would diverge from PDV_e^{PMP} if the wage diverged from the private marginal product. This would happen if wage < PMP because the employer was monopsonistic (e.g., the State has monopolized the activity, as with medicine). In this case, we can argue that the *wage* (< PMP) would get discounted back to its present value for capitalizing the skilled worker: an interpretation that makes sense if we think of this monopsonist as offering a capitalized, current value to the worker for the latter's services over his lifetime.[16] Therefore $PDV_e^{wage} \leqq PDV_e^{PMP}$ according as wage $\leqq$ PMP.

(5) PDV_e^{SMP}: Present discounted value in LDC of emigration, taking the total, social marginal product of the emigrant. This measure would include in the income stream the entire marginal product attributable to the emigrant. This makes sense if we hypothesize a capital market where *countries* are willing to bid for the asset in question: an LDC would then bid so as to impute the *total*, social marginal product to the emigrant and hence the capitalization would reflect this. Naturally, in the presence of externalities, $PDV_e^{SMP} > PDV_e^{PMP}$.

[16]Note however that, in the context of international migration, a measure built on monopsonistic hiring does not make as much sense as when the migration is excluded; the migration itself introduces, as Ray Hill has pointed out to me, the elimination of the monopsony. This observation, of course, recalls to one's mind the proposition that free trade continues to be an optimal policy despite the presence of a distortion through domestic monopoly, as the free trade itself eliminates the monopoly. Secondly, in practice, it is extremely unlikely that the estimate of *PDV* would be undertaken except by reference to the wage earned, so that the distinction between PMP and the wage may not be empirically easy to implement. On the other hand, one cannot rule out the computation of PMP by estimating production functions and solving for PMP by putting in estimated supplies of factors of production.

(6) PDV_i^{PMP}: Present discounted value of the immigrant in the DC of immigration. This is the counterpart of PDV_e^{PMP} and discounts back the income stream, defined by the private marginal product, in the country of immigration. The two measures will diverge insofar as the PMPs, at parity conversion, are unlikely to be equal. The discount rates should generally be different and even the working life spans are not identical between DCs and LDCs.

(7) PDV_i^{wage}: Present discounted value, using the wage, of the immigrant in the DC of immigration. This is then the counterpart of PDV_e^{wage} and similar comments about the differences between these two measures hold as in the discussion just preceding.

(8) PDV_i^{SMP}: Present discounted value of the immigrant in the DC of immigration, taking the social marginal product in the DC. This measure is the counterpart of PDV_e^{SMP} and, for reasons of the kind already spelled out, the two will not generally be identical.

While one may choose from among these measures in estimating the imputed transnational flows of capital, note two things. (1) One could add yet other relevant measures. Thus, for example, one could think of a 'slavery-equivalent' PVD measure where the 'cost of maintaining' the worker would have to be subtracted from, say, the PMP of the worker, since the purchaser of the 'asset' would have to maintain it: there is, in fact, here the paradox that while the worker is regarded in the traditional economic theory of capitalist and socialist societies as using his income to earn satisfaction or *utility* from consumption of goods and services, the slavery system must be analyzed (and indeed is, in all standard treatments in cliometrics, for example) as requiring the slaves' 'minimal' necessary consumption as a *cost*. (2) Next, the different measures of imputed capital above do *not* have any necessary connection with the notion of 'human capital' as understood among economists. Thus, for example, there is nothing in the PDV^{wage} measures that requires that the wage should reflect returns to investment in education or training: the returns may well be 'rent' to talents, or the incremental returns to incremental education may be the result of an Arrow–Spence (1973) screening process or a Bhagwati–Srinivasan (1975) job-ladder and overqualification process. Therefore what we shall mean by imputed capital flows is the present discounted value of 'income' streams, which has no necessary connection with the theory of human capital at all, or to historic cost (which, on the other hand, *is* defined as equivalent to direct and indirect educational costs as in the standard theory of human capital).

4.1.2. Case II: 'Reverse', 'net' vs. 'gross', 'to-and-fro' migrations.

The multitude of possible measures that we discussed above indicate only the difficulties that arise from handling the imputation problems of permanent, once-and-for-all migrations. As we have already noted, however, the skilled immigrants from LDCs do occasionally happen to return to their countries of origin, or to other LDCs, constituting a 'reverse' flow requiring us to distinguish between 'net' and 'gross' flows. They also, most unfortunately for statisticians and economists, do not seem to make up their minds even then and, like the present author, seem sometimes to swing to and fro between DCs and LDCs. This phenomenon raises problems for our computed imputations of capital flows, to which we address ourselves briefly at this point.

Two critical points need to be noted at the outset. (1) From the viewpoint of measurement, it is clear that relatively unambiguous criteria are necessary at each stage of measurement. Thus, since ex ante intentions of migrants are generally *not* reliable, we should stick to ex post migrations. Hence, quite regardless of whether a migrant intends to return to his LDC, he should be classified as a migrant as long as he takes an immigrant visa: much the way short-term capital is regarded even if the intention may be to invest it in that asset for ever. A set of simple and feasible conventions could be surely evolved, to classify immigrants as having 'effectively' migrated from one country to another, taking ex post movements according to well-defined categories into account. The problems here are no greater than those encountered in allocating financial flows to categories such as short-term and long-term movements. (2) Next, since we have already seen that the presence of two countries involves differential valuations, on any one concept, the question naturally arises about possible consistency in measures at different points of migration of the same person. Thus, if historic cost valuation is adopted, one could evaluate the emigrant from LDC, at initial migration, at LDC valuation. When he returns, one could add to this value the incremental cost of education in the DC at DC valuation *or* evaluate the same at equivalent LDC costs. There seems to be no compelling reason to choose among these alternatives except that one may well put some premium on being consistent and evaluate *all* costs at LDC-equivalent values, whether incurred in LDCs or DCs.

Keeping these questions in mind, we can suggest certain procedures or conventions which may be followed in evaluating the flows in the case of reverse migrations.

(1) *Historic cost measures*: Take the complex case where the emigrant is educated in the LDC, acquires further education as a nonimmigrant student in the DC, works in the DC as an immigrant and then returns to the LDC.

(i) Taking consistent HC_e valuation, at costs in the LDC, we would then measure the imputed flow of capital to the DC as the historic costs incurred up to the point of emigration: hence, the educational costs (direct and indirect) of the DC educatio would have to be evaluated at the value of such educational costs if incurred in the LDC, since emigration is not considered to have taken place in the example until *after* the DC education is complete. The reverse flow should then also be measured at the same LDC-equivalent historic cost, HC_e.

(ii) Alternatively, the valuation could be carried through, at each point of cross-over, in terms of DC-equivalent historic costs, HC_i.

(iii) On the other hand, one could take historic values, *as incurred*, evaluating them at the values in the countries where they were incurred, even though this involves adding together values at different 'prices'. Thus, the LDC-educational costs would be recorded at LDC values, HC_e, and the DC-educational costs at DC values, HC_i. Their sum, in our example, would be recorded initially as the flow of imputed capital to the DC and later as the return flow to the LDC.

(2) *Present discounted value measures*: These raise particularly serious computational difficulties, of course, as the valuations must be made (if we stick to the consistency requirement, in the sense of the preceding subsection) entirely with reference to the discount rate, the time-span of remaining working life, and the 'income' (i.e., PMP, Wage or SMP) as relevant to either the LDC or the DC. Thus, with LDC valuations, we would need to compute the imputed flow from the LDC to the DC in the foregoing example at the value of the fully-trained immigrant; and the return flow to the LDC would measure the same value at 'income' over the working-time-span remaining to the immigrant at the point of the reverse migration. And the same, with DC valuations, would hold for PDV_i measures, taken consistently.

The foregoing is by no means an exhaustive analysis of the issues that would be raised in arriving at a set of conventions for measuring the imputed capital flows as implied by the movements of skilled people across national boundaries; but it does indicate clearly the dimensions of the problems that would have to be resolved in arriving at the requisite estimates. We may now turn to the more conventional analysis of the three measures of gains and losses to the LDCs, DCs and the emigrants themselves.

4.2. The gains to the emigrants

The measurement of gains (or, in the 'pathological' case of expulsion, for example, losses) to the emigrants is, *in principle*, a relatively straightforward matter though, *in practice*, it will raise a number of difficulties.[17] Again, let us distinguish between the simpler (but unrealistic) case of once-and-for-all migration and the complex (but realistic) case of reverse and to-and-fro migrations.

4.2.1. Case I: Once-and-for-all migration.

In this case, one is clearly able to use without difficulty the measure of gain

---

[17]The presumption of economic gain to emigrants is also consistent with the somewhat stronger results of econometric studies of the decision to migrate, namely that economic factors do explain this decision. See the Krugman–Bhagwati paper in this volume on these studies.

provided by the present discounted value of the incremental real earnings obtained by the migration. To undertake this computation, familar from the standard economic literature on the decision to migrate, one clearly needs the following information.

(1) The time profile of earnings of the emigrant in the LDC of origin and the DC of destination must be estimated. Note that these profiles will not coincide, not merely because of differences in wage structures, but also because the LDC and the DC are unlikely to offer the same *working* life span (given differences in retirement age, etc.) *and* the migration could also alter life expectancy. Furthermore, in estimating the time profile of earnings in either country, the analyst should take care not to assume that wage structures, by age, are identical across the two countries; evidence collected by Psacharopoulos shows that they do differ. Furthermore, the gains in income over the anticipated time span must be adjusted for possible changes due to inflationary and real changes in the economy, if these can be shown to be systematic; and in converting the values in domestic currencies to a common unit, the analyst should probably also take into account the anticipated consequence of such changes on the exchange rate.

(2) If measures of monetary returns in domestic currency are used, as they must be, in making the calculations, the parity rates should be adjusted to allow for differences in the cost of living between the LDC and the DC.

(3) Allowance should be made further for direct tax liabilities and inputed gains in public consumption in the LDC and the DC.

(4) Anyone familiar with LDC sociology, rooted in extended family and kinship obligations, may well wish to also consider the fact that the obligations in the shape of financial demands for support may be an increasing function of prosperity. Thus a fraction of the remittances may well be regarded as a deductible 'loss' (rather than as a utility-generating expenditure) from the earning stream of the migrant in the DC.

(5) Moreover, the initial cost of moving to the DC must be estimated as well; this is not always negligible.

(6) Finally, a suitable discount rate must be chosen for reducing the stream of net gains to its present discounted value.

4.2.2. Case II: Reverse and to-and-fro migration.

The principles set out for case I carry over here as well; but the complexities are enhanced. To make a sensible estimate of improved real income, thanks to the sojourn(s)/migration(s) to the DCs, one would have to estimate the time-spans spent there and take the differential improvement in real income over *those* time-spans only. Again, one should want to take into account complicating factors such as (i) possible improvements in life expectancy, (ii) increase in access to better jobs back in the LDC owing to what, like the Ghanaians, I like to call the 'been-to' effect,[18] (iii) the fact that savings in DCs will be spent largely in LDCs on return and hence should not be subjected to the cost-of-living deflation, mentioned earlier for conversion into common units, and (iv) the possibility of social security payments being available in LDCs from the sojourns in the DCs.

Three concluding observations are in order.

(1) These *PDV* calculations are tricky, at best, and could yield only broad orders of magnitude; but they do, in some fashion, enter the decision to migrate (see the Krugman–Bhagwati survey of the econometric literature on migration in this volume) and could also be of use as providing a tax base for levying an exit tax on emigrants on the principle that the LDC seeks a fractional share of this income gain, on progressive-income-taxation grounds (as set out above), for spending on those left behind. On the other hand, for a Bhagwati-style income tax on PTK immigrants from LDCs, there would be no need to estimate *PDV*s and one could well work with the estimated improvements as registered in the incremental income stream over the period of migration to the DCs.

(2) Next, note that the *PDV* calculations here, which may be symbolised as PDV_m since they related to the migrants directly, differ from the PDV_e and PDV_i calculations in the preceding subsection on measuring inputed capital flows in two essential respects: (i) PDV_i and PDV_e do *not* subtract out the receipts stream in the LDC from that in the DC but discount back the DC and the LDC streams, respectively; and (ii) the PDV_m measure additionally faces all the problems of putting together the streams in two domestic currencies whereas, with the consistency approach, the PDV_i and PDV_e measures deal with values defined in only one currency unit.

(3) Finally, it is worth stressing that the easier-to-calculate and conceptually more satisfactory *PDV* measures of 'capital' flows for UNCTAD-type purposes are PDV_e and PDV_i, and *not* the gains-measure PDV_m.

We now turn to the question of measuring the gains (losses) to the DCs and LDCs, in turn. First, however, we must dispose of the question as to whether it is meaningful to add together the PDV_m type of measure to the estimated gains to DCs or subtract it from the estimated losses to LDCs. The customary treatment has been to regard all three measures as separate, and to calculate them as such. This is *not* because the migrants were regarded as 'stateless' or owing to oversight. The reasons are plain to anyone who is familiar with the following facts.[19] (i) Skilled migrants in the postwar world, where we are discussing

---

[18]The Indian equivalent for the Ghanaian 'been-to' is 'foreign-returned'. In either case, it often manages to act as a successful competitive instrument for securing better jobs in the job ladder.

[19]For further discussion of the issues raised here, see section 1 of the Bhagwati–Rodriguez (1975) paper in this volume.

'normal' brain drain flows (as distinct from, say, expulsion or refugee migrants), tend to 'return' to their LDC of origin at some stage of their career. The era of once-and-for-all migrations is over thanks to the low transport costs which permit occasional to-and-fro migrations or long vists to countries of origin, thanks to the growth of opportunities in countries of immigration to immigrants *without* citizenship status for holding a great number of lucrative jobs so that immigrants frequently hold onto their citizenships of origin and hence to their political and psychological affiliations, and thanks finally to the greater acceptability of ethnic diversity, as against the melting-pot ethos, in even the United States.[20] In this situation, to regard the migrants categorically as 'part of the DC' population for calculating the 'gains' in DC incomes from the immigration is to betray ignorance of the nature of current PTK immigration *or* to succumb to the desire to come up with large numbers of LDC 'contributions' to DCs in the interest of international negotiation, but in a manner which is calculated to invite ridicule. (ii) Nor should DC advocates resort to the contrary practice of treating the immigrants' incremental welfare as necessarily additive to LDC gains, on the ground that their affiliation continues with LDCs, as indicated by return and to-and-fro flows. The fact of the matter is that migrants are the subject of policy decisions which reflect national concerns about what happens to the economic welfare of those who do not so migrate, as also other considerations of a noneconomic nature; and, in the interest of clarity of the issues involved, as also to allow for the possibility of aggregating the gains and losses in all kinds of alternative ways as required for the specific nature of particular migrations, it is sensible to treat the migrants' welfare as a separate concept, as is in fact the current practice (except for a recent UNCTAD study which falls into the trap of adding the migrants' improved incomes to DC 'gains' to arive at duly impressive estimates of DC gains that will doubtless please the Group of 77, but only add to the disenchantment with such procedures on the part of the DCs).[21]

4.3. The gains to the DCs (excluding immigrants)

In determining the gain to the DCs (excluding the immigrants) from the inflow of PTK manpower from the LDCs, one should construct an appropriate welfare measure. However, in the brain drain literature, one can also come across measures which have really no welfare rationale, contrary to what is often asserted. I therefore start with the latter and go on to the former, more appropriate measures of gains to DCs.

---

[20]It might even be postulated that the PTK immigrants have, in turn, helped to reduce the incidence of the melting-pot ethos because, with their greater mobility *and* desirability as immigrants, they have the option to leave the country of immigration rather than to accept the loss of their ethnic and national identity.

[21]UNCTAD Document TD/B/AC, 1974 (Geneva, Switzerland).

4.3.1. SIC (savings in investment costs).

In the Reubens paper for this conference, as also in some earlier analyses of the effects of skilled migrations on DCs, the measure used is built on the question: how much investment cost is 'saved' by the DCs through having the immigrants' services available to the DCs as against the alternative option of those services being made available from domestic investment? This measure, it should be noted, yields conceptually the same figure as if we were trying to compute the investment cost of *import-substituting for a service or commodity currently being imported.*

Of course, as soon as we note this identity of concept, it is immediately evident that this measure is *not* a welfare measure in any valid economic sense. The diversion of investment from other activities will undoubtedly reduce economic returns elsewhere; but the import of services implied by the immigration alternative *also* requires that the immigrants be paid for their services. Hence, short of eventually comparing these alternative costs, there is nothing really to be gained by computing merely the investment costs in educating 'natives' to 'replace' the immigrants. And, it should be noted that the popular description of such figures of investment costs (in training DC nationals to 'replace' LDC immigrants into the DC's) as 'gains' to DCs is therefore lacking in conceptual clarity and rationale.

However, assuming that the statistician does wish to measure the savings in investment costs (SIC) to the DCs of immigration, differences from the measures considered earlier may now be noted. Thus, the SIC measure would, unlike the HC_i and HC_e measures discussed earlier, require that any DC investment in the LDC immigrant (as when M.I.T. gave me a fellowship for graduate work) be netted out from the computed costs of training a 'substitute' M.I.T. Ph.D. from the native population. Whether the DC or the LDC paid for the immigrant's education, all or part thereof, is a pertinent issue for the SIC measure, while it was not for the measures earlier discussed.[22]

Again, we must note the difference between marginal and average costs in substituting the immigrant with the native PTK. Thus, if there is unemployment in the PTK class of immigrant, the marginal SIC cost of substitution with the native – this marginal cost, of course, is the same as PDV_i^{wage} – could be considered to be zero. On the other hand, this view is possibly a simplistic view once we recognize that (i) significant unemployment rates in a profession rarely persist for long periods, so that the zero replacement cost is likely to be a short-term phenomenon, and (ii) part or all of a long-term unemployment rate may, in any case, be a search-process phenomenon.

Finally, the reverse flow problem must be noted here as elsewhere. At the

---

[22]For what it is worth, one could even compute the direct and indirect capital and labor requirements, a la Heckscher–Ohlin–Leontief, of import-substituting the immigrants' services, using the $[a_{ij}]$, $[b_{ij}]$, and the labor-coefficients matrices.

point of 'migration', defined according to agreed convention, the *SIC* measure can be computed (netting out the estimated investment by the DC in the LDC immigrant) as discussed above. If and when the immigrant leaves the DC, so as to be defined as an immigrant into another country, the DC of original immigration can be shown to have lost the originally-computed *SIC*. However, unlike in the imputed-capital-flow case, I see no particular merit in adopting conventions addressed to ensuring consistency *between* DCs and LDCs: the 'saving' in educational costs from return migration to India is quite naturally measured at Indian costs, whereas the 'savings' in educational costs from the original emigration of the Indian professional to the U.S. and the 'dissaving' from his return to India are naturally measured at U.S. costs.[23]

4.3.2. WG (welfare gain).

The appropriate measurement of the welfare effects of LDC PTK immigration on DCs requires rather different types of conceptualization and data than the *SIC* measure that I have just been discussing. Naturally, it requires the elaboration of a social objective function and the construction of an appropriate model within which the welfare effects of the immigration can be formally investigated. The issues raised by migration for the adoption of a suitable objective function are fairly complex; so are the possible models that can be constructed to analyze the welfare implications of the brain drain once the objective function has been chosen. Hence, both of these topics have been neglected for separate and detailed treatment in the Bhagwati–Rodriguez paper in this volume.

4.4. The losses to the LDCs (excluding emigrants)

The analysis here is perfectly symmetrical to that of gains to the DCs from immigration and hence brevity is called for.

4.4.1. LIC (loss in investment costs).

Corresponding to the *SIC* measure for the DCs, one can develop the *LIC* measure for the LDCs losing the PTK manpower. And it would have exactly the same conceptual limitations and problems as the *SIC* measure for the DCs.

---

[23]We earlier ignored depreciation from the historic cost measures. This was not an oversight but reflected both the difficulty of settling on a convincing formula and the fact that brains will 'appreciate' as often as they will depreciate as they proceed through their span of working life. The ignorance of depreciation, however, may well be an important omission in certain PTK occupations (such as engineering) and for ages beyond a certain maximum, whereas the ignorance of appreciation (after formal education) may well be an important omission in other occupations (such as medicine) and for ages below a certain maximum. Hence, one might well differ on the conventions to adopt in this regard; and whatever convention is adopted, it would be pertinent for both the *HC* and the *SIC* measures when we have reverse and to-and-fro migrations.

Thus, it would not be a welfare-loss measure; not would it distinguish between marginal (PDV) and average (HC) measures, a distinction of considerable importance in situations such as long-term unemployment.

4.4.2. *WL (welfare loss).*

As with the DCs, the appropriate measure of the welfare impact of the emigration on the LDCs requires specification of an appropriate objective function and of a set of relations which characterize the economy within which the emigration is modeled. Again, the analysis of these two aspects of the problem of estimating *WL* on the LDCs is carried out at length in the Bhagwati–Rodriguez paper in this volume.

5. Alternative tax forms and rationales

There is already implicit in the analysis thus far the possibility of taxing either the immigrants *or* the DCs of immigration; and so are the possible rationales for such taxes. In this section, however, these possibilities and rationales are analyzed more systematically and at length.

Tax proposals related to the brain drain can be classified according to the following criteria.

5.1. *Who pays the tax?*

One can distinguish among two principal objects of a brain-drain-related tax: (1) the immigrants themselves; and (2) the DC of immigration.

As for the taxes on immigrants, one can further distinguish among four major types of taxes: (a) a Soviet-style exit tax at the point of emigration; (b) a Bhagwati-style surtax on the income of the immigrant, after the fact of immigration;[24] and two quasi-tax measures presently employed in similar or different contexts; (c) a bond, signed by the potential emigrant, which requires that the act of emigration will imply the imposition of a stated penalty: the effect is virtually similar to that of an exit tax, although the specifics of the two types of levies may be different in particular cases;[25] and finally, (d) tax deductible contributions, which are really voluntary but whose incidence falls, depending on which tax bracket the contributor is in, partly on the contributor and for the remaining part on the DC government's treasury.

[24]The exit tax and the income tax have been contrasted in Bhagwati and Dellalfar (1974). This paper is being reprinted with minor revisions in the Bhagwati–Partington (1976) volume.

[25]Thus, for example, the bonds are typically applied only to those who seem to go abroad for study with the use of public funds, rather than to all professional emigrants, such as was the case with the Soviet exit tax. Also, the exit tax is collected prior to departure whereas the bond is conditional on actual emigration, so that even those who intend to, and actually do, return without emigration have to forego the interest on the bond.

As for taxes on DCs in general, one can think of (a) a straight-forward tax, related to the brain drain, but levied on the tax assessees in the same way as income tax but earmarked for specific brain-drain-oriented purposes; alternatively, (b) some of the generalized revenue, accruing to the treasury in the DCs in the normal way, can be used for brain-drain-oriented purposes; or (c) one may think of tax deduction again as partly constituting a charge on the generalized revenue and being assigned to brain drain objectives.[26]

5.2. Who receives the revenue?

Here, there are again two main possibilities: (1) the revenue may go, bilaterally, to the LDC of origin; alternatively, (2) it may go to a multilateral agency, such as the UNDP, to be disbursed in a generalized fashion on LDCs for developmental purposes.

5.3. Rationale for the tax

The rationale for a tax related to the brain drain can be distinguished again by *who* pays the tax.

(1) Where the immigrants pay the tax – as in case 5.1(1) above – one can think of two alternative rationales: (a) the tax can be thought of as compensation for the loss inflicted on the LDC of emigration by the fact of the emigration; and (b) the tax can alternatively be considered to be an extension of the progressive-taxation principle so that the improvement in the economic wellbeing of the emigrant is taxed for the benefit of those left behind in the poorer LDC of emigration.

(2) Where the DC pays the tax from generalized revenue or revenue collected generally but earmarked for brain drain objectives, one can again distinguish among two alternative rationales: (a) insofar as there are losses inflicted on the LDC of emigration, the moral principle may be invoked that if the rich hurt the poor, they should compensate them;[27] and (b) if the rich DCs benefit thanks to the poor LDCs, they ought to reroute these gains to the LDCs. In the former case, clearly, the tax will be related to LDC losses; in the latter case, to the gains of the DCs.[28]

---

[26]Thus, in their excellent, legal analysis of the Bhagwati tax proposal, being printed in the Bhagwati–Partington volume, Oldman and Pomp consider the possibility of adopting a scheme under which skilled immigrants could make tax-deductible donations to the UN or LDCs of emigration.

[27]By contrast, the foreign aid programmes, as conceived by liberals such as Gunnar Myrdal, have been premised on the moral principle of redistribution, per se. However, the compensation idea is occasionally invoked as an additional justification for aid programmes, though rarely by the donor countries.

[28]In both cases, I am clearly referring to DCs and LDCs, *excluding* the migrants. For a discussion of this point, see Bhagwati and Rodriguez (1975), in this volume.

5.4. *How should the tax rate be chosen?*

The choice of the tax rate will depend, of course, on whether the tax is to be imposed on the immigrants or on DCs of immigration: this is so because, as we have just seen, the rationale in each case, and within the case for that matter, will vary. Furthermore, the professional economist can distinguish between determining the consequences of an arbitrarily-chosen tax rate and determining an optimal tax rate. These general points can be adequately illustrated by considering some alternative possibilities.

(1) Thus, begin by considering the choice of an optimal tax rate when the assessee is the immigrant, the LDC of origin is the recipient of the tax revenue, and the optimal tax rate is desired. In this case, it is possible to distinguish

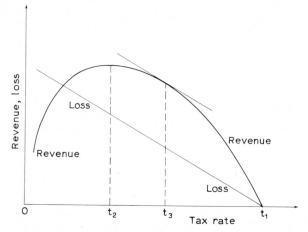

Fig. 1. The tax revenue and welfare loss are plotted as functions of the tax on the brain drain. For simplicity, the loss curve is linear. The revenue and loss are both assumed to fall to zero as the tax rate reaches t_1 and emigration ceases. The tax rates t_1, t_2, and t_3 minimize loss, maximize revenue and revenue-*minus*-loss, respectively.

among three possibilities. (a) If the objective of the tax is to minimize the loss from the brain drain to the LDC of origin, then one would need to identify the loss-causing factors and then suitably choose the tax rate that minimizes this loss.[29] (b) If, however, the objective is to maximize the revenue from the brain drain tax, the optimal tax rate will generally be different. (c) Finally, the most appropriate objective would be to maximize the difference between the revenue and the loss, choosing the tax rate that does this. And then again, this tax rate would be different in general from the other two. This is illustrated in fig. 1, where the optimal tax rates, for cases (a)–(c), are shown as t_1, t_2, and t_3, respectively.

[29]Thus, a suitable model would have to be chosen, as well as an appropriate objective function, as discussed in the Bhagwati–Rodriguez (1975) paper.

(2) Alternatively, take the case where the optimal tax rate is chosen with respect to a generalized DC tax and the LDC of origin is the recipient of the revenue. In this case, one may reasonably assume that the tax would not affect the migration level.[30] If so, only the revenue will shift upwards as the tax rate (say, related to the level of immigration) rises. An arbitrary, upper limit must then be set on the tax rate. Alternatively, one can also derive the tax rate by reference to the rationale underlying the tax. Thus, in the case where the tax is supposed to compensate for LDC loss from the emigration – as in case 5.3(2)(a) above – the tax rate would become, for any given level of migration, the loss divided by the number immigrating into the DC from that LDC. Similarly if the rationale involved the DC gains from the immigration – as in case 5.3(2)(b) above – one would divide these gains by the number of the relevant immigrants.

Clearly, depending therefore on the mix of the rationales, the assessee, and the recipient of the revenue, the reader can work out the implied optimal tax rates that would follow, from the economist's optimizing procedures, in any specific situation. However, one can depart from the optimality framework and consider merely revenue and/or welfare consequences of a specific tax measure related to the brain drain.

This is, in fact, what many of the papers presented at the conference do: investigate a tax that is an income tax levied on the incomes of the migrants in the DCs of immigration. Thus, the McCulloch–Yellen and Rodriguez papers (and the Bhagwati–Hamada paper before them) formally model the consequences of such a tax in general-equilibrium terms, (while, however, *not* feeding back into the LDC the proceeds from the tax, as would be required by a full analysis of such a tax proposal).[31] The econometric papers, by Lucas and Psacharopoulos, are also addressed to the same type of income tax and seek to establish the sensitivity of the immigration flows to the imposition of such a tax via its effects on the inducement to emigrate, since the net-of-tax returns in DCs of immigration would fall with the imposition of the tax.

These theoretical and econometric papers on the possible effects of an income tax on immigrants provide the first systematic analysis of *any* proposal for taxation relating to the brain drain. They are complemented, in turn, by the estimates of tax revenues which could be earned, under various 'plausible' assumptions, from the imposition of such an income tax on immigrants in the U.S. (Bhagwati–Dellalfar), the U.K. (Balacs–Gordon) and Canada (DeVoretz–Maki). Finally, this proposal is examined for its feasibility from legal, constitutional and human-rights viewpoints by the lawyers at the conference: Oldman

---

[30]This assumption could be falsified if the DC of immigration, in view of the tax related to the brain drain, were to restrict the inflow as the tax rate increases and raises the cost of the inflow.

[31]This omission is rather like the omission from the analysis of the effects of PL480 food disposal in LDCs on LDC agricultural production, of the investment-funds-augmenting effects of the PL480 aid. On this, see Fisher's (1963) acknowledgment to Rosenstein–Rodan for pointing out this lacuna in his earlier analysis.

and Pomp examine it from an international tax standpoint as also from the viewpoint of the U.S. Constitution; Partington conducts a systematic analysis from the vantage point of the U.K., taking into account not merely law but also sociological and tax collection aspects; and Newman discusses the tax proposal so as to seek any possible inconsistencies with the existing conventions and 'law' at the U.N. on human rights.[32]

5.5. Who levies the tax?

The legal papers on the proposal to levy a surtax on incomes of immigrants also make clear that one must also ask the question as to which country levies the tax.

From the viewpoint of formal economic analysis, it is clearly unimportant to distinguish between an LDC-imposed and a DC-imposed income tax on immigrants. However, this distinction is of overriding legal importance because the possible lack of constitutionality in the U.S. of a DC-imposed tax, and hence the infeasibility of the proposed tax, are issues which make *this* version of the proposed income tax on immigrants inferior to the alternative version where it is an LDC-imposed tax.

6. Concluding remarks

The preceding review and analysis of what appear to me to be the principal conceptual and empirical problems arising from the objective of brain-drain-related taxation must be complemented, of course, by the interested readers and policymakers by reading the several chapters of this volume that have been cited in this paper. It should however serve to define, and thereby fill a serious lacuna in the economic (as also legal) literature in that regard, the main contours of any logical and focused analysis of the phenomenon of brain drain and taxation related to it.

[32]The three revenue-estimate papers and the three legal papers are being published, as noted above, in the separate, companion volume edited by Bhagwati and Partington (1976), with a detailed introduction and summary by the editors.

References

Arrow, K., 1973, Higher education as a filter, Journal of Public Economics 2, no. 3, 193–216.
Bhagwati, J. and W. Dellalfar, 1974, The brain drain and income taxation, World Development 1.
Bhagwati, J. and M. Partington, 1976, Taxing the brain drain: A proposal (North-Holland, Amsterdam).
Bhagwati, J. and C. Rodriguez, 1975, Welfare–theoretical analyses of the brain drain, Journal of Development Economics 2, no. 3.
Bhagwati, J. and T.N. Srinivasan, 1975, Education in a job-ladder model and the fairness-in-living rule, MIT working paper, no. 159.

De Voretz, D. and D. Maki, 1975, The brain drain and income taxation: Canada, in: J. Bhagwati and M. Partington, eds., 1976, Taxing the brain drain: A proposal (North-Holland, Amsterdam).

Fisher, F., 1963, A theoretical analysis of the impact of food surplus disposal on agricultural production in recipient countries, Journal of Farm Economics 45.

Friedman, S., 1973, The effect of the U.S. immigration act of 1965 on the flow of skilled migrants from less developed countries, World Development 1, no. 8.

Johnson, H., 1972, The effect of the monetary problem on development cooperation: Linking special drawing rights and development, Foreign Policy 8, fall (reprinted).

U.S. House of Representatives, Committee of Foreign Affairs, 1974, Brain drain: A study of the persistent issue of international scientific mobility (GPO, Washington), September.

PART II

ECONOMETRIC ANALYSIS OF THE DECISION
TO MIGRATE

CHAPTER 2

THE DECISION TO MIGRATE

A survey

Paul KRUGMAN and Jagdish BHAGWATI

Massachusetts Institute of Technology, Cambridge, MA 02139, U.S.A.

1. Introduction

The decision to migrate has been the subject of analysis by social scientists with diverse backgrounds. Demographers, sociologists and, in recent times, economists have been examining the problems of both internal and international migration, embracing furthermore skilled and unskilled migrations.

From the viewpoint of the focus on this conference, on Brain Drain and Taxation, it is clear that the most interesting aspect of these studies is the sensitivity of the migrant flows to economic rewards; as is, in fact, clearly stated by Lucas and Psacharopoulos in their papers for the conference prior to their econometric exercises directed at precisely this issue. It should therefore be of interest to review here many of the principal results of *earlier* research in this area of inquiry, directing our attention to the findings on economic motivations, and in particular, to the quantitative estimates of the corresponding elasticities of migration flows in regard thereto.[1]

Furthermore, the main focus of our review will be on systematic, econometric analyses, although some nod will be made in the direction of sociological inquiries with potential interest for economists. This narrowing of our review is appropriate since we intend to provide the reader with the perspective required to come to grips with the conference papers of Lucas and Psacharopoulos, DeVoretz–Maki and Bhagwati–Dellalfar on the Bhagwati-type income tax, where the effect of the proposed tax on yields would depend on the elasticity of the migration flows with respect to the narrowing of the net-of-tax wage differentials between LDCs of origin and DCs of destination.[2]

---

[1] Note however that the economists' studies do not refer exclusively to what might be regarded as 'economic', as distinct from 'noneconomic', factors. Thus, for example, in some of the studies on international migration, factors such as 'professional opportunities' are considered; though few of the econometric, as distinct from questionnaire, studies have managed to use anything except what may be regarded as strictly economic factors.

[2] The sociological and demographic studies, which we mainly ignore, appear to rely essentially on a framework analyzing migration in terms of 'push' and 'pull' factors, with little recognition of the fact, apparent to any trained economist, that it is generally futile to ask

Our survey will divide the studies reviewed by two major categories, internal and international migration, treating the former in section 2 and the latter in section 3.

2. Internal migration

We review here 14 econometric studies on internal migration. At the outset, however, it would be useful to state the principal *qualitative* findings on the explanatory variables that seem to emerge from this research.

2.1. Principal qualitative findings

Note initially that demographic research appears to have found that migration tends to follow 'economic opportunity'. There is dissension as to the relative importance of wage differences and of job openings; however, both question-naire-type and statistical evidence lend support to the view that wage rates matter. Furthermore, migration tends to go to areas of high 'urbanization' (though it is not clear, from Bogue (1969) for example, that this effect is considered independent of income as urbanization increases with income). Finally, educated people appear to be more mobile than the uneducated.

These explanatory variables, i.e., wages, education, and urbanization, also turn up in the 14 econometric studies, though there is additional attention paid to variables such as 'distance', and to defining the dependent variable more carefully. By way of summary classification of the findings of the signs of the coefficients, we have put together table 1. The studies use different dependent variables, as clearly indicated in the appropriate headings to each subset of table 1; thus, a distinction is made between studies dealing with gross flows (A), net flows (B), and destination of the migrants (C). Two studies, Sahota (1968) and Gallaway–Gilbert–Smith (1967), have two models each and hence appear twice in the listing. Finally, note that in each case the question is the effect of a variable on migration from i to j.

Note first that there is complete unanimity on the effect of income on migration to a region.[3] No study here (or anywhere, as far as we can tell) has ever found a perverse effect of destination income on migration. There is also near unanimity on the effect of origin region income, which deters migration; only Vanderkamp (1971) dissents, and we should note that he used only income

which blade of the scissors cuts the paper. While therefore it is relatively easy for the economist to reinforce his customary sense of superiority vis-a-vis these other social sciences by examining the sociological and demographic literature in this area, it is at the same time good to know their findings. The economist reader should find it useful to see for himself the review of these findings in Bogue (1969, ch. 19), as also to consult Parnes (1954), though we briefly report on these in the next section.

[3]In some cases, 'income' is a wage or present discounted value measure. Differences in concepts will be discussed later.

Table 1

Signs of coefficients in 14 econometric studies.[a]

(A) Studies of gross flows

Author	Country	Income in j	Income in i	Education in j	Education in i	Urban in j	Urban in i	Distance
Sahota	Brazil	+	−	+	−	−	+	−
Beals, Levy and Moses	Ghana	+	−	−	−	+	+	−
Greenwood	Egypt	+	−	+	−	+	+	−
Levy and Wadycki	Venezuela	+	−	?	?	+	−	−
Greenwood	India	+	−	0	0	+	+	−
Gallaway, Gilbert and Smith	U.S.	+	−	0	0	0	0	0
Vanderkamp	Canada	+	+	0	0	0	0	−

(B) Studies of net flows (measured in out direction)

Author	Country	Income	Education	Urban
Sjaastad	U.S.	−[b]	−	−
Raimon	U.S.	−[b]	0	0
Schultz	Colombia	−[b]	+	0
Bowles	U.S.	−[c]	0	0
Gallaway, Gilbert and Smith	U.S.	−[c]	0	0

(C) Destination of migrant

Author	Country	Income differential	Education differential	Urban differential	Distance
Sahota	Brazil	+	−	+	−
Greenwood	U.S.	+	+	+	−

[a]For details on the studies, see the discussion in the text. In each case, the question is what effect a variable has on migration from i to j. If a variable encourages migration from i to j, it receives a + sign; if it discourages, it receives a − sign; if the effect is indeterminate, a ? is used. A zero indicates that the variable was not considered in the study.

[b]Income in region considered.

[c]Differential between income in region and in some other region.

as an explanatory variable, whereas others used other factors which are surely not independent of income. Hence it is not unlikely that the reason for the discrepancy is that Vanderkamp has found dM/dY while others have found $\partial M/\partial Y$.

Results on education are generally ambiguous. This is not surprising, since the measure of education deployed is educational attainment of the population, which can be argued to have contradictory effects: (1) education is a public service and thus an opportunity which should attract migrants; and at the same time, (2) educated people are more likely to migrate. Furthermore, there are problems of simultaneity. If a region is attractive to migrants, it may (because of differential mobility) tend to have above-average education. This would generate a positive relationship. On the other hand, an abundance of educated people may make a region unattractive for other educated people, etc. Perhaps we should regard it as a vindication of theory that where theory has nothing to say, neither do empirical results.

To say that the effect of education on migration between regions is ambiguous, however, is not to say that the effect of education on the propensity to migrate is unknown. Two studies, those of Bowles (1970), on the U.S. South, and of Levy and Wadycki (1974), on Venezuela, were able to determine the effect of education on the *responsiveness* to other factors, and both found that responsiveness to economic factors increased with education.

The effects of urbanization are a little clearer, but not much. By and large, migrants appear to have a preference for urban areas over and above the income associated with such areas. Urbanization in the origin region, however, is of less certain effect. Again, two arguments can be made, with opposite implications: (1) potential migrants are less likely to leave regions which have been urbanized to their satisfaction; and (2) urbanites are more likely to be well informed about opportunities elsewhere.

The last column of table 1 lists the effect of distance on migration, which is negative – and quite large – wherever tried. Sjaastad (1962) has argued that the effect of distance is too large to be explained solely by cost, and that social and cultural factors should be allowed as an explanation. However, Sahota (1968) carried out a calculation of the cost of moving, which turned out to be substantial. At the same time, Levy and Wadycki (1974) found educated migrants to be much less affected by distance than others.

These are the principal qualitative conclusions to be drawn from the studies. We will return later to the question of the quantitative significance of income and other factors. But first we give a brief summary of each of the articles. This makes tedious reading, but it is necessary as the studies are in many cases not comparable, but have differences which can be resolved by comparing what they are doing. In particular, researchers investigating the determinants of migration have occasionally been less than careful about both the choice of a dependent variable and the interpretation of results. Some apparently contradictory results have not been about the same thing: some studies have used specifications that are demonstrably incorrect.

2.2. Review of individual papers

To systematize our review of the individual papers, we have grouped the papers under three headings. The reader will recall that there are 7 studies of gross migration flows, 5 of net flows, and 2 of the destination decision of migrants. Under each heading, we will then discuss what we would expect to find and, in light thereof, review the individual papers.

2.2.1. Gross flows between regions.

We have here five studies of LDCs which base their estimates of migration on national censuses in which people were asked where they were born and classified by region. The other two studies in this group are based on somewhat different questions for the U.S. and Canada. The 1960 U.S. census records where people lived in 1955. For Canada, actual annual flows from 1947–1966 were calculated from requests for family allowance transfers. Despite the differences in the measures, we will refer to all kinds of gross flow from i to j as M_{ij}, and introduce other symbols: M_i for total migrants out of i, P_i and P_j for the populations of the two regions, and D_{ij} for the distance.

Now, it would seem evident that M_{ij} is likely to be an increasing function of P_i, the population of i, since that is a measure of the number of potential migrants. On the other hand, one *could* argue that the relationship may not be one of strict proportionality because, as with most economic phenomena, at *some* scale of P_i, for say skilled people in any one occupation (e.g., economists), there may be too few people for any one of them to feel that they can interact efficiently, and hence a large proportion would want to migrate, whereas, at a much larger scale, there may be a crowding effect leading to disproportionately more people wanting to migrate; so that we may have the typical U-curve phenomenon here. Nonetheless, a reasonable approximation may well be to treat the phenomenon as one of proportionality, thus implying that M_{ij}/P_i is the appropriate dependent variable in counting gross flows.

Allowing then for the population effect thus, it is clear that we would expect M_{ij} to be larger if: (i) region j is the more desirable; (ii) region i is the less desirable; and (iii) the people of region i are the more prone to migration.

Factor (i), relating to the country of destination, yields variables which can be expected to have relatively unambiguous signs, of course. On the other hand, factors (ii) and (iii) both relate to the country of origin and can clearly yield common variables which pull in contrary directions, as we have already had occasion to note. A way out of this difficulty would be to deflate M_{ij} by M_i. Then one could work with destination variables only to explain the shares of different j's in the emigration from a given i. This deflation was used by Sahota (1968) and Greenwood (1969), but with a serious flaw in specification which we presently note. Yet another cross-sectional approach could be to sum all the flows into j and treat $\sum_i M_{ij}$ as the dependent variable and only the destination variables as the independent variables.

We may now turn to the econometric studies of gross migration flows, beginning with five that yield elasticities and ending with two that yield more qualitative results.

(1) *Sahota* (1968) studied data on state of birth and state of residence as reported in the Brazilian census of 1950. He estimated log-linear equations explaining migration by males in two different age groups.

Sahota did not deflate M_{ij} by the population of either state of origin or state of destination. Nor did he include either population as an explanatory variable. This is rather puzzling, and is nowhere justified; its effect on the results is not clear. As explanatory variables, Sahota used a large number of characteristics of the states, and the distance between them. Distance had a substantial negative effect. His income variable was the wage rate in some regressions, and the level of per capita income in others. The elasticity of migration with respect to income in the destination state ranged from 1.82 to 2.25; in the origin region it had a negative sign, ranging from -0.77 to -1.69. Other variables are reported in table 1.

(2) *Beals, Levy and Moses* (1967) used the same kind of data from the 1960 Ghana census. The dependent variable was expressed as M_{ij}/P_i, and explained using a log-linear specification. Their explanatory variables included average labor income, population, the fraction who had attended school, and urbanization for both regions. Since population of i appeared on the right-hand side of the equation, the (partial) relationship between M_{ij} and P_i was not restricted to strict proportionality.

The elasticity of migration with respect to home population was significantly greater than one in all regressions; the elasticity with respect to destination population was less than one. No explanation is offered for the latter result; as for the former, they suggest the effect of 'the assured presence of friends of similar background'; presumably they are arguing, then, that Ghanaian regions represent cultural units.

Income in i and j had a negative and positive sign, respectively, and ran from -1.4 to -2.3 for Y_i, from 1.4 to 2.7 for Y_j.

(3) *Greenwood* (1969) carried out a study based on the 1960 Egyptian census which was essentially identical to that of Beals, Levy, and Moses. Using state-of-birth, state-of-residence data from the census, he estimated a log-linear function on M_{ij}, with population of i and j, wage rates, educational level, and

urbanization as explanatory variables. Like the previous study, this paper estimated a coefficient on origin region population significantly greater than one, although the coefficient on destination region population was not significantly different from one. Wage rates had the expected signs, with elasticities of 0.651 for destination and -1.406 for origin.

(4) *Levy and Wadycki* (1974) used a similar technique on migration in Venezuela. The principal differences were that M_{ij} was disaggregated by education level, and the econometric techniques were relatively sophisticated. Once again, population of origin region had an elasticity significantly greater than one, except for those with a secondary education or more; for those with less than a secondary education, population of destination had a coefficient significantly less than one. Wage rates, as usual, had the expected signs; for migrants with a secondary education, the elasticity of migration with respect to origin wage ranged from -1.68 to -3.35; the elasticity with respect to destination wage was about 2.

The most important result of this study was that the educated are less deterred by distance and more responsive to differences in wage rates than the less educated.

(5) *Greenwood* (1971), in another paper, estimated the effects of distance, income, and urbanization on rural–urban and urban–urban migration in India (based on the 1961 census). His dependent variable was M_{ij}/P_iP_j: i.e., he implicitly accepted the 'gravity hypothesis' for this paper. Income, urbanization, and distance were the explanatory variables. For rural areas the effect of income on migration was positive for both region of origin and destination; for urban areas, the effect of origin income was, as usual, negative. Elasticity of migration with respect to destination income lay in the range 1 to 1.5.

These five studies are all somewhat similar, and show remarkable similarity in some results. In particular, the elasticity of migration with respect to destination income generally lies between 1.0 and 2.5. As further evidence, Sahota cites a similar elasticity, in Sjaastad's (1959) unpublished thesis, of 1.52. These are the only really comparable numbers in the migration literature; as we will discuss later, they are not exactly what we might want to assess the likely response of migration to policy changes, but there really is nothing better available.

There are two more studies of gross migration flows, which are not really comparable to the previous five, except for some qualitative effects.

(6) *Gallaway, Gilbert and Smith* (1967) studied U.S. migration based on the 1960 census. Their dependent variable is M_{ij}/P_i. The explanatory variables were the arithmetic differentials in per capita income and unemployment, and distance; the article did not consider P_j's effect on M_{ij}. Although income and unemploy-

ment had the right signs, little of the variance in migration was explained. They did not express their results in elasticity terms, so the relative importance of income here is difficult to judge,

(7) *Vanderkamp* (1971) studied migration flows between Canadian provinces, as measured by requests for family allowance transfers. His dependent variable was $M_{ij}/(P_i+P_j)$, which does not have any obvious rationale. The results are again not expressed in elasticity terms. Income and distance were the only explanatory variables; the coefficients on income in both origin and destination areas were positive, but larger for the latter.[4]

2.2.2. Net flows out of (into) a region.

There are fewer studies on net flows out of (into) a region and, given our interest in international migration where net flows are just not available in any systematic fashion, this is perhaps not too distressing. Of course, the concept of a net flow is not relevant from the viewpoint of individual decision-making. However, ultimately, policy must try to focus on net flows and hence the following five studies are worth reporting on, if for no other reason than that we are interested in policy issues.[5]

(1) *Sjaastad* (1960) studied the percentage gain (loss) in a state's population from 1940–49 due to in-(out-)migration, for the 'lower 48' U.S. states. Independent variables were per capita income, farm population, rate of growth of income, educational level, etc., used in linear regressions. The main result was that income encouraged net in-migration; the results are not easily expressible in elasticity terms, but Sjaastad argues (p. 53) that the effect of income, though significant, is quite small. He also got a uniformly positive coefficient on education, which he argued was the result of an identification problem since educated people are more mobile; states experiencing in-migration tended to have high levels of education.

(2) *Raimon* (1962) used similar data from the 1950s for the U.S., in a straightforward study. He found that states with above-average income tended to experience net in-migration; and that there was a high rank correlation between net in-migration and either per capita income or average earnings per worker.

---

[4]It should be noted that Vanderkamp spends much of his paper discussing return flows, which will not concern us here.

[5]A major problem with interpreting net flows is that net figures can be very misleading if care is not taken about what is being added up. For example, the substantial net migration out of the U.S. South since World War II is the difference between a large outmigration of unskilled labor and a smaller immigration of highly skilled labor, so that in some sense migration out of the South is greatly exaggerated by the net figure. Also, the analysis of net migration can sometimes be subject to identification problems, as will be seen later in our discussion.

(3) *Schultz* (1970) studied net migration out of rural areas of Colombia. He found an elasticity of migration with respect to the rural wage rate of about -0.5. The percentage of population aged 10–14 with a primary education was positively related to out-migration; however, the percentage educated in the age group 5–9 had the opposite effect.

(4) *Bowles* (1970) applied a 'human capital' approach to differential migration of age–income–race groups out of the U.S. South. His principal explanatory variable was the estimated present value of the income to be gained by migration. The specification allowed the effect of this variable to change with age and education; separate analyses were run for blacks and whites. He found that: (1) migration was positively affected by the discounted earnings stream; (2) the effect of this stream increased with education and decreased with age; and (3) blacks were more likely to move than whites, but less responsive to economic incentive.[6]

(5) *Gallaway, Gilbert and Smith* (1967), in the second part of their paper, used as a measure of net migration between U.S. states the expression $[M_{ij}/P_i - M_{ji}/P_j]$. They then took as observations only the flows in a direction in which it is positive, regressing them on income and unemployment differentials. This is rather puzzling but they nonetheless got the 'expected' positive co-efficient on income.[7]

2.2.3. Migrants' choice of destination.

We mentioned above that it might be a good idea to use M_{ij}/M_i as a dependent variable, because it would eliminate those effects on M_{ij} which reflect effects of the propensity to migrate in i. The following two studies did use that variable.

(1) *Sahota* (1968), in the second part of his study of Brazil, regressed (M_{ij}/M_i) in a log-linear equation on differentials in income, wages (i.e., Y_j/Y_i, W_j/W_i), etc. Income had the expected effect, but with a greatly reduced elasticity. He also had a simultaneous model in which migration and wage rates were simultaneously determined, with the resulting elasticity with respect to wages lying between 0.10 and 0.15.

But in the event, these results cannot be accepted because the equation is mis-specified. Let $m_{ij} = (M_{ij}/M_i)$. Then Sahota has $M_{ij} = F(Y_j/Y_i, \text{ etc.})$, with $\partial F/\partial(Y_j/Y_i) > 0$. But this says that if, say, income in i should rise, the proportion

---

[6]These results should be compared with those of Levy and Wadycki (1974) in the previous section.

[7]A very low R^2 plagues their results and may be due to the omission of any variable representing population of destination.

of migrants going to any given destination (and thus to all destinations) must fall.

(2) *Greenwood* (1967), in a study of interstate mobility in the U.S., uses the same formulation. And he makes the same mistake. Even so, his initial estimate of the elasticity of migration with respect to income in j over income in i is 0.54. Other explanatory variables are distance, education, urbanization, unemployment, and temperature, but not P_j. He introduces as an explanatory variable the number of persons born in state i and living in j, which he calls the 'migrant stock'; and, indeed, its influence is plausible. When it is introduced it is significant, and causes the income coefficient to fall to 0.16.

2.3. *Conclusions to be drawn from the econometric literature*

What may we conclude then from the foregoing review of the several econometric studies of internal migration?

Clearly, the one clear reason for migration that emerges is, as Ravenstein wrote long ago, 'the desire inherent in most men to "better" themselves in material respects'.[8]

The evidence that migration is influenced by economic incentives is so uniform and secure that, if anyone should argue for any particular case that economic gain has *no* effect, one should be skeptical; particularly where migrants do in fact gain economically from their move. Furthermore, such evidence as there is suggests that education makes people more responsive to the possibilities of gain from migration.

This is not to deny the importance of noneconomic motives, which are clearly important; income variables rarely explain even as much as half of the variance in these studies, and social factors such as race or education (which can be regarded as much as a noneconomic as an economic factor) seem to affect responsiveness to economic incentives. For the individual migrant, income considerations may be relatively minor, but the effect of income is nearly always significant and never perverse. So, if, as in some of the brain drain literature which we review presently, an author asserts that there is no relationship between the economic gain from migration and the decision to migrate, one may confidently assume that there is a prima facie case that the author had only been flirting with his analysis, and not making the scholarly efforts necessary to test the hypothesis adequately.

How large is the effect of income on migration? One should beware of comparing results from widely different sources, but there does not seem to be any alternative. The largest group of more or less comparable studies is the group of studies of gross migration above. These generally imply an elasticity of migration with respect to destination income of, say, between 1.00 and 2.5.

[8]Quoted in Lee (1966).

Presumably, for highly educated migrants the value should be on the high side of that range, in view of the results in the papers by Bowles (1970) and Levy and Wadycki (1974).

Unfortunately, there is an upward bias in these estimates, since they involve only migration to one region out of several. Presumably an increase in income in *j* would draw migrants from *i*, not only from those who would not otherwise have migrated, but also from those who would have migrated to other regions. We might call these effects 'migration creation' and 'migration diversion'. Migration diversion is clearly of negligible interest for the brain drain problem; poor countries would feel no better if their doctors went to Britain instead of the U.S. Conceivably, an estimate of the diversion effect could be taken from a study using M_{ij}/M_i as dependent variable. For what it's worth, the studies by Sahota (1968) and Greenwood (1969) using it found relatively low elasticities of migration diversion with respect to income, i.e., around 0.5 or less; but those studies were, as mentioned above, marred by a serious misspecification. If we subtract this figure from the estimates of total effect on migration, we end up with a migration creation elasticity of, say, 0.5 to 2.0. Needless to say, this range has been arrived at by making logical jumps which few would gladly share; but those familiar with the theory and policy of second-best, and those who believe that fiction founded on facts is superior to ignorance, could find these numbers of some use.

But, in using them for analysis of the international brain drain, we need to remember two additional caveats. (1) The differentials in incomes between LDCs and DCs are far more substantial than those built into the studies reviewed above. So the elasticities are estimated from data that fall into a range of observations which do *not* span the values that we are interested in. But the degree of extrapolation involved here is certainly not extraordinary, especially when one recalls that many economists can be found who will argue, for example, that surplus labour (in the sense of zero social marginal product to labour) is impossible at any factor endowment because the production function for agriculture, estimated from the observed range of values, is Cobb–Douglas. (2) Next, in the context of international migration of skilled labour, it is pertinent to remember that one is dealing with restricted access and queues, so that the elasticity of (actual) migration with respect to reduced wage differentials, thanks to a Bhagwati-type income tax, could well be significantly lower than the range indicated above.

We turn our attention now to precisely the issue of the migration of skilled manpower, chiefly from the LDCs to the DCs, and review the contributions in that area.

3. International migration: The brain drain

Most of the many studies of high-level migration do a once-over-lightly on the motivations of migrants, doing no more than listing a number of plausible reasons before going on to policy questions. One report on a conference stated the reasons quite plainly: 'Statistical analyses and studies of motivation both require surveys and factual information. Policy recommendations, on the other hand, could be made on the basis of assumptions about statistics and motivations, and hence this part of the problem provided greater opportunity for discussion' [Oldham (1968, p. 17)].

By and large, adequate data is lacking on migration itself, let alone on likely determinants. So in spite of the immense number of papers that have been written on high-level migration, only a handful provide any useful information about the decision to migrate. Before we turn to these, however, it would be useful to cite Scott's (1970) earlier and most useful review, which groups the reasons for skilled migration under four categories:

(1) *Income differentials*: This is straightforward enough. There are several points that have to be watched carefully, though. (i) It is the whole stream of earnings, discounted to the present in some way, that probably matters. Thus a figure for income at only one po'nt, such as after 5 years of employment, while useful, may be misleading. (ii) If, as is common, there is unemployment among high-level people in the home country, a comparison of earnings if employed may lead to misleading ideas about the income to be gained from migration. (iii) Per capita income is not a very useful guide to earnings of professionals and scientists. As Psacharopoulos (1973, p. 132) has shown, the position of graduates of higher education in the wage structure varies considerably among countries.

(2) *Professional opportunities:* It is certainly reasonable to suppose that at least some people move because they cannot do what they would like in an LDC because of a lack of openings or sufficient diversity. Nobody really has any idea how important this is; but our guess is that it affects only a small number of people, but that these people may be exceptionally important.

(3) *Living conditions:* This includes everything from the political environment to the availability of peanut butter. One of the major findings of a UNITAR study (1973) was that members of ethnic minorities are especially liable to emigrate, presumably because of discrimination in the home country.

(4) *Working conditions:* Many scientists who emigrate give the availability of research facilities, libraries, etc., as a reason, and it must surely have some effect.

Scott had very little empirical evidence on which to draw. At this point, a few years later, there is more evidence, though still not very much. We have altogether six studies, of which only the first two were available to Scott: (1) a book by Hatch and Rudd (1968) on British students; (2) a first rate book by Myers (1972) on foreign students in the U.S.; (3) a book by Psacharopoulos (1973) on returns to education generally; (4) a major sociological UNITAR study by Glaser (1973); (5) a useful article by Kao and Lee (1973) on Taiwan students in the U.S.; and finally, (6) a rather unsatisfactory piece by Sen (1971) on immigration into the U.S. We will go through these studies, looking for evidence on various motives, then try to sum up what the present state of knowledge is.

(1) *Hatch* and *Rudd* (1968) devote one chapter of their book on 'graduate education and after' to a study of Britons with graduate education going overseas. Their analysis consisted purely of a questionnaire, which was answered by 678 one-time graduate students who had been overseas at some time between 1957 and 1966. It is a little difficult to be sure what respondents meant, but what is interesting is that many of those who were still overseas in 1966 gave reasons that appear to relate either to income or, less often, to openings and opportunities. (A diehard economic determinist might argue that 'dissatisfaction with Britain' means income, too.)

(2) *Myers'* (1972) work is an extremely helpful piece of research, making the most of inadequate data. What Myers is out to explain is the nonreturn of students educated in the U.S., what he calls the 'untrained brain drain'. There are four major parts to his analysis.

(i) The rate of nonreturn (as measured by statements of intent) for a number of countries was calculated; the rate of nonreturn was defined as nonreturnees as a proportion of students in the U.S. Myers used the multiple regression technique to analyze variation in this rate, with two interesting results: the rate of nonreturn was positively associated with per capita income in the home country and was negatively related to 'political elitism'. Note that the rate of nonreturn is not an appropriate measure of the magnitude of brains being drained: if France sent only 2 students to the U.S., and they both stayed, France would have a 100 percent nonreturn rate. So there is not necessarily anything perverse about the finding on income. It may even make sense a priori, since poor countries may not be able to provide adequate education at home, whereas if a European comes to the U.S. to study it may be only because he has a particular reason for wanting to be in the U.S.

In any case, Myers found that the conditions of financial sponsorship were the principal determinant of differences in nonreturn rates among countries.

(ii) In order to get an index of manpower loss, i.e., brains drained, Myers divided the number of nonreturning students by the total number of students at home and abroad who were citizens of the home country. This new index turned out to be essentially unrelated to either per capita income or political factors, which is interesting; at least this part of the brain drain seems to afflict rich and poor alike.

(iii) Myers discussed at some length an unpublished study by Herve on nonreturn. Herve attempted to use an 'effective demand' model of decisions by students. He first calculated a regression equation relating the number of students per capita to per capita income; then compared ac.ual to predicted values to arrive at a 'surplus' or 'deficit'. The idea was that the number of students a nation can employ depends on income; thus nonreturn should be related to surplus or deficit. One might argue that what Herve was actually doing was indirectly estimating the return to education in countries, since his surplus countries presumably should have had low earnings for college grad-uates, either because of competition driving down salaries or because of unem-ployment. In any case, the analysis did not work for all countries taken as a group, but if Latin America was deleted it did.

(iv) Finally, a questionnaire study was carried out on Peruvian students. They were asked to give, not merely intentions and reasons for their decision, but also estimates of their lifetime earnings streams in the U.S. and Peru, and their subjective estimates of the relative cost of living. There were two surprising results: (a) according to the figures given by the respondents, the present discounted value of income in Peru would *exceed* that in the U.S.; and (b) the comparison between the U.S. and Peru was least favorable to the U.S. for those planning to remain in the U.S. These results are hard to believe, and Myers was properly skeptical, arguing in particular that his respondents discounted the possibility of unemployment when judging Peruvian incomes.

Myers did not draw any firm conclusions from all this. He failed to find clear evidence that income matters, but argued himself that he was not able to test this properly.

(3) *Psacharopoulos'* (1973) book is concerned with returns to education generally, but in the course of the book, he arrived at two sets of figures which allowed him. to carry out an analysis of the brain drain problem. These are: (i) estimates of rates of return to higher education for a number of countries (Psacharapoulos did not compute these himself, rather, he selected them from estimates made by others); and (ii) 'cross' rates of return, which were internal rates of return on the income stream which would be earned if someone were to be educated in a country, then migrate permanently to the U.S. For his dependent variable, Psacharapoulos worked with the number of professional, technical, and related (PTK) workers admitted to the U.S. in 1969, dividing this by the number of students in higher education in the home country (using the latter, like Myers, as a proxy for the number of potential migrants).

In his first calculations, Psacharapoulos did not use these rates of return. Instead, he regressed migration on home country per capita income and distance, and duplicated the result of Myers in finding no significant effect. But he then pointed out, as mentioned above, that this was not surprising, since per capita income is a poor predictor of earnings of college graduates.

The estimation was then repeated, with log of migration explained by logs of the two rates of return. The elasticities with respect to cross and home country rates of return were, respectively, 1.563 and -1.072, both significantly different from zero. This is, as far as we can tell, the only estimate available on the effect of economic conditions on the migration of professionals (except for the results reported by Psacharopoulos and Lucas in their papers for this conference itself) and should therefore be treasured as one small candle in a vast darkness, whatever its faults. What is even more remarkable is that the size of the estimated effect is in the same general range as that which characterized the internal migration studies covered above.

Given a set of hard numbers, it would be pleasant just to accept them. But Psacharapoulos' work must be treated with some caution, for a number of reasons. (i) The sample is very small; the need for comparable data reduced the number of usable countries to 13. (ii) The rates of return to higher education are not calculated on a comparable basis; they are taken from a variety of sources, although Psacharopoulos did try to choose studies using similar definitions and techniques. (iii) The correct variables to use in a human capital analysis are not rates of return but present values; these cannot always be used interchangeably. Psacharopoulos presumably had to use rates of return because of data limitations. (iv) Finally, there is something which is not the author's fault, but inherent in the problem, and this is that none of his variables measures quite what we would like it to measure. Immigration of professional and technical workers, as measured by the U.S. Immigration Service, is not really an accurate measure of how many brains the U.S. has drained (as noted in Bhagwati's survey in chapter 1 of this volume). The number of college students is not really a measure of potential migrants. And the rates of return are based on average figures for earnings by age and education in each country, whereas those who choose to migrate are probably neither typical of those in the home country with the same education, nor comparable to Americans with the same educational qualifications. (There is some indication that they may be more talented, on the average, than stay-at-homes in either country.)

(4) *Glaser's* (1973) mammoth study for UNITAR is based on a questionnaire, but the questionnaire was designed in such a way as to allow at least rudimentary statistical analysis. Some 20,000 people replied to a long, fairly specific set of questions. (The results reported by Glaser, however, are based only on the first 5,500 replies.) Those questioned fell into three groups: LDC students currently studying in developed countries, professionals who had received overseas training and then returned ('returnees') and professionals who had not returned ('stay-ons').

Intentions were gauged by asking whether respondents 'definitely' or 'probably' would either stay or return. With the 'undecided' category, this gave a total of five categories. For many of the analyses, this ordinal variable was transformed into a cardinal variable by letting 'definitely return' = 2.0, 'probably return' = 1.0, etc.

The greater part of the analysis consists simply of cross-tabulations of intentions with various characteristics of migrants. These produced a number of interesting results, of which some are summarized below:

(1) Members of religious, cultural, or ethnic minorities have a relatively high tendency to emigrate; a conclusion which had been suspected before, but never conclusively shown.

(2) Contrary to some previous suspicions, there does not appear to be any systematic relationship between emigration and social class.

(3) It appear that the least able students are the least likely to emigrate.

(4) Respondents generally cited working conditions and professional needs as reasons to emigrate and personal relations as reasons to remain home.

After examining these cross-tabulations, Glaser carried out a more sophisticated statistical analysis; reasons named by respondents and intentions on migration were formed into trichotomous variables and compared using the statistic 'gamma'. The results of this analysis were that income, quality of jobs, and number of jobs were invariably strong reasons for migration. Opportunity to contribute to one's profession had strong association with migration decisions, but could work in either direction. Friends, family, and patriotism were associated with return. Professional needs turned out to be only weakly associated with the decision on emigration.

Also included was a brief analysis of the effect of income differentials on migration. Respondents were asked to estimate their income after five years of full-time employment at home or in the country of education. These figures were converted into dollars at official exchange rates. The intention to migrate was turned into a cardinal variable, from 1 = definitely return home to 5 = definitely emigrate, and regressed on the proportional gain in expected income from emigration. The estimated coefficient was significantly positive but, Glaser asserts, not very large (there are problems in deciding what is large); only a very small part of variance was explained ($R^2 = 0.033$).

Glaser's mammoth work will probably become a standard reference on motivations of emigrants, so some care should be taken to point out where it appears to be less than satisfactory.

(1) The cross-tabulations and correlations which make up most of the study do not show reasons for emigration; they show associations between the citing of reasons and emigration, which cannot be properly interpreted without some

sort of causal model. If X and Y are associated, it may be because Y affects X, but it may also be because Z affects both X and Y. It is odd that this problem is ignored, since the first chapter contains extensive strictures against confusing association and causation. In all fairness, though, Glaser's technique of grouping reasons into 'clusters' probably reduces the danger from this problem; but more analytical and empirical discussion of these issues (than is available in Glaser's work so far) is called for.

(2) Because of this problem, Glaser really should have done one of two things: (a) cross-tabulate in more than two dimensions, which is probably the best procedure with ordinal data; but even with 20,000 respondents, any reasonable sized four or five dimensional cross-tabulations will start having empty or nearly empty boxes; or (b) used some sort of multivariate technique; it is not just that, as Glaser says, such techniques give better prediction; if such a technique is really appropriate, simple correlations will give biased results.

(3) Because of this, we should hesitate to accept at face value the assessments of the relative importance of various factors, although it is not obvious in what ways they may be biased.

(4) Finally, it is rather peculiar that, on the one hand, income-related questions such as salaries, quality and availability of jobs were among the best predictors of emigration; while on the other hand, the actual income differential explained very little variance. There may be several reasons for this. (a) The question asked of respondents was what they thought they would earn after five years of employment. This ignores both the problem of unemployment, which may vary widely among countries, and the differences in salary patterns by age in different countries (i.e., U.S. salaries tend to start high and grow slowly, while in many countries salaries rise relatively rapidly with age). (b) The business of turning an ordinal into a cardinal variable leaves us uneasy. To illustrate, the quantitative meaning of, say, a shift from 'definitely' to 'probably' return is not clear. (c) The problems of purchasing power are difficult, but one would like a little more information. There is one problem that is particularly worrisome: respondents were asked for estimates of income after five years, in their national currency. How was inflation taken into account? To ask, say, a Brazilian for his income in five years, and convert it to dollars at *current* exchange rates, could overstate what he could earn in Brazil by a factor of two or three.

UNITAR will undoubtedly do some more detailed analysis on their incredible data bank. What Glaser has done so far is more a survey of the data and of the associations found in it than a serious analysis of the decision to migrate.

(5) *Kao* and *Lee* (1973) carried out what amounts to a miniature Glaser-type study of Nationalist Chinese migration to the U.S. They asked about 'propensity to stay in the U.S.', scaled from 0 to 9, and a number of other variables which were either binary or integer-scaled. These were then treated as cardinal variables in a number of linear multiple regressions. 'Satisfaction with the American

way of life' and 'income satisfaction in the United States' were generally the most important. These are certainly not surprising results; they indicate that both income and noneconomic motives matter, which is reassuring.

(6) *Sen*'s (1971) paper takes a cross-section of 47 countries and examines the relationship between various characteristics of a country and emigration of natural scientists, social scientists, engineers, and doctors to the U.S. He rejects the hypothesis that per capita income of sending countries matters, and finds the determinants of emigration to be the number of students in the field, and especially the number of graduate students in the U.S. This latter relationship is so strong that, in the case of doctors, it could not result even if every graduate students in the U.S. stayed there, which leads Sen to suggest the possible importance of information flows. Unfortunately, little of this can be taken at face value for several reasons, of which we spell out a few here.

(1) Sen's result that income does not matter is based on the use of regressions which use presumably the PTK migrants by different categories deflated by total population in the origin country *or* the total number of PTK migrants, as an absolute number, as the dependent variable, while per capita income in origin country is used as the independent variable. For one thing, the use of total migrants is not advisable for reasons which should be apparent from our earlier discussion of the literature on internal migration. Moreover, even the use of the deflated migrants raises the question: why should the deflation with total population (rather than with the population of the PTK class of migrants being analyzed) be correct? Only a systematic examination of the correlation between total and PTK population, if any, and its extent, could indicate the kind of bias that such a deflating procedure would imply. Also, the unsuccessful use of income per capita as the independent variable should not be taken as tantamount to explaining away the role of 'economic' factors. Sen should have explored the success of variables such as present discounted values, or relative wage rates, as in the standard literature on migration. The implied rejection of economic motivation in Sen's results must therefore be taken with serious reservations; this is particularly so when we consider the more successful and imaginative use of immigration data in the 1973 work of Psacharopoulos and the work by him and by Lucas in the papers for this conference.

(2) It is *not* correct econometric practice to take zero-order correlations, discard variables with low R^2, then do a multiple regression on those that remain. The correct way to it is to include all variables in the multiple regression to start with, and use t-statistics to test significance.

(3) Nor is Sen's relationship between graduate students and immigration levels meaningfully assessed. To infer that this implies an information network whereby more graduate students lead to more information and hence to more immigration is to bypass the far more plausible hypothesis that both are non-

causally associated for reasons such as the following. (i) Countries which produce a large number of, say, natural scientists would presumably have a large number of students in the field, which would presumably lead to a large number of students overseas as well as at home. And it would also presumably lead to larger emigration, if only because there would be more potential migrants. (ii) Moreover, for countries with cultural ties to the U.S., the U.S. would be a natural destination for both study and migration. If nothing else, the division of the Third World into francophone and anglophone areas would insure some relationship between overseas graduate study and emigration.[9]

The casual econometrics of this paper merits it, at best, only a minor place in our inventory of useful contributions to the analysis of the brain drain and the associated identification of the variables that matter in the decision to migrate.

4. Concluding remarks

The foregoing review of the literature on the decision to migrate is somewhat staggering in its implication that, despite the enormous amount written on the subject of the brain drain, we are forced to rely on the expedient of drawing analogies with a few studies of internal migrations and on literally no more than a mere handful of direct estimates [to be precise, three, of which two (Lucas and Psacharopoulos) have been prepared for this conference and ironically two are by one man]. What have we learned from them?

Starting with the analogy first: in the studies of internal migration, the elasticity of migration with respect to income at the destination was always positive, generally greater than one, never more than three. There was some evidence that highly educated people were more responsive to the possibility of income gains from moving than others. It is tempting to assume that international migration, which is more difficult both physically and psychically, has a lower elasticity with respect to income at the destination. But this does not follow; it is a confusion of the level of a curve – i.e., fewer people migrate abroad – with its slope.

The direct estimates are by Psacharopoulos. His earlier estimate explained migration by internal rates of return; and the elasticity of migration to the U.S. with respect to such a rate was 1.5. This must imply a somewhat higher elasticity with respect to the wage, say 2.0. His later estimate, for the conference, uses wages directly, with an estimated elasticity with respect to the U.S. wage of 0.543. Both estimates are based on small samples and imperfect data; taking this into account, they establish a range of reasonable values not too different from that found in the internal migration literature.

[9]The 'information flow' hypothesis itself is, of course, familiar in the migration literature and has been explicitly postulated, for example, in Greenwood (1967).

Does this allow us to put any bounds on the elasticity (ε)? The effect of income is surely positive, but it might be quite small for all we know; so we cannot really give any lower bound other than $\varepsilon > 0$. At the same time, the only estimated value for the elasticity of migration with respect to income we have seen that is greater than three was by Quigley (1972) for the exceptional case of 19th century Swedish migration to the U.S., so that one might put the upper bound at 3.0.

Whether one wishes to use any specific estimates, such as those of Psacharopoulos, or a broad range such as 0 to 3.0, must depend on one's taste. Whether these values are considered 'high' or 'low', on the other hand, must of course depend on the uses to which they are put.

References

Beals, R.E., M.B. Levy and L.N. Moses, 1967, Rationality and migration in Ghana, Review of Economics, November.

Bowles, S., 1970, Migration as investment: Empirical tests of the human investment approach to geographical mobility, Review of Economics and Statistics, November.

Bogue, D.J., 1969, Principles of demography (Wiley, New York).

Gallaway, L.E., R.F. Gilbert and P.E. Smith, 1967, The economics of labor mobility: An empirical analysis, Western Economic Journal, June.

Glaser, W., 1973, The migration and return of professionals, Colombia University Bureau of Applied Social Research, A study for the United Nations Institute for Training and Research (UNITAR).

Greenwood, M.J., 1969a, An analysis of the determinants of geographic labor mobility in the United States, Review of Economics and Statistics, May.

Greenwood, M.J., 1969b, The determinants of labor migration in Egypt, Journal of Regional Science, no. 9.

Greenwood, M.J., 1971, A regression analysis of migration to urban areas of a less developed country: The case of India, Journal of Regional Science, no. 2.

Kao, C.H. and J.W. Lee, 1973, An empirical analysis of China's brain drain into the United States, Economic Development and Cultural Change, April.

Lee, E.S., 1966, A theory of migration, Demography 3.

Levy, M.B., and W.J. Wadycki, 1974, Education and the decision to migrate: An econometric analysis of migration in Venezuela, Econometrica, March.

Myers, R.G., 1972, Education and emigration (McKay, New York).

Oldham, C.H.G., 1968, International migration of talent from and to the less developed countries (report of a conference at Ditchley Park).

Parnes, H.J., 1954, Research on labor mobility (Social Science Research Council, New York).

Psacharopoulos, G., 1973, Returns to education (Elsevier, Amsterdam).

Quigley, J.M., 1972, An economic model of Swedish emigration, Quarterly Journal of Economics, February.

Raimon, R.L., 1962, Interstate migration and wage theory, Review of Economics and Statistics, November.

Rudd, E. and S. Hatch, 1968, Graduate study and after.

Sahota, G.S., 1968, An economic analysis of internal migration in Brazil, Journal of Political Economy, March/April.

Schultz, T.P., 1971, Rural–urban migration in Columbia, Review of Economics and Statistics, May.

Scott, A., 1970, The brain drain – Is a human capital approach justified?, in: W.L. Hansen, ed., Education, income, and human capital (NBER, New York).

Sen, A.K., 1971, A quantitative study of the flow of trained personnel from the developing countries to the United States of America, Journal of Development Planning (UN), no. 3.

Sjaastad, L., 1959, The relationship between migration and income in the United States, Regional Science Association Papers and Proceedings.

Sjaastad, L., 1961, Income and migration in the United States, unpublished Ph.D. dissertation, Chicago.

Sjaastad, 1962, The costs and returns of human migration, Journal of Political Economy, October.

Vanderkamp, J., 1971, Migration flows, their determinants, and the effects of return migration, Journal of Political Economy, September/October.

CHAPTER 3

ESTIMATING SOME KEY PARAMETERS
IN THE BRAIN DRAIN TAXATION MODEL

George PSACHAROPOULOS*

London School of Economics, London, England

This paper attempts an estimate of the supply function of qualified emigrants from 23 countries into the U.S. by comparing the wages of professionals in the country of destination to those in the country of origin. The results have shown that the relative wage is a strong explanatory variable, the implied supply elasticity being of the order of 0.4. Among the other variables tried, distance was found to be unimportant, while relative per capita income had one half the explanatory power of relative wages. It was also found that a surtax of the Bhagwati type would have a negligible deterrent effect on the number of emigrants, therefore providing a pure revenue source to LDCs.

1. Introduction

The otherwise dormant literature on the brain drain has been recently shaken by a new immigration tax proposal. This proposal is an income tax, levied as a surtax, on skilled emigrants from LDCs into DCs, to be collected by the DCs of immigration and handed over to either the LDCs of origin or, in a preferred version, to an international agency such as UNDP for generalised spending for developmental purposes in the LDCs en bloc. This proposal was advanced by Bhagwati (1972) and preliminary, illustrative estimates of the tax revenue that could be collected were made in a subsequent paper by Bhagwati and Dellalfar (1973). At the same time, the economic implications of such a tax have been explored, in the context of a theoretical model embodying unemployment in the country of origin, by Bhagwati and Hamada (1974).

The theoretical elaboration yields the result that the effect of the tax on those left behind depends upon two crucial parameters: firstly, upon the elasticity of emigration with respect to a tax of this nature and, secondly, upon the elasticity of emigration with respect to foreign wages. The reason is that, on the one hand, the tax revenue will be greater to the extent that emigrants are not highly responsive to the tax. On the other hand, the country of origin would save higher

*This paper has benefited from the advice of my colleague Christopher Dougherty, the detailed criticisms made by Jagdish Bhagwati and from the comments of other participants in the Bellagio Conference on Brain Drain and Income Taxation and the Research Seminar on the Economics of Education at the London School of Economics.

training costs of professionals to the extent that emigrants are highly responsive to foreign wages.

The main purpose of this paper is to estimate the above-mentioned elasticities, the one, in fact, being a simple transformation of the other. In the process of so doing, however, we investigate empirically the more general behavioural question of the determinants of intercountry movements of educated labour.

2. Previous literature

The existing literature is not very helpful in assessing the responsiveness of emigrants to foreign wages. Empirical analyses of the relationship between differential economic rewards and the decision to emigrate have been mainly limited to labour movements within a single country [e.g., Sahota (1968) and Greenwood (1969)]. Analyses of the determinants of the brain drain have chiefly used qualitative scale variables, like the satisfaction derived from higher income abroad [e.g., Kao and Lee (1973) and Scott (1970, p. 246)], which would be inadequate for estimating the elasticities in question. The reason for this differential empirical treatment of interregional versus international migration must be attributed to the scarcity of data on the wages of professionals in the country of origin which might be compared with corresponding data in the country of destination.

In an earlier empirical study [Psacharopoulos (1971)] such data were used to answer a different (but related) question, namely, what are the returns to someone who graduates in his home country and then emigrates to the United States. The rate of return to this *combined* graduation–emigration decision was used to explain the brain drain into the United States from a limited number of countries.

In this paper I expand and slightly revise the earlier set of data on the wages of professionals in various countries in order to assess the responsiveness of emigrants to economic rewards.[1]

3. The data

Table 1 shows the basic data on which the analysis in this paper is based. The 23 countries of origin appearing in this table represent the intersection of the countries for which we have data on the earnings of professionals and for which the U.S. Immigration and Naturalization Service publishes detailed immigration statistics. Column 2 of this table shows the number of immigrants (Z) admitted into the United States in 1969, and this will be the dependent variable in what follows. The year 1969 was chosen for this purpose as it represents a 'quota free'

[1]In this sense I also reply to Scott's (1971) criticism that I should have used relative wages instead of rates of return as the independent variable in the emigration function. But see also Psacharopoulos (1972).

Table 1

Immigration of professionals into the U.S. and related statistics by country of origin.[a]

Country of origin (i) (1)	Immigrants absolute annual flow Z_i (2)	Immigration propensity Z_i/H_i (3)	Wage of professionals in the country of origin (in $) W_i (4)	Wage ratio $\bar{W}_f/W_i$ (5)	Per capita income ratio $\bar{Y}_f/Y_i$ (6)	Distance factor (in $) D_i (7)
Mexico	484	2.52	5,993	2.16	6.91	137
Colombia	647	11.16	5,027	2.57	12.58	255
Chile	116	2.19	2,530	5.11	7.31	448
Brazil	157	0.55	3,344	3.87	12.62	471
India	2,857	2.71	1,430	9.05	47.03	926
Thailand	398	10.21	3,043	4.25	24.06	851
Philippines	7,138	13.75	1,358	9.53	19.25	708
South Korea	1,062	7.48	1,678	7.71	19.16	708
Turkey	266	1.86	5,518	2.34	10.95	561
Iran	482	8.31	2,842	4.55	14.47	752
Morocco	57	5.18	5,136	2.52	21.01	358
Israel	383	8.51	2,293	5.64	2.87	649
Greece	585	8.01	2,128	6.08	4.38	541
Italy	501	1.19	5,888	2.20	2.88	466
Spain	411	2.60	4,710	2.75	5.18	378
Japan	400	0.26	2,864	4.52	2.93	627
Norway	134	3.19	6,433	2.01	1.93	399
Sweden	53	0.46	14,359	0.90	1.23	427
Netherlands	221	1.21	6,944	1.86	2.06	378
France	252	0.41	9.464	1.37	1.63	378
Canada	2,431	4.83	9,209	1.40	1.33	73
United Kingdom	2,513	6.08	6,224	2.08	2.26	365
Australia	300	1.82	7,431	1.74	1.69	842

[a]*Sources:* Column 2 – 1969 immigrants flow, from United States, Department of Justice (1969, table 8).

Column 3 – Col. 2 × 1000/Enrollment in higher education in the country of origin in 1967/68, from UNESCO (1970, table 2.12).

Column 4 – Mexico, Colombia, Chile, Brazil, Philippines, Turkey, Israel, Greece, Norway, Netherlands, Canada and U.K. from Psacharopoulos (1973, p. 185). India from Blaug et al. (1969, p. 171). Average salary of graduates in arts and engineering. Thailand from Blaug (1971, p. A-14). Average of nine higher education fields at the 35–39 age group. S. Korea from Kim (1968, p. 9, item 5). Corresponds to those with 15 years of service. Iran from Psacharopoulos and Williams (1973, p. 46). Refers to contractual employees with B.A. Morocco from Psacharopoulos (forthcoming, table 6). Regression-derived corresponding to 40-year-old males with university degree. Italy from Bank of Italy (1972, table 10). Spain from Grifoll (1969, table 21). Before tax average salary of five higher education specialties. Japan from Stoikov (1973, table 3). Regression-derived corresponding to male college graduates with 5 years previous experience and 15 years

Notes for table 1 (*continued*)

> service with the present firm. Sweden from Klevmarken (1972, p. 119). Read off the age-earnings profile of a 40-year-old graduate in 'science, business and economics'. France from Lévy-Garboua (1973, table 6). Refers to males, all diplomas. Australia from Blandy and Goldsworthy (1973). Lifetime earnings of male graduates divided by 45.
>
> Column 5 – W_f = $12,938 divided by W_i.
>
> Column 6 – U.S. per capita income ($4,139) divided by the per capita income of the country of origin; from United Nations (1973, table 182).
>
> Column 7 – Pan American Airlines.

year relative to the old U.S. immigration system. Furthermore, this year comes closer to the date of the wage data which, for most countries, refer to the late sixties.

Evidently, one needs to standardise the absolute number of immigrants for the size of the country of origin. The number of students enrolled in higher education (H) in 1968 was chosen for this purpose. What we would have liked, ideally, is the stock of professionals in the country of origin, a statistic that is not available in all countries of the sample. Note, however, that the size of the higher education student body is a more relevant standardising factor than, say, the country's population or labour force as a whole. The resulting standardised variable, labelled 'immigration propensity', appears in column 3 of table 1.

Column 4 of the same table shows the mean annual before-tax wage (W) of professionals in the country of origin, assembled from a variety of sources. Given that the corresponding statistic for the United States is $\overline{W}_f$ = $12,938, the reader can judge for himself how well (or badly) some LDC Joneses are keeping up with U.S. Joneses.[2] Of course, note that the comparison of $\overline{W}_f$ to W_i cannot yield the extent of the upward pull (if any) on the domestic wage level resulting from the alleged international integration of professionals [Bhagwati and Hamada (1974)]. The additional information we would need for a conclusion of this kind is the shadow, competitive market clearing wage of professionals in the country of origin.[3] But regardless of the within-country distortion in the market of professionals, the U.S.-to-the-country-of-origin wage differential can form the basis of a behavioural model to explain the international movement of educated labour.

4. Alternative specifications of the emigration function

The immigration propensity was related to economic incentives by means of

---

[2]This figure refers to 1968 and corresponds to those with 4+ years of higher education [U.S. Bureau of the Census (1972, p. 114)].

[3]This is of course another scanty statistic and furthermore subject to criticism regarding its derivation. For examples on how to arrive at market clearing wages using different methodologies, see Psacharopoulos (1970) and Harberger (1971).

the following simple linear forms,

$$Z_i/H_i = a + b(\overline{W}_f/W_i),\tag{1}$$

where $\overline{W}_f/W_i$ is the ratio of the wage of professionals in the U.S. relative to the wage of professionals in the country of origin (table 1, column 5).[4] A variant of this model is

$$Z_i/H_i = a + b(\overline{W}_f/W_i) + D_i,\tag{1a}$$

where D_i is a distance factor from country i to the United States, measured as the one way air fare from the country of origin to Chicago, Illinois (table 1, column 7).

The above model was contrasted to the more traditional ones,

$$Z_i/H_i = a + b(\overline{Y}_f/Y_i)\tag{2}$$

$$Z_i/H_i = a + b(\overline{Y}_f/Y_i) + cD_i,\tag{2a}$$

where $\overline{Y}_f/Y_i$ is the ratio of per capita income of the U.S. relative to the per capita income of the country of origin (table 1, column 6).[5]

Finally, the following model was tried,

$$Z_i/H_i = a + bR_i,$$

where the independent variable R is a transformation of the relative wages which may be interpreted as an approximate measure of the internal rate of return to emigration, namely,

$$R_i = \frac{\overline{W}_f - W_i}{2D_i}.$$

[4]Eq. (1) is given in such form for expository simplicity. In the actual run all wages are after conventional income tax (T) and corrected for the differential cost of living (L) between the United States and the country of origin [United Nations (1969)]. Therefore, the actual form fitted was

$$\frac{Z_i}{H_i} = a + b\frac{L_i W_f(1 - \bar{t}_f)}{W_i(1 - t_i)} = a + b\frac{L_i(\overline{W}_f - \overline{T}_f)}{W_i - T_i},\tag{1'}$$

where t and T represent the tax rate and absolute amount of tax, respectively. The income tax rate for the United States was taken equal to 11.75 percent [from Bhagwati and Dellalfar (1973, table 6)], while a flat 10 percent tax rate was assumed to apply in all countries of origin.

Admittedly, the correction for the cost of living is very crude. The regression results were rather insensitive to the inclusion of the L adjustment factor.

[5]In the actual run, the per capita income ratio was adjusted for the cost of living.

The numerator of this expression shows the annual additional income stream accruing to the emigrant over his lifetime, while the denominator shows the cost of acquiring this income stream, assumed equal to twice the cost of moving.[6]

Table 2 shows the resulting rates of return. Bearing in mind that these are conservative measures, they can be interpreted in two ways. Firstly, their overall size justifies the behaviour of LDC professionals who apply for an immigrant's visa to the United States. Secondly, if these rates are not a temporary pheno- menon and have persisted over time, their size suggests that the international market for professionals, far from being well integrated, is in a state of extreme disequilibrium. To put it another way, these rates reflect the mobility-inhibiting distortions, caused by lack of information, family ties or immigration restrictions.

Table 3 shows the overall sample means and parameter values.

Table 2

Internal rates of return to immigration into the U.S.[a]

Country of origin *i*	Rate of return (%) R_i
Mexico	1100
Colombia	555
Chile	489
Brazil	522
India	284
Thailand	287
Philippines	419
South Korea	398
Turkey	238
Iran	296
Morocco	417
Israel	319
Greece	496
Italy	305
Spain	452
Japan	492
Norway	443
Sweden	negative
Netherlands	266
France	163
Canada	1007
United Kingdom	338
Australia	200

[a]Rates of return are after tax and adjusted for the cost of living and the shape of the age– earnings profiles. For sources see text.

[6]In the actual run, wages were after tax and adjusted for the cost of living. Furthermore, the rate of return was adjusted downwards by 30 percent. The reason is that, as has been shown elsewhere [Psacharopoulos (1973, appendix A)], the above approximation to the true rate of return overstates it by about one-third (as the approximation assumes a horizontal and infinitely lasting age–earnings profile).

Table 3

Sample means and parameter values.[a]

Variable or constant		Symbol	Mean or value
Propensity to emigrate (emigrants per 100 students enrolled in higher education)		$\overline{(Z/H)}$	4.58
U.S. before-tax professional earnings	($)	$\bar{W}_f$	12,938
U.S. tax rate (percent)		$\bar{t}_f$	11.75
Annual professional taxes in the U.S.	($)	$\bar{T}_f$	1,520
U.S. after-tax professional earnings	($)	$\bar{W}_f - \bar{T}_f$	11,418
Cost of living adjustment factor		L	0.84
U.S. after-tax professional earnings adjusted for the cost of living	($)	$(\bar{W}_f - \bar{T}_f)L$	9,591
Before-tax earnings of professionals in the country of origin	($)	$\bar{W}_i$	5,037
Country-of-origin tax rate (percent)		$\bar{t}_i$	10
Annual taxes of professionals in the country of origin	($)	$\bar{T}_i$	504
After-tax professional earnings in the country of origin	($)	$\bar{W}_i - \bar{T}_i$	4,533
Rate of return to emigration (percent)		$\bar{R}_i$	338
Distance factor	($)	$\bar{D}_i$	509
Wage ratio, after tax and cost of living adjustment		$\left[\dfrac{(\bar{W}_f - \bar{T}_f)L_i}{\bar{W}_i - \bar{T}_i} \right]$	3.04
Per capita income ratio		$\overline{(\bar{Y}_f L_i / Y_i)}$	7.96

[a]*Sources:* Based on tables 1 and 2. See text also.

Table 4

Regression results.[a]

Model	Constant term	Wage ratio W_f/W_i	Per capita income ratio $\bar{Y}_f/Y_i$	Distance D_i	Rate of return R_i	R^2
(1)	1.694	0.950 (2.49)				0.23
(1a)	2.346	1.115 (2.21)		-0.0023 (-0.51)		0.24
(2)	3.408		0.147 (0.09)			0.11
(2a)	2.930		0.130 (0.12)	0.0012 (0.00)		0.11
(3)	3.942				0.157 (0.78)	0.01

[a]The dependent variable in all cases is the propensity to emigrate (Z_i/H_i). Wages are after tax and adjusted for the cost of living. Numbers in parentheses are t-statistics.

5. Regression results

The three alternative models performed as shown in table 4. Relative wage is the most significant variable, accounting for about one-fourth of the variation in the propensity to emigrate. Given the simplicity of the model, the crudity and cross-sectional character of the data, we consider this to be a strong result.

Relative per capita income and distance, in particular, are not statistically significant. The poor performance of distance accounts also for the non-significant result on the rate of return variable (which incorporates the distance factor). It seems that, given the large profit margin involved, the fare represents so small a proportion of the emigrant's expected gain as to become a negligible factor in the emigration decision.

6. The value of the elasticities

The results presented above can now be used to estimate the value of the elasticities in the Bhagwati–Hamada model. For this purpose let us first rewrite the basic estimating equation as

$$\frac{Z_i}{H_i} = a + b \frac{L_i(\overline{W}_f - \overline{T}_f - T_b)}{W_i - T_i}, \tag{1''}$$

in order to distinguish between the two kinds of taxes immigrants pay: $\overline{T}_f$ is the conventional U.S. income tax per immigrant, T_b is the Bhagwati surtax per immigrant, their sum being equal to the total tax revenue per immigrant ($T = \overline{T}_f + T_b$). Then we may define the elasticity of emigration with respect to the surtax revenue per immigrant as

$$\eta_f^T = - \frac{dZ}{dT_b} \cdot \frac{T_b}{Z},$$

and the elasticity of emigration with respect to the effective foreign wages per immigrant as

$$\varepsilon_f = \frac{dZ}{d(\overline{W}_f - T)} \cdot \frac{\overline{W}_f - T}{Z}.$$

Differentiating (1'') with respect to T_b and ($\overline{W}_f - T$), and utilising the first regression result in table 4 (i.e., $b = 0.95$), we arrive at the following elasticity values:[7]

$$\eta_f^T = 0.044,$$

$$\varepsilon_f = 0.395.$$

[7]Estimated at the mean of $(W_i - T_i)$, L_i and (Z_i/H_i).

7. Interpretation of the results

Bhagwati and Hamada note the 'direct' and 'indirect' effects of their poll tax (which is identical to the Bhagwati surtax in steady state), on the incomes of those left behind. The direct effect relates to the tax revenue effect, that is, to the total surtax collected and returned to the country of origin. Clearly, this effect will be positive when $\eta_f^T < 1$, as $d(T_b Z)/dT_b = (1 - \eta_f^T) \cdot Z$ represents the revenue change as the surtax is changed.

As for the indirect effect, Bhagwati and Hamada (1974, p. 40, eq. 38) show that in the variant of their model chosen for this analysis, the *total* direct plus indirect effect will also be positive if $\eta_f^T < 1$, the latter thus being a sufficient (but not necessary) condition for this outcome. It follows therefore that our estimated elasticity value $\eta_f^T = 0.044$ shows that this sufficiency condition for the Bhagwati surtax improving the incomes of those left behind is well met.

We can also readily calculate the 'direct' effect component of this improvement. Using the elasticity value $\eta_f^T = 0.044$, a stock of taxable PTK immigrants (into U.S. from LDCs) $Z = 41,435$,[8] and $\Delta T_b = \$1,142$ (representing a 10 percent poll tax of the emigrants' after-conventional-tax earnings), we arrive at an annual direct revenue effect on the order of $45 million to be distributed to LDCs from one recipient country alone.

[8] From Bhagwati and Dellalfar (1973, table 1).

References

Bank of Italy, 1972, Quindicinale di note e commenti, Anno VIII, N. 162–63, May.

Bhagwati, J., 1972, The United States in the Nixon era: The end of innocence, Daedalus, fall.

Bhagwati, J. and W. Dellalfar, 1973, The brain drain and income taxation: A proposal, World Development 1, no. 1.

Bhagwati, J. and K. Hamada, 1974, The brain drain, international integration of markets for professionals and unemployment: A theoretical analysis, Journal of Development Economics 1, no. 1.

Blandy, R. and T. Goldsworthy, 1973, Private returns to education in South Australia, mimeo (The Flinders University of South Australia, Bedford Park, Australia).

Blaug, M., 1971, The rate of return to investment in education in Thailand, A report to the National Planning Committee on the Third Educational Development Plan (National Education Council, Bangkok).

Blaug, M., R. Layard and M. Woodhall, 1969, The causes of graduate unemployment in India (Allen Lane, The Penguin Press, London).

Greenwood, M.J. 1969, An analysis of the determinants of geographic labour mobility in the United States, Review of Economics and Statistics, May.

Grifoll, G.J., 1969, Aspectes economicas de l'educacio (Banca Cataláña, Barcelona).

Harberger, A., 1971, On measuring the social opportunity cost of labour, International Labour Review, June.

Kao, C.H.C. and J.W. Lee, 1973, An empirical analysis of China's brain drain into the United States, Economic Development and Cultural Change, April.

Kim, K.S., 1968, Rates of return on education in Korea, mimeo (USAID, Washington).

Klevmarken, A., 1972, Statistical methods for the analysis of earnings data with special application to salaries in Swedish industry (The Industrial Institute for Economics and Social Research, Stockholm).

Lévy-Garboua, L., 1973, Les profils age-gains correspondant à quelques formations-type en France (CREDOC, Paris).

Psacharopoulos, G., 1970, Estimating shadow rates of return to investment in education, Journal of Human Resources, winter.

Psacharopoulos, G., 1971, On some positive aspects of the economics of the brain drain, Minerva, April.

Psacharopoulos, G., 1972, Letter to the editor, Minerva, January.

Psacharopoulos, G., 1973, Returns to education: An international comparison, (Elsevier–Jossey Bass).

Psacharopoulos, G. and G. Williams, 1973, Public sector earnings and educational planning, International Labour Review, July.

Psacharopoulos, G., (forthcoming), Earnings determinants in a mixed labour market or, The premium for being a foreigner, in: W. Van Ricjckeghem, ed., Employment problems and policies in developing countries – The case of Morocco, (Rotterdam University Press, Rotterdam).

Sahota, G.S., 1968, An economic analysis of internal migration in Brazil, Journal of Political Economy, March.

Scott, A.D., 1970, The brain drain – Is a human capital approach justified?, in: W. Lee Hansen, ed., Education, income and human capital (National Bureau of Economic Research, New York).

Scott, A.D., 1971, Letter to the editor, Minerva, October.

Stoikov, V., 1973, The structure of earnings in Japanese industries, Journal of Political Economy, March/April.

UNESCO, 1970, Statistical yearbook 1970.

United Nations, 1969, Monthly Bulletin of Statistics, December.

United Nations, 1973, Statistical yearbook, 1973.

United States Department of Justice, 1969, Annual report of the Immigration and Naturalization Service.

United States Bureau of the Census, 1972, Statistical abstract of the United States, 1972.

CHAPTER 4

THE SUPPLY-OF-IMMIGRANTS FUNCTION
AND TAXATION OF IMMIGRANTS' INCOMES

An econometric analysis

Robert E. B. LUCAS*

U.C.L.A., Los Angeles, CA 90024, U.S.A.

This paper considers the derivation of the commonly estimated macro supply-of-migrants equation from a discrete choice-of-location theory, in which tastes are stochastic. This approach highlights a number of economic and econometric problems inherent in popular forms of this equation. A logit specification of the supply function of U.S. immigrants is presented, using aggregated data on applications for labor certificates rather than observed movements. A modest simulation then follows, reporting the sensitivity of migration flows, hours worked by immigrants, and tax revenues, under alternative rates of Bhagwati's proposed tax on U.S. immigrants' incomes.

1. Introduction

Bhagwati (1972) proposes the imposition of a tax on incomes of professional, technical and kindred (PTK) immigrants from less developed countries (LDCs), working in the developed nations, the revenue to be collected by the host country and, in a desired variant, delivered to an international agency for developmental spending in LDCs. In a subsequent paper, Bhagwati and Dellalfar (1973) estimate the amount of revenue which might be collected by such a tax on LDC immigrants who entered the U.S. from 1962 to 1969. Further, Bhagwati and Hamada (1974) explore the consequences of skilled persons' emigration on source-country welfare in the context of a general equilibrium model embracing unemployment, wage rigidity, and wage emulation, and suggest that a Bhagwati-type tax may be welfare enhancing as a mechanism for internalizing any external costs inherent in the brain drain.

A central parameter in these analyses is, of course, the responsiveness of migration flows to the tax. The purpose of this paper is to present an econometric analysis of this question and to proceed then to simulate the sensitivity of tax revenues to alternative rates of a tax comparable to Bhagwati's. The

*The author is grateful to J.N. Bhagwati, K. Hamada and R. McCulloch for comments on an earlier draft.

analysis relates to U.S. immigration, being the case to which the Bhagwati–
Dellalfar estimates are originally addressed.

The outline of the paper is as follows. Section 2 presents a discrete choice-
of-location theory, the utility function being of the type considered by McFadden
(1974). Although this is rather a natural framework within which to consider
migration, the analysis seems to be novel and a number of interesting econometric and economic problems arise, particularly pertaining to the aggregated
or macro migration equation. Section 3 sketches the current U.S. immigration
system, focussing on those aspects of relevance to the regression analysis in
later sections. Section 4 contains estimates of the wage responsiveness of the
supply of migrants to the U.S., relying upon data reporting applications for
labor certification rather than numbers admitted. Although there exists a
number of such estimates for internal migration, the work of Psacharopoulos
(1973) is apparently the only precursor of this investigation into international
movements. Finally, the simulated effects of a Bhagwati-style tax upon numbers
of migrants, hours worked, and tax revenues, are given in section 5, followed by
a listing of certain limitations of this study in the closing section.

2. Micro foundation for macro migration equation

2.1. Towards a theory

Most existing general equilibrium models explicitly incorporating migration
suggest, as a fundamental equation, that the flow of migrants from one location
to another depends upon some measures of alternative wages in the two locations.[1] One might perceive such macro migration functions as differential
equations postulated, ad hoc, to be disequilibrium dynamic adjustments of
labor quantities in pursuit of factor price inequalities. However, the difficulties
of founding any such equation in decision theory are well known, their residual
ad hoc nature thus being rather unsatisfactory.

As an alternative basis, let us envision each individual (or family) selecting,
at any moment in time, a location with finite dimensions from some set of
alternatives, and suppose that in making this discrete choice the individual takes
account, amongst other things, of the discounted wage-streams offered by each
locale, and the transition costs between locales.[2] Further, we shall follow
McFadden (1974) in assuming that tastes have two components: the representative consumer part, in which tastes vary systematically with some vector
of measured attributes of persons; and a stochastic disturbance element,

---

[1]See, for example, Harris and Todaro (1970).
[2]In contrast to Sjaastad (1962), attention is here focussed on wage-rates rather than earnings
since part of the benefit to migration may be increased leisure. The omission of leisure opportunity is a common oversight in human capital theory, as noted by Lindsay (1971).

reflecting individuals' idiosyncrasies. Thus,

$$U^\alpha = U(w^\alpha, \delta^\alpha, \gamma^\alpha, \varepsilon^\alpha), \tag{1}$$

where U^α is person α's utility, w^α is α's discounted wage-rate, δ^α is transition cost incurred by α, γ^α is a vector of measured attributes of α, and ε^α is a stochastic disturbance term. α's problem is to pick from a set of locations with given wage-offers, and transition costs available to α, so as to maximize (1). The probability of any person α, drawn randomly from the population, choosing location i is then some function:

$$\pi_i^\alpha = \pi(W^\alpha, D^\alpha, \gamma^\alpha, \varepsilon^\alpha), \tag{2}$$

where W^α is the vector of locational discounted wage-streams available to α and D^α is a similar vector of transition costs. Compare now a popularly estimated macro migration equation:[3]

$$P_{ji} = P(\bar{w}_i, \bar{w}_j, d_{ji}, \bar{\gamma}, u), \tag{3}$$

where P_{ji} is proportion of location j's population which moves to i, $\bar{w}_i$, $\bar{w}_j$ are mean wages in i and j, d_{ji} is distance from j to i, $\bar{\gamma}$ is a vector of mean attributes of j's population, and u is a stochastic disturbance term. The distance variable is commonly thought to be a proxy for transition costs, varying directly with transportation costs, psychological costs of removal to an unfamiliar milieu, and costs of information acquisition.[4] With this in mind, and ignoring discrepancies between current and discounted wages,[5] consider then the transformation of (2) into (3).

If *both* (2) and (3) are linear, then taking the expected value of the micro migration decision function for those persons originally located in j easily yields (3). Note even here though that mean wages and distances for all locations other than j and i are relegated to the disturbance term u, and one must assume that these omitted terms are uncorrelated with those included if absence of bias is to be asserted.[6] Linear specification of (3) is not popular, and indeed linearity does embody certain problems. In particular, since the left-hand variable in (3) is constrained to lie in the interval zero–one, it is well known that the distribution of disturbances is heteroskedastic.[7] Thus, t-tests are strictly

---

[3]For a recent survey of such estimates, see Greenwood (1975).

[4]The consensus of opinion seems to be leaning towards dominance of the last. The one-shot transportation costs, possibly with a high fixed component, represents a minor fraction in the present value calculations of migration at moderate discount rates. Further, the work of Schwartz (1973) favours information over psychic costs interpretations.

[5]That is, taking the former as proxies for the latter.

[6]Across which observations these are to be uncorrelated will be considered shortly.

[7]Theil (1971).

inappropriate, though sufficiently large t-values might be defended on a robustness principle.[8] Also, as we shall see later, it is not uncommon for linear probability equations to predict outside of the zero–one range for the probabilistic dependent variable.

The standard reaction to the heteroskedasticity and prediction pathologies is to take something like a logit transformation of the probability variable. In doing so, however, linearity in the underlying migration decision function must be abandoned, but then such linearity is really no more than a convenience.

Once nonlinearity of (2) is admitted, taking expected values is no longer such a trivial matter: both the functional form of (2) and the joint distribution of the underlying variables must now generally be known. Although mean wages may remain as arguments of the expectational form (3), higher moments of the joint distribution of distances and wages are also likely to appear.[9] To ignore such higher moments in the specification of the macro migration regression equation, one must maintain that the first and other moments are uncorrelated, otherwise bias again ensues.

By way of closing this section, let it be noted that our decision theoretic approach to the migration equation does not, by itself, explain continuing labor flows in the absence of changes in the independent variables, and consequently is not intended as a foundation for differential disequilibrium adjustment equations more generally. Steady flows may be attributed to population taste changes (either through changing personal attributes such as age or through idiosyncratic component variations) or to steady changes in wage differentials, though these would probably be in the wrong direction in the absence of demand shifts. An interesting extension of the above model may, however, contribute a further factor tending to slow adjustment towards equilibrium. For a number of reasons, one might suppose that the probability of a person migrating to some spot depends on the magnitude of such prior movement from his community – because information is more readily transmitted, settling-in costs defrayed, and the hostility of an alien environment stilled. Thus, one might introduce the integral of past quantities moved into (2), in a fashion reminiscent of the learning-by-doing models.[10] Continuing migration in the face of unaltered wage differentials and tastes is then explicable, and a quantity adjustment equation of the Samuelson differential equation type may even be generated.

---

[8] Malinvaud (1966).

[9] For example, if

$$\pi_i^\alpha = \pi_i \cdot w_i^{\alpha 2} + \pi_j \cdot w_j^{\alpha 2},$$

with π_i, π_j nonstochastic, then

$$E[\pi_i^\alpha] = \pi_i \cdot [\bar{w}_i^2 + \sigma_{w_i}] + \pi_j \cdot [\bar{w}_j^2 + \sigma_{w_j}],$$

where σ_w is the variance of w.

[10] Or rather learning-by-others-doing. Any externality inherent in such a phenomenon can, of course, tend towards migration rates below those required for a world Pareto optimum.

2.2. Eligible data bases

In the absence of suitable micro data for estimating the micro decision function (2) directly, and in the absence of sufficient time-series aggregate data for estimating (3), attention naturally turns to cross-sectional aggregated data. A difficulty with the latter is one of choosing appropriate observation units, and a moment's reflection will suffice to demonstrate that a popular solution is quite clearly unsatisfactory.

In particular, it is not uncommon to deploy measures of the proportions of one location's population moving to many alternative destinations as observations on the left-hand variable in (3), with the respective locational average variables on the right. For example, in examining rural–urban migration, several studies look at the fractions of rural population moving to town 1, town 2, etc. But the probabilities of person α moving to town 1, town 2, or of staying put, reflect mutually exclusive decisions, taken simultaneously, the outcomes summing to one. In other words, the system of equations with the probabilities of moving to different destinations is not a series of observations on independent experiments, as assumed in deriving regression formulae, but an over-simplified reduced form of a simultaneous structural model.

The alternative, and that administered here, is to observe the proportions of population moving from several original locations to one destination. If the representative portions of taste are assumed common to every location of origin, then the parameters of the macro migration equation are independent of the observational index. Otherwise, if it is felt that such a hypothesis is overly strong, then (3) may be treated as a random coefficient equation, discrepancies between the coefficients for each location of origin and the mean coefficients being dismissed to the disturbance terms in the usual fashion.

2.3. On destination wage

A fundamental problem emerges in the application of the technique proposed in the last paragraph, namely that of measuring destination wage-rate. Consider, for example, the exercise treated hereafter relating proportions of populations moving from various countries to the U.S. There exists just one average wage-rate in America at any moment in time, so apparently there will be no multi-fariousness in this variable, and precisely the parameter which interests us most is seemingly inestimable. Fortunately such reasoning is in error, for the appropriate measure of expected destination wage is not the prevailing average wage. Remember that the W^α in (2) are wage-offers to α in the various locations, and the expected values of these offers for the population of any country of origin is almost certainly not the U.S. average wage, if only because average skill levels differ across countries. Indeed the average, imaginary, U.S. wage-offer to citizens of another realm cannot be observed directly, and the empirical sections which follow must tackle the issue of predicting such average offers.

3. The American immigration system

3.1. Basic facts

During 1973, the U.S. admitted some 400,000 persons on immigrant visas. The geographical distribution of these persons by country or region of birth is shown in the first column of table 1, from which it is seen that approximately three-quarters of U.S. immigrants are born in the major less developed regions.[11]

Apparently, much step migration occurs en route to the U.S., as reflected in column 3 of table 1, which reports U.S. immigrants by territory of birth as a percentage of immigrants reporting the same territory as last permanent residence. Of particular note here are the low values in this column for the European Socialist Bloc and China, with correspondingly high values for Austria and Hong Kong, the recipients of transient refugees from the former areas. The few African emigrants to the U.S. commonly seem to proceed via other continents, but, for the most part, step migration towards the U.S. is apparently within the continent of birth.

Possibly of greater interest to the emigrant nations are the fractions of their populations departing. Accordingly, the fourth column of table 1 measures number of U.S. 1973 immigrants reporting a territory as last permanent residence per 100,000 inhabitants of that territory. The range in this value, both within and across continents, is indeed large, varying from almost seven persons in every thousand from Trinidad and Tobago, to less than one per 100,000 from most of Africa, Indonesia, and China. Our later regression analysis examines these cross-country variations, but first it is necessary to briefly outline the U.S. system of restricting entry by immigrant visas.

3.2. U.S. immigration laws

The current U.S. immigration restrictions, as established by the Immigration Amendments of 1965, comprise an intricate system of preferences and eligibilities, differing between the Eastern and Western hemispheres, with ceilings of 20,000 immigrants per year on each Eastern Hemisphere country, overall limits on each hemisphere, and separate ceilings on each Eastern Hemisphere preference category. Essentially, however, there are three major ways to obtain an immigrant visa: by being a relative of a citizen or resident alien in the U.S. (though the definition of 'relative' differs between hemispheres), by admission

---

[11]That is, Africa, Asia, and the Americas other than Canada.

Table 1

Geographical distribution of U.S. immigrants and labor certification beneficiaries for 1973.[a]

	Number of immigrants by country or region of birth (a)	Number of immigrants by country or region of last permanent residence (b)	$\frac{b}{a}$ (%)	b/population ($\times 10^5$)	Number of nontemporary labor certification beneficiaries by country or region of birth (c)	$\frac{c}{a}$ (%)	c/number of nontemporary labor certificate applications decided (%)
World Totals	400,063	400,063	100.00	11.49	28,289	7.07	64.04
Europe	92,870	91,183	98.18	12.76	5,839	6.29	64.05
Austria	528	1,589	300.95	21.26	85	16.10	59.86
Czechoslovakia	1,552	910	58.63	6.28	50	3.22	56.82
Denmark	428	439	102.57	8.79	70	16.36	58.82
France	1,845	2,587	140.22	5.00	284	15.39	65.74
Germany (E)	6,600	7,565	114.62	9.35	20	6.30	71.43
Germany (W)					403		64.81
Greece	10,751	10,348	96.25	122.03	589	5.48	52.40
Hungary	1,624	1,008	62.07	9.69	54	3.33	55.67
Ireland	2,000	1,588	79.40	52.69	318	15.90	74.65
Italy	22,151	22,264	100.51	40.97	490	2.21	75.38
Netherlands	1,016	966	95.08	7.25	127	12.50	61.06
Poland	4,914	4,136	84.17	12.51	229	4.66	52.89
Portugal	10,751	10,019	93.19	116.64	604	5.62	75.88
Romania	1,623	1,106	68.15	5.33	63	3.88	62.38
Spain	4,134	5,538	133.96	16.05	503	12.17	75.64
Sweden	573	597	104.19	7.35	85	14.83	53.13
Switzerland	577	704	122.01	10.96	126	21.84	68.48
USSR	1,248	918	73.56	0.37	72	5.77	58.06
UK	10,638	11,860	111.49	21.26	1,309	12.30	62.54
Yugoslavia	7,582	5,213	68.75	25.10	160	2.11	54.42
Other Europe	2,335	1,830	78.37	5.94	205	8.78	60.12

Table 1 (continued)

	Number of immigrants by country or region of birth (a)	Number of immigrants by country or region of last permanent residence (b)	b/a (%)	b/population (×10⁻⁵)	Number of nontemporary labor certification beneficiaries by country or region of birth (c)	c/a (%)	c/number of nontemporary labor certificate applications decided (%)
Asia	124,160	119,984	96.64	5.79	14,201	11.44	67.17
China (Mainland)	17,297 }	1,625	52.92 }	0.20	1,087	13.63 }	73.40
China (Taiwan)		7,528		66.96	1,271		74.41
Hong Kong	4,359	10,283	235.90	252.16	97	2.23	61.39
India	13,124	11,975	91.25	2.13	2,826	21.53	64.49
Indonesia	449	278	61.92	0.23	41	9.13	56.94
Iran	2,998	2,853	95.16	9.34	294	9.81	67.28
Iraq	1,039	692	66.60	9.16	58	5.58	72.50
Israel	1,917	2,879	150.18	93.47	261	13.62	65.41
Japan	5,461	6,104	111.77	5.71	634	11.61	75.21
Jordan	2,450	2,120	86.53	85.93	40	1.63	52.63
Korea (N)	22,930 }	22,313	97.31	47.43	158	16.16 }	69.60
Korea (S)					3,547		78.95
Lebanon	1,977	2,567	129.84	86.64	162	8.19	69.83
Philippines	30,799	30,248	98.21	77.48	1,974	6.41	54.43
Syria	1,128	796	70.57	11.93	121	10.73	75.62
Thailand	4,941	4,915	99.47	13.55	467	9.45	76.31
Turkey	1,899	1,447	76.20	3.91	281	14.80	69.55
Vietnam (N)	4,569 }	4,532	99.19	11.66	14	0.92 }	63.64
Vietnam (S)					28		68.29
Pakistan	6,823 }	2,350	100.09	2.35	578	12.31 }	46.43
Yemen (San'a)		1,057		13.95	9		45.00
Other Asia		3,422		3.21	253		59.95
North America	152,788	157,181	102.88	136.64	5,178	3.39	57.95
Canada	8,951	14,800	165.34	67.74	652	7.28	51.10
Mexico	70,141	70,411	100.38	133.76	449	0.64	26.04
Barbados	1,448	1,402	96.82	584.17	392	27.07	78.56

Cuba	24,147	22,537	93.33	257.60	153	0.63	48.42
Dominican Republic	13,921	14,011	100.65	325.46	76	0.55	41.99
Haiti	4,786	4,641	96.97	91.48	215	4.49	61.60
Jamaica	9,963	9,615	96.51	500.00	1,750	17.56	75.24
Trinidad and Tobago	7,035	7,168	101.89	686.59	722	10.26	27.56
Costa Rica	901	962	106.77	52.20	63	6.99	57.27
El Salvador	2,042	2,036	99.71	54.15	115	5.63	56.65
Guatemala	1,759	1,793	101.93	33.15	128	7.28	59.81
Honduras	1,329	1,367	102.86	50.87	80	6.02	56.74
Nicaragua	670	674	100.60	33.90	66	9.85	55.00
Panama	1,612	1,734	107.57	113.78	113	7.01	70.62
Other N.A.	4,083	4,030	98.70	201.30	204	5.00	63.35
South America	20,335	22,423	110.27	11.37	2,156	10.60	63.51
Argentina	2,034	2,869	141.05	11.99	307	15.09	65.74
Brazil	1,213	1,780	146.74	1.80	98	8.08	61.64
Chile	1,139	1,135	99.65	14.15	125	10.97	51.23
Colombia	5,230	5,287	101.09	23.51	507	9.69	59.72
Ecuador	4,139	4,178	100.94	64.20	171	4.13	52.62
Guyana	2,969	2,852	96.06	378.25	539	18.15	75.49
Peru	1,713	1,806	105.43	12.49	177	10.33	59.80
Uruguay	617	700	113.45	23.68	120	19.45	72.73
Venezuela	640	1,183	184.84	10.78	19	2.97	76.00
Other S.A.	641	633	98.75	7.67	93	14.51	61.59
Africa	6,655	5,537	83.20	1.51	667	10.02	56.29
Egypt	2,274	1,727	75.95	4.96	155	6.82	51.16
Ghana	4,381	457	86.97	5.03	38	11.69	51.35
Nigeria		673		1.16	101		48.10
South Africa		546		2.38	82		71.30
Other Africa		2,134		0.89	291		60.25
Oceania	3,255	3,755	115.36	21.50	248	7.62	62.00
Australia	1,400	1,969	140.64	15.19	130	9.29	63.11
New Zealand	1,855	497	96.28	17.11	75	6.36	63.03
Other Oceania		1,289		80.61	43		57.33

[a] *Data sources:* Immigrants – U.S. Immigration and Naturalization Service (1973, tables 6 and 6a);
Population – U.N. (1973, table 18), Columbia Encyclopedia (1976);
Labor Certification – Unpublished U.S. Department of Labor data.

as a refugee, or by obtaining a labor certificate.[12] The numbers admitted under these major headings during 1970 are as follows.[13]

Relatives	284,347
Refugees	22,071
Labor certification beneficiaries	60,566
Members of other categories	6,342

Although relatives clearly form the dominant group, for reasons to be given later, attention will focus here on the labor certification beneficiaries.

The fraction of U.S. immigrants admitted on the basis of labor certification has been declining recently,[14] the number of certificates granted for non-temporary entry being only 7 percent of the number of immigrants by 1973 (as can be seen from the sixth column of table 1). However, reading down this column, one again finds considerable variation across countries, the numbers of labor certificates awarded for nontemporary entry to persons born in Switzerland, India, and Barbados, being more than one-fifth of the numbers of immigrants born in those countries, in contrast to less than one percent for Vietnam, Cuba, and the Dominican Republic.

The last column of table 1 calculates the numbers of labor certificates granted per hundred applications with outcome determined. The mean probability of receiving a certificate, given that one applies, is 0.64. It is intriguing to notice though that the band of variation around the mean is far from negligible, this probability being less than half for Pakistan, Yemen, Mexico, Cuba, Dominican Republic, and Nigeria, but greater than three-quarters for several nations.

4. Estimates of a U.S. immigration equation

This cursory glance at the intricacies of the American immigration system warns that some care must be taken in picking a strategy to study the wage sensitivity of U.S. immigration. The vast majority of immigrants are relatives either of citizens or of resident aliens, and many – particularly the immediate relatives – probably shift chiefly to unite the family, with only very minor regard for wage differentials. The prime mover in the family is the one on whom we shall then focus, for the relatives cannot follow until an initial entry is gained.

There are, as we have seen, two basic methods for the first member of a

---

[12]Labor certification is also required for certain temporary work visas.
[13]*Source*: U.S. Department of Labor (1974, p. 9).
[14]Ibid.

family to acquire a U.S. immigration visa: as a refugee, or as a labor certification beneficiary. The motivations of the former may again be presumed to be largely noneconomic, which brings us to the labor certification beneficiaries. It seems entirely plausible that for this group, the type of decision theory modeled in section 2 is applicable, and the task of this section is to test this hypothesis.

In testing, it must be remembered that the decision theory is one of supply responses and, as we have seen, supply may differ substantially from quantity of certificates granted, the gap varying considerably from country to country. To adhere to the earlier theory, the dependent variable must be measured in terms of certificates sought which, fortunately, is possible using a U.S. Department of Labor tape reporting information about each individual applicant for labor certification during fiscal 1973.[15] This tape includes data on sex, country of birth, whether for temporary or immigrant visa, and the certified/not-certified status of each applicant. Even this fine micro data file does not permit direct estimation of (2), the probabilistic decision function, because everyone in the file, by definition, has the dependent dummy turned on – they have decided to move. Nor can this source be fused legitimately with another hypothetical micro file on nonmovers, for the sample must always then be defined in terms of the left-hand variable and generate biased estimates.

Resorting then to an aggregate form, the left-hand variable used is the number of male applicants for labor certificates divided by the size of the male labor force, the units of observation being countries of origin.[16] Three comments are necessary on this. The study is restricted to males because measures of the female labor force are notoriously unreliable for purposes of international comparisons. Secondly, labor force rather than population is used as denominator mostly because the varying age structures and schooling retentions across countries would introduce superfluous and unnecessary perturbations. Thirdly, our theory is one of movement from present location, whereas the measured dependent variable here refers to country of birth, the last permanent residence for certificate applicants not being available. As section 3 showed for immigrants more generally, this discrepancy does introduce substantial error, but such errors-in-variables in the dependent variable need not concern us here, for the mean error may be taken as zero (which must be true if all countries were included), and there is no reason to suppose that these errors are correlated with included variables.

The next step, as explained previously, is to develop a prediction of a wage

[15]I am very grateful to the U.S. Department of Labor for the use of this computer tape of material transcribed from BES form 71-30.

[16]Both applications for temporary and permanent status certification are included, being a model of supply. Also, in a sense, it might be desirable to subtract from the denominator those adult males who move for 'prior' reasons, such as family, given no data on supply responses by such persons. To omit this adjustment probably introduces error only of the second order of smalls however. The source of data on male labor forces is ILO (1973, table 2B).

which the members of each foreign country's male labor force could command in the U.S. The reason this is likely to vary from country to country is mostly one of skill distribution, but measures of skill distributions are not available for very many countries on any consistent basis. The distributions of males across major occupational categories for some 103 countries are, however, available, and as a first approximation these may be supposed to reflect the broad dispersions of marketable skills.[17] Wage data are then taken from the corresponding major occupational classes in the U.S. and two measures of available wage dispersion computed by associating the U.S. wage for an occupation class with the members of that class in each of the other countries.[18] The two measures are: (a) average available wage in the U.S. in dollars per year – the cross-cell weighted average; and (b) variance of U.S. available wages – the cross-cell variance.
Other included variables are:

(1) National income per capita (U.S. $) in country of origin, intended as a proxy for expected wage in the initial location.[19]

(2) Global distance in miles from the capital of each country to New York.

(3) Whether (1) or not (0) the country is English speaking is included, on the grounds that the American milieu is likely to be less hostile, and job access simpler, if one speaks English.

(4) Determination, the proportion of applications refused for each country, is introduced to test for a 'discouraged applicant' effect, though such an effect relies both on good information and non-negligible time or money costs of application.

Table 2 presents estimates of a linear specification of this migration equation, omitting of course the variance of available wages from this strictly linear case.[20] All of our hypotheses are accepted, save the last, if one is willing to trust the fairly strong *t*-statistics in the face of heteroskedasticity:[21] higher available

---

[17]ILO (1973, table 2B).

[18]The source of wage data is U.S. Census (1970, table 227). The actual measure is median earnings of total male, experienced labor force who worked 50–52 weeks. By taking full-time earnings, one may hope that our measure reflects hourly wage (the variable we should like to measure) up to an irrelevent scalar transformation.

[19]See U.N. (1973, table 182).

[20]Ordinary least squares is used to estimate the migration equation, implying an assumed absence of simultaneity between locational wages and migration flows. In this context this does not seem unreasonable. From 1969–72, 192 thousand working immigrants entered the U.S. per year, which is only 0.2 percent of the U.S. labor force [U.S. Dept. of Labor (1974, p. 5)]. Note that the use of application data in this study rules out any concern over identification of the supply as opposed to demand forces.

[21]Having developed this migration equation as a supply response by adult males not eligible for immigration as family or refugees, the left-hand variable is measured with error by omission of illegal migrants out of this category. Unfortunately, no reliable data are available on such movements. An alternative specification, not reported here, includes a dummy variable for Mexico and Canada, but this generates no significant change in the wage coefficients in either the linear or logit cases and the dummy itself has an insignificant coefficient. One might be willing to accept this as a crude indication of lack of bias from omission of illegal migrants.

U.S. wages encourage certificate applications; greater incomes in the country of origin act in the opposite direction; the various costs associated with longer distances deter certification seeking; the English speaking nations do apply for relatively more certificates; although greater average probabilities of rejection do act as a deterrent to aspiration, this tendency is not significantly different from zero. Overall, some 40 percent of the cross-country variance in applications is explained by these few variables, and the results seem quite pleasing, *until* one tries to predict. At first sight, the coefficients in table 2 may seem rather small, but then so is the dependent variable's mean. Ceteris paribus, a ten percent reduction in the available U.S. wage, under the Bhagwati tax, predicts

Table 2

A linear immigration equation (dependent variable: male certification applicants/male labor force).

Independent variable	Estimated coefficient	Standard error of coefficient	Absolute t-ratio
Constant	-0.363×10^{-4}	0.258×10^{-3}	0.14
Average available wage in U.S.	0.810×10^{-7}	0.370×10^{-7}	2.19
NNP per capita	-0.992×10^{-7}	0.400×10^{-7}	2.48
Distance	-0.599×10^{-7}	0.102×10^{-7}	5.85
English speaking	0.259×10^{-3}	0.528×10^{-4}	4.90
Determination	-0.174×10^{-3}	0.170×10^{-3}	1.03

Number of observations = 103
Sum of squared residuals = 0.575×10^{-5}
$R^2 = 0.406$
Mean value of dependent variable = 0.179×10^{-3}

negative fractions of applicants for many countries: a common pathology for linear probability equations.[22]

To take the logit of the dependent variable immediately places us in a non-linear world, and such a form is estimated in table 3. Again, it is found in the first column that the two mean wage indicators are statistically significant (t-tests now being quite justifiable) bearing signs consistent with the usual hypotheses, though the effect of home national income is now quite weak. The English speaking nations retain their positive coefficient, though, fascinatingly, the role of distance goes to zero. Of particular interest to the models of section 2 is the relevance of the second moment of available wages inserted experimentally in equation 1 of table 3. The log of this variance is found to have a coefficient insignificantly different from zero, but then no hypothesis about this

[22]The assertion that the available U.S. wage is reduced proportionately by the tax, used here and in section 5, relies on the earlier assumption of infinitely elastic demand for immigrants' labor services.

coefficient has been mentioned, only that to omit the variable might generate bias. The latter seems to be borne out in equation 2 of table 3, for dropping the second moment reduces the coefficient on the first to being insignificantly different from zero.[23]

Table 3

Two logit immigration equations (dependent variable: logit [male certification applicants/ male labor force]).

Independent variable	Equation 1 Estimated coefficient (t-ratio)	Equation 2 Estimated coefficient (t-ratio)
Constant	−39.64 (1.44)	−53.82 (2.22)
Log_e (mean U.S. available wage)	6.01 (2.08)	5.14 (1.85)
Log_e (variance U.S. available wage)	−1.43 (1.07)	
NNP per capita	−0.001 (2.18)	−0.001 (1.98)
Distance	−0.0001 (0.64)	−0.00005 (0.41)
English speaking	1.19 (2.05)	1.29 (2.23)
Number of observations	103	103
Sum of squared residuals	739.27	747.95
R^2	0.12	0.11
Mean value of dependent variable	−8.97	−8.97

5. Simulating the consequences of a tax on U.S. immigrants' earnings

This section examines the sensitivity of migration flows, hours worked by immigrants and revenue levels, under alternative rates of a proportional tax on immigrants' earnings. The foregoing regressions, bowing to data limitations, are for all occupational classes from both developed and underdeveloped nations, so the tax to be considered here is one imposed on all immigrants rather than just PTKs from LDCs as in the original Bhagwati proposal. The techniques employed, and particularly the simplifying assumptions necessitated by the lack of alternative data, are outlined in the following subsections before the results are presented.

[23]The inclusion of determination in the equations of table 3 produces no significant difference in the reported coefficients and has itself an insignificant coefficient at the five percent level.

5.1. Immigration rates

Two stories at polar extremities might here be told, though the truth no doubt resides somewhere between.

Variant 1. Both Western and Eastern hemisphere quotas are presently oversubscribed, so any deterrent effect of the tax may simply serve to shorten the queue yet leave the quotas filled. The post hoc flow of immigrants may then be unaffected by the tax and revenue calculations thereby much simplified.[24] Paradoxically, potential movers, discouraged from joining the queue for immigrant visas only to pay extra taxes on arrival, may elect to seek entry in other categories (temporary worker, exchange visitor, or illegal), thus possibly actually swelling the outflow from countries of origin.

Variant 2. Alternatively, if the tax only applies to some portion of potential immigrants (such as PTKs from LDCs), their discouragement reduces the fraction in the queue of elligible immigrants represented by them. If the drawing from the queue to fill the quota is essentially random in the steady state, then the proportionate reduction in admissions of taxed immigrants is approximated by the proportionate reduction in their numbers joining the queue, as the initial contribution of this group to the total queue goes to zero.

Revenue calculations founded on both variants are presented below, but it remains for this section to consider predicting changes in immigration flows under variant 2.

The story told by way of a prologue to section 4 is meant to suggest that U.S. immigrants probably fall into two broad categories: those who enter irrespective of the labor certification system; and those entering as, or on the coattails of, nontemporary certification beneficiaries, being some multiple of such beneficiaries. The magnitude of this multiplier is likely to vary from country to country, if only because family unit size so varies, generating a random coefficient equation. This may provide a partial explanation of the cross-country discrepancies observed in column 6 of table 1. These ideas are subjected to a modest test in table 4, in which estimates of the mean cross-country coefficients are reported for this relationship, the size effect being eliminated by dividing through by population.[25] Given the magnitudes of the computed t-ratios, our story may be accepted with some degree of enthusiasm, despite heteroskedasticity; something like 4.6 persons are emigrating to the U.S., from a typical country, for every extra permanent labor certificate granted.

[24]See Bhagwati and Dellalfar (1973).
[25]This approach results in estimation of the unweighed cross-country mean coefficients rather than representative coefficients for the world as a unit. It should be recognized that, to the extent that the U.S. INS chooses groupings for its published data on the basis of immigration per capita rates, our estimates are in danger of bias from sample selection on values of the left-hand variable, but there seems little alternative at this stage.

Combining these results with equation 1 of table 3, together with a few conversion ratios, now allows simulation of the potential consequences of a Bhagwati-type tax on U.S. immigration rates. This is achieved in three steps:

(1) The first supply equation in table 3 is used to predict reductions from the initial, cross-country, unweighted, mean value of male permanent certification seekers per male labor force participant, as the net average available U.S. wage is diminished by alternative tax rates.[26]

(2) These predicted values are then multiplied by a conversion factor which is essentially the product of three cross-country average components: male labor force/population; labor certificates granted/certificates sought; total licenses sought/males seeking licenses. The conversion factor, and hence each of these components, is presumed to be invariant to the new tax imposed, the multiplication resulting in predictions of total licenses granted to nontemporary seekers per inhabitant of original location.

(3) This last is then substituted into the equation in table 4 to generate predictions of the number of U.S. immigrants per person from a typical country.

Table 4

The multiple effect of certification on immigration (dependent variable: U.S. immigrants by country of birth/thousand persons).

Independent variable	Estimated coefficient (standard error)	t-ratio
Constant	0.36 (0.0958)	3.78
Labor certificates granted to nontemporary applicants/ population (in thousands)	4.64 (0.36)	12.72

Number of observations = 66[a]
Sum of squared residuals = 35.124
$R^2 = 0.717$
Mean value dependent variable = 0.74

[a]The number of observations here is less than in table 3 since immigrants by country of birth are not published for every separate country used in table 3. Otherwise, sources are as before.

5.2. Hours worked

The study of hours worked is a massive undertaking in its own right and clearly beyond the capacity of this exercise.[27] Fortunately, others have already

[26]Notice here the reliance on a zero coefficient on the log variance of available U.S. wages, which measure is also affected by a proportional tax.
[27]The effect of the proposed tax on hours worked is neglected in the calculations of Bhagwati and Dellalfar (1973).

done much of the work, and it remains only to apply their results to the present case. In particular, the two-equation model of Hall (1973) is selected, being rather suitable for our intentions.[28]

The first equation of Hall's model estimates adults' hourly wage-rates in the U.S. as a function of selected characteristics of each adult.[29] Average values for these characteristics of immigrants are then substituted here, and a value for gross hourly wage-rate predicted.[30] Next, this value is converted into net, real hourly wage-rate, and after deflation by a Bhagwati tax, inserted into Hall's hours-worked equation to predict the required number.[31] A great advantage of Hall's piece is that no distinction is made between labor force participants and nonparticipants in estimating the hours of work equation, so participation changes need no separate prediction here.

5.3. Revenues

Revenues are calculated here for both variants of the supply-of-immigrants story. Multiplying predicted population fractions migrating to the U.S. by the proportion of current migrants who are adults provides estimates of adult immigrants per capita.[32] Under the suppositions that this last conversion element is exogenous to the tax system, and that no children work, revenue per person in a typical country is then computed as the product of wage-rate net of U.S. taxes, the tax rate, hours worked per adult, and adult immigrants per inhabitant, the last being held constant at the zero tax rate under variant 1.

5.4. The results

Table 5 presents the simulated results for alternative tax rates from zero to fifty percent. No turning point for revenue is discovered over this range, for either variant. One reason for this is the lack of elasticity demonstrated by

[28]There exists, though, some considerable discrepancy in estimates of wage elasticity of hours supplied amongst the many studies.

[29]Hall (1973, table 3.1).

[30]In the performance of this prediction, the following characteristics of adult immigrants are assumed: race = white, mean age group = 25–34 [USINS (1973, table 10)], years of U.S. schooling equivalent completed = 12, U.S. residence = New York, resided abroad at age 16, healthy, probability of union membership = 0.31 (male), 0.16 (female), [Hall (1973, table 3B)].

[31]The following assumptions are made in this context: probabilities of positions in family – single male = 0.14, married male = 0.32, single female = 0.11, married female = 0.40, female head = 0.03 [USINS (1973, table 10) and USDL (1974, table 6)]; race = white; mean age group = 20–59, (see earlier); 2 adults per family; children of both school and nonschool age in family; marginal federal income tax rate = 0.15; cost of living deflator for New York = 109 [Hall (1973, appendix)]. Whole income per adult is assumed to be available hours (2000) multiplied by wage-rate net of the Bhagwati tax, thus assuming zero unearned income. See Hall (1970, table 6.2).

[32]See USINS, (1973, table 10).

hours worked according to this study's manipulations of Hall's equations. Such inelasticity ought to be of interest to the U.S. in the context of a Bhagwati-type proposal, for it indicates a lack of erosion of tax base for the U.S. and consequently no increase in tax burden imposed by immigrants on U.S. citizens, though very low wage elasticities are not common to all estimates of supply-of-hours functions.

In contrast, male labor certification seekers are discouraged quite easily, even with only modest tax rates. Of course the conversion ratios mute the impact on immigration under variant 2, yet the remaining effect is still large, as may be seen from column 3 of table 5. This, unfortunately, leaves a substantial range between the two variants, within which the truth most likely lies.

Table 5

Simulated results.

Tax rate	Hours worked per adult immigrant	Adult emigrants to U.S. per thousand inhabitants	Revenue per thousand inhabitants per vintage of immigrants (1966 U.S. $)	
		Variant 2	Variant 2	Variant 1
0	1133	0.429	0	0
0.05	1129	0.386	40.80	45.27
0.10	1123	0.354	74.34	90.10
0.20	1091	0.311	126.85	175.01
0.30	1087	0.288	175.46	261.48
0.40	1083	0.276	223.86	347.26
0.50	1078	0.271	273.74	432.36

This gap naturally generates a widening discrepancy between simulated revenues under the two alternatives in the last columns of table 5, with some considerable braking force from discouraged post hoc migration under the second variant. The term 'vintage' at the head of the revenue columns refers to one year of migration flows, but the original Bhagwati suggestion is to tax for ten years after migration. If the numbers simulated here referred to a steady-state net flow, then such a tax applied to all immigrants' earnings at a ten percent rate would probably result in a revenue of between 7.5 and 9 million 1966 U.S. dollars for a typical country with ten million inhabitants. This results from each adult immigrant, working or not, paying an average of about $210 per year in taxes over and above their U.S. taxes.

6. A summing up

In lieu of a conclusion, some of the primary limitations of the preceding ought to be emphasized. Following Bhagwati and Dellalfar, attention is focussed here on revenues from taxation of immigrants' earned incomes, but it should be remembered that these are not the only source of payments to the countries of origin. Both taxation of unearned incomes and voluntary remittances by emigrants form alternative sources, and both are likely to be reduced eventually by taxation of earnings through the propensities to remit and to save.

The neglect of reverse migration flows by prior immigrants places a severe restriction on the generalities of this study, but no suitable data seem to be available. The use of gross flows to estimate revenues, as here and in Bhagwati and Dellalfar, clearly produces upward bias. But the effect of taxation on net migrant flows need not necessarily be underestimated by viewing gross flows only, for on the one hand net wages are reduced producing an incentive to return home, but on the other hand immigrants may be target savers and return flows reduced by taxation on this account.

Finally, this study is constrained to estimate a macro migration equation, despite the specification problems outlined in section 2, owing to a lack of such micro data as are desirable for estimating relocation decision functions in an international context. One ramification of the technique deployed above in estimating this macro function is that our results apply to an earnings tax imposed on all immigrants, rather than just the PTK workers from LDCs as in Bhagwati's original proposal.

References

Bhagwati, J.N., 1972, United States in the Nixon era: The end of innocence, Daedalus 101.

Bhagwati, J.N. and W. Dellalfar, 1973, The brain drain and income taxation, World Development 1.

Bhagwati, J.N. and K. Hamada, 1974, The brain drain, international integration of markets for professionals and unemployment: A theoretical analysis, Journal of Development Economics 1, 19–42.

Columbia Encyclopedia, 1976 (Columbia University Press, New York).

Greenwood, M.J., 1975, Research on internal migration in the U.S., A survey, Journal of Economic Literature 13, 397–433.

Hall, R.E., 1970, Wages, income and hours of work in the U.S. labor force, M.I.T. Working Paper 62.

Hall, R.E., 1973, Wages, income and hours of work in the U.S. labor force, in: G.G. Cain and H.W. Watts, ed., Income maintenance and labor supply (Rand McNally, Chicago), 102–162.

Harris, J.R., and M.P. Todaro, 1970, Migration, unemployment and development: A two-sector analysis, American Economic Review 60, 126–142.

International Labor Office, 1973, Yearbook of Labor Statistics.

Lindsay, C.M., 1971, Measuring human capital returns, Journal of Political Economy 79, 1195–1215.

Malinvaud, E., 1966, Statistical methods of econometrics, (North-Holland, Amsterdam).

McFadden, D., 1974, Conditional logit analysis of qualitative choice behavior, in: P. Zarembka, ed., Frontiers in econometrics (Academic Press, New York), 105–142.

Psacharopoulos, G., 1973, Returns to education: An international comparison, (Elsevier–Jossey Bass).

Schwartz, A., 1973, Interpreting the effect of distance on migration, Journal of Political Economy 81, 1153–1169.

Sjaastad, L.A., 1962, The costs and returns of human migration, Journal of Political Economy 70, 580–93.
Theil, H., 1971, Principles of econometrics (Wiley, New York).
United Nations, 1973, Statistical yearbook.
United States Department of Labor, Manpower administration, 1974, Immigrants and the American labor market, Manpower Research Monograph 31.
United States Bureau of the Census, 1970, Census of population, United States summary, vol. 1, part 1, section 2.
United States Immigration and Naturalization Service, 1973, Annual report.

PART III

THEORETICAL ANALYSIS OF THE
CONSEQUENCES OF THE BRAIN DRAIN

CHAPTER 5

WELFARE–THEORETICAL ANALYSES OF THE BRAIN DRAIN*

Jagdish BHAGWATI

M.I.T., Cambridge, MA 02139, U.S.A.

Carlos RODRIGUEZ

Columbia University, New York, NY 10027, U.S.A.

The paper reviews and synthesises the theoretical analyses of the brain drain in the earlier literature and in the present symposium in the Journal on the subject. Static analysis and dynamic analysis are distinguished, critical issues are raised relating to how welfare changes should be discussed in the context of migration, and possibilities of fruitful future research are outlined.

1. Introduction

This paper reviews the literature on the theoretical analysis of the welfare effects of the brain drain. The different theoretical analyses, with their occasionally divergent conclusions, can be illuminatingly classified according to whether: (i) they deal with comparative-static or dynamic formulations; (ii) they assume a perfectly competitive model or one with endogenous market or policy-imposed distortions; and (iii) they address themselves to the welfare of the country of emigration or of immigration, or take a world-welfare viewpoint.

In the following review, we begin (section 2) briefly with a discussion of the last set of issues distinguished above, namely, whose welfare should be considered and how welfare should be defined. We next turn, in section 3, to the early, theoretical literature which has focussed on comparative-static analyses in perfectly competitive models. In section 4, we turn to analyses which allow for distortions: policy-imposed (e.g., educational subsidies) and endogenous (e.g.,

*Earl Grinols and Asim Dasgupta have provided excellent research assistance in the course of writing this paper. The first author took primary responsibility for preparing the preliminary drafts of the sections on static analysis and the second author for the section on dynamic analysis; the final outcome is however jointly authored in the full sense of the term. Thanks are due to Harry Johnson and Al Berry for helpful comments.

rigid or sticky real wages). Finally, in section 5, we review the dynamic analyses of the effects of the brain drain.[1]

In reviewing the literature, we naturally synthesise and marginally extend it. Also, we provide an analytical taxonomy into which the theoretical contributions in this volume can be, and are, appropriately fitted, and hence their relationship to the foregoing contributions and to one another is more readily assessed by the reader.

2. Welfare: Whose and how defined

2.1.

A central problem in the analysis of migration relates to the question: whose welfare is being assessed? Even if we assume away intergenerational welfare problems (such as those raised by Rawls (1971) recently), the modern migration of skilled personnel raises in an acute form the question as to whether the welfare of these migrants is to be considered part of the welfare of the LDC (or, for that matter, as in a recent UNCTAD study (1974), part of the welfare of the DC).

If migration were permanent, so that the immigrant could be taken to have left the LDC and arrived in the DC on a for-ever basis, then it would make some sense to consider the question as to what has happened to 'LDC welfare' as identical to the question as to what has happened to the 'welfare of those left behind in the LDC'. However, skilled (PTK in U.S. immigration terminology: professional, technical and kindred) migrants today – including those who take permanent-residence visas in the DC of immigration and are immigrants in the juridical sense as well as in popular parlance – typically move to and fro between the LDC of origin and the DC of destination (and indeed, en route, to other DCs and LDCs at times). Hence, PTK immigrants are not really permanent migrants in many cases.

However, even in the case of permanent, for-ever migrants, it is not entirely clear that they should be excluded altogether from the definition of 'LDC welfare'. Skilled immigrants today enjoy low transport costs which permit frequent returns to the LDCs of origin and hence retention of LDC loyalties and affiliations. Their job opportunities also now tend to cut across different DCs, increasing their capacity to resist the assimilative pressures of the DC in which they reside – a passionate immigrant into the UK, who will not adapt to British phlegm, may be able to migrate to the back-slapping friendliness of the U.S. or to a convex combination of the two cultures in Canada. The identification with the DC of

---

[1] We should enter the caveat explicitly that our review is by no means exhaustive but touches rather on what appear to us to be interesting contributions from the viewpoint of our focus in this paper. Furthermore, we confine ourselves to explicitly theoretical analyses, using formal models in one way or another: hence we do not review early writings of interest such as Johnson's (1965) article on the Canadian brain drain.

destination is not quite so inevitable in consequence. Furthermore, the melting pot now has itself melted in the U.S., the principal DC of immigration: ethnic diversity is encouraged and Dr. Kissinger finds his Realpolitik hamstrung by ethnic groups whose political and emotional affiliation to countries of emigration is considered a thoroughly acceptable part of the domestic political process.

Thus, several factors have combined to make a continuing link to LDCs of origin and failure to fuse into DCs of destination important aspects of modern, PTK migration from LDCs to DCs. This observation, plus the fact of extensive 'to-and-fro' migration, make it somewhat implausible to assert that, if one is interested in LDC welfare, one must exclude the welfare of the migrants from the analysis. Identically, any procedure which defines 'DC welfare' as inclusive of the PTK immigrants' welfare runs into the same difficulties plus the additional fact that, despite the selective regulation of immigration in the national interest by the legislative and executive branches of DC governments, the average citizen of a DC is more likely to regard the immigrant's welfare as a 'favour' to the immigrant at the DC-citizens' 'expense' than as an augmentation of DC welfare!

It is best therefore to analyse the welfare issues separately for three groups: (i) LDC nonemigrants; (ii) migrants; and (iii) DC non-immigrants. Then, depending on what is appropriate for the analysis of any specific situation, one can add together any of the three components to arrive at what is considered to be 'LDC welfare' or 'DC welfare': clearly, no general rules will apply to all situations.

Among the other implications of to-and-fro migration by migrants, we might also note one consequence of some analytical interest. While the *theoretical* models to be reviewed presently allow for migration from the LDC to the DC in the context of a variety of models of the LDC, none of them allow for the 'return of the native'. Once the return migration is allowed for, one can open up interesting possibilities for theoretical analysis: the modelling of the DC, implying possible learning effects for the (temporary) migrant, for example, could become relevant so that the two-way migration relates to the same (physical) migrant but implies unequal flows in the two directions from the viewpoint of welfare analysis. A 2-period analysis of the welfare impact of such to-and-fro migration would then be called for and would involve the effect of changing locations on the efficiency and wealth of the migrant in an essential way.

2.2.

Next, we ought to distinguish explicitly between the conventional economist's objective function, which admits only goods and services, and augmented objective functions, which allow 'noneconomic' arguments in the objective function as in the analysis of optimal policy intervention to achieve noneconomic objectives in Bhagwati and Srinivasan (1969).

The explicitly theoretical literature to be presently reviewed is exclusively focussed on the conventional objective function. However, the fact that societies may value the presence of technical personnel per se in the interest of modernisation or the possibly associated increase in the size of the 'modern', industrial sector's activity level is manifestly an important aspect of societal concerns, and the economist evaluating the welfare effects of the brain drain must come to terms with these traditionally political, sociological, 'noneconomic' objectives. This is indeed what McCulloch and Yellen (1975) do when they discuss the possible 'demodernisation' effect of an emigration tax in their model of the brain drain at the Bellagio conference.

2.3.

At a different level, the economic analyst may not be able to continue using a well-ordered social utility function because there are no fiscal policy instruments by which incomes can be redistributed in the desired manner. In this event, explicit attention to the (actual) income distributions before and after migration is required for welfare analysis. Thus, in Hamada's (1975) Bellagio contribution, incomes *can* be redistributed but, in the absence of lump-sum taxation as a feasible alternative, only via the income tax: hence income distribution and per capita income levels are *both* to be analysed for examining the welfare consequences of emigration.

2.4.

Similarly, if we depart from the assumption of full employment of factors of production, then the effect of emigration on the unemployment levels (or rates) could well be an additional, 'economic' argument in the objective function: as is done in the Bhagwati–Hamada (1974) paper.

2.5.

Finally, we may note that dynamic welfare analyses would necessarily take the theorist into intertemporal optimisation: and, in this case (as is evident from our detailed analysis in section 5), the welfare presumptions established from static, welfare analysis do not necessarily carry over.

3. Static, welfare theorising without distortions

The focus of most theoretical analyses has been on LDC nonemigrants' welfare, using comparative statics and models without distortions, and assuming permanent migration. These contributions can be reviewed in ascending order of complexity.

3.1. Model 1: One-product, one-factor-emigration model

The simplest neoclassical model which has been used for analysing the impact of migration on the welfare of the LDC nonemigrants is the one-product model with just one factor (labour) migrating at the margin in a closed economy.

In this model, used by Grubel and Scott (1966), it was argued correctly that, for infinitesimal changes, the emigrant will neither harm nor help the non-emigrants: the emigrant will have been contributing his marginal product to national income and earning it as well, so that his presence or absence is irrelevant to the nonemigrants' welfare. To put it graphically, the emigrant will be merely sailing away with his own marginal product.

However, for *finite* changes, as was noted by Berry and Soligo (1969) and later independently by Tobin (1974), there is the familiar 'surplus' that the nonemigrants lose. This is seen readily in fig. 1, where the marginal product of labour (MPL) curve is drawn, falling as a consequence of the usual concave production

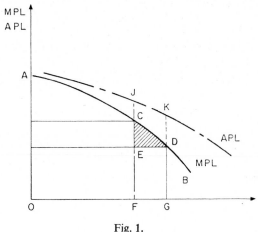

Fig. 1.

function. The finite emigration of *FG* amount of labour then results in a loss of surplus of the shaded area *CDE*.

Note one more point that is sometimes the source of critical confusion. If we draw in an average product of labour (APL) schedule, it is clear that, for both infinitesimal and finite changes, the *per capita income* of the *economy* will rise (from *KG* to *JF* in fig. 1) with emigration as a simple consequence of the assumed diminishing returns. How does this reconcile with the conclusion that the infinitesimal migration does not affect the welfare of those left behind? The paradox is only apparent: the emigrant earns not the per capita income in the pre-migration situation, but rather the marginal product. The per capita income comparison, to be a correct welfare index of the impact on those left behind, would have to presume that the migrant earned average, rather than marginal, product: in this case, since the average exceeds the marginal product, the migrant was contributing less to national income than earning and making demand on it, so that his migration helps those left behind.[2]

3.2. Model 2: Two-product, two-factor, one-factor-emigration model

The extension of the preceding analysis of one-factor-emigration to the standard trade-theoretic model of two products and two primary factors has been carried out by Kenen (1971) in the Kindleberger Festschrift. Its substance can be readily derived as follows.

For a closed economy, start with given equilibrium. When labour migrates infinitesimally, the Rybczynski theorem implies that, at constant commodity prices, the output of the labour-intensive commodity will fall and that of the capital-intensive commodity will rise. Since domestic income and expenditure fall, however, the assumption of noninferiority in consumption, combined with stability, will yield in the post-emigration, full-equilibrium situation a reduced (relative) commodity price for the capital-intensive commodity. Next, turn to fig. 2a, which sketches the production possibility set of the nonemigrants as AB. In the before-migration situation, the commodity price-ratio is PQ and the welfare of the nonmigrant group is at U_b. With the emigration, the commodity price-ratio shifts, as just argued, to SR and the nonemigrants get worse off ($U_b > U_a$). It is easy to see the source of this loss: the 'trade opportunity' of the

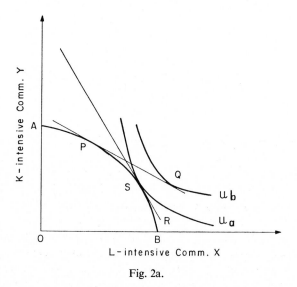

Fig. 2a.

[2]For those familiar with peasant-family-farming models in the Lewis-type literature on dualism, where average product rewards to family members are assumed, the per capita income of the farming *sector* would become the relevant welfare index. It does not seem relevant, however, to the problem of international migration.

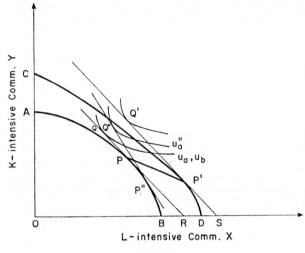

Fig. 2b.

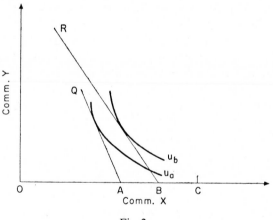

Fig. 2c.

nonmigrants, from the presence of (and with) the migrants, disappears with the emigration.

Consider now the extension to an open economy. If international prices are fixed by the 'small country' assumption, let $PQ = P'Q'$ be the given international prices in fig. 2b. PP' is the Rybczynski-line for changing labour supply. Before the migration, the *total* population has the production set CD, the nonmigrants have the production set AB, the nonmigrants' welfare is at U_b and potential emigrants earn income RS in terms of commodity X. When migration occurs, the migrants essentially disappear with their constant marginal product and, at the unchanged commodity price-ratio, the nonmigrants are left as well off as before ($U_b = U_a$). The presence or the absence of the migrant group in the population implies the same terms of trade, and hence the same trade opportunity, for the nonmigrants: hence the no-impact result (for infinitesimal *and* finite migration).

If the terms of trade can vary, however, it follows similarly that the welfare of the nonmigrants will improve or worsen according as the terms of trade improve or worsen.[3] In the case illustrated in fig. 2a, the nonmigrants export commodity X for commodity Y and the after-migration improvement in the terms of trade improves their welfare ($U_a'' > U_b$).

Note finally that this strict relationship between the terms of trade behaviour and the nonemigrants' welfare will not hold for Model 1, for finite emigration, because whereas the emigration at constant prices implies in Model 2 a constant marginal product for labour owing to the Rybczynski theorem, recall that in the one-good Model 1 we have a *declining* marginal product to labour schedule. Hence, for Model 1, we have to set off the loss of the surplus (CDE in fig. 1) against the terms of trade gain, if any, to arrive at the net impact of the migration on nonemigrants' welfare. Thus, in fig. 2c, OA represents the production possibility set of the nonemigrants, with specialisation throughout on producing X as required by Model 1; AC represents the production attributable to the potential migrants; and AB represents the surplus (CDE in fig. 1) that accrues to the nonemigrants. Thus, prior to emigration, with terms of trade BR, we have nonemigrants' welfare at U_b. With the migration, the terms of trade improve to AQ but the surplus is lost so that the nonmigrants' budget line is now anchored on A rather than B. Fig. 2c shows that $U_b > U_a$, i.e., that the terms of trade gain is outweighed by the loss of the surplus. The contrary possibility also exists and could equally well have been illustrated.

3.3. Model 3: One-product, two-factor, two-factor-emigration model

A different extension of the closed-economy Model 1, retaining the one-product framework but permitting two factors to emigrate in a two-factors framework, is due to Johnson (1967). It is derived, in turn, from the Berry–Soligo paper and is best set out in terms of fig. 3.

Assume two groups: nonemigrants (1) and emigrants (2). The former group has K_1 and L_1 units of capital and labour whereas the latter has K_2 and L_2 such units. The overall wage–rental ratio (ω/γ) is a function of the *overall* K/L ratio, k, where $K = K_1 + K_2$ and $L = L_1 + L_2$. In fig. 3, we then have the post-emigration-of-group-2 equilibrium at Q and $(\omega, \gamma)_{k_1}$ is the wage–rental ratio tangent

---

[3]This conclusion naturally holds only insofar as the trade pattern for the nonmigrant group is not reversed by the migration. This qualification, explicitly noted by Kenen, has its counterpart in our review of the dynamic analyses where the effects of dissimilar *savings* behaviour by migrants and nonmigrants are considered.

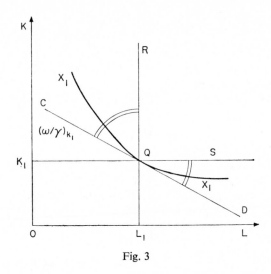

Fig. 3

to the X_1 isoquant. X_1 is therefore the post-migration income of group 1. How does this compare with the pre-migration income level? There are two possibilities to consider but both show a worsening of welfare (except for a singular case of no impact) from the migration. The entire range of feasible (ω/γ) ratios before migration can be divided into (i) the range spanned by QR and QC, which would materialise clearly if $k_2 > k_1$ (where $k_2 = K_2/L_2$ and $k_1 = K_1/L_1$) and thus $k > k_1$; and (ii) the range spanned by QS and QD which would materialise if $k_2 < k_1$. The singular case is where $k_2 = k_1 = k$ and therefore $(\omega/\gamma)_{k_1} = (\omega/\gamma)_k$. It follows immediately that, when $k_2 > k_1$, so that it is the richer group that emigrates, the wage-to-rental ratio will *fall* to $(\omega/\gamma)_{k_1}$; in the other case, where $k_2 < k_1$, it will *rise* to $(\omega/\gamma)_{k_1}$. In *either* case, the 'budget line' for group 1 will shrink in the relevant range and will imply *loss* of income. To read off this loss of income, all that one has to do, in the case where $k_2 > k_1$ for example, is to draw the $(\omega/\gamma)_k$ line through Q and take its tangency with respect to the X_k isoquant; clearly ,$X_k > X_1$ and $(X_k - X_1)$ is the loss of income to group 1 from the migration of group 2.

It follows equally that the nonemigrant group 1 will become *better off* if the wage–rental ratio rises (falls) when $k_2 > k_1 (k_2 < k_1)$. This can happen if, when $k_2 > k_1$ for example, the emigrants leave a sufficient amount of their capital behind to *raise* (instead of lowering) the overall capital–labour ratio, k, with emigration.

The same conclusions can be readily derived in the context of yet another familiar diagrammatic technique.[4] Take fig. 4. It measures the capital–labour

---

[4]Asim Dasgupta suggested this diagrammatic treatment to us, independently of having seen fig. 5 in section 5, after seeing the preliminary draft of section 3.

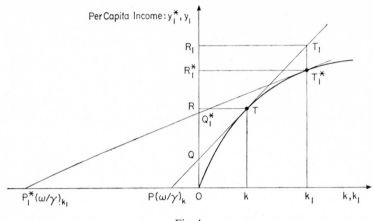

Fig. 4.

ratios along the horizontal axis to the right and per capita incomes y_1^* and y_1 (overall and group 1, respectively) on the vertical axis. Writing the aggregate, constant-returns-to-scale production function in the intensive form as $y = f(k)$, with $f' > 0$ and $f'' < 0$ as usual, we can easily show that the factor rewards, γ and ω, in the premigration situation are

$$\gamma = f'(k) = OQ/PO$$

and

$$\omega = f(k) - kf'(k) = OQ,$$

and therefore

$$\omega/\gamma = PO,$$

so that the wage–rental ratio can be measured as the length of the intercept, on the horizontal axis to the left, of the tangent to the $y = f(k)$ curve OTT_1^* in fig. 4.

Now, $y_1 = \omega(k) + \gamma(k) \cdot k_1$ before migration and $y_1^* = \omega(k_1) + \gamma(k_1) \cdot k_1$ *after* migration. In fig. 4, it is then readily shown that

$$y_1^* = OR_1^*$$

and

$$y_1 = y_1^* + T_1 T_1^*,$$

so that the migration leads to a decline in the per capita income of the non-emigrant group 1 by $T_1 T_1^*$. As with fig. 3, then, we can also think of two possibilities: where $k < k_1$ and $k > k_1$. In the latter case as well, if fig. 4 is so redrawn, there will be a measure $T_1 T_1^*$ of per capita income loss for group 1.[5]

Finally, note that it should be possible to derive the results of Model 1 as a special case of Model 3: for Model 1 is where one may think of two factors emigrating, but with one factor (capital) taking zero value. With the emigrant group 2 then being labour-abundant, we have the case where $k < k_1$ and the wage–rental ratio rises after emigration: so we are in the range $(QS - QD)$ in fig. 3 and in the configuration shown in fig. 4 and, in each instance of course, we get the expected loss of income for the nonemigrant group 1.

Consider next the extension to an open economy. For the simplest case (considered by Johnson) of a small country with fixed terms of trade, and staying within the Samuelson range of incomplete specialisation in production, it is immediately obvious that the emigration of group 2, for $k \gtreqqless k_1$, will leave group 1 no better or worse off than before the migration.

3.4. Model 4: One-product, three-factor, two-factor-emigration model

In his contribution to the Bellagio conference, Grubel (1975) works with a simple model where skilled workers, unskilled workers and capital combine to produce a single output and the skilled workers ('engineers') migrate with the capital embodied in their acquired skills. The main results of his geometrical analysis are readily derived, while relaxing his assumption that skilled and unskilled labourers must be used in fixed proportions, as follows. Thus, consider the system:

$$\theta = \theta(K_0, L_e, L_w), \tag{1}$$

$$\bar{L} = L_e + L_w, \tag{2}$$

$$\bar{K} = K_0 + kL_e, \tag{3}$$

where θ is output, L_e is the number of engineers, L_w the number of workers, $\bar{L}$ the stock of total labour, $\bar{K}$ the capital stock, k the units of capital required (i.e., used up) to train an engineer, and K_0 the capital left over to be employed with L_e and L_w to produce output θ.

Assuming that the system will work efficiently so as to maximise output, we can then easily determine the effect of emigration on per capita income. The implication of the efficiency assumption can be first spelled out simply by using the envelope theorem. Thus substitute the constraints (2) and (3) into $\theta(\cdot)$:

$$\theta = \theta(\bar{K} - kL_e, L_e, \bar{L} - L_e). \tag{4}$$

---

[5]The above results can also be simply derived by noting that $dy_1/dk = (k_1 - k)(d\gamma/dk)$. From this it also follows that, for infinitesimal emigration, the cost of the emigration to the nonemigrant group goes to zero *in the limit* and may virtually be treated as zero.

For a maximum, it is necessary that

$$[\theta_1(-k)+\theta_2+\theta_3(-1)] = 0, \tag{5}$$

where θ_i is the ith partial derivative and 1, 2, 3 refer to the first (K_0), second (L_e) and third (L_w) arguments in the function $\theta(\cdot)$.

3.4.1. First consider the emigration of unskilled labour. Now:

$$\frac{d\theta}{d\bar{L}} = \theta_1(-k)\frac{dL_e}{d\bar{L}}+\theta_2\frac{dL_e}{d\bar{L}}+\theta_3(-1)\frac{dL_e}{d\bar{L}}+\theta_3$$

$$= [\theta_1(-k)+\theta_2+\theta_3(-1)]\frac{dL_e}{d\bar{L}}+\theta_3$$

$$= \theta_3 \quad \text{(using (5))}. \tag{6}$$

Hence, if unskilled labour emigrates, the loss of national income will be equal to the marginal product of the labour; thus an infinitesimal move will not harm these left behind. Next, we may examine the impact of the emigration on per capita incomes:

$$\frac{d(\theta/\bar{L})}{d\bar{L}} = \frac{\bar{L}(d\theta/d\bar{L})-\theta}{\bar{L}^2} = \frac{\theta_3}{\bar{L}}-\frac{\theta}{\bar{L}^2} = \frac{1}{\bar{L}}\left(\theta_3-\frac{\theta}{\bar{L}}\right). \tag{7}$$

As one would intuitively expect, therefore, the per capita product will rise or fall according as the marginal product to labour (θ_3) falls below or exceeds the average product of labour ($\theta/\bar{L}$).

3.4.2. Next, consider the emigration of an engineer, implying the 'loss' of the k units of capital *along with* a unit of labour.
    Therefore,

$$\frac{d\theta}{d\bar{L}} = \theta_1\left(k-k\frac{dL_e}{d\bar{L}}\right)+\theta_2\frac{dL_e}{d\bar{L}}+\theta_3(1-dL_e/d\bar{L})$$

$$= \theta_1 k+\theta_3 \quad \text{(again using (5))}. \tag{8}$$

And then

$$\frac{d(\theta/\bar{L})}{d\bar{L}} = \{\theta_3+\theta_1 k\}-\frac{\theta}{\bar{L}}, \tag{9}$$

where, now, the bracketed term includes the marginal product of labour plus the 'lost' marginal product of the capital emigrating via the engineer. Again, we have the intuitive results on the impact of infinitesimal emigration of skilled labour on the national income (and hence zero-impact on those left behind) and on the per capita income of the society.

It is futile to talk of 'presumptions' of loss or gain from emigration. But the weight of the arguments above is that, except for the no-impact outcome for infinitesimal emigration, the different models seem to lead to a prima facie presumption of a loss to those left behind even under conditions of perfect competition. The *magnitude* of this loss is of course conditional on the production functions assumed for the analysis; and as every undergraduate student of economics now must know, 'high' or 'low' costs can emerge depending on whether the elasticity of substitution in production is assumed to be low or high, in turn.[6]

4. Static, welfare theorising with distortions

The theoretical literature embodying distortions, whether policy-imposed or endogenous (in Bhagwati's (1971) terminology), is rather sparse, although the awareness that such distortions can affect the welfare analysis of the brain drain is fairly widespread.

The first paper to consider distortions in a systematic, general-equilibrium framework was by Bhagwati and Hamada (1974). It considers two distortions: an educational subsidy (which is a policy-imposed distortion) and a sticky wage (which is an endogenous distortion). The model, in view of the sticky wage, permits unemployment in the Harris–Todaro (1970) fashion. At the same time, the model enables the authors to analyse the consequences of what is aptly called the 'emulation' effect: the possibility that migration of educated labour can raise the sticky wage as the LDC Joneses emulate and try to keep up with the DC Joneses.

An interesting variation on this model is provided by McCulloch and Yellen (1975) in their Bellagio paper. They modify the Harris–Todaro approach so as to enable the sticky wage to respond *partially* to the degree of unemployment; at the same time, as in one of the Bhagwati–Hamada (1974) variants, they assume that all educational costs are privately borne (i.e., that there is no policy-imposed distortion via an educational subsidy).[7]

---

[6]This must be kept in mind by any unsophisticated reader of Johnson's (1967, app. III) illustrative, 'small', cost calculations for the Cobb–Douglas case, even though one is only belabouring the obvious here. It is perfectly clear that, by assuming a different production function (e.g., the fixed-coefficients Leontief variety), one can generate 'large' losses. One important implication, again hardly unobvious, is that the cost of the brain drain could very well vary with the kind of professionals one is discussing.

[7]There are other points of difference between the Bhagwati–Hamada and the McCulloch–Yellen models which the readers can note for themselves: they are not pertinent to the discussion in the text.

Both papers lead to more complex welfare analysis than the models without distortions in section 2. They enable one to consider, for example, unemployment as an argument in the objective function. Moreover, there is no longer any necessary equality between the income lost to a country by migration and the wage that the (infinitesimal) migrant earns: the Grubel–Scott proposition is predictably invalid.

Finally, two important results from this type of analysis may be noted. First, it is often argued that if only the emigrant paid for the educational subsidy he had received, that would suffice to leave no adverse welfare impact on those left behind; the Bhagwati–Hamada analysis – of the cases where the educational cost is internalised, and where it is not but the country of immigration compensates the LDC for the educational cost of the immigrant – shows that this is not a valid conclusion.

Second, there is a school of thought which argues that the emigration of PTK manpower from LDCs, when there is unemployment, will not harm the LDCs: that, in fact, we have here an 'overflow' or 'safety-valve', rather than a 'drain', phenomenon. Graphically, as Walter Adams put it to the first author of this paper, 'I saw doctors driving taxicabs in Manila; why should we worry about their migrating abroad?' It is clear from the Bhagwati–Hamada analysis that the emigration, by raising the *expected* return to doctors, can cause further expansion of education and hence lead to loss of income; and that the emulation effect can make even *actual* returns to doctors higher than they might have been, thus reinforcing the loss in income.

Further, as the Hamada–Bhagwati (1975) analysis at Bellagio models the point at issue, it is not really meaningful to think of that doctor as driving taxicabs in Manila forever. He is almost certainly 'waiting' to clear his ECFMG to migrate to the U.S. If the possibility of migration to the U.S. were not available, he would at some stage stop wasting his skills and being a cabdriver and, since returns to being a doctor in Manila are clearly low, he would migrate internally: to the smaller cities where he could practice medicine. The external brain drain (from Manila to New York) therefore inhibits the (desirable) internal diffusion (out of Manila into the hinterland).[8] And, even if one pretends that doctors earn the value of their marginal product (in and out of Manila, in the Philippines), the above argument shows that the social marginal product of the doctor who is 'unemployed' qua doctor is *not* zero, contrary to the argument of Adams.

In short, the assumption that PTK personnel who are unemployed at any one point of time can therefore emigrate at no loss of marginal product to their

---

[8]The diffusion of doctors from Manila into the hinterland is the slow, capitalist equivalent of the Maoist policy of 'sending' doctors to the countryside. In India, there is growing evidence that doctors in major cities are now opening offices in the adjacent towns, visiting there for periods such as one day a week, thus effectively 'migrating' partially to the hinterland: flirting is easier than marriage!

society is based on the faulty reasoning which assumes that they will forever so remain and omits taking into account the 'search process' aspect of the labour market. And, it ignores additional welfare implications which could follow from phenomena such as the Bhagwati–Hamada emulation effect.[9]

5. Dynamic analyses of international migration

The dynamic treatment of the consequences of migration, whether unskilled or skilled, is more recent; besides, the number of contributions in this framework is yet relatively small.

The dynamic models naturally divide into those which concentrate on steady-state analysis, such as Berry and Soligo (1969), McCulloch and Yellen (1974) and Rodriguez (1975a), and those which additionally or exclusively describe the transition of the economy outside the steady state, as in Mishan and Needleman (1968) and Rodriguez (1975b).

At the same time, their common dynamic feature is the explicit introduction of capital as a factor of production and the ability of the economy to change the level of its capital stock by means of savings: domestic or foreign. Furthermore, the papers addressed to the brain drain, as distinct from what might be called Ricardian labour migration of the purely unskilled variety, incorporate a second produced factor of production: education as human capital. Moreover, all the papers reviewed focus *not* on world-welfare effects, but on the welfare implications of the migration on the nonmigrant populations of the countries of immigration or emigration. Finally, in regard to the measures of welfare changes, the most widely used are the per capita income of native residents together with the relative factor rewards as indicators of the income distribution, although Berry–Soligo and Rodriguez (1975a) follow a utilitarian approach and proceed to evaluate the full changes in the levels of utility enjoyed, the former by means of consumer surplus analysis and the latter by the first-order change in the stationary level of utility enjoyed by each individual in the context of a life-cycle model of saving.[10]

Finally, we must note that, in contrast to the static analyses reviewed in earlier sections, labour mobility in a dynamic context can be analysed (i) as a once-and-for-all labor movement, or instead (ii) as a rate of migration per unit of time which may, in turn, be either constant or varying over time according to the changing domestic or foreign conditions.

---

[9]The precise implications of building these interpretations of unemployment into the model used for analysing the effects of brain drain will depend, of course, on how the rest of the model is put together. This should be obvious to the reader from contrasting the analyses in, say, Bhagwati–Hamada (1974), McCulloch–Yellen (1975) and Hamada–Bhagwati (1975).

[10]In none of the dynamic models either, therefore, is the issue of to-and-fro migration addressed: emigrants leave for good and the welfare of those left behind is what is considered.

In case (i), it is clear that a once-and-for-all labor movement will not affect any of the steady-state values of the relevant per capita variables, provided we assume that migrants have the same preferences as those of the indigenous population. Under those circumstances, the labor movement can be considered as a change in one of the initial conditions (i.e., initial population) such that the steady state of the economy (if it exists) will be unaffected by it. If, however, a steady state does not exist (as in one of the cases discussed by Mishan–Needleman because of their inclusion of Hicks-neutral technological progress in a Solow-type growth model), even a once-and-for-all inflow of labor with the same preferences as the indigenous population will have permanent effects on the long-run paths of the per capita variables. When migrants have different preferences from those of the rest, however, even a once-and-for-all migration will change the preference structure of the population and will thus have both short- and long-run effects on the economy (provided, of course, that those preferences are transmitted to their children). With the exception of McCulloch–Yellen (1974) and Mishan–Needleman, all the other articles reviewed here introduce differences in preferences in one way or another.

In case (ii), where migration is a continuous process through time, we again have to distinguish between two different problems: (a) a constant or variable migration rate will change the rate of population growth and thus the steady-state requirements of per capita savings, and (b) the preferences of the migrants may differ from those of the rest. In either case it is clear that a continuous migration process will affect both the transition and the steady-state behaviour of the economy.

5.1. The dynamic models of Ricardian labour migration

This subsection concentrates on the models that treat labour as a homogeneous input (contrary to those, discussed in the next subsection, which additionally consider skilled labour).

5.1.1. Of the analyses treating international migration in a dynamic context, the Mishan–Needleman paper is probably the one which provides the clearest link between the static and dynamic models. Their production structure is the same as that of the Solow-type growth model: one-sector, neoclassical technology with two inputs: capital and labor. Savings (equated to investment) are a constant fraction of income and population reproduces at a constant exponential rate. Immigrants have the same preferences (i.e., savings ratio) as the natives and are assumed to enter the country of immigration in a constant number per year. After the immigrant group of a given year enters the country, it starts reproducing itself at the same exponential rate as the natives. Since one of the main objectives of the analysis is to investigate the effects of immigration on the welfare of the indigenous population, they incorporate those born to the immi-grants (i.e., their descendants) into the stock of the immigrant population.[11]

These simple assumptions provide an ideal framework to test in a dynamic model the static propositions that a discrete labor inflow (outflow) will decrease (in-crease) aggregate per capita income but raise (reduce) the per capita income of those who were previously in the country (left behind). In this case, of course, the focus of analysis is on the *time-paths* of the different measures of per capita income.

Mishan and Needleman do not solve explicitly their model in order to find out the qualitative properties of the growth path but rather they postulate a CES production function and, using various sets of parameters values presumably appropriate to the UK, they proceed to simulate the paths of the relevant vari-ables for a thirty-year horizon. Some of their results seem to confirm those of the static analysis: for all of the 30 years aggregate income per capita falls short of that under no immigration, while the wage–rental ratio is consistently lower under the immigration regime. However, their results for the effects on the per capita income of the indigenous population do, in some cases (notably, when the production function is Cobb–Douglas), differ from what would be expected: in the Cobb–Douglas case the per capita income of the indigenous population falls short (instead of being in excess) of that under no immigration for the first 21 years. This seems an unusual conclusion in light of the neoclassical nature of the assumptions. We think, however, that a possible explanation for that lies in their treatment of overhead capital. They assume that a constant fraction of total savings is required for the formation of overhead capital, which is not directly productive; although in the text they assume that such savings are provided by the immigrants, the equations that they simulate do not show it but rather imply that the immigrants' savings for overhead capital are provided by the indigenous population at the expense of their own accumulation of physical capital, which of course tends to reduce their own per capita income [Mishan and Needleman (1968, eqs. 13 and 18)]. Furthermore, the moment the immigrant settles in the country there is an additional requirement for overhead capital, which is assumed to be provided by the indigenous population.

Abstracting from the formation of overhead capital and their assumption of a positive constant rate of technical progress, the effects of a once-and-for-all immigrant inflow in the Mishan–Needleman model can be described, in a perhaps more illuminating way, as follows.

Let $Q = F(K, L) = Lf(k)$ be the neoclassical production function for the composite good Q which can be either consumed or transformed into physical capital. The total labor force can be divided into that of indigenous origin, L_d,

---

[11]Again, there is room here for debate. Even where the immigrants are treated as different from the country of immigration, would it not be unrealistic to assume that those born of first-generation immigrants will still be 'second-class' citizens forever (in the unfolding of our dynamic model)?

and that of immigrant origin, L_{m}. Since both immigrants and indigenous reli-
dents have the same savings ratio, the capital–labor ratio of the economy
changes through time according to the standard formula,

$$\dot{k} = s \cdot f(k) - n \cdot k, \tag{10}$$

where n is the rate of population growth. At time t_0, when the once-and-for-all
immigration takes place, there is a jump in the capital–labor ratio from $k_0 = K(t_0)/L_{\mathrm{d}}(t_0)$ to $k_1 = K(t_0)/\{L_{\mathrm{d}}(t_0) + L_{\mathrm{m}}(t_0)\}$, where $L_{\mathrm{m}}(t_0)$ is the size of the
immigrant inflow. From t_0 on, immigration ceases but the initial immigrant
population starts reproducing itself at the rate n, while at the same time they
save the same fraction of their income as the rest of the population. In consequence, the capital–labor ratio of the economy, after the initial jump at t_0, starts
changing through time according to (10).

The amount of capital per head *owned* by the immigrant population then
changes according to

$$(2)\dot{k}_{\mathrm{m}} = s \cdot y_{\mathrm{m}} - n \cdot k_{\mathrm{m}}, \tag{11}$$

where y_{m} is the per capita income of the immigrant population and equals the
sum of their wage earnings, $\omega(k)$, plus the earnings from the capital they own,
$\gamma(k)k_{\mathrm{m}}$. Notice that given competition and constant returns to scale the wage
rate and the rental rate, ω and γ, are functions only of the economy's aggregate
capital–labor ratio k. In fig. 5, per capita income and savings are represented on
the vertical axis and ratios of capital to population on the horizontal axis. The
curve $q = f(k)$ shows the aggregate per capita income as a function of the
aggregate capital–labor ratio; the curve nk shows the steady-state investment
requirements; and finally, the curve $sf(k)$ shows the aggregate per capita savings.

We assume that, before the immigration, the economy had reached the steady-
state level of the capital–labor ratio k_0. After the immigration, the capital–labor
ratio falls instantaneously to k_1 and aggregate income per capita consequently
falls to k_1B from the higher level k_0D. The reduction in the capital–labor ratio
increases the rental rate and reduces the wage rate (which is now given by the
distance OA along the vertical axis). Since initially immigrants have no capital,
their income is equal to the wage rate OA, clearly lower than the aggregate per
capita income which also includes the earnings from the capital stock. Even
though the aggregate capital–labor ratio has been reduced, the per capita amount
of capital *owned* by the indigenous population remains unchanged at k_0. Thus,
the per capita income of the indigenous population immediately after the immigrant inflow is equal to the new wage rate, OA, plus the rental rate (the slope
of the line AC times their per capita holdings of capital, or the distance k_0C
which exceeds the per capita income they had before the immigration by the

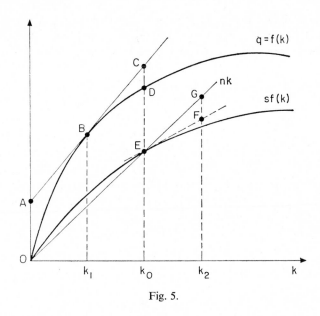

Fig. 5.

amount CD. Thus, the short-run effect of immigration is to raise the per capita income of the indigenous population.[12]

Following the impact effect, it is clear that for the new capital–labor ratio k_1, aggregate savings exceed the amount of investment required to keep it at the same level and thus it will start rising, according to eq. (10), until eventually it will reapproach the pre-immigration steady-state value k_0. There are thus no long-run effects on the aggregate per capita income or capital–labor ratio from a once-and-for-all immigrant inflow. Initially, however, the per capita income of the indigenous population has been increased above the original steady-state level; thus, their per capita savings will exceed the amount required to keep the amount of capital per-head they own constant. In consequence, the ratio of capital per head owned by the indigenous population, k_d, will start rising. It is clear that during the transition process for which $k < k_0$ it will also be $k_d > k_0$, and thus the per capita income of the indigenous residents will exceed its pre-immigration steady-state value. Eventually, however, the aggregate capital–labor ratio will approach k_0 and remain there. At this moment k_d may be also equal to k_0 or still larger. If it is equal, the income per capita of the indigenous population will be the same as the aggregate per capita income, and thus k_d will behave in the same way as k and will remain constant. If k_d still exceeds k_0 while $k = k_0$, then k_d must be falling and finally approaching k_0: for the set of factor rewards implied by $k = k_0$, any k_d larger than k_0 implies that the per capita

---

[12]The reader may here profitably recall our analysis of fig. 4.

savings of the indigenous residents fall short of the investment required to keep it constant. For example, for $k = k_0$ and $k_d = k_2 > k_0$, per capita savings of the indigenous population are $k_2 F$ (the line EF is tangent to the function $sf(k_0)$ at the point k_0; thus the slope of the line is $s\gamma(k_0)$) while the steady-state investment requirements are Gk_2, which clearly exceed $k_2 F$; thus, k_d must be falling and eventually approaching the pre-immigration level k_0.

To conclude, following a once-and-for-all inflow of foreign labor into the country, the basic assumptions of the Mishan–Needleman model imply that the income per capita of the indigenous population will be raised above the pre-immigration level and remain above it during all the transition period until the economy again reaches the pre-immigration steady-state level for all per capita variables.

5.1.2. To the extent that the assumption of equal tastes helped to rule out any steady-state effects of migration, the most natural extension at this point is to inquire about the nature of steady-state effects when the preferences of migrants differ from those of the rest (in particular, when the saving ratios differ). As it happens, this is precisely the question addressed by Berry–Soligo (1969) and Rodriguez (1975a), to whose analyses we now turn.

Both papers differ from Mishan–Needleman in at least two basic respects:

(1) Savings behavior is derived from the individual's maximisation of life-time utility. This, in general, implies that the saving ratios are not constant but rather depend on factor rewards. Individuals do not all have the same utility function.

(2) Both papers are concerned with the effects of emigration on the welfare of those left behind rather than the effects of immigration on the welfare of the indigenous population of the receiving country; it is obvious, however, that both questions are different sides of the same coin.

Basically, their behavioral assumption is that of a life-cycle model of savings where individuals work when they are young and save for their retirement. In this context, the interest rate not only plays the role of being the return to the factor of production 'capital' but also determines the trade-off between present (working period) and future (retirement period) consumption. As proved elsewhere [Samuelson (1958), Diamond (1965)], a competitive market will in general fail to attain the optimal 'golden rule' level of the capital–labor ratio (for which the interest rate equals the rate of population growth) at which society's consumption potential is maximised and the optimal distribution of consumption among generations is attained. To the extent therefore that emigration or immigration changes the aggregate savings ratio of the population, and thus the steady-state level of the capital–labor ratio, there can be aggregate social gains or losses depending on whether the move is towards or away from the golden rule level of the capital–labor ratio.

For the members of each individual group (characterised by a set of preferences) these aggregate gains or losses must be modified to the extent that the
individual differs from the average: the change in the steady-state capital–labor
ratio brings about changes in relative factor rewards which in turn redistribute
income in favor of the group which is relatively better endowed with the factor
whose reward has increased in relative terms. For example, if there are only two
groups of individuals, high savers and low savers, emigration of some members
of the high-savers group will in general reduce the new steady-state capital–
labor ratio (through the reduction in the aggregate savings ratio of the population). If the capital–labor ratio was initially below its golden rule level (i.e., the
interest rate was larger than the rate of population growth), this move must
decrease welfare in the aggregate. The lower capital intensity, in turn, decreases
the wage–rental ratio and thus redistributes income towards those remaining
members of the high-savers group (those with a higher preference for the ownership of capital) and away from the low savers. It follows that, on both counts,
the members of the low-savings group tend to be worse off while the remaining
members of the high-savings group may be either worse off or better off. When
low savers emigrate, the capital–labor ratio will be increased and, if the movement is towards the golden rule ratio, there is a gain in the aggregate and a
redistribution of income towards the remaining low savers (the wage–rental
ratio rises). Thus, on both counts, the remaining low savers are better off while
the effect on high savers is ambiguous.

It follows from the above analysis that if the capital–labor ratio is below its
golden rule level, in the long run emigration of high savers (which decreases the
capital–labor ratio even further) will make at least one group worse off, while
emigration of low savers will make at least one group better off. If, however, the
capital–labor ratio was above the golden rule level, those conclusions should
be reversed since in this case reductions in the capital–labor ratio are beneficial
in the aggregate.

5.1.3. To summarise, in this section we have concentrated on the description
of dynamic models of labor migration where migrants may or may not differ
from the rest of the population in regard to their preferences for the accumulation of physical capital. If everyone's preferences are identical and migration is
a once-and-for-all phenomenon, there are in general no steady-state effects of
migration; the gains of the population of the receiving country (or losses to those
remaining in the country of origin) which appear in the static models also appear
in this case, except that these gains (or losses) occur in the transitional period
during which the economy approaches the original steady state. These transitional gains or losses are shown to depend critically on the per capita ownership
of capital by the economic agents and the transitional change in the economy's
factor proportions (and factor rewards) brought about by the migration.

When migrants differ from the rest of the population in their savings habits, we have not merely the transitional gains or losses referred to above, but also the permanent changes in the steady state of the economy due to the now different aggregate savings behavior. These effects can be divided into two parts: (i) effects of movements in the steady-state capital–labor ratio towards or away from the golden rule ratio; and (ii) effects of changes in the steady-state distribution of income due to the new prevailing set of factor rewards and the different preferences of members of the population for the ownership of factors of production.

5.2. The dynamic models of the brain drain

We turn next to the brain drain models whose basic feature is that human capital, in addition to unskilled labor and physical capital, appears as a distinctive factor of production. Human capital is assumed to be accumulated through an educational process which uses up some of society's scarce resources.

To the extent that competition prevails everywhere, including the educational market, it is clear that allowing for the international mobility of educated people amounts to little more than an extension of the issues discussed in the previous section to the context of a three-factor model. Neither of the two papers in this area [McCulloch–Yellen (1974) and Rodriguez (1975b)], however, could be described as a straightforward three-factor extension of the models analysed so far. The main differences are:

(1) The educational market is not assumed to be perfect, either because education is not competitively supplied or because, thanks to the existence of capital market imperfections or information costs, the rates of return to physical and human capital are not equalised.

(2) Rather than considering an exogenous population movement or migration rate, the two papers consider as exogenous the foreign rewards of the internationally mobile factors and the migration preferences of those factors in response to the rates of return from international emigration. Since these rates of return depend not only on the foreign rewards but also on the domestic rewards and the costs of the move, it follows that the actual migration rates will be endogenously determined within the system.

(3) The Rodriguez (1975b) analysis also includes the case of labor market distortions of the type analysed in Harris–Todaro (1970), which were also discussed in a static framework in Bhagwati–Hamada (1974) and Hamada–Bhagwati (1975).

The paper which most closely approximates the other dynamic models previously discussed is McCulloch–Yellen (1974), which concentrates on the study of the steady-state effects on the distribution of income of migration of educated (skilled) people within the context of the following basic assumptions:

(1) Only one good is produced, with a constant-returns-to-scale technology and three factors: physical capital, skilled (educated) labor and unskilled labor.

(2) Education (the acquisition of skills) is carried on until the point where the skilled–unskilled wage differential equals the cost of acquiring the education which, in turn, increases with the fraction of the newly-born population getting educated. The educational cost may be either the marginal or average cost depending on the kind of market structure which prevails in this sector. For the purposes of making the comparison, they convert the once-and-for-all education cost into a constant flow per time unit, using an exogenously given discount rate.

(3) Migration is carried on until the foreign–domestic wage differential for skilled labor equals the flow-equivalent migration cost. Unskilled labor does not migrate.

(4) The domestic rate of return on physical capital is equalised with the foreign rate of return by assuming perfect international mobility of foreign capital at constant rental.

Given these assumptions and a constant rate of population growth, the result is, in general, a nonzero migration rate for skilled labor. This is so because there is no reason why the steady-state output of the educational sector will be consistent with the maintenance of that particular stock of skilled labor relative to the other factors which precisely generates a domestic skilled wage such that emigration or immigration is not attractive. There is, however, a band equal to the foreign skilled wage plus or minus the migration cost such that if the steady-state domestic skilled wage falls within it, no migration will occur.

The steady-state factor rewards for skilled and unskilled labor, migration rate and education rate will then depend on certain exogenous parameters, among them the foreign wage for skilled labor, the foreign rental on capital, the migration cost and the interest rate used for discounting investments in human capital or migration. In fact, reduced to its barest essentials, the basic assumptions of this model imply the following steady-state relationships. Assuming that the steady state is consistent with net emigration of skilled labor (a similar analysis follows easily in the case of immigration), the domestic skilled wage is pegged at the world level minus the migration cost (converted into a constant-flow equivalent). The thus-determined skilled wage *plus* constant rental on capital (equal to the world rental) suffice to determine all the steady-state factor proportions in production (the ratios of capital to skilled and unskilled labor) and therefore, by implication, the unskilled wage and also the skilled–unskilled wage differential. The wage differential, in turn, determines the fraction of the newly-born population acquiring education via assumption (2) above. Since for a steady state the growth rate of the skilled labor force must equal that of the total labor force (such that factor proportions remain constant), the equilibrium migration rate is then obtained as the difference between the growth rate in the stock of skilled people, implied by the already-determined equilibrium factor proportions and the fraction of those newly-born getting educated, and the rate of population growth.[13]

From these relatively simple relationships it is then easy to derive the steady-state responses of several endogenous variables to changes in the exogenous parameters. For example, an increase in the cost of emigration (or equivalently, an emigration tax or a fall in the foreign skilled wage) reduces the domestic skilled wage by the same amount. Given the constant rental on capital and the constant-returns-to-scale technology, reductions in the skilled wage are associated with increases in the unskilled wage; thus the skilled–unskilled wage differential must unambiguously fall. The fall in the skilled–unskilled wage ratio makes skilled labor more attractive for use in production than unskilled labor and thus the ratio of skilled to unskilled labor is increased. Similarly, the lower wage differential makes education less attractive and thus the fraction of the newly-born getting educated falls. The lower output of the educational sector plus the higher steady-state requirement of skilled labor relative to the unskilled unambiguously implies a reduction in the rate of emigration.

The only other dynamic analysis of skilled migration is by Rodriguez (1975b). It concentrates on the *differential attitudes* of individuals regarding the decisions of capital accumulation, education and migration. Rather than postulating that education is carried on by everyone up to the point where the wage differential equals the (flow-equivalent) education cost, he assumes that all those born to educated (skilled) parents will get educated *irrespective of* costs and returns (at least within the relevant range), while only a fraction of those born to uneducated parents will seek education (this fraction depending on the pecuniary rate of return to education). Similarly, migration does not necessarily close the gap between foreign and domestic wages (allowing for the migration cost) but rather the fraction of the skilled population which chooses to migrate is assumed to be a function of the rate of return to such a move. It is further assumed that investment in physical capital is a constant fraction of profits earned. On the technology side, Rodriguez assumes two sectors whose outputs are traded at a fixed international relative price, as in Bhagwati–Hamada (1974) and McCulloch–Yellen (1975), but, and in contrast to both, physical capital is used in both sectors while only one type of labor (skilled or unskilled) is used in each sector. The mobility of capital between the sectors and the fixed terms of trade imply a

---

[13]Denote by S, U and $P = S + U$ the skilled, unskilled and total population, respectively; by g and e the gross rate of population growth and the fraction of those just born getting education; and by m the ratio of skilled migrants to total population. Then, the growth rates in the stocks of skilled labor and total population are

$$(1/S)(\mathrm{d}S/\mathrm{d}t) = (eg - m)(P/S),$$

$$(1/P)(\mathrm{d}P/\mathrm{d}t) = g - m.$$

Since both growth rates must be equal in the steady state, the equilibrium migration rate will be given by

$$m = -g(1 - e)(S/U) + ge.$$

technologically-determined *positive* relationship between the returns to both kinds of labor. This makes the income distribution predictions of this model essentially different from those of McCulloch–Yellen (1974), where the assumptions about technology and international mobility of capital implied a *negative* relationship between the skilled and unskilled wage rates. Education is assumed to be supplied by a third sector at a constant cost and capital goods are assumed to be imported from abroad or produced in one of the two domestic sectors.

The paper analyses the stability of the model, the nature of the steady-state solution and comparative statics, proceeding then a la Bhagwati–Hamada to analyse the long-run effects of sticky real wages in the context of a Harris–Todaro (1970) labor market, while also exploring the short- and long-run effects of the implementation of a migration tax on factor rewards and unemployment.

When wages are flexible, the most distinctive result of the model is the complete independence of all steady-state factor rewards from the costs of migration or the foreign wage and thus also from a migration tax. The reason for this result can be easily shown as follows. Denote by x the fraction of those born to unskilled parents who get educated, n the growth rate of population, U and K the stocks of unskilled labor and capital, and s and r the savings ratio out of profits and the interest rate, respectively. Then, the growth rate in the stock of the unskilled population equals

$$(1/U)(dU/dt) = n(1-x), \tag{12}$$

and the growth rate in the stock of capital is

$$(1/K)(dK/dt) = s \cdot r. \tag{13}$$

In the steady state, both these growth rates must be equalised and thus, in the steady state, we must have

$$s \cdot r = n(1-x) \tag{14}$$

Since x depends only on the constant education cost and the skilled–unskilled wage differential which, in turn, depends only on the interest rate r, it follows that the above condition by itself determines the steady-state interest rate and, by implication, all other factor rewards as functions only of the educational costs s and n. Since none of these three variables depends in any way on the foreign wage or the migration cost, it follows that steady-state factor rewards are independent of these two variables. Notice, however, that if workers were also to save, the rate of growth of the capital stock would *also* depend on their savings ratio and the shares of the different factors in national income. Since these shares will depend on the ratios of the different factor endowments (which are endogenous variables in the steady state), the above steady-state condition would not suffice to determine all factor rewards which will now depend also on the other parameters of the system, including the foreign wage and the migration cost.

As for the short run, Rodriguez returns to the original assumptions, showing that the steady-state independence of factor rewards from a migration tax does *not* prevail in the short run and that, following the imposition of such a tax, the returns to *both* types of labor will fall during the transitional period while the return to capital is increased.

In conclusion, Rodriguez notes for the sticky-wage variant of his model that, with this amendment, it is rather the long-run rate of unemployment that is independent from the foreign wage or the migration cost. However, in the transitional period, following an increase in the migration cost, the unemployment rate is increased; note, however, that since Rodriguez shows that the model is always unstable when there is a minimum wage for skilled labor, this result strictly applies only to unskilled wages and unskilled unemployment.

6. Concluding remarks

Clearly, the preceding review suggests that the theoretical analysis of the brain drain, once dormant after the Grubel–Scott–Berry–Soligo–Johnson phase, has received a fresh lease on life with the analysis of distortions (beginning with Bhagwati–Hamada) and of explicitly dynamic formulations (in Rodriguez). The explicit examination of policy options, in general-equilibrium formulation, is also recent: especially the Bhagwati-type surtax on migrants has been examined, for its welfare impact, in several of the recent papers.

Where can we suggest fruitful avenues for future theoretical work? The following would seem to be rewarding areas for general-equilibrium analysis:

(1) The welfare of the nonemigrants may be examined for to-and-fro migration (as noted earlier) be permitting the migrant to acquire skills, wealth, etc., during the migration to the DCs.

(2) The case of the migration accentuating distortions (e.g., through the emulation effect in Bhagwati–Hamada) may be extended to the case where migration *reduces* distortions (e.g., if a state monopsony is under-remunerating the emigrants' skills, the migration could reduce the monopsonistic power).

(3) The possibility that the migration could affect the foreign trade possibilities (i.e., the foreign offer curve) via its effect on the LDCs overall national income, and hence on its bargaining power in a world of unequal partners or via the efforts exerted by the migrants in their DCs of destination on behalf of their LDCs of origin (e.g., Greek PTK emigrants influencing the U.S. Congress in favour of Greece in matters of importance to Greece), may also be formalised.

References

Berry, R. and R. Soligo, 1969, Some welfare aspects of international migration, Journal of Political Economy, 77.

Bhagwati, J., 1971, The generalized theory of distortions and welfare, in: J. Bhagwati, R. Jones, R. Mundell and J. Vanek, eds., Trade, balance of payments and growth (North-Holland, Amsterdam).

Bhagwati, J. and T.N. Srinivasan, 1969, Optimal intervention to achieve non-economic objectives, Review of Economic Studies, 27–38.

Bhagwati, J. and W. Dellalfar, 1973, The brain drain and income taxation, World Development 1, no. 1.

Bhagwati, J. and K. Hamada, 1974, The brain drain, international integration of markets for professionals and unemployment: A theoretical analysis, Journal of Development Economics 1, no. 1.

Diamond, P.A., 1965, National debt in a neoclassical growth model, American Economic Review 55, December.

Grubel, H., 1975, Evaluating the welfare effects of the brain drain from developing countries, paper presented at the Bellagio Conference on Brain Drain and Income Taxation, Bellagio, Italy.

Grubel, H. and A. Scott, 1966, The international flow of human capital, American Economic Review, May.

*Hamada, K., 1975, Efficiency, equality, income taxation and the brain drain: A second-best argument, paper presented at the Bellagio Conference on Brain Drain and Income Taxation, Bellagio, Italy.

*Hamada, K. and J. Bhagwati, 1975, Domestic distortions, imperfect information and the brain drain, paper presented at the Bellagio Conference on Brain Drain and Income Taxation, Bellagio, Italy.

Harris, J. and M. Todaro, 1970, Migration, unemployment and development: A two-sector analysis, American Economic Review, March.

Johnson, H.G., 1965, The economics of the 'brain drain': The Canadian case, Minerva.

Johnson, H.G., 1967, Some economic aspects of brain drain, Pakistan Development Review 3.

Kenen, P., 1971, Migration, the terms of trade and economic welfare in the source country, in: J. Bhagwati, R. Jones, R. Mundell and J. Vanek, eds. Trade, balance of payments and growth (North-Holland, Amsterdam).

McCulloch, R. and J. Yellen, 1974, Factor mobility and the steady state distribution of income, Discussion paper no. 369 (Harvard Institute of Economic Research, Cambridge, MA).

*McCulloch, R. and J. Yellen, 1975, Consequences of a tax on the brain drain for unemployment and income inequality in LDCs, paper presented at the Bellagio Conference on Brain Drain and Income Taxation, Bellagio, Italy.

Mishan, E.J. and L. Needleman, 1968, Immigration: Some long-term economic consequences, Part A and part B, Economia Internazionale 21, nos. 2 and 3.

Rawls, J., 1971, A theory of justice (Harvard University Press, Cambridge, MA).

Rodriguez, C., 1975a, On the welfare aspects of international migration, Journal of Political Economy, forthcoming.

*Rodriguez, C., 1975b, Brain drain and economic growth: A dynamic model, paper presented at the Bellagio Conference on Brain Drain and Income Taxation, Bellagio, Italy.

Samuelson, P.A., 1958, An exact consumption-loan model of interest with or without the social contrivance of money, Journal of Political Economy, December.

Sjaastad, L., 1962, The costs and returns of human migration, Journal of Political Economy, October (supplement).

Tobin, J., 1974, Notes on the economic theory of expulsion and expropriation, Journal of Development Economics 1, no. 1.

UNCTAD, 1974, The reverse transfer of technology: Economic effects of the outflow of trained personnel from developing countries (brain drain), Trade and Development Board, Inter-governmental group on transfer of technology, Third session, Geneva, July 15.

CHAPTER 6

THE BRAIN DRAIN, INTERNATIONAL INTEGRATION OF MARKETS FOR PROFESSIONALS AND UNEMPLOYMENT
A theoretical analysis*

Jagdish BHAGWATI and Koichi HAMADA

Massachusetts Institute of Technology, Cambridge, MA 02139, U.S.A.

1. Introduction

Nearly the entire *theoretical* literature on the effects of the 'brain drain' from the less developed countries on their welfare has been undertaken in the framework of neoclassical models of the Hicks–Samuelson value-theoretic variety.[1]

While the analysts in this genre have greatly clarified certain issues such as the nature of the objective function to be specified, their analysis and prescriptions have been constrained by the theoretical model which they work with. The central result of their analysis, attributable to Grubel and Scott (1966), that brain drain prima facie should not be a cause for worry as the drained person will only take away the value of his marginal product which he himself earns anyway, can be rather obviously shown to be subject to the limitations that (i) for finite, rather than infinitestimal, shifts of labour, there would still be a loss to those left behind;[2] (ii) if the social marginal product exceeds the private marginal product, thanks to strong externalities, as would seem to be the case with doctors and exceptionally gifted academics about whose emigration typically the underdeveloped countries seem to worry, then again there *is* a loss to those left behind;[3]

*Thanks are due to the National Science Foundation for financial support of the research underlying this paper. The paper was written while K. Hamada (University of Tokyo, Bunkyo-ku, Tokyo) was visiting M.I.T. on a Fellowship from the American Council of Learned Societies. Helpful comments on the paper were received from T.N. Srinivasan, Robert Solow, Herbert Grubel and an anonymous referee. An appendix has been added for this volume.

[1] See, in particular, Grubel and Scott (1966) and Johnson (1972).

[2] On the other hand, depending on the size of the emigration and the nature of the production function, this loss may still be very small.

[3] On the other hand, one could stretch things a great deal and argue that, for some emigrants, their contribution to social product still continues to accrue to the home country: e.g. an Indian scientist's achievements abroad 'inspire' his countrymen at home; and that this happens *without* their earning their private product from the home-country's GNP and also that their social product may even *increase* if their achievements improve in a more efficient and productive environment than the one found in their home country.

and (iii) if the State has financed the education which is embodied in the skilled worker who migrates, *and* if it is assumed that the State would have taxed this skilled worker – a realistic assumption when there is progressive taxation – partially or wholly to 'recover' the return on this investment, then his emigration does deprive those left behind of this return and thus worsens their welfare.

These are useful insights into the problem of the 'brain drain'. However, admittedly, the analysis is overly simple and could be extended in many directions. An obvious growth-theoretic extension would be to bring in savings behaviour and maximization of welfare over time for those left behind. Or, within the confines of the Hicks–Samuelson model, the analysis could be enriched to allow for remittances from the emigrated people: an argument which qualifies the conclusions in favour of permitting the brain drain. The neoclassical model could further be extended *fully* in the direction of trade-theoretic models with factor movements: the effect of the labour migration on the commodity terms of trade of the labour–losing country could be readily analysed along the lines of the recent Jones (1967) and Kemp (1966) contributions to the welfare theory of international capital movements.[4]

But few of these extensions of the Hicks–Samuelson value-theoretic model are anything but analytic modifications which admit into the model the kinds of complexities which the model itself, rather than reality, suggests. It is necessary therefore to see whether an alternative value-theoretic model can be devised which comes closer to reality as observed in certain underdeveloped countries.

In particular, certain important aspects of the educated-manpower problem in underdeveloped countries have been noted by the non-theorists:

(1) The presence of international income-inequality implies that, for the educated elite which is better informed about the developed world, and more integrated therewith regarding notions of a 'good life' and related values, the salary levels demanded *and* fixed by the elite groups themselves tend to reflect the salary levels of comparable groups in the more developed countries. René Dumont (1969) has argued for French Africa:

> 'During the last phase of colonialism, the policy was to equalize salaries of Africans and Europeans in similar jobs, a defensible position only in the framework of 'assimilation'. The native civil servant, in addition to his regular salary, received a colonial supplement. This has been reduced in some cases, but not abolished. At independence, this pseudoequality has led to flagrant disparity with the rest of the population, whose standard of living is often a fifteenth of the French.

---

[4]Johnson (1967) has extended the analysis of the problem in a yet different direction, by assuming that skilled-labour migration reduces *both* the labour and the capital stock of the emigrating country. However, his analysis is limited by his assumption that human capital and physical capital are perfect substitutes – an assumption that would naturally provide a downward bias to the damaging effects of brain drain.

Massive departure of the French resulted in a high rate of promotion of subordinate African civil servants, who thus earn even more now than before, for the same qualifications. The student returning from France is appointed director if he is the only African technician or graduate in his field.' (p. 80)

Indeed, this phenomenon has been noted by Osvaldo Sunkel (1971) for Latin America and by Dudley Seers and Richard Jolly (1972) for a wider group of countries. Thus, we can postulate a socio-economic situation in which the real wage levels of the educated elites are set by fiat, legislation, unionisation, etc., at levels which reflect the degree of response to the international-elite-integration effect just outlined.

(2) This phenomenon of educated-elite wages, 'way out of line with the average per capita income of the underdeveloped countries', is next regarded as often leading to a 'leap-frogging' process under which the lowest wages tend to get pulled up by the highest: hence the phenomenon of such institutionally defined wages tends to run through the entire labour-market.

(3) With these institutionally defined wages, it is inevitable that the labour-market must work so as to have open unemployment of labour (except in singular cases); and this too is an observed phenomenon: educated and also uneducated people are often unemployed in the developed countries.

(4) At the same time, the phenomenon of high wages, accruing to the (employed) educated elite, creates a political demand for education. René Dumont (1969) has again described the French African situation vividly:

Present education obstructs progress

'This statement may appear paradoxical to many readers, particularly coming from the pen of a professor, since education was the essential foundation of development in Europe, America, Japan, the Soviet Union and China. In Africa it has a certain utility, but this is greatly curtailed by the social *milieu* on to which the educational system was grafted. For most African children, in town and country alike, school represents above all a means of entering the *elite* class. Even in the most backward areas of the bush everyone has grasped the fact that the official with clean hands earns more and works much less.

Pushed by his parents, a peasant child realizes that he can never go very far in agriculture; the only way to get ahead is to get out. He goes to school and works very hard, to this end, sometimes at the price of incredible sacrifices. I have heard of a child in Chad who walks twice a day the twenty kilometres separating his house from school.

. . . Before long, these young people end up in the shanty-towns of the capitals and become social parasites. Their days are spent writing requests for jobs, requests that pile up in all the administrations.' Some of them, in Douala for example, join the underground.' (pp. 88–89)

But this is a situation which is to be found in a large number of underdeveloped countries, indeed.

(5) And the demand for education is translated into educational expenditures by the State, in these underdeveloped countries, with visible alacrity. In India, for example, the number of colleges expands, with little time lag, to accommodate the students who qualify with 'passing marks' from the high schools: and the standards in the latter have, in turn, fallen to accommodate the larger flows of students seeking educational qualifications.

A value-theoretic model which accounts for these phenomena is clearly more relevant for analysis of the questions pertaining to the labour market, such as the welfare effect of the brain drain, in several underdeveloped countries than the neoclassical model (which assumes fully flexible wages, for example).

We proceed therefore to the construction of precisely such a model in sect. 2 and then analyse the phenomena of brain drain and increasing international integration of elite groups in its framework in sect. 3. In sect. 4, we discuss a number of variants of this basic model. In sect. 5, we draw together the welfare implications of emigration in the framework of our model and its variants, also examining the effects of taxing emigrants – a policy that has sometimes been advocated in the literature.[5] In particular, since our model allows for the existence of unemployment for both educated and uneducated labour, our discussion of welfare will involve examination not merely of the (conventional) impact on the domestic availability of goods and services for final use but also of the effect of each policy measure on the level and the degree of unemployment, if any, of each class of labour.[6]

2. The basic model

The simplest general equilibrium model, incorporating the features described above, which can be constructed for our analysis is set out below.

Assume two commodities m_1 and m_2. Let their outputs M_1 and M_2 be related to the inputs by the following production functions which possess the standard properties including twice differentiability and linear homogeneity,

$$M_1 = F_1(L_1),\tag{1}$$

$$M_2 = F_2(L_2),\tag{2}$$

where L_1 is the quantity of skilled/educated labour employed in producing m_1,

---

[5]See, for example, Bhagwati and Dellalfar (1973).

[6]We might as well note explicitly that the kind of model we build and analyse in this paper is not universally valid, even on casual empiricism. Thus, for example, in Japan, the (relative) wage level of intellectuals in Japan has managed to remain virtually unaffected by the significantly higher level of remuneration for their counterparts in the West. This may be one of the many respects in which Japan has apparently differed from the other 'latecomers' in the process of industrialization and integration of the world economy and polity, exhibiting a remarkable ability to adhere to an 'inner-directed' posture in her political and cultural methods.

and L_2 is the quantity of unskilled/uneducated labour employed in producing m_2. Note that educated labour enters only m_1-production and uneducated labour enters only m_2-production. Diminishing returns to L_1 and L_2 are postulated, implying implicit, specific 'non-labour' factors. We further assume that the country is a 'small' country, in Samuelson's sense, so that the commodity price ratio $p_1/p_2 = \pi$ is exogenously fixed and commodity m_2 is the numeraire.

We next assume that the real wage of educated labour is fixed, by international emulation and associated union-fixation or wage legislation, at level $\bar{w}_1$ in m_2-units. Note that this automatically defines $(\partial F_1/\partial L_1)\pi$ and hence L_1 and M_1. Similarly, assume that the 'leap-frogging' process fixed the minimum wages of unskilled labour L_2 at $\bar{w}_2$ ($= \partial F_2/\partial L_2$), and hence also L_2 and M_2. Thus we can write the following two factor market equations:

$$\partial F_1/\partial L_1 = \bar{w}_1/\pi, \quad \text{or } L_1 = g_1(\bar{w}_1/\pi), \tag{3}$$

$$\partial F_2/\partial L_2 = \bar{w}_2, \quad \text{or } L_2 = g_2(\bar{w}_2). \tag{4}$$

Then with U_1 and U_2 denoting the unemployed, educated and uneducated labour respectively, N_1 and N_2 denoting educated and uneducated labour supply respectively, and $\bar{N}$ representing the total fixed labour supply, we have three balance equations:[7]

$$L_1 + U_1 = N_1, \tag{5}$$

$$L_2 + U_2 = N_2, \tag{6}$$

$$N_1 + N_2 = \bar{N}. \tag{7}$$

But we next need to know how the available labour supply will divide between N_1, and N_2. To do this, we need to introduce equations to determine the supply of educated labour N_1. We shall assume that there will be a positive inducement to get educated as long as the expected wage for educated labour exceeds the expected wage for uneducated labour.

Let the expected wage for educated labour Ew_1 then be the *average* wage for it, namely,

$$Ew_1 = \bar{w}_1(L_1/N_1), \tag{8}$$

and the expected wage for uneducated labour Ew_2 be the *average* wage for it:

$$Ew_2 = \bar{w}_2(L_2/N_2), \tag{9}$$

---

[7]Bhagwati and Srinivasan (1972) have analysed an alternative adjustment mechanism for the labour market, where the unemployment of skilled labour is not permitted as long as there are enough jobs in the unskilled labour market. Under this theory, the available supply of skilled labour first gets absorbed in the skilled labour market, and the spillover then takes the available jobs in the unskilled labour market (where the two kinds of labour are equally productive but the employers sociologically prefer giving jobs to skilled over unskilled applicants). The Bhagwati–Srinivasan model is designed to study the phenomenon of 'overqualification', whereby the educated seem to get into the uneducated-level jobs over time: a phenomenon which has sometimes also been called the 'upgrading' of jobs.

and the equilibrium condition then is:

$$Ew_1 = Ew_2.\tag{10}$$

Note that this equilibrium condition makes sense insofar as we are assuming that the State undertake the cost of education, and not labour itself. It is assumed therefore that as long as $Ew_1 > Ew_2$, there will be a politically effective excess demand for State-financed educational facilities to be opened up, for N_2 to be turned into N_1 until $Ew_1 = Ew_2$. However, to analyze the effect of this assumption on the level of national income, we may simply subtract the cost of this education from national production of m_1 and m_2 to arrive at the national income available for consumption:

$$Y = (\pi M_1 + M_2) - kN_1,\tag{11}$$

where k is the fixed educational cost, in m_2-units, per person; this cost being subtracted from total output of M_1 and M_2 to arrive at the net output available for consumption Y.[8] It follows that increasing Y is tantamount to increasing the value of a conventional social welfare function defined in terms of goods and services available for domestic consumption.

This basic model thus has eleven equations and eleven unknowns: M_1, M_2, L_1, L_2, U_1, U_2, N_1, N_2, Ew_1, Ew_2, and Y. It is also a model in terms of which we can analyze meaningfully a number of questions relating to the brain drain problem and the phenomenon of international integration of the educated-labour markets.

3. Brain drain and international integration of market for professionals

This basic model can be easily contrasted with the case where both wages are flexible and labour pays for the cost of education. Note first that we have here *three* sources of economic inefficiency: the two sticky wages plus the free education. In the absence of these three inefficiencies, the economy would have reached the standard Pareto-optimal equilibrium with the following first-order conditions:

$$w_1 - k = (\partial F_1/\partial L_1) - k = (\partial F_2/\partial L_2) = w_2,\tag{12}$$

with full employment of labour. In analysing the model with the three inefficiencies which we have noted, we now proceed through successive possibilities, analysing the effects on unemployment and national income in four alternative cases:

Case I. Our-Joneses-keeping-up-with-their-Joneses: This is the case where the country's educated/skilled labour, on integrating with the outside-world's

---

[8]To ensure proper dimensionality in the analysis that follows, this educational cost must be regarded as the 'annual' flow-equivalent of the educational cost incurred to train a man. Also, to simplify the analysis, we do not introduce private educational expenditure until sect. 4.

educated/skilled labour, demands and achieves an increment in its salary level: this is therefore the case where there is primary increase in w_1.

Case II. Keeping-up-with-our-Joneses: This is the case where we have the well-observed 'leap-frogging' process, so that the rise in w_1 (the wage of skilled labour) leads to a sympathetic rise in w_2 (the wage of unskilled labour).

Case III. Emigration-of-our-Joneses: This is the case where the emigration of skilled labour to higher-wage areas abroad leads to higher expected wage to skilled labour: *either* via mere reduction in unemployment of skilled labour at home and consequent increased assurance of the domestic wage $(\bar{w}_1)$ *or* via pushing up the expected wage because the wage-rate abroad is higher than the domestic wage.

Case IV. The general case of emigration and rise of wages: This is the general case where the emigration of skilled labour is also accompanied by a sympathetic rise in the domestic wage $(\bar{w}_1)$: a case that is plausible because more emigration could imply more integration of the professional markets for skilled labour internationally. This general case therefore considers the totality of effects from Case II and Case III: the emigration effect of Case III being combined with the dual wage-increase effect of Case II.

We now analyse these cases, in turn. The following analysis is carried out on the assumption that a marginal change in wages or emigration still leaves some unemployment in each sector; otherwise, neoclassical competitive analysis would become applicable.

Case I. Our-Joneses-keeping-up-with-their-Joneses

This is the case where the educated labour force is getting culturally integrated internationally, and the effect is to exercise an upward pull on its domestic salary level. This phenomenon of 'our-Joneses-keeping-up-with-their-Joneses' can be analysed simply then by analysing the effect of a shift in w_1.

We can see the effect of the increase in $\bar{w}_1$ on employment by differentiating (3) and (4):

$$dL_1/d\bar{w}_1 = (1/\pi)g_1'(\bar{w}_1/\pi) < 0, \text{ because } g_1'(\bar{w}_1/\pi) = (\partial^2 F_1/\partial L_1^2)^{-1} < 0,$$
(13)

$$dL_2/d\bar{w}_1 = 0.$$
(14)

The employment in m_1-sector will decrease in response to the rise in wages in its own sector and the employment in m_2-sector remains the same.

However, unemployment in both sectors depends on how labour divides into the two types of labour. We can readily see the effect of the wage increase in m_1-sector on the division of labour supply into the two types, by deriving:

$$dN_1/d\bar{w}_1 = (1 - \eta_1)N_2L_1/(\bar{w}_1L_1 + \bar{w}_2L_2),$$
(15)

where $\eta_1 \equiv (\bar{w}_1/L_1)(dL_1/d\bar{w}_1)$ is the elasticity of the demand for labour in m_1-industry. Further, (15) simplifies to:

$$dN_1/d\bar{w}_1 = (1-\eta_1)N_1 N_2/(\bar{N}\bar{w}_1), \qquad (16)$$

or, in elasticity terms,

$$(\bar{w}_1/N_1)(dN_1/d\bar{w}_1) = (1-\eta_1)N_2/\bar{N}. \qquad (17)$$

Thus the supply of educated labour increases or decreases depending on whether the elasticity of demand for labour in m_1-industry, is less or more than unity. This result is easy to understand, of course, because the outcome regarding the supply of educated labour depends on the impact effect of the wage change in m_1 on the expected wage (Ew_1) in that sector: and the expected wage will rise insofar as the actual wage rises but fall insofar as (educated) labour is laid off by profit-maximising entrepreneurs in m_1 in consequence. The net outcome is determined by whether the elasticity of demand for labour in m_1 is higher or lower than unity: in the former case, the net effect is to lower the expected wage Ew_1; in the latter case, the net effect is to increase it.[9]

We can now analyze the effect on absolute and relative unemployment of each sector.

(a) *Absolute level of unemployment of educated labour*

$$(d/d\bar{w}_1)(N_1-L_1) = (1-\eta_1)N_1 N_2/(\bar{w}_1 N)+\eta_1 L_1/\bar{w}_1. \qquad (18)$$

Thus if the elasticity of demand for educated labour is less than unity, the absolute level of unemployment increases because the supply of educated labour increases while the demand decreases. However, even if the elasticity of demand for educated labour is greater than unity, so that the supply of educated labour is reduced (owing to reduced expected wage Ew_1), the absolute unemployment of educated labour would increase if the demand for such labour reduces even more; this would be the case if:[10]

$$L_1/N_1 \geqq N_2/\bar{N}, \qquad (19)$$

or

$$L_1/N_1 < N_2/\bar{N}, \quad \text{but} \quad \eta_1 < [1-(L_1/N_1)/(N_2/\bar{N})]^{-1}. \qquad (20)$$

---

[9]At the same time, it is easy to see that the elasticity of demand for labour, η_1, is the ratio of the elasticity of substitution of the production function, σ_1, and the capital share, α_1:

$$\eta_1 = -\frac{\bar{w}_1}{L_1}\frac{dL_1}{d\bar{w}_1} = -\frac{F_L{}^1}{L_1 F_{LL}{}^1} = \frac{F_L{}^1}{\bar{K}_1 F_{LL}{}^1} = \frac{F_L{}^1 F_K{}^1}{F^1 \cdot F_{KL}{}^1} \cdot \frac{F^1}{F_K{}^1 \bar{K}_1} = \frac{\sigma_1}{\alpha_1}.$$

We may therefore restate the above proposition: the supply of educated labour increases or decreases depending on whether the elasticity of substitution in m_1-industry is smaller or larger than the capital share in m_1-industry.

[10]This can be seen by rewriting eq. (18) as:

$$(d/dw_1)(N_1-L_1) = \{1-\eta_1+\eta_1(L_1\bar{N}/N_1 N_2)\}N_1 N_2/(\bar{w}_1\bar{N}).$$

In developing countries the elasticity of substitution in industrial sectors seems to be low, so that it is likely that the elasticity of demand for labour in m_1-sector is less than unity. Moreover, (22) is quite likely to be satisfied unless the unemployment rate in m_1-industry is extremely high. Therefore, we can conclude that the absolute unemployment in educated labour will most probably increase if the wage of educated labour increases.

(b) *Relative unemployment of educated labour*

Similarly, from (14) and (17), we can derive:

$$\frac{N_1}{L_1}\frac{\mathrm{d}}{\mathrm{d}\bar{w}_1}\left(\frac{L_1}{N_1}\right) = -\frac{N_2}{\bar{N}}\frac{1}{\bar{w}_1}\left\{\left(\frac{\bar{N}}{N_2}-1\right)\eta_1+1\right\} < 0. \tag{21}$$

Thus the relative unemployment of educated labour will always increase when the wage in m_1-industry increases.

(c) *Unemployment of uneducated labour*

Since the employment of uneducated labour depends on its unchanged wage, it will clearly not change. However, the *unemployment* of uneducated labour will increase or decrease, depending on whether the supply of uneducated labour increases or decreases. Thus if $\eta_1 < 1$, so that the resulting improvement in Ew_1 has led to increase in educated labour, the stock of uneducated labour (N_2) will have been reduced and hence also the unemployment of uneducated labour. Similarly, if $\eta_1 > 1$, the unemployment of uneducated labour will have increased.

(d) *National income*

Next, it is easy to see that:

$$\mathrm{d}Y/\mathrm{d}\bar{w}_1 = -L_1\eta_1 - k(1-\eta_1)(N_1N_2/\bar{N}\bar{w}_1). \tag{22}$$

National income will therefore change, when $\bar{w}_1$ rises, because of two effects: (i) the decline in employment of (educated) labour will diminish output of m_1 without any offset from increment in output in m_2 where the employment has not changed; and (ii) the cost of educating labour will change, depending on whether the supply of educated labour increases or decreases. Clearly, therefore, when $\eta_1 < 1$, the increase in the supply of educated labour will work to accentuate the reduction in income from the first effect: thus the result must be unambiguously to reduce national income, as is evident from (22). Moreover, even if we take the other case where $\eta_1 > 1$, provided that condition (19) or (20) is satisfied *and* $k < \bar{w}_1$, the *net* effect will be to reduce national income, again as is evident from (22). The only case when income will increase is where k is large, η_1 is extremely large and the initial unemployment rate of educated labour is large and violates eq. (19). The results in this case are summarized under the column (Effect I) in table 1.

Table 1
Effects of rise in wages.

Impact on:	Symbol	*Effect I* Our-Joneses-keeping-up-with-their-Joneses	*Effect II* Keeping-up-with-our-Joneses $\theta \equiv dw_2/dw_1$
Educated labour	$\dfrac{dN_1}{d\bar{w}_1}\left(=-\dfrac{dN_2}{d\bar{w}_1}\right)$	$(1-\eta_1)N_1N_2/(\bar{w}_1\bar{N})$	$-\theta(1-\eta_2)N_1N_2/(\bar{w}_2\bar{N})$
Unemployment of educated labour	$\dfrac{d}{d\bar{w}_1}(N_1-L_1)$	$(1-\eta_1)N_1N_2/(\bar{w}_1\bar{N})+\eta_1 L_1/\bar{w}_1$	$-\theta(1-\eta_2)N_1N_2/(\bar{w}_2\bar{N})$
Rate of employment of educated labour	$\dfrac{N_1}{L_1}\dfrac{d}{d\bar{w}_1}\left(\dfrac{L_1}{N_1}\right)$	$-\eta_1/\bar{w}_1-(1-\eta_1)N_2/(\bar{w}_1\bar{N})$	$\theta(1-\eta_2)N_2/(\bar{w}_1\bar{N})$
Unemployment of uneducated labour	$\dfrac{d}{d\bar{w}_1}(N_2-L_2)$	$-(1-\eta_1)N_1N_2/(\bar{w}_1\bar{N})$	$\theta\{(1-\eta_2)N_1N_2/\bar{w}_2\bar{N}+\eta_2 L\bar{w}_2/_2\}$
Rate of employment of uneducated labour	$\dfrac{N_2}{L_2}\dfrac{d}{d\bar{w}_1}\left(\dfrac{L_2}{N_2}\right)$	$(1-\eta_1)N_1/(\bar{w}_1\bar{N})$	$\theta\{-\eta_2/\bar{w}_2-(1-\eta_2)N_1/(\bar{w}_2\bar{N})\}$
National income	$\dfrac{dY}{d\bar{w}_1}$	$-\eta_1 L_1-k(1-\eta_1)N_1N_2/(\bar{w}_1\bar{N})$	$\theta\{-\eta_2 L_2+k(1-\eta_2)N_1N_2/(\bar{w}_2\bar{N})\}$

Case II. Keeping-up-with-our-Joneses

The next question we ask is what happens if the rise in $\bar{w}_1$ leads, in turn, to a sympathetic rise in $\bar{w}_2$ *via* the well-observed 'leap-frogging' process: this may be called the 'keeping-up-with-our-own-Joneses' phenomenon. We can indeed explore all the questions considered for Case I, for the case where *both* $\bar{w}_1$ and $\bar{w}_2$ rise.

The effect on employment in m_1-sector naturally remains the same as above; but there is now an additional negative effect on employment in m_2-sector, thanks to the induced rise in w_2. Instead of (14) we have

$$dL_2/d\bar{w}_1 = g_2'(\bar{w}_2)(d\bar{w}_2/d\bar{w}_1) < 0. \tag{23}$$

Thus, defining $d\bar{w}_2/d\bar{w}_1 \equiv \theta(\theta > 0)$ and $\eta_2 \equiv -(\bar{w}_2/L_2)(dL_2/d\bar{w}_2)$, we get the results tabulated in table 1.

In addition to the effect through the rise in w_1 (Effect I), the effect through the rise in w_2 (Effect II) is superimposed.

Note that, in contrast to Case I, the directions of the impacts are ambiguous because the induced rise in $\bar{w}_2$ can offset the effects of the primary increase in $\bar{w}_1$. Take, for example, the impact of the increase in $\bar{w}_1$ on the level of the educated labour force (N_1). For Effect I, the level of N_1 will rise if $\eta_1 < 1$; however, for Effect II, the induced rise in $\bar{w}_2$, implying $\theta > 0$, will work to .reduce N_1 if $\eta_2 < 1$, thus making the direction of the combined effect indeterminate. An interesting implication of the impact on national income in the last row of table 1 is that it is more difficult to exclude the possibility of increased income from the process of wage-increases. For example, take the extreme case where $\eta_1 = \eta_2 = 0$, and $d\bar{w}_1 = d\bar{w}_2$, i.e. $\theta = 1$. Then

$$dY/d\bar{w}_1 = k(\bar{w}_1 - \bar{w}_2)N_1N_2/(\bar{w}_1\bar{w}_2\bar{N}) > 0.$$

In this special case where the elasticities are zero, and where the factor intensities are consequently fixed, the simultaneous wage rise will increase national income because less people will get educated, thus reducing the cost of education, while employment in each sector is kept constant.

Case III. Emigration-of-our-Joneses

We can now turn to the issue of actual emigration of educated labour. We can set up the problem by assuming an exogenous emigration of educated labour, Z, which does not *in itself* lead to a simultaneous rise in the (actual) wage $\bar{w}_1$ for educated labour; only in Case IV will we consider the fully general case where the emigration causes rise in $\bar{w}_1$ as also an induced rise in $\bar{w}_2$ as per Case II.

Eq. (5) must then be rewritten as:

$$L_1 + U_1 + Z = N_1, \tag{24}$$

so that the total educated labour is now the sum of domestically employed and unemployed plus emigrated labour.[11]

There are alternative ways in which we can explore now the impact of such emigration on the system, but all of them must operate through the primary impact on expected wage in the educated-labour market. Let us take three possibilities.

(I): We may assume that the migration of a few educated members of the working force does not have any impact on the expected wage, as the migration is not wage-induced and does not lead to similar expectations. Then, in this singular case, *as long as* the migration of labour still leaves *some* unemployment of educated labour, the division of labour into the two types of labour is unaffected, so that the only effect is a reduction in the unemployment of educated labour. Clearly, moreover, production and national income are unchanged. However, since per-capita income and the relative employment rate of educated labour are increased, social welfare should be increased by the 'brain drain' for any reasonable social welfare function. If, therefore, the migration is welfare-improving for the migrants – an assumption that seems reasonable if they are pursuing self-interest – the emigration is a 'good' event, causing welfare improvement for both the migrants and those left behind.

(II): But this 'well-behaved' result will no longer carry through if we assume that the expected wage to educated labour will improve with the migration. This may happen in at least two plausible ways. *Either* the emigration may be treated as reducing the unemployment in the market for educated labour, so that the emigration is treated as raising the wage merely by increasing the number employed, without taking into consideration the incremental wage accruing to those employed abroad as distinct from those employed at home: this may be called the *incremental-employment-effect* variant of the model. *Alternatively*, we may assume that the fact that the emigrants earn a differentially higher wage also affects the expected wage: this may be called the *incremental-employment-and-differential-wage* variant. We examine the former variant first.

For the *incremental-employment* variant, the effect of the emigration is to change the equation for the expected wage in m_1 as

$$Ew_1 = \bar{w}_1(L_1 + Z)/N_1. \tag{25}$$

---

[11]We should note here the delicate problem of the timing of education and emigration. There would be little difficulty of interpretation, however, if we regard this analysis as the comparison of two stationary states with and without migration, or more precisely one with some migration and the other with marginal increase in migration.

Thus the division of total labour between the two groups (educated and un-educated) is determined now by:

$$\bar{w}_1(L_1+Z)/N_1 = \bar{w}_2 L_2/N_2. \tag{26}$$

Noting that the employment of labour in neither sector is affected by dZ, we can next show that

$$dN_1/dZ = N_1 N_2/\{(L_1+Z)\bar{N}\}. \tag{27}$$

We thus see, from (27), that the increase of educated labour supply will be less than the amount of migration of educated labour if $(L_1+Z)/N_1 > N_2/\bar{N}$ [which is a relation very similar to (19) earlier]. Thus, under the above inequality, the unemployment of educated labour increases, and the unemployment of un-educated labour decreases, due to the effect of an increase in N_1.[12]

The effect on *national income* is quite simply:

$$dY/dZ = -k(dN_1/dZ). \tag{28}$$

National income is seen, from (28), to diminish unambiguously because of the cost of educating the increment in educated labour.

But we may well ask what happens to *per-capita income*, as the total amount of labour in the system is diminished too. Now, clearly:

$$\frac{d}{dZ}\left(\frac{Y}{\bar{N}-Z}\right) = \frac{kN_2}{(\bar{N}-Z)^2}\left(-\frac{(\bar{N}-Z)}{\bar{N}}\frac{N_1}{L_1+Z}+\frac{Y}{kN_2}\right).$$

Hence, if $kN_2/Y < (L_1+Z)N_1$, for example, the average income will increase with the emigration. That is, if the ratio of the hypothetical educational cost of training all uneducated labour to national income is smaller than the employment rate of educated labour, the national income per labour will increase. Another way of looking at it is to see that $d(Y/(\bar{N}-Z))/dZ > 0$ if $k(dN_1/dZ) < Y/(\bar{N}-Z)$, i.e. the per-capita income would increase if the increase in the education cost is less than the per-capita income.

(III): We may finally explore the *incremental-employment-and-differential-wage* variant. We thus assume now that the labour force will indeed take into

---

[12]If the unemployment is defined as $U_1/N_1 = 1-(L_1+Z)/N_1$, we can show that

$$\frac{d}{dZ}\left(\frac{U_1}{N_1}\right) < 0, \text{ because: } \frac{d}{dZ}\left(\frac{L_1+Z}{N_1}\right) = \frac{1}{N_1}\left(1-\frac{(L_1+Z)}{N_1}\frac{N_1 N_2}{(L_1+Z)\bar{N}}\right)$$

$$= \frac{1}{N_1}\left(1-\frac{N_2}{\bar{N}}\right) > 0.$$

account the foreign wage level at which the emigrants get hired. If we then denote the foreign wage as $\bar{w}_f$, we can write the expected wage in m_1 as:

$$Ew_1 = (\bar{w}_1 L_1 + \bar{w}_f Z)/N_1. \tag{29}$$

In this case, we now can derive the following modified results:

$$dN_1/dZ = \bar{w}_f N_2/(\bar{w}_1 L_1 + \bar{w}_2 L_2 + w_f Z) = \bar{w}_f N_1 N_2/\{N(\bar{w}_1 L_1 + \bar{w}_f Z)\}, \tag{30}$$

$$dY/dZ = -k(dN_1/dZ) = -k\bar{w}_f N_1 N_2/\{N(\bar{w}_1 L_1 + \bar{w}_f Z)\}. \tag{31}$$

It is then easy to see that the change in the level of the educated labour force (N_1) in the new equilibrium will readily exceed the emigration if $\bar{w}_f$ is large enough relative to $\bar{w}_1$. Therefore in the case when the high wage rate in foreign countries is taken account of in assessing the expected wage rate, it is quite probable that unemployment in educated sector increases in both absolute and relative sense.

In addition, as is evident from (31), national income will go down; and it is easy to see that the possibility of decreasing per-capita income as well is more likely than before.[13] Therefore in the society whose welfare function depends on per-capita income and unemployment rates, national welfare will quite possibly go down unless the evaluation of reducing unemployment rate in the m_2-sector more than offsets the loss due to decreasing per-capita income and increasing unemployment in the m_1-sector.

Case IV. The general case of emigration and rise of wages

If the wage of educated labour is rigidly fixed because it reflects the salary levels of comparable groups in the more developed countries, it is quite conceivable that $\bar{w}_1$ itself is affected by the amount of migration of educated labour. The more migration there is, the more then could be the upward pull from the internationalization of this educated elite to domestic wage fixation. This rise in $\bar{w}_1$ may in turn trigger additional wage rise in $\bar{w}_2$, as analyzed in Case II.

Thus the effects of migration on employment, supply of educated labour and national income in this fully general case can now be decomposed as the sum of

---

[13]This is seen readily as follows. For a unit of emigration, population decreases by $1/(N-Z)$ per cent. On the other hand, national income decreases by $k\bar{w}_f N_1 N_2/\{N(\bar{w}_1 L_1 + \bar{w}_f Z) Y\}$. The fact that the latter may exceed the former can then be readily seen as follows. Let us take the special case of the impact of initiating emigration, that is, $Z = 0$. If the following, quite possible, relationship holds:

$$\bar{w}_f/\bar{w}_1 > (L_1/N_1)(Y/kN_2),$$

then the relative rate of decrease in national income is larger than that of decrease in population, thus leading to the reduction of per-capita income.

Table 2

Total effects of migration.

Impact on:	Symbol	Direct effects of migration	Indirect effects through:	
			Effect I — Rise in $\bar{w}_1$	Effect II — Rise in $\bar{w}_2$
Educated labour	$\dfrac{dN_1}{dZ}\left(=-\dfrac{dN_2}{dZ}\right)$	$\dfrac{\bar{w}_t}{\bar{w}_1}\dfrac{N_1 N_2}{\bar{N}L_1}$	$\dfrac{(1-\eta_1)N_1 N_2}{\bar{w}_1\bar{N}}\theta\dfrac{d\bar{w}_1}{dZ}$	$-\dfrac{(1-\eta_2)N_1 N_2}{\bar{w}_2\bar{N}}\theta\dfrac{d\bar{w}_1}{dZ}$
Employment of educated labour	$\dfrac{dL_1}{dZ}$	0	$-\eta_1\dfrac{L_1}{\bar{w}_1}\dfrac{d\bar{w}_1}{dZ}$	0
Unemployment of educated labour	$\dfrac{d}{dZ}(N_1-L_1)$	$\dfrac{\bar{w}_t}{\bar{w}_1}\dfrac{N_1 N_2}{\bar{N}L_1}$	$\dfrac{(1-\eta_1)N_1 N_2}{\bar{w}_1\bar{N}}+\eta_1\dfrac{L_1}{\bar{w}_1}\dfrac{d\bar{w}_1}{dZ}$	$-\dfrac{(1-\eta_2)N_1 N_2}{\bar{w}_2\bar{N}}\theta\dfrac{d\bar{w}_1}{dZ}$
Employment of uneducated labour	$\dfrac{dL_2}{dZ}$	0	0	$-\eta_2\dfrac{L_2}{\bar{w}_2}\dfrac{d\bar{w}_1}{dZ}$
Unemployment of uneducated labour	$\dfrac{d}{dZ}(N_2-L_2)$	$-\dfrac{\bar{w}_t}{\bar{w}_1}\dfrac{N_1 N_2}{\bar{N}L_1}$	$-\dfrac{(1-\eta_1)N_1 N_2}{\bar{w}_1\bar{N}}\dfrac{d\bar{w}_1}{dZ}$	$\left\{\dfrac{(1-\eta_2)N_1 N_2}{\bar{w}_2\bar{N}}+\eta_2\dfrac{L_2}{\bar{w}_2}\right\}\theta\dfrac{d\bar{w}_1}{dZ}$
National income	$\dfrac{dY}{dZ}$	$-k\dfrac{\bar{w}_t}{\bar{w}_1}\dfrac{N_1 N_2}{\bar{N}L_1}$	$-\left\{\eta_1 L_1+\dfrac{k(1-\eta_1)N_1 N_2}{\bar{w}_1\bar{N}}\right\}\dfrac{d\bar{w}_1}{dZ}$	$\left\{-\eta_2 L_2+\dfrac{k(1-\eta_2)N_1 N_2}{\bar{w}_2\bar{N}}\right\}\theta\dfrac{d\bar{w}_1}{dZ}$

(1) the *direct* effect of migration keeping wage levels constant and (2) the *indirect* effect of the resulting wage increases. The latter component is in turn decomposed into (1) the effect of the wage increase in the m_1-sector and (2) the effect of a wage increase in the m_2-sector that it induces. Thus taking the *incremental-employment-and-differential-wage* variant, and evaluating for simplicity the expression for the initial impact, namely, at the point where $Z = 0$, we may summarize the expressions for the total effect of emigration as in table 2.

The following observations, based on these results, are in order concerning the effects of emigration of educated labour in our model.

(1) Note that the *direct* effect of emigration on employment in either sector is nil. However, if the foreign wage level is taken into account in calculating the expected wage (Ew_1), this increases the supply of educated labour (N_1) and will reduce national income by the incremental educational cost. If the foreign wage level ($\bar{w}_f$) is high enough, we could also have increased unemployment of educated labour and reduced per-capita income.

(2) The induced wage-increase of educated labour, if any, will work to reduce the employment of educated labour. If the elasticity of demand for educated labour (η_1) is below unity, the supply of educated labour will increase, thus increasing unemployment of the educated, both absolutely and relatively; further, national income will also be likely to reduce.

(3) Finally, if we have the leap-frogging process, such that $\bar{w}_2$ also rises in response to the rise in $\bar{w}_1$, the effect thereof will be towards reducing the employment of uneducated labour. This effect would thus work to increase the expected wage (Ew_2) in this sector (if $\eta_2 < 1$) and thus to mitigate the increase in the supply of educated labour (when $\eta_1 < 1$): the net result could even be to reduce, in the new equilibrium, the supply of educated labour. The loss of national income would also be reduced insofar as the supply of educated labour is reduced; however, unless the effect of reducing the cost of education is large, it is unlikely that it will offset the loss in national income caused through the contraction of output of m_1 and m_2 resulting from the rise in $\bar{w}_1$ and $\bar{w}_2$ respectively.

Thus, in our model, even without invoking the presence of 'externalities' (leading to differences between the private and social marginal product of the emigrants), we see that the emigration of educated labour can easily lead to unfavourable effects on national income, per-capita income and on the unemployment (absolute and relative) of educated and uneducated labour through the effect of the migration on expected-wage formation in the market for educated labour, the upward pull on the (actual) wage of educated labour, and the leap-frogging upward pull on the (actual) wage of uneducated labour. And, as we proceed now to discuss in more detail in sect. 4, the internalization of the cost of education will not necessarily reduce the income–cost of the migration. Nor will the payment by the foreign country of the cost of education of the im-migrants eliminate the adverse effect of the migration.

4. Alternative assumptions

Before we proceed to an explicit welfare analysis of the effects of brain drain in sect. 5, we now sketch briefly the effects of varying some of the assumptions in the model of sects. 2 and 3.[14]

4.1. Internalizing the cost of education

The reader may well ask what happens if we let people pay for their own education, so that the educational cost is 'internalized'. In this case, instead of (10), we will have:

$$Ew_1 - k^* = Ew_2, \tag{10'}$$

where k^* is the amount of educational cost that is internalized ($k^* \leq k$).

Since employment depends on the *actual* wage, however, the employment effects in the model are unchanged whereas the allocation of the labour force between the two groups (educated and uneducated) will be directly affected. In consequence, we now have:

$$\mathrm{d}N_1/\mathrm{d}\bar{w}_1 = (1-\eta_1)N_2L_1/[\bar{w}_1L_1 + \bar{w}_2L_2 - k^*(N_1 - N_2)]. \tag{15'}$$

Since it is easy to show that the denominator is positive,[15] the behaviour of N_1 continues, as in the earlier case of free education, to depend on the elasticity of demand for labour.

The resulting impact on the other comparative-statics results established for the case of free education can be readily worked out by the reader. It may be noted, however, that, contrary to general intuition, the internalization of the educational cost does not necessarily reduce the undesirable impact effect of the brain drain in our model: the welfare impact of an increment in $\bar{w}_1$ under free education ($k^* = 0$) is given by (22) for Case I, and under internalized cost by:

$$\mathrm{d}Y/\mathrm{d}\bar{w}_1 = -L_1\eta_1 - k(1-\eta_2)N_2L_1/[\bar{w}_1L_1 + \bar{w}_2L_2 - k(N_1 - N_2)], \tag{22'}$$

and, in general, when a welfare cost is involved (as when $\eta_1 < 1$), the two costs cannot be uniquely ranked.

---

[14]Incidentally, none of our quantitative conclusions depend on the assumption of allowing only two sectors. In fact, even in the presence of many sectors, we still obtain:

$$(\bar{w}_1/N_1)(\mathrm{d}N_1/\mathrm{d}\bar{w}_1) = [(\bar{N} - N_1)/\bar{N}](1 - \eta_1)$$

and

$$(w_1/N_j)(\mathrm{d}N_j/\mathrm{d}\bar{w}_1) = -(N_1/\bar{N})(1 - \eta_1),$$

where

$$\bar{N} \equiv \sum_{j=1}^{n} N_j, \quad \text{for } n \geq 2. \qquad \text{(See the appendix.)}$$

[15]By (10'), we have: $\bar{w}_1L_1 + \bar{w}_2L_2 - k^*(N_1 - N_2) = \bar{w}_2(L_2/N_2)\bar{N} + k^*N_2$.

Similarly, for Case III, we may note again that the adverse effect of emigration on employment and income is not necessarily reduced if the cost of education is internalized as in (10'). Thus, for example, (27) is modified in the case of internalized educational cost ($k^* = k$) to:

$$dN_1/dZ = \bar{w}_f N_2 / \{\bar{w}_1 L_1 + \bar{w}_2 L_2 + \bar{w}_f Z - k(N_1 - N_2)\}, \tag{27'}$$

and it is clear that the new, additional term $-k(N_1 - N_2)$ could, in principle, work in either direction. Also, eq. (31) for impact on national income would modify to:

$$dY/dZ = -k\bar{w}_f N_2 / \{\bar{w}_1 L_1 + \bar{w}_2 L_2 + \bar{w}_f Z - k(N_1 - N_2)\}. \tag{31'}$$

And this means that the effect of internalizing the cost of education could well be to *increase*, rather than diminish, the cost in national income from the emigration in our model: this being yet another instance of second-best theory.

All this, of course, is not to deny that, for any *given* levels of $\bar{w}_1$, $\bar{w}_2$ and Z, the *progressive* internalization of the cost of education will be employment-and-income-*improving*. We can show that the increased internalization of the cost of education will, while leaving unchanged the employment in each sector, reduce the supply of educated labour (N_1) and hence its (total) cost (kN_1):

$$dN_1/dk^* = -N_1 N_2 / \{w_2(L_2/N_2)N + K^* N_2\} < 0. \tag{32}$$

Therefore, as long as unemployment in educated labour exists, increasing the education cost borne by labour itself will save the education cost by $-k\,dN_1$. Note further that, even if the cost paid by labour (i.e., k^*) approaches the 'true value' of k, the unemployment of educated labour may still exist.[16] In such a case, the imposition of higher cost ($k^* > k$) for education may turn out to be optimal in this second-best problem with wage rigidities![17]

4.2. Irreversibility of education

We may next address ourselves to the question of what happens in the 'short run' when the educated labour force cannot be reduced. The effect of this clearly is to accentuate – by eliminating the possibility of reducing the educated-labour supply, N_1, and thus saving on its cost, kN_1 – the loss possibilities in the model. There is thus no relief for the 'let-us-not-worry-about-brain-drain' economists from shifting to the short run!

---

[16]Suppose $\bar{w}_1$ and $\bar{w}_2$ are fixed higher than the equilibrium full employment wage rate indicated by (12). Then the phenomenon discussed in the text could readily occur.

[17]Note again that the saving in educational costs, which we have been discussing, applies only in the 'long run', for comparison of two stationary states in our model.

4.3. The case where the labour market in m_2-sector is competitive

Next, what happens if the 'uneducated-labour' sector is 'competitive', so that the sticky-wage assumption applies only to educated labour? In this case, instead of (10) we will now have:

$$(L_1/N_1)\cdot \bar{w}_1 = w_2, \tag{10''}$$

and

$$N_2 = L_2.$$

Further, since w_2 is no longer fixed, it will now be determined by:

$$w_2 = g(L_2), \qquad g' < 0.$$

Finally, we will have the total labour supply constraint as:

$$N_1 + N_2 = \bar{N}.$$

Solving these four equations, we would then get now:

$$dN_1/d\bar{w}_1 = L_1(1 - \eta_1)/(w_2 - N_1 g'), \tag{33}$$

and it is easy to see that (33) has the same qualitative property as (16) in our basic model in sects. 2 and 3.[18]

4.4. Cost of education paid by country of immigration

It is sometimes asserted that if the host country pays the cost of education, brain drain would cease to be harmful. In our model, this is easily allowed for, of course, by assuming that the country of emigration recovers (kdZ) worth of transfer income from the country of immigration. It is again easy to see, as already noted in sect. 3, that all this does is to modify the last row of table 2 by the addition of the term (kdZ) and that the net effect on income, and the effects on unemployment, can still be adverse.

5. Welfare effects of brain drain and integration of markets for professionals

We may now draw together the main analytical results of sect. 3 to derive welfare conclusions. To do this, however, we need to specify the social welfare function explicitly.

It is our contention that the traditional trade-theoretic analysis of the Grubel–Scott–Johnson variety yields conclusions more favourable to the phenomenon of brain drain and integration of markets for professionals, not merely because

---

[18]It may be interesting to note, however, that the change in $\bar{w}_1$ will now endogenously change w_2. And, in the case where $\eta_1 < 1$, $dw_2/d\bar{w}_1 = -g'(dN_1/dw_1) > 0$, since $dN_2 = -dN_1$, so that a rise in $\bar{w}_1$ leads to a rise in w_2. This is, of course, not the same as the 'leap-frogging' in our Case II, a phenomenon that is ruled out by the 'competitive' assumption for section m_2.

the model used for analysis is simplistic. It is also because the social welfare function used for analysis is really limited in confining itself to arguments which rule out many relevant variables.

In fact, we think that it could make much sense to define a social welfare function which has at least the following arguments:

(1) *National income*: The sense of security, bargaining power in trade and economic negotiations, the need for defense, and a number of political and economic variables of importance could depend, not just on per-capita income, but on national income as an aggregate.

(2) *Level of emigration*: Those who have lived in the less developed countries know that the emigration of skilled manpower in certain occupations, such as scientific research in particular, creates a sense of inadequacy, which may stiffle creative endeavour in domestic environment.

(3) *Level of educated/professional manpower*: The technological ability of the population may matter much to the independence and creativity of the population; hence a fall in the (short-run and long-run) level of the educated labour force due to the phenomena being discussed by us could cause an adverse effect on social welfare.

(4) *Unemployment*: Unemployment, whether absolute or its rate, is also of importance to social welfare. More directly, it affects political stability and social cohesion, if nothing else, and is of immediate concern to the developing countries. In this regard, the unemployment among the educated may be even more explosive than among the uneducated, as is evident from the fact that the leadership of the revolutionary movements in Calcutta, for example, has derived from the unemployed, educated students.

(5) *Income distribution*: In the absence of fiscal ability to redistribute incomes, the direct income distributional impact of the phenomena under discussion will also often be the final effect. And it should clearly enter the social welfare function. In the context of our model, we could thus include in the arguments of the social welfare function, for example, the relative share of wage income in total national income: $(\bar{w}_1 L_1 + \bar{w}_2 L_2)/Y$.[19]

Thus, a realistic social welfare function should probably read as follows:

$$U = U\{Y, Y/(N-Z), Z, N_1, L_1/N_1, L_2/N_2, (\bar{w}_1 L_1 + \bar{w}_2 L_2)/Y\}. \quad (34)$$

We forego a taxonomic exercise, exploring the outcomes on welfare and possible tradeoffs among alternative arguments in this welfare function, for different parametric combinations of the elasticities η_1, η_2 and other parameters such as θ and k appearing in the expressions in table 2. The reader can readily

---

[19]Alternatively, we could use as an argument the weighted sum of per-capita utilities: e.g. where $U(w_i)$ is the per-capita utility in labour class i with $U' > 0$ and $U'' < 0$, the social welfare function could have the argument: $\Sigma\, U_i(w_i)L_i$.

do this for himself; and we have already discussed briefly in sect. 3 some of the possible outcomes with regard to national income, per capita income, supply of educated labour and the level and rates of unemployment in both classes of labour.[20]

Emigration tax

Rather, we may sketch here the answer to the question as to what would happen if the country of emigration were to impose a tax on emigration. To analyse this policy, assume that a recurring poll tax (that would be paid annually by the migrant) is levied on each emigrant.[21] Restricting our analysis to the effect on the income of those left behind (for reasons of space), we should expect a twofold effect: (i) the direct effect of the tax on revenue, which may then be treated as income redistributed to those left behind; and (ii) the indirect effect on unemployment levels, income, etc., which would operate through the effects on expected and actual wage levels.

(i) If we take T as the (recurring) poll tax paid by the emigrants (Z), the tax revenue will be TZ. As T is changed, this revenue will change by:

$$Z(1 - \eta_f^T), \tag{35}$$

where η_f^T is the elasticity of emigration with respect to the poll tax (i.e., $-T/Z \cdot dZ/dT$). Clearly, this *revenue effect* will be positive or negative, depending on the elasticity of emigration with respect to taxation.

(ii) As for the 'indirect' effect, this can be indicated *via* the simplified Case III assumption of the *incremental-employment-and-differential-wage* variant: i.e., by assuming that (only) the expected wage is modified downwards by the tax. Thus, we must rewrite (29) as follows:

$$Ew_1 = [\bar{w}_1 L_1 + (\bar{w}_f - T)Z]/N_1. \tag{29'}$$

---

[20]The only effects, which we have not worked out in sect. 3, relate to income distribution. This, however, can be readily worked out. Thus, for the general Case IV, we can write:

$$\frac{Y}{\bar{w}_1 L_1 + \bar{w}_2 L_2} \frac{d\{(\bar{w}_1 L_1 + \bar{w}_2 L_2)/Y\}}{dZ} = \frac{1}{\bar{w}_1 L_1 + \bar{w}_2 L_2} \left(L_1(1 - \eta_1) + L_2(1 - \eta_2)\theta \frac{d\bar{w}_1}{dZ} \right)$$

$$+ \frac{k\bar{w}_f N_1 N_2}{Y\bar{N}\bar{w}_1 L_1} + \frac{1}{Y} \left\{ \eta_1 L_1 + \frac{k(1 - \eta_1)N_1 N_2}{\bar{w}_1 \bar{N}} \right\} \frac{d\bar{w}_1}{dZ}$$

$$+ \frac{\theta}{Y} \left[\eta_2 L_2 - \frac{k(1 - \eta_1)N_1 N_2}{\bar{w}_1 \bar{N}} \right] \frac{d\bar{w}_1}{dZ}.$$

[21]The effect of the usual poll tax would be of a once-for-all nature. However, in order to conform to our analysis in terms of flows, it would be useful to conceive of a recurring poll tax along the lines of the Bhagwati–Dellalfar (1973) proposal (which relates to an income tax related to the income of the emigrant, a difference of unimportance if we assume a unique $\bar{w}_f$).

Substituting (29') into (10) and differentiating with respect to T, we obtain

$$\frac{\mathrm{d}N_1}{\mathrm{d}T} = -\frac{N_2 Z - N_2(\bar{w}_\mathrm{f} - T)(\mathrm{d}Z/\mathrm{d}T)}{\bar{w}_1 L_1 + \bar{w}_2 L_2 + (\bar{w}_\mathrm{f} - T)Z},$$

which can be written as

$$\frac{\mathrm{d}N_1}{\mathrm{d}T} = -\frac{N_2 Z(1 + \varepsilon_\mathrm{f})}{\bar{w}_1 L_1 + \bar{w}_2 L_2 + (\bar{w}_\mathrm{f} - T)Z} < 0, \tag{36}$$

where ε_f is the elasticity of emigration with respect to effective foreign wages $(w_\mathrm{f} - T)$.[22] Thus an increase in T will always decrease the supply of educated labour in the long run, and this effect is strengthened if the emigrant is responsive to the recurring poll tax. As before, the income change is then:

$$\frac{\mathrm{d}Y}{\mathrm{d}T} = -k \frac{\mathrm{d}N_1}{\mathrm{d}T} = \frac{k N_2 Z(1 + \varepsilon_\mathrm{f})}{\bar{w}_1 L_1 + \bar{w}_2 L_2 + (\bar{w}_\mathrm{f} - T)Z} > 0. \tag{37}$$

Thus, the net impact on the income of those left behind will be given by the sum of these two, direct and indirect, effects (36) and (37):

$$Z(1 - \eta_\mathrm{f}^T) + \frac{k N_2 Z(1 + \varepsilon_\mathrm{f})}{\bar{w}_1 L_1 + \bar{w}_2 L_2 + (\bar{w}_\mathrm{f} - T)Z}. \tag{38}$$

A sufficient (but not necessary) condition for the per capita income of those left behind to improve thanks to the emigration tax, therefore, would be that $\eta_\mathrm{f}^T < 1$.[23]

The reader could readily extend the analysis of the poll tax on emigration to examine the impact on the other arguments in the social welfare function; space considerations prevent us from undertaking this task ourselves.

6. Concluding remarks

It is clear, of course, that our results are in contrast with those of the traditional, fully neoclassical model because of the assumptions of 'rigid' wages and resulting unemployment. Under the conventional assumptions of flexible wages and absence of unemployment, the results of emigration are both simpler and easily stated: (i) for internalized cost of education ($k^* = k$), the emigration will reduce national income but, in increasing the average product of labour, will also raise per-capita income under the 'normal' assumption of diminishing

---

[22] Note that $(\bar{w}_\mathrm{f} - T/T)\eta_\mathrm{f}^T = \varepsilon_\mathrm{f}$.

[23] Note that the 'indirect' effect works only in the long run. Furthermore, we have ruled out the more general case where the emigration may affect the *actual* wage as well. If this were allowed, then the emigration tax might well reduce the *actual* wage in the m_1, and possibly m_2, sectors and hence moderate the income loss on that account.

marginal productivity of labour;[24] and (ii) for free education ($k^* = 0$), the other polar case, and no compensation for educational costs by the country of immigration, it is possible (though not inevitable) that the average product of labour, and hence per-capita income, falls as a result of emigration of educated labour.

Our results are both more complex and less comforting than these. They are also more realistic. They should suffice to raise doubts about the complacency concerning the brain drain phenomenon resulting from the analysis in the existing literature.[25]

Appendix: Many sectors

Some readers may consider the assumption of only two sectors somewhat unnatural because the brain drain phenomenon in the real world occurs in rather limited and specific industrial or professional classifications of jobs. But none of our qualitative conclusions depend, given the simple structure of the system, on the assumption of only two sectors. This is readily seen by indicating how the analysis can be extended to n ($n > 2$) sectors.

Let w_i, N_i, L_i, k_i^* and λ_i represent the fixed wage, labour supply, employment, the privately-incurred educational cost and the ratio of employment to the

---

[24]The *apparent* contradiction between this statement and the earlier Grubel–Scott argument that emigration leaves unchanged the welfare of those left behind is easily resolved. The Grubel–Scott result is based on the fact that the emigre was earning w (the wage) and thus everyone other than him was getting ($Y - w$), whereas his departure reduces Y itself by w: hence the result for those left behind is the sum of the reduction in income due to emigration ($dY/dL = -w$) and the increment in available income as the emigrant loses his claim on income defined by his wage ($+w$), which means no-impact. On the other hand, $d(Y/L)/dL = (1/L)[w - (Y/L)] > 0$ as the wage, which equals the marginal product, will be below the average product: hence emigration will *raise* per-capita income, i.e. *improve* the welfare of those left behind. This contradiction is easily resolved, however, once it is seen that the Grubel–Scott argument assumes that the income accruing to the emigre prior to emigration is w, the wage, whereas the per-capita-income argument in effect assumes it to be $Y/L(> w)$: the former assumption thus yields no impact whereas the latter yields improvement, for those left behind. In this paper, we have examined the impact on *both* income and per-capita income; results under the Grubel–Scott assumption can however be readily derived by taking the impact on income and adding to it the consumption of the emigrant, defined as his wage rate ($\bar{w}_1$), on the assumption that the emigrant was employed prior to emigration, or possibly a lower sum if we assume that he was unemployed and was subsisting on someone else's income.

[25]We have not modelled here, as an anonymous referee has pointed out, some of the real-world complexities which arise on a different dimension from those (e.g. sticky wages and unemployment) considered in this paper: for example, the effects of the quality and content of higher education and professional training in the advanced countries on the phenomenon of brain drain. Thus, it is well known that the brain drain occurs in part *via* the settling down abroad of LDC students who have been receiving higher education abroad. To some extent, this phenomenon results from the fact that the type of training received abroad makes these students somewhat ill-suited at times to any useful work at home and, if they do return, makes them conduits of disequilibrating disturbances in the domestic economy. We would need however a different model to study these kinds of relationships and effects: to admit everything into one model would be to make it too complex.

labour supply (L_i/N_i) in the ith sector, respectively. Then, we can write the system determining labour employment and supply as:

$$L_i = \lambda_i N_i, \qquad \text{for } i = 1, 2, \ldots, n;$$

$$\lambda_i w_i - k_i^* = \lambda, \qquad \text{for } i = 1, 2, \ldots, n;$$

$$\sum_i N_i = \bar{N};$$

where λ is an additional variable to keep the symmetry of the system. Then the division of labour into many categories in response to the initial wage rise in the first sector is given by the following equations:[26]

$$
n\left\{\begin{bmatrix}
\overbrace{\begin{matrix} \lambda_1 & & 0 \\ 0 & & \\ & & \lambda_n \end{matrix}}^{n} & \overbrace{\begin{matrix} N_1 & & 0 \\ & 0 & \\ & & N_n \end{matrix}}^{n} & \begin{matrix} 0 \\ \vdots \\ 0 \end{matrix} \\
\begin{matrix} w_1 & & \\ & 0 & \\ & 0 & \\ 0 & & w_n \\ 1 & 1 & 0 \end{matrix} & \begin{matrix} & & \\ & & \\ & & \\ & & -1 \\ 0 & & 0 \end{matrix} & \begin{matrix} -1 \\ \vdots \\ \vdots \\ \vdots \\ 0 \end{matrix}
\end{bmatrix}\right.
\begin{bmatrix} dN_1 \\ \vdots \\ dN_n \\ d\lambda_1 \\ \vdots \\ d\lambda_n \\ d\lambda \end{bmatrix} = \begin{bmatrix} 0 \\ \vdots \\ 0 \\ -\lambda_1 \\ 0 \\ \vdots \\ 0 \\ 0 \end{bmatrix} dw_1. \tag{39}
$$

From this, we can derive the relevant comparative static relations. For example, (denoting $\mu_i \equiv dL_i/d\bar{w}_i$),

$$
\frac{dN_1}{d\bar{w}_1} = \frac{\mu_1\left(\bar{w}_1 - \dfrac{N_1}{\mu_1}\lambda_1\right)\displaystyle\prod_{i=2}^{n}(\lambda_i\bar{w}_i)\left(\displaystyle\sum_{i=2}^{n}\dfrac{N_i}{\lambda_i\bar{w}_i}\right)}{-\displaystyle\prod_{i=1}^{n}(\lambda_i\bar{w}_i)\left(\displaystyle\sum_{i=1}^{n}\dfrac{N_i}{\lambda_i\bar{w}_i}\right)}
$$

$$
= \frac{(L_1 - \lambda_1\mu_1 w_1)\left(\displaystyle\sum_{i=2}^{n}\dfrac{N_i}{\lambda_i w_i}\right)}{\lambda_1\bar{w}_1\left(\displaystyle\sum_{i=1}^{n}\dfrac{N_i}{\lambda_i\bar{w}_i}\right)} = \frac{N_1}{\bar{w}_1}(1-\eta_1)\frac{\left(\displaystyle\sum_{i=2}^{n}\dfrac{N_i}{\lambda_i\bar{w}_i}\right)}{\left(\displaystyle\sum_{i=1}^{n}\dfrac{N_i}{\lambda_i\bar{w}_i}\right)},
$$

[26]If $dw_j/dw_1 \neq 0$, then the column on the right-hand side will obviously read

$$
\begin{bmatrix}
dL_1/dw_1 \\
dL_2/dw_2 \cdot dw_2/dw_1 \\
\vdots \\
dL_n/dw_n \cdot dw_n/dw_1 \\
1 \\
dw_2/dw_1 \\
\vdots \\
dw_n/dw_1 \\
0
\end{bmatrix}.
$$

which simplifies, if k_i^* is zero (i.e., all educational cost is state-financed as in sections 1 and 2), to

$$\frac{dN_1}{d\bar{w}_1} = \frac{(\bar{N}-N_1)N_1}{N\bar{w}_1}(1-\eta_1),$$

or, in the elasticity form,

$$\frac{\bar{w}_1}{N_1}\cdot\frac{dN_1}{d\bar{w}_1} = \frac{\bar{N}-N_1}{\bar{N}}(1-\eta_1). \tag{40}$$

The result in (40) is, of course, identical to that in (17) for the two-sector case, once we realize that $(\bar{N}-N_1) = N_2$ when there are only two sectors: and this is indeed as it should be, since the effect on labour supply in section m_1 naturally depends, as before, on the impact of the rise in $\bar{w}_1$ on the expected wage in m_1, and this impact is independent of the number of sectors from (to) which the labour flows in (out).

Other results of some interest can also be spelled out. Thus,

$$\frac{d\lambda}{d\bar{w}_1} = \frac{\displaystyle\prod_{i=1}^{n}(\lambda_i\bar{w}_i)\left(\frac{\mu_1}{\lambda_1}-\frac{N_1}{\bar{w}_1}\right)}{-\displaystyle\prod_{i=1}^{n}(\lambda_i\bar{w}_i)\cdot\left(\sum_{i=1}^{n}\frac{N_i}{\lambda_i\bar{w}_i}\right)} = \frac{\left(\dfrac{N_1}{\bar{w}_1}-\dfrac{\mu_1}{\lambda_1}\right)}{\displaystyle\sum_{i=1}^{n}\frac{N_i}{\lambda_i\bar{w}_i}}$$

From this, it follows that

$$\frac{dN_j}{d\bar{w}_1} = \frac{d}{d\bar{w}_1}\left(\frac{L_j w_j}{\lambda}\right) = -\frac{\bar{w}_j L_j}{\lambda^2}\frac{\left(\dfrac{N_1}{\bar{w}_1}-\dfrac{\mu_1}{\lambda_1}\right)}{\displaystyle\sum_{i=1}^{n}\left(\dfrac{N_i}{\lambda_i\bar{w}_i}\right)},$$

which again simplifies, if k^* is zero, to

$$= -\frac{N_j N_1}{N\bar{w}_1}(1-\eta_1),$$

or, in elasticity terms,

$$\frac{\bar{w}_1}{N_j}\frac{dN_j}{d\bar{w}_1} = -\frac{N_1}{\bar{N}}(1-\eta_1). \tag{41}$$

Again, therefore, nothing of substance has really changed with the introduction of $n > 2$ sectors.

References

Bhagwati, J., 1972, Overqualification, education and welfare: A theoretical analysis, mimeo. (M.I.T., Cambridge, Mass.).

Bhagwati, J. and W. Dellalfar, 1973, The brain drain and income taxation: A proposal, World Development 1, no. 1.

Dumont, R., 1969, False start in Africa (Praeger, New York).

Grubel, H. and A. Scott, 1966, The international flow of human capital, American Economic Review, May.

Johnson, H.G., 1967, Some economic aspects of brain drain, Pakistan Development Review 3.

Johnson, H.G., 1972, Labour mobility and the brain drain, in: G. Ranis, ed., The gap between rich and poor nations, Proceedings of the 1970 IEA Conference at Bled, Yugoslavia (Macmillan, New York).

Jolly, R. and D. Seers, 1972, The brain drain and the development process, in: G. Ranis, ed., The gap between rich and poor nations, Proceedings of the 1970 IEA Conference at Bled, Yugoslavia (Macmillan, New York).

Jones, R., 1967, International capital movements and the theory of tariffs and trade, Quarterly Journal of Economics, Feb.

Kemp, M., 1966, Gains from international trade and investment, American Economic Review, Sept.

Sunkel, O., 1971, Latin American underdevelopment in the year 2000, in: J. Bhagwati, ed., Economics and world order: From the 1970's to the 1990's (Macmillan, New York).

CHAPTER 7

DOMESTIC DISTORTIONS, IMPERFECT INFORMATION AND THE BRAIN DRAIN*

Koichi HAMADA

Tokyo University, Tokyo, Japan

Jagdish BHAGWATI

M.I.T., Cambridge, MA 02139, U.S.A.

An earlier paper by Bhagwati and Hamada (1974) presented a theoretical analysis of the brain drain in the context of wage rigidity and unemployment. This paper extends the analysis by modifying the model to incorporate the phenomena of overqualification, internal diffusion of labor from urban to rural areas and imperfect information about the quality of labor. The welfare effect of the brain drain in the presence of these phenomena is analyzed.

1. Introduction

The traditional, theoretic analysis of the welfare effects of the brain drain, initiated by Grubel and Scott (1966) and developed by Berry and Soligo (1969), Johnson (1967) and Kenen (1971) among others, has been based on the assumption of perfect competition, including perfect information and full wage flexibility.

A departure from these assumptions was made in an earlier paper of ours – Bhagwati–Hamada (1974) – by permitting the presence of wage rigidity and unemployment. In the context of this model, the basic Grubel–Scott contention that (infinitesimal) emigration would not affect the welfare (conventionally defined) of those left behind was clearly not valid and a welfare loss could well be imposed on the nonmigrant group. In addition, the Bhagwati–Hamada analysis introduced the possibility of the 'emulation effect' whereby the migration could raise the wage levels of the class of migrants by virtue (or rather, vice) of the implied, consequent integration internationally of this class of labor: such a 'distortion-augmenting' emulation effect could accentuate then the welfare loss imposed on those left behind.

*Thanks are due to the National Science Foundation for partial financial support of the research underlying this paper. The paper was prepared for the Bellagio Conference on The Brain Drain and Income Taxation, 15–19 February 1975. It is best read as a companion piece to the Bhagwati–Hamada (1974) paper, whose analysis it extends.

In this paper, we utilize the same basic model, but extend it in three directions which bring it closer to alternative facets of reality in the LDCs.

First, we consider the phenomenon of 'overqualification', i.e., where jobs have been upgraded and the educated are working in jobs that, objectively speaking, do not 'require' the education.[1] The extension of our analysis to the situation where overqualification is present shows that, in the absence of the emulation effect, brain drain from the class of skills characterized by over-qualification can help, rather than hurt, those left behind.

Secondly, we extend our analysis to the phenomenon that has sometimes been described as the 'internal brain drain' but is more aptly called the 'internal diffusion' of professionals. Thus it is well known that doctors tend to congregate in the urban areas and rural areas tend not to attract doctors. However, there is also a process of internal diffusion going on, with doctors, as the congestion in the cities increases and cuts into average incomes, increasingly moving to the countryside partially or fully.[2] This internal diffusion process is likely to be in-hibited as the possibility of external brain drain from the LDC (cities) is opened up. We will model this phenomenon and demonstrate formally the welfare-reducing impact of migration in such a context.

Thirdly, we introduce an element of imperfect information into the analysis of the brain drain. Arrow (1973) and Spence (1974) have developed a 'screening' theory of education.[3] In its simplified form, the theory states that education is important not so much because it increases the productivity of workers as because it plays the role of filtering efficient labor from labor in general. We utilize this notion and consider the case where the brain drain serves to identify, and thus screen, the more efficient from the less efficient. It turns out that if the domestic labor market cannot discriminate as effectively as the international market for professionals, then the economy tends to lose, essentially because emigrants are picked up from the category of the more efficient.

This analysis of market distortions and imperfect information will demon-strate that the welfare effects of the brain drain, and accordingly the nature of the policy intervention necessary, differ significantly depending on the nature of distortion or imperfection that the LDC economy is facing; in fact, within each LDC, different classes of professional emigrants (e.g., doctors, engineers, etc.) may correspond to different models. While this analysis takes the domestic distortions as given exogenously, we raise in our concluding section the signifi-

[1] For a statement of this basic model, see Bhagwati (1972) and the systematic, general-equilibrium analysis of education in this framework in Bhagwati and Srinivasan (1975). The latter paper rechristens the overqualification model as the 'job ladder' model.

[2] The partial movement frequently occurs through opening up clinics or offices in the neigh-boring towns, with the city doctor spending part of the month there.

[3] A concise statement of four alternative theories of education (the Schultz-Becker 'human capital' theory, the radical 'socialization' theory, the Arrow–Spence screening theory and the Bhagwati–Srinivasan 'job ladder' and fairness-in-hiring theory) is provided in Bhagwati and Srinivasan (1975).

cant possibility that migration itself could influence these distortions, accentuating or moderating them.

2. The basic framework and the welfare criterion

We initially state the basic Bhagwati–Hamada (1974) model, with its special features such as the presence of wage rigidity and unemployment.[4] Consider an economy satisfying the small country assumption such that the relative commodity price-ratio between two tradeable commodities is fixed internationally. Let there be two kinds of labor: uneducated and educated. Uneducated labor can be transformed into educated labor at constant costs. Corresponding to the two goods, there are two sectors in the economy: the traditional sector that normally employs uneducated labor, and the developed sector that normally employs educated labor.[5] Wages are assumed to be exogenously given by the international emulation process and possibly by the 'leap-frogging' process discussed in the Bhagwati–Hamada (1974) paper.[6] It is also assumed that unemployment exists in both of the sectors.

The production function of the traditional sector is given by

$$F_0(L_0) \qquad [\text{with } F_0' > 0, F_0'' < 0],$$

where L_0 is the employment of labor in the traditional sector. The production function of the developed sector is given by

$$F_e(L_e) \qquad [\text{with } F_e' > 0, F_e'' < 0],$$

where L_e is the employment of labor in the developed sector. We shall assume that $F_e'(L_e) > F_0'(L_0)$ for an identical amount of labor $L_e = L_0$.

The total labor force N is divided into two categories: uneducated labor N_0 and educated labor N_e, in such a way that

$$N_0 + N_e = N. \tag{1}$$

Under the 'normal' assumption that excludes the over-qualification of labor, $(N_0 - L_0)$ and $(N_e - L_e)$ indicate, respectively, the unemployment in the traditional sector and that in the developed sector, in the absence of brain drain. Let us suppose now that brain drain occurs only from educated labor. In the presence

---

[4]Only the barest details are provided here; the reader can consult the original Bhagwati–Hamada paper for a more leisurely statement of the model.

[5]The use of the qualifying adverb 'normally' is pertinent to our analysis in the next section.

[6]Bhagwati and Hamada (1974). Most of the results below remain valid so long as the wage of educated labor is determined exogenously. The wage of uneducated labor may be determined by marginal or average productivity.

of brain drain equal to Z, $(N_e - Z - L_e)$ then indicates the unemployment in the developed sector.

Wages are fixed as $\bar{w}_0$ and $\bar{w}_e$, and labor is employed to the point of equality with its marginal product, i.e.,

$$F_0'(L_0) = \bar{w}_0,\tag{2}$$

$$F_e'(L_e) = \bar{w}_e,\tag{3}$$

assuming the international price ratio to be normalized to unity. When $\bar{w}_0$ and $\bar{w}_e$ are given, L_0 and L_e will clearly be determined from eqs. (2) and (3).

People decide whether to educate themselves by comparing the expected wage rate for uneducated labor and that for educated labor. That is, in the absence of any constraints on the expansion of education facilities, and if educational cost is provided by the government, the equality

$$\frac{L_0}{N_0}\bar{w}_0 = \frac{L_e}{N_e - Z}\bar{w}_e\tag{4}$$

will determine the amount of educated people. In certain institutional settings discussed below, there will then be permanent excess demand to get educated: in this case, the number of educated people will have to be limited exogenously by governmental fiat.

Let us now turn to the welfare criterion to judge the welfare effect of the brain drain in this economy. We will take the average income of those left behind as the welfare criterion. The resulting formula for welfare change is then readily derived as follows.

The GNP, Y, of the country of emigration can be expressed as

$$Y = F_0(L_0) + F_e(L_e) - kN_e = G(N-Z),\tag{5}$$

where k is the constant cost of education, noting again that the international commodity price-ratio is normalized at unity, and GNP is a function of the available labor force. As soon as we shift, however, to the GNP accruing to those left behind, i.e., Y_d, their income *after* migration becomes

$$Y_d = G(N-Z),$$

and, before migration, it is

$$Y_d = G(N) - vZ,$$

where v is the average income that emigrants are receiving prior to the emigration. It follows immediately then, denoting per capita income of those left behind by y_d, that

$$\frac{dy_d}{dZ} = \frac{1}{N-Z}\left\{v + \frac{dG}{dZ}\right\},\tag{6}$$

and, evaluated at $Z = 0$, we have[7]

$$\frac{dy_d}{dZ}\bigg|_{Z=0} = \frac{1}{N}\left\{v + \frac{dG}{dZ}\right\}.\tag{6'}$$

Therefore we must look at the value of $[v + (dG/dZ)]$ in order to assess the welfare effect of the brain drain. All that this formula says is that if the marginal loss due to the reduction of labor is larger than the payment that was received by the marginal emigrant, then those left behind will lose; otherwise they will gain.

We shall not repeat the comparative static analysis of the system of eqs. (1)–(4) that was developed in our earlier paper.[8] It is necessary to note, however, that if the brain drain results (only) in a rise in the wage of educated labor (thanks to the emulation effect), then the effect on GNP will now become

$$\frac{dG}{dZ} = -k\frac{L_0\bar{w}_0}{L_e\bar{w}_e + L_0\bar{w}_0} - \left\{\eta_e L_e + \frac{k(1-\eta_e)N_eN_0}{\bar{w}_e N}\right\}\frac{d\bar{w}_e}{dZ},$$

where η_e is the wage elasticity of the demand for educated labor.[9] Having noted this, we now turn to the extension of the analysis to the phenomena of overqualification, internal diffusion and imperfect information.

3. The overqualification phenomenon

The labor market may function, in response to excess supply, not by cutting the wage as in the usual neoclassical analysis, but rather in the context of a 'job ladder' model, with sticky wages, where the excess supply then spills over from the 'best' to the 'next-best' job. Thus educated labor, on finding no more employment in the educated-labor category of jobs, can be postulated as moving down

[7]This welfare criterion, as Berry and Soligo (1969) noted, is of course different from that which would result if we were comparing, before and after migration, the per capita incomes (as distinct from the per capita incomes of those left behind). For the former case, the criterion would modify to

$$\frac{dY/(N-Z)}{dZ} = \frac{1}{N-Z}\left(\frac{dG}{dZ} + \frac{Y}{N-Z}\right).$$

[8]Bhagwati and Hamada (1974, p. 33, table 2). Note merely that there is a minor difference between eq. (25) there and eq. (4) in this paper concerning the treatment of Z. But this is for the purpose of simpler exposition and does not affect the substance of our analysis.

[9]See Bhagwati and Hamada (1974, p. 33); the difference in the first term in the RHS comes from our new eq. (4), which replaces the earlier eq. (25).

the job ladder and taking the jobs which do not require the education. Bhagwati and Srinivasan (1975) further argue that, in this case, a 'fairness-in-hiring' principle may also be sociologically invoked whereby employers, faced by excess demand for the no-educational-requirement jobs from both educated and uneducated labor, prefer to hire the educated because they think it is 'fair' to reward those who have put in extra effort, as it were. Thus, although both kinds of labor are equally productive in the no-education-requirement jobs, the educated applicants are hired in preference over the uneducated ones.

In the analysis that follows, we then modify our basic model to incorporate this job ladder phenomenon with overqualification (or upgrading of jobs in terms of hiring practice) characterizing the hiring in the sector where educated and uneducated labor have identical productivity. Thus, assume now (as before) that the educated labor may be in excess supply in its market, in the *developed* sector; however, when the expected wage in this sector is equalized with the wage in the *traditional* sector, the educated labor spills over into employment in the traditional sector. And, given the number of jobs in the traditional sector at the exogenously-fixed wage therein, we assume that the incidence of unemployment then falls on uneducated labor. Formally, the model then modifies as follows.

Let L_{ee}, L_{e0} and L_{00} denote respectively the educated labor *employed* in the developed sector, educated labor *employed* in the traditional sector, and uneducated labor *employed* in the traditional sector. Then, by definition, we have

$$L_{ee} = L_e,$$

and

$$L_{e0} + L_{00} = L_0,$$

for labor employment in the two sectors. Now, the assumption that everyone will get educated as long as the expected wage to educated labor exceeds that to uneducated labor (since the educational cost is borne by the government and its indirect tax cost not taken into account by atomistic labor), implies that in this modified model there would be an endless incentive to get educated: the expected return to educated labor would always exceed the expected return to uneducated labor. Hence, we must impose an *exogenous* constraint on how many get educated: i.e., $N_e = \bar{N}_e$ by policy decision.

It is immediately obvious then that, thanks to the constancy of $\bar{w}_e$ (and hence of L_e) and $\bar{N}_e$, the effect of the migration is to create an *identical* reduction in the unemployment of uneducated labor:

$$dL_{e0} = -dZ \quad \text{and} \quad dL_{00} = dZ,$$

so that we have

$$dG/dZ = 0. \tag{7}$$

The loss of educated labor is fully offset, at the margin, by unemployed uneducated labor getting employed in their place in the traditional sector, without loss of productivity (as postulated), so that both L_e and L_0, the employment levels in both sectors, and hence the output levels in both sectors are unaffected.[10] It follows therefore that

$$\left\{ v + \frac{\mathrm{d}G}{\mathrm{d}Z} \right\} > 0, \tag{8}$$

unless we introduce other complexities into the analysis.

Such a complication, for example, is when the wage $\bar{w}_e$ in the developed sector rises due to the emulation effect, in the presence of migration, and the accompanying move towards integration of the labor market for the migrant class of labor. The number being educated will remain constant (at $\bar{N}_e$) again by assumption; however, GNP will now be reduced by the induced fall in L_e (as $\bar{w}_e$ rises) in the developed sector:

$$\frac{\mathrm{d}G}{\mathrm{d}Z} = -L_e \eta_e \frac{\mathrm{d}\bar{w}_e}{\mathrm{d}Z}. \tag{9}$$

Yet another complication could be introduced if we were to postulate that the governmental educational policy is aimed at providing a constant educational labor force *net* of emigration. In this event, the emigration of educated labor would lead to an identical, offsetting expansion of the educated labor force, so that we must modify eq. (7) as follows:

$$\mathrm{d}G/\mathrm{d}Z = -k, \tag{10}$$

because, while output in the two sectors remains constant, the cost of education increases as more get educated to offset the emigrated educated labor. In this case, again, the welfare criterion $[v + (\mathrm{d}G/\mathrm{d}Z)]$ will become ambiguous unless we postulate (as seems reasonable) that $v > k$.

In conclusion, it would appear that, under the conditions postulated, the over-qualification phenomenon tends to mitigate the welfare loss, if any, of the brain drain. In fact, if the brain drain is not accompanied by an induced rise in the wage-level in the developed sector or by an offsetting expansion of domestic educational facilities, the brain drain will increase (rather than decrease) the per capita income of those left behind in the country of emigration.

---

[10]This argument presupposes, of course, that the magnitude of emigration does not exceed the spillover of educated labor into the traditional sector in the pre-emigration situation.

4. The internal diffusion process

The diffusion of the emigrant class of professionals (e.g., doctors) from the urban to the rural areas, from areas of 'low' to areas of 'high' social marginal product, is a phenomenon that again can be modelled as an extension of our basic framework, leading to the conclusion that the brain drain in the presence of such a diffusion process could harm those left behind.

Suppose now that there are two subsectors in the developed sector, and hence two opportunities for the educated labor therein: urban and rural employment. In the urban occupation, wage $\bar{w}_{eu}$ is paid and is higher than the wage $\bar{w}_{er}$ in the rural occupation; the latter, in turn, is still higher than the wage in the traditional sector $\bar{w}_0$. Educated labor thus chooses between rural and urban occupations such that

$$\bar{w}_{er} = \frac{L_{eu}}{N_e - L_{er} - Z} \bar{w}_{eu}, \tag{11}$$

where L_{er} and L_{eu} indicate employment in rural and in urban occupations, respectively. Again, since $\bar{w}_{er} > \bar{w}_0$ and educational costs to individuals are nil, we must contend with excess demand for getting educated. Hence we will assume, as in the preceding section, that the size of the educated labor force N_e is exogenously fixed by the government, consistent with eq. (11).

We further postulate that, in the rural occupation, there is a shortage of educated labor. Formally, the social marginal product in the rural occupation is higher than the wage,

$$F'_{er}(L_{er}) > \bar{w}_{er},$$

while, in the urban occupation, the wage is equal to its marginal product:

$$F'_{eu}(L_{eu}) = \bar{w}_{eu}.$$

If emigration occurs now, without any additional emulation-induced effects on the wages in both occupations, then the constancy of N_e implies that

$$dL_{er} = -dZ,$$

and

$$\frac{dG}{dZ} = -F'_{er}(L_{er}).$$

Essentially, this means that the educated labor employed in the *rural* occupation decreases by the amount of the emigration: the emigration raises the expected wage in the urban occupation, pulling the educated labor out of the rural occupation. The welfare criterion then is

$$v + \frac{dG}{dZ} = v - F'_{er} \tag{12}$$

which has a positive sign if F'_{er} is smaller than v, but can be negative if the social marginal product in the rural occupation is substantially higher than the wage in the rural occupation and further exceeds the wage that was paid to the emigrant.

Introduce now the emulation effect, so that the brain drain induces a rise in $\bar{w}_{eu}$. In this case, clearly the production loss is aggravated. For, in the urban occupation, L_{eu} is reduced by $(\eta_{eu}L_{eu}/\bar{w}_{eu})d\bar{w}_{eu}$, where η_{eu} is the elasticity of demand for labor in the urban occupation. On the other hand, the labor shortage is increased in the rural occupation because L_{er} is reduced as follows:

$$dL_{er} = -dZ - \frac{L_{eu}(1-\eta_{eu})}{\bar{w}_{er}} d\bar{w}_{eu}.$$

Therefore, the shortage of educated labor in the rural occupation increases by more than the size of emigration if $\eta_{eu} < 1$. The total production loss is then

$$\frac{dG}{dZ} = -F'_{er}\left\{1 + \frac{L_{eu}(1-\eta_{eu})}{\bar{w}_{er}}\frac{d\bar{w}_{eu}}{dZ}\right\} - L_{eu}\eta_{eu}\frac{d\bar{w}_{eu}}{dZ}. \tag{13}$$

Thus, in spite of the fact that the employment of the urban occupation reduces, the shortage in the rural occupation increases.

If our analysis accurately reflects the reality in some LDCs, then we must consider to be somewhat optimistic the following view of Myint (1968) on the effects of the brain drain of doctors from large cities in the LDCs:

> The pressure of excess demand from the advanced countries is most likely to affect the doctors in private practice in the bigger towns in the underdeveloped countries. In so far as this is true, the welfare effects are less catastrophic than if the doctors were being taken away from the rural areas and the development effect is probably negligible.

The analysis of this section shows that the effect of the brain drain could be significantly harmful even though the direct source of the emigrants was the urban population.

5. Brain drain and the screening process

Consider now the question as to who is likely to emigrate. Several 'high-level' emigrants are individuals who possess some special skills such as language ability, study and experience in the developed countries. They are therefore likely to be specialists who have some special ability 'needed' in the recipient country.[11] Suppose now that these kinds of characteristics or ability are also productive at home. In this case, we have the possibility that the brain drain functions as a screening device of more efficient from less efficient labor.

If these individuals receive their full marginal productivity at home, there is no problem. Or if the fact that a person has a foreign offer for job and emigration results in his getting a correspondingly higher wage, there is no problem either. But does the employer know who possesses differentially higher ability? Or, if he knows this, does he or can he offer higher wages to such people? In other words, if a category of educated labor contains both 'emigrable' and 'non-emigrable' labor, and if the former is more efficient, does the price mechanism duly take account of the difference?[12] This section therefore deals with the possible imperfection of information in the market of educated labor and the consequences it has for the welfare effects of the brain drain.

The basic Arrow (1973)–Spence (1974) framework for analyzing education as a screening (or, as Arrow calls it, filtering) device eliminates any productivity effects of, say, the human-capital variety. In our framework, however, we admit the productivity effect, but at the same time allow for the possibility that the (domestic) market cannot discriminate between the highly-gifted (and consequently 'emigrable') labor and the commonly-educated (and consequently 'non-emigrable') labor.

Now let us return to our basic model. Assume again that educated labor works only in the developed sector, but that educated labor consists of two categories: 'commonly-educated' labor L_c and 'highly-gifted' labor L_h. L_h is λ times more productive than L_c, the difference being of the labor-augmenting type. However, let us assume that employers cannot discriminate between L_c and L_h, so that all the educated labor receives the *average* marginal productivity. Therefore,

$$\bar{w}_e = \{(1-p)+p\lambda\}F'_e(L_e), \qquad \lambda > 1, \tag{3'}$$

where p is the ratio of the highly-gifted labor to all the educated labor: $p = L_h/L_e = L_h/(L_c+L_h)$. In other words, p may be regarded as the probability of educated labor turning out to be highly gifted.

Then, in the system of the basic model (1)–(4), with the only modification that (3) is replaced by (3'), we obtain the same qualitative properties for given values of $\bar{w}_0$ and $\bar{w}_e$ as the basic model. The rise in $\bar{w}_e$ also creates the same qualitative impact as in the basic model.

---

[11]The labor certification process which is necessary for 'normal' professional immigration in many countries would tend to produce this outcome, of course.

[12]In Japan, for example, all college graduates in a company receive almost the same salary until several years after the graduation. If somebody is offered a higher-paid position in a foreign country, it does not follow that the company pays him a higher wage.

Suppose now that the individuals who emigrate are picked up only from the highly-gifted category. Then, with a given number of educated labor, the *marginal* loss to the economy is

$$\lambda F'_e(L_e),$$

while the emigrant before emigration was receiving the weighted *average*,

$$v = \bar{w}_e = \{(1-p)+\lambda p\}F'_e(L_e).$$

Therefore the direct loss to those who remain behind is given from our welfare criterion as follows:

$$v + \frac{dG}{dZ} = -\lambda F'_e(L_e) + \bar{w}_e$$

$$= (1-\lambda)(1-p)F'_e(L_e) < 0, \tag{14}$$

assuming that the number of the educated labor is held constant.

Naturally eq. (14) indicates only the direct impact. When the marginal outflow of highly-gifted labor occurs, however, the vacancy will be filled with new labor with the expected value of productivity equalling $\bar{w}_e$. Moreover, from (1) and (4), the number of educated labor will then increase by

$$dN_e = \frac{L_0 \bar{w}_0}{L_0 \bar{w}_0 + L_e \bar{w}_e} dZ,$$

thus imposing on the economy the education cost $k dN_e$. Therefore, the *total* effect (ruling out other effects such as emulation-induced wage increases) is given by

$$v + \frac{dG}{dZ} = -\lambda F'_e(L_e) + 2\bar{w}_e - k \frac{L_0 \bar{w}_0}{L_0 \bar{w}_0 + L_e \bar{w}_e}$$

$$= \{1 - (\lambda-1)(1-2p)\}F'_e - k \frac{L_0 \bar{w}_0}{L_0 \bar{w}_0 + L_e \bar{w}_e}. \tag{15}$$

Eq. (15) has no definite sign but it is easy to see that it can quite easily be negative.

It is worth noting that the direct-impact effect in eq. (14) is valid even if we work with a model with flexible wages in both the educated and the uneducated labor markets. Moreover, in an economy equipped with competitive labor market and the amount of education optimally given by the government, eq. (14) will indicate the *total* effect of emigration in such an economy. For, if N_e is determined optimally,

$$\frac{dG}{dZ} = \frac{\partial G}{\partial Z}\bigg|_{N_e:\text{const}} + \frac{\partial G}{\partial N_e}\frac{dN_e}{dZ}$$

$$= \frac{\partial G}{\partial Z}\bigg|_{N_e:\text{const}} = (1-\lambda)(1-p)F_e' < 0,$$

by the envelope relationship.

So far we have worked with the assumption that the emigrating labor is necessarily from the highly-gifted category. Suppose now instead that the probability of an emigrant being highly-gifted is q. Then the expected value of the direct impact on the economy is

$$v + \frac{dG}{dZ} = \bar{w}_e - \{(1-q)+\lambda q\}F_e'$$

$$= (q-p)(1-\lambda)F_e', \qquad (16)$$

which is negative as long as $q > p$. As long as the screening power of brain drain has *some* informational value, i.e., $q > p$, the impact effect is clearly negative.

We have also assumed thus far that the ratio or the probability of highly-gifted labor is independent of the brain drain. Suppose, however, that the probability of an individual turning out to be highly-gifted is related positively to some trait such as the high school grade. Then, the probability of turning out highly-gifted for the *marginal* student who comes into the educational system because of the emigration will be lower than the *average* probability for the educated. In this case, p is a decreasing function of Z, and this factor gives rise to yet further welfare-reducing effects.

In conclusion, we may note the possible dynamic externality aspects involved in the emigration of the highly-gifted. It is possible that such emigration affects, *via* adverse impact on domestic availability of the highly-gifted (who are not inspired and taught into full maturity of their talent in the absence of the senior highly-gifted people), the welfare of those left behind by affecting the ratio p adversely. Thus, suppose that it takes one period to educate the younger generation for skilled labor. Suppose also that $p(t)$ depends on the density of the preceding generation $p(t-1)$ such that

$$p(t) = \alpha + \beta p(t-1) \qquad [\alpha > 0, 0 < \beta < 1].$$

Then it is easy to show that if brain drain is occurring every period, affecting

$p(t)$ by δ, the stationary value of p will be reduced by $\beta\delta/(1-\beta)$.[13] Even a once-and-for-all emigration of highly-gifted labor will have a decaying but enduring effect on the future path of $p(t)$.

6. Brain drain and institutional change

It should be clear by now that the welfare effects of the brain drain differ significantly depending on the institutional setting from which labor is emigrating. If the phenomenon of overqualification exists, then the brain drain may work to improve the welfare, provided that we exclude the emulation effect on the wage level of the emigrant class of labor. On the other hand, if the domestic market for the labor is characterized by the internal diffusion process, the brain drain will harm those remaining behind, regardless of whether or not the emulation effect leads to a rise in the wage level. Finally, if emigrants are chosen from the highly-gifted category and are not so identified in the domestic market, then the brain drain could cause a welfare loss even with flexible wage rates.

The institutional setting concerning wage levels and changes therein and informational structure differs from country to country. Even within a country, it must surely differ from occupation to occupation. Risking oversimplification, we might argue that overqualification is likely to occur most with social scientists and (for certain countries, chiefly India) with engineers; the internal diffusion process is most serious for doctors and nurses, and imperfect information is pertinent to scholars and researchers. Therefore, depending on which LDC is being discussed, and which occupation is the object of attention, the analysis of the welfare effects of the brain drain is likely to vary; and a generalized analysis could well be misleading. Our analysis should be taken as an attempt to underline the importance of setting out the nature of institutional rigidities or imperfect information in the labor prior to analyzing the welfare effects of such emigration.

Note finally that our analysis in this paper has proceeded almost exclusively on the assumption that the institutional distortions in the domestic economy of the LDC of emigration are exogenous to the emigration process. The only exception made was for the Bhagwati–Hamada emulation effect: emigration from a class of skilled labor would raise the (sticky) wage of that labor, thus accentuating the sticky-wage distortion in the labor market.

But we can, and indeed must, ask the question whether the emigration process can be expected to influence, and if so in what direction, each of the market imperfections that we have analyzed in this paper. The analysis of the emulation effect in Bhagwati–Hamada (1974), and in the present paper, demonstrates the significance of modelling this kind of linkage into one's theoretical framework. But this can also be seen from at least two other areas of inter-

---

[13]Even without considering the above-mentioned mechanism of reducing p, p will be immediately reduced by the emigration of highly-gifted because it takes time to replenish highly-gifted labor in the situation considered here.

national economic analysis. Thus, in tariff theory, it is well known that while a domestic monopoly is distortionary, it does not compromise the case for free trade since the introduction of free trade itself can be regarded as destroying the monopoly: the free trade policy is distortion-destroying and hence continues to be optimal. To take the other example, the welfare effect of foreign investment by MNCs (multinational corporations) may be considered in light of its effects on an 'imperfect' domestic entrepreneurship: it may inhibit and stunt its growth or it may encourage it to be competitive and efficient.[14]

In the present context, we must eventually ask questions such as the following, distinguishing in each case between the 'malign impact' and the 'benign impact' hypotheses:

(1) Will the brain drain accentuate a domestic distortion such as a sticky wage (that exceeds the shadow wage as in Bhagwati–Hamada or falls below it as with monopsonistic pricing of a skill such as medicine under a nationalized health service) or will it promote increased flexibility in wage-setting in the country of emigration (as implied by Johnson (1972))?

(2) Will the brain drain, in the presence of unemployment, reduce the possible subsidy to education or will it lead to greater demands for increasing it?

(3) Will the screening function exercised in the brain drain process induce the domestic labor market to do better screening in the future or will it demoralize it into indiscriminate escalation of the entire wage level regardless of differential productivity?

These are all yet additional instances of the unsettled debate among development economists whether international integration into the world economy leads to development in the LDCs or to their domestic disintegration.[15] The issues raised here are not purely economic; they necessarily encompass sociological, political, ethnic and historical facets. Complex as they therefore are, and almost intractable to conventional economic analysis, they are equally necessary to address and resolve if the analysis of the brain drain is to be complete.

---

[14]For a discussion of these possibilities of 'malign impact' and 'benign impact' models in analyzing MNCs, see Bhagwati (1975).
[15]This phrasing is from Sunkel; see, for example, his long essay (1973) on import substitution.

References

Arrow, K.J., 1973, Higher education as a filter, Journal of Public Economics 2, no. 3.
Berry, R. and R. Soligo, 1969, Some welfare aspects of international migration, Journal of Political Economy, September–October.
Bhagwati, J., 1972, Overqualification, education and welfare: A theoretical analysis, mimeo (M.I.T., Cambridge, MA).

Bhagwati, J., 1975, What we need to know, contributed at the Princeton Conference on International Trade and Finance, March 1973, forthcoming in: Peter Kenen, ed., Volume of papers and proceedings (Cambridge University Press, Cambridge).

Bhagwati, J. and K. Hamada, 1974, The brain drain, international integration of markets for professionals and unemployment: A theoretical analysis, Journal of Developmental Economics 1, no. 1.

Bhagwati, J. and T.N. Srinivasan, 1975, Education in a job-ladder model and the fairness-in-hiring rule, mimeo (M.I.T., Cambridge, MA).

Grubel, H. and A. Scott, 1966, The international flow of human capital, American Economic Review, May.

Johnson, H.G., 1967, Some economic aspects of brain drain, Pakistan Development Review 3.

Johnson, H.G., 1972, Labor mobility and the brain drain, in: G. Ranis, ed., The gap between rich and poor nations (Macmillan, London).

Kenen, P.B., 1971, Migration, the terms of trade and economic welfare in the source country, in: J. Bhagwati et al., eds., Trade, balance of payments and growth (North-Holland, Amsterdam).

Myint, H., 1968, The underdeveloped countries: A less alarmist view, in: W. Adams, ed., The brain drain (Macmillan, New York).

Spence, A.M., 1974, Market signalling: Informational transfer in hiring and related screening processes (Harvard University Press, Cambridge, MA).

Sunkel, O., 1972, Latin American underdevelopment in the year 2000, in: J. Bhagwati, ed., Economics and world order (Macmillan, New York).

CHAPTER 8

CONSEQUENCES OF A TAX ON THE BRAIN DRAIN FOR UNEMPLOYMENT AND INCOME INEQUALITY IN LESS DEVELOPED COUNTRIES*

Rachel McCULLOCH and Janet L. YELLEN

Harvard University, Cambridge, MA 02138, U.S.A.

Welfare implications of an income tax paid by emigrant skilled workers are analyzed in a model which assumes international capital mobility and allows for unemployed labor in the modern sector of a developing country. The tax discourages overinvestment in education and also contributes to the welfare of those remaining through the direct revenue effect. However, expected earnings of unskilled workers decline as a result of the tax, while those of non-migrant skilled workers rise. The tax may thus exacerbate domestic income inequality. In addition, modern sector employment, output, and capital stock may fall.

1. Introduction

Neoclassical analysis of the brain drain leads to the laissez-faire conclusion that emigration of skilled workers in response to economic incentives increases world income without reducing the welfare of those left behind.[1] This conclusion is undermined by the existence of distortions or externalities which are troublesome for any free market policy. For example, in a model which relaxes the neoclassical full employment assumption, Bhagwati and Hamada (1974) have shown that when wages are set exogenously and education is available to all who wish it, brain drain may well be deleterious even if each factor is paid its marginal product. Bhagwati (1972) has proposed a surtax to be paid by emigrant skilled workers to their country of origin, and Bhagwati and Dellalfar (1973) have estimated the revenue from such a tax. The rationale for this proposal rests in part on the direct revenue effect – a kind of foreign aid tied to emigration flows – and in part on desirable indirect effects on the economies of the LDCs, including those spelled out in the Bhagwati–Hamada analysis.

Our earlier work,[2] while it embodies all the neoclassical assumptions questioned by Bhagwati and Hamada, also provides some support for the migration tax

---

*The underlying research for this paper was supported by National Science Foundation Grant No. SOC74-19459. The authors are indebted to Jagdish Bhagwati for many useful comments and suggestions.

[1]See especially Grubel and Scott (1966) and Johnson (1967). The marginal analysis underlying these conclusions has been criticized by Berry and Soligo (1969).

[2]McCulloch and Yellen (1974).

proposal. There, we assume that flexible wages maintain full employment of both skilled and unskilled labor, and skilled workers are free to migrate whenever net returns to doing so are positive. A tax on migration is shown to lower the domestic skilled wage by the amount of the tax, reduce the fraction of the population acquiring education, decrease the percentage migrating, and increase the wages of unskilled workers. Where each individual pays the average cost of education (despite assumed differences in 'native ability' which show up as differences in the cost of education), net earnings of skilled and unskilled workers are equal, and both groups thus gain as a result of the tax on migration. This outcome reflects the inefficiency of the initial equilibrium. Where each individual pays the average cost of education, there will be overinvestment in education and an associated loss in national welfare unless entry is restricted. The migration tax is a second-best policy which lowers private returns to education by pulling down the skilled wage rate. This reduces overinvestment in education and thus produces a welfare gain for labor.

In this paper we modify our previous neoclassical approach to allow for un-employed skilled and unskilled labor in the 'modern' sector of a developing economy. Wage determination in the modern sector embodies the Bhagwati–Hamada suggestion of administratively determined wage rates which for skilled workers emulate the compensation of foreign workers, and for unskilled workers emulate the compensation of domestic skilled workers. However, we make these sticky wage rates themselves endogenous variables in the system, with demands for high wages moderated by the level of unemployment. We also incorporate possibilities of factor complementarity and substitution through use of a three-factor production process. The stock of capital in the modern sector is endo-genous, allowing for longer-run impact of emigration policy on new investment. In the traditional sector, unskilled labor is the only variable factor, and flexible wages ensure full employment.

Our analysis has mixed implications for the emigration tax proposal. As suggested by Bhagwati–Dellalfar and Bhagwati–Hamada, the tax is likely to raise the income of those left behind, both through reduction in the number of workers acquiring education and through the revenue effect of the tax. However, total labor earnings (gross of educational expenditures) will, under plausible assumptions, fall. And other effects on the LDC economy are also worrisome. The wage rate of domestic skilled workers rises, along with the skilled employ-ment rate, while the wage rates of unskilled workers in both the modern and the traditional sector fall. Thus, domestic income inequality, measured either by the skilled–unskilled wage differential or by the gap between expected earnings of skilled and unskilled workers, is exacerbated. A further disturbing consequence is that the migration tax causes 'demodernization' – the size of the modern sector labor force declines and output may also fall, while in the traditional sector, employment and output increase. If, as often argued, labor in the traditional sector receives more than its marginal product, demodernization reinforces the

existing misallocation of labor between sectors and national welfare is correspondingly reduced.

On the basis of these findings, we conclude that the migration tax is a mixed
blessing. It must be paired with internal redistribution or other palliatives if
increased domestic income inequality is to be avoided.

2. The model

We consider two sectors: a modern sector employing L_1 skilled workers, L_2
unskilled workers, and K units of internationally mobile capital; and a traditional
sector employing L_T unskilled workers along with fixed supplies of land and
capital. Output in the modern sector is given by

$$X = F(L_1, L_2, K), \tag{1}$$

where F is a linear homogeneous production function satisfying the usual neoclassical conditions. Traditional sector output is given by

$$T = G(L_T), \qquad G' > 0, G'' < 0. \tag{2}$$

The diminishing marginal product of labor reflects our assumption of fixed land
and capital in the traditional sector. Both goods are traded at fixed international
prices and measured in units such that $p_T/p_X = 1$.[3]

Following the formulation of Bhagwati and Hamada (1974), the skilled wage
rate is fixed by 'international emulation' and associated union or government
action. However, in view of the threat to social stability posed by high unemployment rates, the strength of the emulation effect also depends on the percentage
e_1 of available skilled workers actually finding employment. Thus

$$w_1 = A^1(w_1^f, e_1), \qquad A_1^1 > 0, A_2^1 > 0, \tag{3}$$

where w_1 is the wage set for domestic skilled labor and w_1^f is the corresponding
wage rate abroad. Similarly, fixing of the modern sector unskilled wage rate w_2
represents a tradeoff between emulation of the wages of skilled workers (the
'leap-frogging' process) and social instability produced by high unemployment
rates. Thus,

$$w_2 = A^2(w_1, e_2), \qquad A_1^2 > 0, A_2^2 > 0, \tag{4}$$

where e_2 is the percentage of unskilled workers actually finding employment.

---

[3]If the traditional sector produces a nontraded good, shifts of resources between the two
sectors will change relative prices and thus have important distributional implications in
addition to those discussed in this paper.

The functions A^1 and A^2 are homogeneous of degree 1 in the first argument, i.e., a rise in the wage rate of the group emulated evokes a proportional change in the set wage w_1 or w_2. The traditional sector wage is assumed to be flexible, adjusting to maintain full employment in that sector.

The third factor used in the modern sector, capital, is assumed to be internationally mobile with a required rate of return r. This required return depends on considerations such as the rate of return elsewhere, taxation, risk differentials, and the cost of information about investment opportunities. The assumption of mobile capital, which is important to much of our analysis, is based on the observation that foreign multinational firms typically provide the bulk of the capital used in the 'modern' sector of many developing countries. In contrast, other writers frequently assume that the capital stock changes over time only through domestic saving. The usual argument that international capital markets are imperfect can be interpreted in our model as a large differential between the necessary rate of return r and similar rates in the developed world.[4] As noted earlier, the stock of capital available to the traditional sector is assumed fixed, presumably the result of past saving by the local population.

The total (fixed) labor force $\bar{N}$ is divided between skilled and unskilled workers,

$$\bar{N} = N_1 + N_2. \tag{5}$$

Unskilled workers may be employed in the modern sector, unemployed, or employed in the traditional sector, so

$$N_2 = L_2 + U_2 + L_\mathrm{T}, \tag{6}$$

where U_2 is the number of unemployed unskilled workers. Similarly, skilled workers may be employed in the modern sector, unemployed, or working abroad, and

$$N_1 = L_1 + U_1 + Z, \tag{7}$$

where U_1 is the number of unemployed skilled workers and Z is the number of emigrant skilled workers.[5] The modern sector employment rates e_1 and e_2, used in the wage setting equations (3) and (4), and the corresponding unemployment rates are then given by

$$e_1 = L_1/(N_1 - Z) = 1 - U_1/(N_1 - Z) = 1 - u_1, \tag{8}$$

$$e_2 = L_2/(N_2 - L_\mathrm{T}) = 1 - U_2/(N_2 - L_\mathrm{T}) = 1 - u_2. \tag{9}$$

---

[4]The assumption of a fixed rate r is most appropriate in the case of a small LDC which maintains an open-door policy toward foreign investment. Our analysis could be generalized by assuming that the country faces an upward-sloping supply of capital schedule.

[5]It is assumed here that only skilled workers have the opportunity to emigrate.

Like Bhagwati and Hamada, we assume that individuals are risk-neutral and acquire education whenever the expected net return is positive. Similarly, unskilled workers choose between modern and traditional sector employment on the basis of expected earnings. These two assumptions can be expressed as

$$w_T = w_2 L_2 / (N_2 - L_T) = w_1 L_1 / N_1 + (w_1^f - M) Z / N_1 - k^*,$$

where w_T is the wage rate in the traditional sector, M is the private cost of migration and k^* is the private cost of education.[6]

The expected earnings of a skilled worker are an average of the modern sector skilled wage, weighted by the probability that a skilled worker will find employment there, and the wage paid to emigrant skilled workers (net of migration cost), weighted by the probability of emigrating. The expected net income of a skilled worker is equal to expected earnings less the private cost of education. We take skilled workers as a group to be homogeneous, so that each individual has the same probability of finding modern sector employment or of migrating, in each case equal to the average for the group as a whole.[7] Using eqs. (8) and (9), the expected income conditions can be rewritten as[8]

$$w_2 e_2 = w_T, \tag{10}$$

$$w_2 e_2 = w_1 e_1 (N_1 - Z) / N_1 + (w_1^f - M) Z / N_1 - k^*. \tag{11}$$

As a result of profit maximization by modern sector firms, marginal products

---

[6]In equilibrium, education and emigration are undertaken prior to the working life of the individual. M and k^* should be interpreted as *amortized* costs, i.e., annual payments equivalent to the total lump-sum cost of emigration and education. The endogeneity of the supply of skilled labor is crucial to the results of the model.

[7]Similarly, we take the probability of a given skilled worker finding modern sector employment in a particular period to be the average for the entire modern sector skilled labor force, and independent of his previous employment history. Hence, a currently unemployed skilled worker has the same expected future income as an employed skilled worker. We assume that the expected *gross* earnings of a nonmigrant skilled worker, $w_1 e_1$, exceed $w_2 e_2$, so that no educated individuals choose to seek unskilled employment. However, see Bhagwati (1972) and Bhagwati and Srinivasan (1975) for an alternate treatment.

[8]It is also illuminating to express the expected income condition in the form

$$w_2 e_2 - w_1 e_1 + k^* = ((w_1^f - M) - w_1 e_1) Z / N.$$

The left-hand side is the differential between the expected wage of an unskilled worker and the expected net earnings of a nonmigrant skilled worker; the right-hand side is the differential between the net earnings of an emigrant and a nonmigrant skilled worker, weighted by the probability of being able to emigrate. For the expected net returns to unskilled and skilled workers (including migrants) to be equal, the expected net earnings of nonmigrant skilled workers must fall short of those of unskilled workers by an amount which compensates for the contribution of emigrants' net income to expected skilled earnings. Since $w_2 e_2 - w_1 e_1 + k^* > 0$ and $w_2 e_2 - w_1 e_1 < 0$ by assumption (see footnote 7), k^* must exceed the difference between gross expected earnings of domestic skilled and unskilled workers, i.e. $k^* > w_1 e_1 - w_2 e_2$.

are equated to factor prices:

$$F_1(L_1, L_2, K) = w_1,$$ (12)

$$F_2(L_1, L_2, K) = w_2,$$ (13)

$$F_3(L_1, L_2, K) = r.$$ (14)

Linear homogeneity of F implies that only two of these three equations are independent.

From (10), the *actual* wage in the traditional sector is equal to the *expected* unskilled wage in the modern sector. Traditional sector employment is then determined by

$$G'(L_T) = e_2 w_2,$$ (15a)

if labor is paid its marginal product in the traditional sector, or by

$$G/L_T = e_2 w_2,$$ (15b)

if labor receives its average product.[9] Total labor supply to the modern sector is given by

$$\bar{N} - L_T - Z = (N_1 - Z) + (N_2 - L_T).$$

The model thus consists of fourteen independent equations in fourteen unknowns: X, T, L_1, L_2, K, w_1, w_2, e_1, e_2, N_1, N_2, U_1, U_2, and L_T. The values of these variables depend on the parameters w_1^f, $\bar{N}$, Z, M, k^*, and r. In the following section we derive by substitution a simplified three-equation version of this system, which is then used to investigate the effects of changes in the parameters on the key variables.

3. Determination of equilibrium wage rates and skilled labor supply

From the model presented in section 2, we can derive by substitution three relationships which together determine w_1, w_2, and N_1. For any given value of N_1, the first relationship indicates combinations of w_1 and w_2 (and implied employment rates) which are consistent with the wage determination equations

---

[9]It is often asserted that workers in traditional agriculture receive wages in excess of their marginal product as a result of joint ownership of land by family or community groups. See Fei and Ranis (1964).

and availability of education at a given private cost. The second determines values of w_1 and w_2 which are consistent with profit maximization by firms when capital is mobile. The third relationship indicates combinations of w_1, w_2, and N_1 such that expected unskilled earnings in the modern and traditional sectors are equated.

To derive the first relationship, we begin with the wage determination equations, (3) and (4), linking wages and employment rates. These may alternatively be expressed as

$$e_1 = B^1(w_1, w_1^f), \qquad B_1^1 > 0,\ B_2^1 < 0, \tag{3'}$$

$$e_2 = B^2(w_1, w_2), \qquad B_1^2 < 0,\ B_2^2 > 0. \tag{4'}$$

Eq. (11) can now be rewritten as

$$w_2 B^2(w_1, w_2) = w_1 B^1(w_1, w_1^f)(N_1 - Z)/N_1 + (w_1^f - M)Z/N_1 - k^*. \tag{16}$$

This equation combines the effects of emulation and induced employment rates in wage setting with access to education at a fixed price k^*.

A second relationship between w_1 and w_2 is imposed by profit-maximizing behavior on the part of firms in the modern sector, who face an exogenously determined required rate of return on capital. The linear homogeneity of F allows us to express the production function in the intensive form,

$$X/K = (1/K)F(L_1, L_2, K)$$

$$= f(L_1/K, L_2/K) = f(l_1, l_2), \tag{1'}$$

where l_1 and l_2 are the ratios of skilled and unskilled labor to capital in modern sector production, and

$$F_1 = f_1(l_1, l_2) = w_1, \tag{12'}$$

$$F_2 = f_2(l_1, l_2) = w_2. \tag{13'}$$

These two equations can be used to solve for l_1 and l_2:

$$l_1 = l_1(w_1, w_2), \tag{17}$$

$$l_2 = l_2(w_1, w_2), \tag{18}$$

with

$$\partial l_1/\partial w_1 = l_{11} = f_{22}/(f_{11}f_{22} - f_{12}^2) < 0, \tag{19}$$

$$\partial l_1/\partial w_2 = l_{12} = -f_{12}/(f_{11}f_{22}-f_{12}^2), \tag{20}$$

$$\partial l_2/\partial w_1 = l_{21} = -f_{21}/(f_{11}f_{22}-f_{12}^2) = l_{12}, \tag{21}$$

$$\partial l_2/\partial w_2 = l_{22} = f_{11}/(f_{11}f_{22}-f_{12}^2) < 0. \tag{22}$$

Profit maximization also implies

$$F_3 = r = f - f_1 l_1 - f_2 l_2, \tag{14'}$$

or

$$r = f(l_1(w_1, w_2), l_2(w_1, w_2)) - w_1 l_1(w_1, w_2) - w_2 l_2(w_1, w_2). \tag{23}$$

Eq. (23) provides a second basic relationship between w_1 and w_2. For a fixed value of r, differentiation of (23) yields

$$dw_2/dw_1 = -l_1/l_2. \tag{24}$$

This implies a unique *inverse* relationship between w_1 and w_2 for a given rate of return. Thus a policy change which does not affect r must move w_1 and w_2 in opposite directions.[10]

To complete the system we need a third equation relating w_1, w_2, and N_1. For this purpose we begin with the identity

$$e_1 l_2/(e_2 l_1) = (N_2 - L_T)/(N_1 - Z).$$

Using the constraint

$$N_1 + N_2 = \bar{N},$$

this becomes

$$e_1 l_2/(e_2 l_1) = (\bar{N} - N_1 - L_T)/(N_1 - Z).$$

The ratios l_1, l_2, e_1, and e_2 can all be expressed as functions of w_1, w_2, and exogenous variables. From eq. (15a) we have

$$G'(L_T) = w_T = w_2 e_2 = w_2 B^2(w_1, w_2),$$

---

[10]It should be noted also that capital mobility implies that, for given wage rates, l_1 and l_2 are determined (and thus $L_1/L_2 = l_1/l_2$), but not the actual employment levels L_1 and L_2 separately.

so that L_T can also be expressed in terms of w_1 and w_2 with[11]

$$\partial L_T/\partial w_1 = L_{T1} = w_2 B_1^2/G'' > 0, \tag{25}$$

$$\partial L_T/\partial w_2 = L_{T2} = (e_2 + w_2 B_2^2)/G'' < 0. \tag{26}$$

Thus we have

$$N_1 = ((\bar{N} - L_T)l_1 e_2 + Z l_2 e_1)/(l_2 e_1 + l_1 e_2), \tag{27}$$

where the right-hand side depends only on w_1, w_2, and the exogenous variables.

We now have three equations, (16), (23), and (27), which can be solved for w_1, w_2, and N_1 in terms of the parameters. To determine the effects of parameter changes, the system is differentiated totally (see the appendix). The qualitative

Table 1

Effects of changes in exogenous variables on w_1, w_2, and N_1.

	dw_1	dw_2	dN_1
dM	$+$	$-$	$-$
dZ	$-$	$+$	$+$
$d\bar{N}$	$+$	$-$	$+$
dw_1^f	$?^a$	$?^a$	$+$ if $e_1/(w_1 B_1^1) \gtreqless (N_1 - Z)e_1 w_1/(Z w_1^f)$
dr	$-$ if $F_{13} \gtreqless 0^a$	$-$ if $F_{23} \gtreqless 0^a$	$?$
dk^*	$+$	$-$	$-$

^{a} w_1 and w_2 must move in opposite directions.

effects of changes in each of the exogenous variables on w_1, w_2, and N_1 are summarized in table 1. Corresponding changes in other endogenous variables can be calculated from dw_1, dw_2, and dN_1. Expressions for these changes in the case of a migration tax are presented in table 2.

4. Effects of a migration tax

Using the results of the previous section, we can now examine in detail the effects of a migration tax on an economy experiencing a net outflow of skilled workers. In our analysis the size of the outflow Z is taken as exogenous. In effect, we assume that sufficient barriers to emigration already exist so that emigration does not represent a marginal decision – i.e., there remains a positive net return to migration. This assumption is consistent with present policies used by most

[11]When traditional sector labor is paid its average product (15b), L_T can again be expressed in terms of w_1 and w_2; L_{T1} and L_{T2} have the same signs as indicated.

E

Table 2

Effects of a rise in the cost of emigration.

Effect	Sign
$dw_1/dM = -Zl_2J/\Delta$	$+$
$dw_2/dM = Zl_1J/\Delta$	$-$
$de_1/dM = -Zl_2JB_1^{1}/\Delta$	$+$
$de_2/dM = ZJV/\Delta$	$-$
$dN_1/dM = (Zl_1/\Delta)\{e_2R - F_{33}/Ql_1 + Kl_2^{2}B_1^{1}/e_1 + Kl_2V/e_2\}$	$-$
$dL_T/dM = -ZJR/\Delta$	$+$
$dY/dM = (-Z/\Delta)\{(DD+E'-k^{*})(l_1e_2R - F_{33}/Q) + Kl_1l_2B_1^{1}(e_2H+kl_2)/e_1$ $\quad - l_2KV(e_1H - kl_1)/e_2\}$	?
$dY^{*}/dM = (-Z/\Delta)\{(2DD+E'-k^{*})(l_1e_2R - F_{33}/Q) + l_1l_2KB_1^{1}(2e_2H+l_2(E'+k^{*}))/e_1$ $\quad + (l_2KB_2^{2}H/w_1e_2)(2DDl_1 + l_1(E'-k^{*})) + (N_1/(N_2-L_T)-1)w_2J)$ $\quad + J(l_2l_1K + l_1e_2N_1)\}$	?
$dK/dM = (Z/\Delta)\{(e_1F_{13} - e_2F_{23})/Q + e_1e_2R - Kl_1l_2e_2B_1^{1}/e_1 + Kl_2e_1V/e_2\}$	?
$dX/dM = (Z/Q\Delta)\{r(e_1F_{13} - e_2F_{23}) - F_{33}(e_1w_1 - e_2w_2) + FQ(e_1e_2R/K + l_2e_1V/e_2$ $\quad - l_1l_2e_2B_1^{1}/e_1)\}$	?
$dL_1/dM = (e_1l_1Z/\Delta)\{-F_{33}/l_1Q + e_2R - Kl_1l_2e_2B_1^{1}/e_1^{2} + Kl_2V/e_2\}$	?
$dL_2/dM = (e_2l_2Z/\Delta)\{F_{33}/l_2Q + e_1R - Kl_1l_2B_1^{1}/e_1 + Kl_2e_1V/e_2^{2}\}$	?

$\Delta = F_{33}/Q - DDe_2l_1R + V(l_1l_2KDD/e_2 + N_1w_2J) - B_1^{1}l_1l_2K(l_2DD + w_1J)/e_1 - l_1N_1e_2J < 0$

$J = e_2l_1 + e_1l_2 > 0 \qquad\qquad R = l_2L_{T1} - l_1L_{T2} > 0$

$H = w_1l_1 + w_2l_2 > 0 \qquad\qquad DD = w_2e_2 - w_1e_1 + k^{*} > 0$

$Q = F_{11}F_{22} - F_{12}^{2} > 0 \qquad\qquad V = l_1B_2^{2} - l_2B_1^{2} > 0$

developed countries to restrict the inflow of skilled workers from abroad. While the returns to emigration are reduced by a tax, this reduction may not be sufficient to deter even the marginal emigrant.

4.1. Wage rates and employment

As indicated by table 1, a rise in the cost of emigration (as a result of a tax or other similar measure) increases the domestic skilled wage, reduces the supply of skilled labor, and lowers the unskilled wage. From eqs. (3′) and (4′), the percentage e_1 of skilled workers finding employment is seen to rise, while that of modern sector unskilled workers must fall. The fall in expected modern sector earnings of unskilled labor, resulting from both a fall in the set wage and in the employment rate, pushes some unskilled labor back into the traditional sector. As a consequence of the tax, a smaller skilled labor class thus earns higher expected incomes, while a larger unskilled labor class earns lower expected incomes, whether in the modern or the traditional sector.[12]

[12]The effects of a tax which also deters some potential emigrants should be analyzed by treating Z as an explicit function of the net returns to emigration. See McCulloch and Yellen (1974) for details of this approach. As indicated in table 1, a rise in M and an *exogenous* reduction in Z have the same qualitative consequences for w_1, w_2, and N_1. Hence a policy which combines a reduction in immigration quotas with the migration tax tends to reinforce the effects achieved by the tax alone.

These surprising results can best be understood in terms of eq. (16). The migration tax reduces the net income of emigrant skilled workers and thus the expected returns to education. Therefore N_1 must fall. At given wage rates, the reduction in N_1 and the corresponding rise in N_2 raise e_1 and lower e_2. Through the wage setting relationships w_1 is pushed upward, while w_2 tends to fall. This fall in w_2 is reinforced by the inverse relationship between skilled and unskilled wage rates for a given rate of return on capital.

The consequences of the tax for employment and unemployment levels are, however, ambiguous. As a result of the altered wage structure, the number of skilled workers employed and total modern sector employment (skilled plus unskilled) tend to fall. Sufficient conditions for L_1 and $L_1 + L_2$ to fall are: (a) the elasticity of the skilled wage demand with respect to the skilled employment rate is at least as high as the corresponding elasticity for the unskilled wage demand, *and* (b) $e_1 \geqq e_2$. The likely reduction in modern sector employment is offset at least in part by an increase in traditional sector employment; thus the total number of unemployed workers in the economy as a whole may rise or fall.

The results in table 1 indicate that in our model a tax on migration and an increase in the private cost of education have exactly the same effects on w_1, w_2, and N_1. This is true because both changes affect the variables in the model only by reducing the expected net income of skilled workers.[13] However, the *ex post* distributional consequences are not identical.[14] Where migration is taxed, the *expected* returns to education fall, but only migrants *actually* receive lower net incomes; the incomes of domestic skilled workers rise. The migration tax therefore reduces the gap between the earnings of emigrant and domestic skilled workers. Where the private cost of education is increased, however, the differential between the earnings of migrants and nonmigrants falls by less, since the increase in cost affects both groups equally. Thus, the migration tax is more effective in reducing the inequality of actual incomes earned between emigrant and domestic skilled workers.

4.2. Income

We have seen that the emigration tax increases domestic income inequality while reducing the gap between incomes earned by emigrant and domestic skilled workers. It is also worth considering the effects of the tax policy on aggregate income measures. (Because of our assumption that Z remains fixed, per capita

[13]If the number of emigrants Z were determined endogenously, a rise in M, the cost of migration, would affect not only the decision to acquire skills but also the decision to migrate. When, as here, Z is determined exogenously, the migration tax has effects on expected earnings exactly equivalent to those of increasing the part of educational costs which are borne by those acquiring skills.

[14]While ex ante returns to education are identical for all (by assumption), there is an ex post distribution of outcomes, as some skilled workers emigrate, others are employed domestically or unemployed.

and total income move together.) One interesting measure of national income accruing directly to residents of the country is modern sector labor income plus total traditional sector income, less educational expenditures. Thus we define

$$Y = W_1L_1 + w_2L_2 + T - E(N_1),$$

where $E(N_1)$ is the social cost of education.[15] We exclude from this measure the income earned by capital in the modern sector because this capital is likely to be owned by foreigners.[16] However, modern sector capital may affect national welfare through the indirect channel of revenue from taxation of profits. For this reason, we analyze below the probable effects on the size of the equilibrium capital stock, as a proxy for the change in tax revenue derived.

The change in Y induced by the emigration tax is

$$\mathrm{d}Y = \mathrm{d}(w_1e_1(N_1 - Z)) + \mathrm{d}(w_2e_2(N_2 - L_T)) + G'\mathrm{d}L_T - E'\mathrm{d}N_1. \quad (28)$$

The last term in (28) measures the resources saved as a result of reduced educational expenditures. The first three terms represent the changes in modern sector skilled labor earnings, modern sector unskilled labor earnings, and total traditional sector income, respectively. The sum of these three changes may be positive or negative. A sufficient condition for the sum to fall is that the elasticity of the skilled wage demand with respect to the skilled employment rate be greater or equal to the corresponding elasticity for the unskilled wage demand.[17] In this case $\mathrm{d}Y$ may also be negative.

The possibility of a fall in Y is increased if the traditional sector wage exceeds the marginal product of labor. Eq. (28) can be rewritten as

$$\mathrm{d}Y = (N_1 - Z)\mathrm{d}(w_1e_1) + (N_2 - L_T)\mathrm{d}(w_2e_2) + (w_1e_1 - w_2e_2 - E')\mathrm{d}N_1$$

$$+ (G' - w_2e_2)\mathrm{d}L_T.$$

The first term is positive and the second negative. The third term is positive if the

---

[15]This cost is measured in terms of either final output. Since both goods are traded internationally at fixed prices, it makes no difference which good is 'consumed' in the educational process.

[16]In contrast, Bhagwati and Hamada (1974) include returns to capital in their measure of income; the (fixed) stock of capital is assumed to be domestically owned.

[17]A slightly weaker sufficient condition is

$$\eta_2/\eta_1 < (1 + l_2w_1/l_1w_2)e_1w_1/(e_2w_2),$$

where

$$\eta_1 = (\partial w_1/\partial e_1)(e_1/w_1) = e_1/(B_1{}^1w_1),$$

$$\eta_2 = (\partial w_2/\partial e_2)(e_2/w_2) = e_2/(B_2{}^2w_2).$$

social marginal cost of education, E', exceeds the private cost k^*.[18] If traditional sector labor is paid its marginal product, then $G' = w_2 e_2$, and the last term is zero. But if traditional sector labor is paid its average product, the last term is negative and depends on the extent to which the wage rate, $w_T = w_2 e_2$, exceeds the marginal product of labor in the traditional sector. This negative term indicates the economic loss resulting from a reflux of unskilled labor into the traditional sector.

In addition to its consequences for resource allocation in production and education, the migration tax affects income directly through the tax proceeds. Thus we define

$$\mathrm{d}Y^* = \mathrm{d}Y + Z\mathrm{d}M,$$

where $\mathrm{d}M$ is the increase in the cost of emigration corresponding to imposition of the migration tax. It is worth mentioning that some policies can act like a tax on emigration from the point of view of the potential drained brains, but yield no gain to those left behind. Lengthy administrative delays, typical both on the part of the LDC nations of emigration and the developed countries admitting immigrant brains, are a good example of this. Sufficient (but not necessary) conditions for Y^* to rise as a consequence of the emigration tax are that $E' > k^*$ *and* (a) N_1, the total number of skilled workers (including emigrants), is greater than $N_2 - L_T$, the number of unskilled workers in the modern sector labor force, *or* (b) the elasticity of the skilled wage demand with respect to the skilled employment rate e_1 is no greater than the corresponding elasticity for the unskilled wage demand, and skilled labor constitutes at least one third of the total modern labor force.[19]

4.3. Modern sector capital stock and output

The size of the modern sector capital stock, and thus the base for taxation of profits,[20] may rise or fall. The effect on the capital stock can be divided into two components. The reduction in the size of the modern sector labor force decreases capital requirements for given wages and employment rates. In addition, the changed wage structure induces alterations in l_1 and l_2 which may reinforce or offset the scale effect. Sufficient conditions for the equilibrium capital stock of the modern sector to fall are: (a) $F_{23} = \partial^2 F/\partial K \partial L_2 < 0$, i.e., an increase in L_2

---

[18]This condition is likely to be satisfied unless there remain unexhausted scale economies in education, so that marginal cost is below average cost.

[19]More precisely, the sufficient condition is

$$2\eta_2/\eta_1 + (N_1/(N_1 - Z) - 1) > (N_2 - L_T)/(N_1 - Z) - N_1/(N_2 - L_T).$$

[20]Foreign-owned capital may also represent undesired dependence on external powers.

decreases the marginal product of capital,[21] *and* (b) the elasticity of the skilled wage demand with respect to the skilled employment rate is at least as high as the corresponding elasticity for the unskilled wage demand. However, the scale effect may be outweighed by changes in factor proportions, yielding a rise in the capital stock. This is more likely to occur if $F_{13} < 0$, i.e., capital and skilled labor are good substitutes in production, the elasticity of the skilled wage demand with respect to e_1 is low relative to the corresponding elasticity for the unskilled wage demand, and the traditional sector production function exhibits strongly diminishing returns to labor.

Because modern sector employment and capital stock may fall as a result of the tax, there is a corresponding tendency for modern sector output to be reduced. Conditions (a) and (b) above for a fall in K are also sufficient to guarantee a decline in output.

5. Conclusions

The analysis presented above raises important questions concerning the emigration tax proposal. As suggested by Bhagwati and Hamada (1974), the tax can increase national income when both educational expenditures and tax revenue are taken into account. However, Bhagwati and Hamada do not consider explicitly the effects of the tax on wages and employment. In our model, expected earnings of unskilled workers are adversely affected by the tax, while those of domestic skilled workers rise. This implies that income inequality, a focus of social unrest in many developing countries, may be increased by such a tax. On the other hand, the tax would reduce the gap between the earnings of domestic and emigrant skilled workers.

The demodernization effect – diversion of labor from the modern to the traditional sector – resulting from the tax may be accompanied by other undesirable consequences. Associated with demodernization is the possibility of declines in modern sector output, employment, and capital stock. The total number of workers unemployed may also rise. Further, if the traditional sector wage exceeds the marginal product of labor, demodernization aggravates the existing misallocation of labor between sectors. Thus we have shown that an emigration tax would have far-reaching economic implications, even when the volume of emigration is unaffected.

Appendix

Differentiation of eqs. (16), (23), and (25) yields

[21]A weaker sufficient condition is
$$e_1F_{13}-e_2F_{23} > 0,$$
which is automatically satisfied if $F_{23} < 0$.

$$
\begin{bmatrix}
DD & N_1 w_2 B_1^2 - (N_1 - Z)(e_1 + w_1 B_1^1) & N_1(e_2 + w_2 B_2^2) \\
0 & l_1 & l_2 \\
e_1 l_2 + e_2 l_1 & (N_1-Z)(l_{21}e_1 + l_2 B_1^1) + L_{T1} l_1 e_2 & (N_1-Z)l_{22}e_1 + L_{T2}l_1 e_2 \\
& -(N_2 - L_T)(l_{11}e_2 + l_1 B_1^2) & -(N_2 - L_T)(l_{12}e_2 + l_1 B_2^2)
\end{bmatrix}
$$

$$
\cdot
\begin{bmatrix}
dN_1 \\
dw_1 \\
dw_2
\end{bmatrix}
=
\begin{bmatrix}
((N_1 - Z)w_1 B_2^1 + Z)dw_1^f - Z dM + FD dZ - N_1 dk^* \\
-dr \\
l_1 e_2 d\bar{N} - l_2 B_2^1 (N_1 - Z) dw_1^f + l_2 e_1 dZ
\end{bmatrix},
$$

where

$$DD = w_2 e_2 - w_1 e_1 + k^*,$$

$$FD = (w_1^f - M) - w_1 e_1,$$

and the other variables are defined as in sections 3 and 4. We solve this system to obtain the entries in table 1. The values of dw_1/dM, dw_2/dM, and dN_1/dM are then used to derive the entries in table 2. In simplifying these expressions, we make use of the following relationships between $F(L_1, L_2, K)$ and $f(l_1, l_2) = F/K$:

$$F_{11} = f_{11}/K,$$

$$F_{22} = f_{22}/K,$$

$$F_{12} = F_{21} = f_{12}/K = f_{21}/K,$$

$$F_{33} = (l_1^2 f_{11} + l_2^2 f_{22} + 2 l_1 l_2 f_{12})/K,$$

$$F_{13} = F_{31} = -(l_2 f_{12} + l_1 f_{11})/K,$$

$$F_{23} = F_{32} = -(l_2 f_{22} + l_1 f_{12})/K.$$

References

Berry, R.A. and R. Soligo, 1969, Some welfare effects of international migration, Journal of Political Economy 77, 778–94.

Bhagwati, J., 1972, Overqualification, education, and welfare: A theoretical analysis, mimeo (M.I.T., Cambridge, MA).

Bhagwati, J. and W. Dellalfar, 1973, The brain drain and income taxation: A proposal, World Development 1, 94–101.

Bhagwati, J. and K. Hamada, 1974, The brain drain, international integration of markets for professionals and unemployment: A theoretical analysis, Journal of Development Economics 1, 19–42.

Bhagwati, J. and T. N. Srinivasan, 1975, Education in a job ladder model and the fairness-in-hiring rule, mimeo (M.I.T., Cambridge, MA).

Fei, J.C.H. and G. Ranis, 1964, Development of the labor surplus economy (Irwin, Homewood, IL).

Grubel, H.B. and A.D. Scott, 1966, The international flow of human capital, American Economic Review 56, 268–74.

Johnson, H.G., 1967, Some economic aspects of brain drain, Pakistan Development Review 7, 379–411.

McCulloch, R. and J.L. Yellen, 1974, Factor mobility and the steady state distribution of income, Discussion paper 369 (Harvard Institute for Economic Research, Cambridge, MA).

CHAPTER 9

BRAIN DRAIN AND ECONOMIC GROWTH

A dynamic model

Carlos Alfredo RODRIGUEZ*

Columbia University, New York, NY 10027, U.S.A.

The problem of the international migration of educated people is analyzed in the context of a dynamic economy where individuals are faced with three basic decisions: education, acquisition of physical capital and migration. The paper discusses the transitional and steady-state behaviour of such an economy, and in addition incorporates a detailed dynamic analysis of the effects of minimum wages and of the implementation of a migration tax.

1. Introduction

Although the brain drain problem has drawn considerable attention in recent years, most of the work done has concentrated either on the description of the magnitudes and countries involved or, at a theoretical level, on the analysis of the problem in a fundamentally static framework. This is the case of a recent paper by Bhagwati and Hamada (1974) where they choose to ignore the effects of a growing population and capital accumulation in order to concentrate on the effects of minimum wage fixation in the context of a Harris–Todaro model. Yet another recent paper, by McCulloch and Yellen (1974), describes a one-sector, three-factors economy (capital, skilled and unskilled labor), but, in postulating perfect international mobility of capital, they assume away some of the interesting questions associated with capital accumulation; furthermore they restrict themselves to the analysis of comparative static changes of steady states, and an analysis of the dynamic properties of the model, including stability and the behavior of the economy during the transition period, is lacking.[1]

The model presented here borrows on the two previously mentioned papers while modifying them by giving a central role to capital accumulation and explicitly introducing dynamic analysis into the framework. The economy

---

*I would like to thank, without implication of responsibility, J. Bhagwati, G. Calvo, R. Findlay and K. Hamada for their helpful comments and suggestions.

[1] Other related theoretical works in the area of the international migration of labor can be found in Berry and Soligo (1969), Grubel and Scott (1966), Johnson (1967), Kenen (1971) and Rodriguez (1975).

described is at every moment endowed with three factors of production: capital, skilled (educated) labor and unskilled labor. Skilled labor and capital produce one good and unskilled labor and capital produce another good. Both goods are traded at a fixed international relative price. Thus the basic production structure is similar to that of Bhagwati–Hamada with the exception that a third factor, capital, mobile between sectors but not internationally (contrary to McCulloch–Yellen), is introduced.

Population is assumed to reproduce naturally at a constant rate n – migration will, however, introduce a difference between the reproduction rate and the effective rate of population growth. I distinguish between those born to skilled (educated) parents and those born to unskilled parents. It is assumed that all the children born to educated parents get educated, while only a fraction of those born to uneducated parents gets educated, this fraction depending on the pecuniary rate of return to education. Although these assumptions could be easily modified, I feel that they give a closer representation of what actually happens: after a family has acquired education, the education of their children becomes more a question of status and intra-family justice than an investment decision based only on pecuniary returns; furthermore, education possibly carries with it nonpecuniary returns which can seldom be perceived ex ante by those still uneducated. Our assumption is thus the extreme version of a situation where the demand for education for children born to educated parents is more inelastic with respect to the rate of return to education than the demand for education for children born to uneducated parents.

Only those educated are assumed to be able to migrate. At every moment a fraction of the stock of educated people migrates; this fraction depends on the rate of return to migration,[2] and thus on the difference between the foreign and domestic wage for skilled labor and the once-and-for-all migration cost. If taxes on the foreign income earned by the migrants are imposed by the source country, as suggested in Bhagwati–Dellalfar (1973), their net present value should be added to the migration cost or, alternatively, the flow tax paid per period can be deducted from the foreign wage; whichever way we consider this tax, the net effect is to reduce the rate of return to migration and thus the migration rate.

With respect to capital accumulation, it is assumed that in every period the desired acquisition of capital goods by the households is a constant fraction s of profits earned. Due to the small country assumption (fixed terms of trade), capital goods can be assumed to be produced in either sector or, alternatively, to be imported from abroad.

The basic behavioral relations in the model are thus specified by three functions: education, migration and savings. Education is assumed to be privately supplied by a third sector which transforms goods into human capital at a constant cost e and with no additional use of inputs. To the extent that some

---

[2] For an analysis of migration as an investment decison see Sjaastad (1962).

education may be provided free by the government, this acts as a decreased private cost of education and thus increases the private rate of return to it.

Section 2 describes algebraically the basic model used and its dynamic properties. Section 3 analyzes the long-run effects of changes in several parameters: foreign wage, savings ratio, education costs, migration costs, and the rate of population growth. Section 4 describes the effects of minimum wages in the context of a Harris–Todaro labor market, and thus extends the results of Bhagwati and Hamada since the model allows for a third factor, capital, which is mobile between sectors.[3] Finally, section 5 analyzes some differences between the short- and long-run response of different endogenous variables to a tax on the income of migrants.

2. The basic model

The two goods are produced under constant-returns-to-scale production functions:

$$Q_s = F(K_s, L_s) = L_s f(k_s), \qquad f' > 0, f'' < 0,$$

$$(f' = df(k_s)/dk_s, \text{ etc.}),$$

$$Q_u = G(K_u, L_u) = L_u g(k_u), \qquad g' > 0, g'' < 0,$$

where L_s = skilled labor force, totally employed in the production of Q_s; L_u = unskilled labor force, totally employed in the production of Q_u; K_s and K_u = capital used in each sector; and k_s and k_u = capital–labor ratios. Both goods are traded in the international market at a fixed relative price, assumed equal to one for simplicity. Since capital is freely mobile between sectors, its rate of return in both sectors, under incomplete specialization, must be equalized,

$$r = f'(k_s) = g'(k_u), \qquad (1)$$

where r is the real rental on capital.[4]

Each sector uses only one kind of labor and there is no need for the returns on both kinds of labor to be the same. From (1) there is a relationship between both capital–labor ratios; there is, however, a similar relation between both types

---

[3]Although the original Harris–Todaro formulation does not allow for capital to be mobile between sectors, a later paper by Corden and Findlay (1975) does, but it does not address itself to the problems of education, capital accumulation or migration; otherwise, the production structure of this paper is essentially the same as theirs.

[4]To the extent that I assume a constant and equal-to-unity price of capital goods and static expectations with respect to future rentals, r is also the real rate of interest.

wages. Wages are determined according to the marginal productivities of labor,

$$w_s = f(k_s) - k_s f'(k_s), \tag{2}$$

$$w_u = g(k_u) - k_u g'(k_u), \tag{3}$$

of where w_s and w_u are the wages for skilled and unskilled labor, respectively. Throughout the analysis it is assumed that $w_s > w_u$. The relation between both types of wages can be obtained from differentiation of (1)–(3):

$$dw_s = -f'' \cdot k_s dk_s, \tag{4}$$

$$dw_u = -g'' \cdot k_u dk_u, \tag{5}$$

and

$$f'' dk_s = g'' dk_u, \tag{6}$$

thus it follows that

$$dw_s - dw_u = \left(\frac{k_s - k_u}{k_s}\right) dw_s, \tag{7}$$

or, alternatively,

$$dw_s - dw_u = f'' \cdot (k_u - k_s) dk_s = g'' \cdot (k_u - k_s) dk_u. \tag{8}$$

It is clear from the above that as long as the economy is producing both goods, there is a direct relation between the skilled–unskilled wage differential and skilled wage or either capital–labor ratio. Notice from (7) that if the unskilled sector is relatively more capital intensive, that is, if $k_u > k_s$, increases in the skilled wage will be associated with decreases in the skilled–unskilled wage differential. This case, as we will see later, is associated with a unique and stable long-run equilibrium, contrary to the case where $k_s > k_u$ where multiple steady states, some stable and some unstable, may exist.

Assuming competitive factor markets, their rewards will be determined such that full employment prevails; this in turn implies

$$hk_s + (1 - h)k_u = k, \tag{9}$$

where h is the ratio of the skilled labor force to the total labor force and k is the ratio of the total capital stock of the country to the total population, independently of whether they are skilled or unskilled. The relation between labor force and population is assumed constant and equal to one for simplicity. The variable h, which I will call the human capital ratio is, at every moment, a constant parameter determined by past decisions on education and migration. Similarly, the economy's capital–labor ratio k is also given at every moment, its level depending on past accumulation decisions and the actual level of population.

The net addition to the stock of skilled people is equal to the sum of those new educated born to educated parents, nL_s, plus those new educated born to unskilled parents, $x \cdot n \cdot L_u$, minus the number of educated people who decide to migrate, $z \cdot L_s$, where x is the fraction of those born to unskilled parents who get educated and z is the fraction of those already educated who decide to migrate. The migration rate z could be easily applied only to those just educated, implying that the decision to migrate is only made by those young persons who have just finished their education, but this is not done here. Algebraically, the change over time in the stock of skilled people is given by

$$dL_s/dt = nL_s + xnL_u - zL_s, \tag{10}$$

or, in terms of rates of change,

$$(1/L_s)dL_s/dt = n - z + n \cdot x(1-h)/h. \tag{10'}$$

The migration and education functions are specified as follows:

$$x = x(w_s - w_u, e), \qquad x_1 > 0, x_2 < 0, \tag{11}$$

$$(x_1 = \partial x/\partial(w_s - w_u), \text{ etc.}),$$

$$z = z(w^* - w_s, M) \qquad z_1 > 0, z_2 < 0, \tag{12}$$

where w^* is the foreign wage for skilled labor and M is the once-and-for-all migration cost.

The actual rate of change in the population is equal to the reproduction rate minus the contribution of those migrating,

$$(1/L)dL/dt = n - h \cdot z = \bar{n}. \tag{13}$$

The human capital ratio h changes over time according to the difference between the rates of growth of skilled and total population, given by (10') and (13),

$$(1/h)dh/dt = (1-h)(nx - hz)/h. \tag{14}$$

The capital–labor ratio, in turn, changes through time according to the difference between the gross rate of capital formation (assuming no depreciation) and the actual rate of population growth,

$$(1/k)dk/dt = s \cdot r - \bar{n} = s \cdot r - n + h \cdot z. \tag{15}$$

Eqs. (14) and (15) describe the dynamic behavior of the two state variables of the model, the human capital ratio and the capital–labor ratio. These two equations need to be complemented with expressions determining the dependence of x, z and r on h and k, which can be easily obtained from (4)–(9):

$$\mathrm{d}x = x_1(k_u - k_s)(f''/A)\mathrm{d}k + x_1(k_u - k_s)^2(f''/A)\mathrm{d}h, \tag{16a}$$

$$\mathrm{d}z = z_1 k_s(f''/A)\mathrm{d}k + z_1(k_u - k_s)k_s(f''/A)\mathrm{d}h, \tag{16b}$$

$$\mathrm{d}r = (f''/A)\mathrm{d}k + (k_u - k_s)(f''/A)\mathrm{d}h, \tag{16c}$$

where

$$A = h + (1 - h)f''/g'' > 0.$$

Thus, (14)–(16) define a system of two differential equations in two variables, h and k, which can, in principle, be solved for the dynamic paths of the variables. I will first analyze the nature of the steady-state solution(s). Equating (14) and (15) to zero, implying that neither h nor k are changing, we obtain a necessary condition for a steady-state solution:

$$n - s \cdot r = n \cdot x, \tag{17}$$

that is, the excess of the reproduction rate over per capita savings must equal the product of the reproduction rate and the education ratio for the children of unskilled parents. Notice that since both sides of (17) can be represented as a function of the skilled wage rate, the solution(s) to it give the steady-state value for w_s and indirectly, using (4)–(8) and (15), also the values for w_u, k_s, k_u, h, k and r. The left-hand side of (17) is

$$n - sr = a(w_s), \qquad \mathrm{d}a/\mathrm{d}w_s = s/k_s > 0,$$

and the right-hand side of (17) can be represented as

$$nx = b(w_s), \qquad \mathrm{d}b/\mathrm{d}w_s = nx_1(k_s - k_u)/k_s \gtrless 0.$$

Since x_1 is positive, it is clear that a unique intersection (if any) of the $a(\cdot)$ and $b(\cdot)$ schedules, and thus a unique solution to (17), can only be guaranteed if $k_s < k_u$, which would imply an upward sloping $a(\cdot)$ schedule and a downward sloping $b(\cdot)$ schedule. If $k_s > k_u$, both schedules are upward sloping and the possibility of multiple intersections arises. Thus uniqueness and, as we will see later, stability of the long-run solution can only be guaranteed if the unskilled sector is relatively more capital intensive. Since both sectors are paying different wages, and in fact using different labor inputs, the relative capital intensity must be defined at any interest rate r which is the reward to the factor that both sectors use in common. As we will see, the capital intensity assumed to prevail will have a bearing not only on the uniqueness and stability of the steady-state solution but also on the qualitative effects of changes in various parameters on the steady-state values of the variables of the system.

Assuming a steady-state solution exists, we can analyze the local stability properties of it by linearizing (14) and (15) in the neighborhood of the solution; the coefficients of the linear approximation are the partial derivatives of (14) and (15) with respect to h and k, all evaluated at the steady-state solution. The expressions for these partial derivatives are:[5]

$$\partial \dot{h}/h = (1-h)\{-z+(k_u-k_s)(f''/A)[x_1 n(k_u-k_s)-hz_1 k_s]\} \gtrless 0, \quad (18\mathrm{a})$$

$$\partial \dot{h}/k = (1-h)(1/A)[x_1 n(k_u-k_s)f''-hk_s f''z_1] \gtrless 0, \quad (18\mathrm{b})$$

$$\partial \dot{k}/\partial h = zk+k(k_u-k_s)(f''/A)(s+hk_s z_1) \gtrless 0, \quad (18\mathrm{c})$$

$$\partial \dot{k}/\partial k = skf''/A+hkk_s f''z_1/A < 0. \quad (18\mathrm{d})$$

Local stability requires the trace of the matrix formed with the partial derivatives,

$$X = \begin{bmatrix} \partial \dot{h}/\partial h & \partial \dot{h}/\partial k \\ \partial \dot{k}/\partial h & \partial \dot{k}/\partial k \end{bmatrix}$$

to be negative and the determinant to be positive. The expressions for the trace and the determinant of X are:

$$\mathrm{Tr}\cdot X = (1-h)x_1 n(k_u-k_s)^2(f''/A)-z(1-h)+sk(f''/A)$$

$$+hk_s^2 z_1(f''/A) < 0,$$

$$(18')$$

$$\mathrm{Det}\cdot X = -zk(1-h)(f''/A)[s+x_1 n(k_u-k_s)] \gtrless 0.$$

Clearly, the trace is always negative whereas the determinant can only be proved to be unambiguously positive if $k_u > k_s$; it is clear, however, that for k_s equal to or slightly larger than k_u, the determinant must still be positive since the positive term in s will still dominate.

---

[5] A dot over a variable denotes its change over time, i.e., $\dot{y} = \mathrm{d}y/\mathrm{d}t$.

Fig. 1 illustrates the dynamic paths of h and k under the assumption that $k_u < k_s$ but stability prevails. The curves $\dot{h} = 0$ and $\dot{k} = 0$ are derived from (14) and (15) and the directions of the arrows come from the signs of the partial derivatives in (18). As shown, the (h, k) plane is divided into four regions by the $\dot{h} = 0$ and $\dot{k} = 0$ schedules. In region I, the country is poorly endowed with both physical and human capital (relative to the steady state) and, as depicted by the arrows, both h and k tend to increase over time, whereas in region III, where h and k are above their steady-state values, both decrease through time. Regions II and IV are intermediate situations where h and k move in opposite directions. From the directions of the arrows it follows that once the system enters into regions I or III it must converge to the steady state without leaving that region; thus a country which starts poorly endowed with physical and human capital will experience a continuous rise in both the human capital and capital–labor ratios

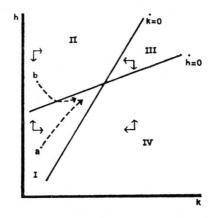

Fig. 1.

until it reaches the steady state (this case is represented by the path starting at point a in the diagram). For a country initially well endowed with human capital but poorly endowed with physical capital, such that the initial position is in region II, this case predicts an initial fall in the human capital ratio, probably followed by a period of increases in it and a continuous increase in the capital–labor ratio. This case is represented by the path starting at point b in the diagram.

The case where $k_u > k_s$, although always locally stable, cannot be represented by a single phase diagram. There are three possible ways in which the $\dot{h} = 0$ and $\dot{k} = 0$ schedules can intersect, all consistent with $k_u > k_s$. These cases are represented in figs. 2–4. In each figure, the path for a country which starts poorly endowed with both physical and human capital is indicated. In the case of fig. 4 the approach to the steady state must be asymptotic, whereas in the other two cases a cyclical approach cannot be ruled out.

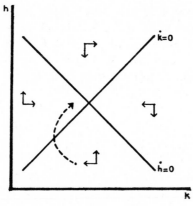

Fig. 2.

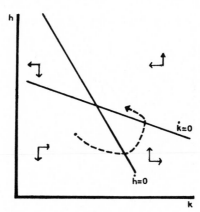

Fig. 3.

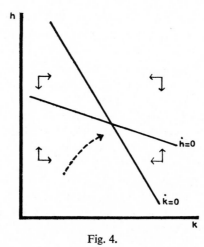

Fig. 4.

It can be shown that the existence of four possible cases consistent with stability is due to the behavior of the capital–labor ratio and that in fact there are only two possible dynamic behaviors for the human capital ratio. This can be done by observing that, from (4)–(9), the skilled wage w_s is only a function of h and k and that it changes over time according to

$$\dot{w}_s = -k_s(f''/A)[\dot{k}+(k_u-k_s)\dot{h}].$$

Since both $\dot{k}$ and $\dot{h}$, in the neighborhood of a steady-state solution, can be represented as only functions of h and w_s, it follows that $\dot{w}_s$ is also only a function of h and w_s in that neighborhood. We can thus transform our dynamic system from the (k, h) plane into the (w_s, h) plane for values of the variables close to the steady-state solution. The expressions for the partial derivatives of the transformed system, evaluated around the steady state, are:

$$\partial\dot{w}_s/\partial w_s = (f''/A)[sk+hk_s^2z_1+(k_u-k_s)^2(1-h)nx_1] < 0,$$

$$\partial\dot{w}_s/\partial h = -f''\cdot k_s^2z/A > 0,$$

$$\partial\dot{h}/\partial w_s = (1-h)[hz_1-nx_1(k_u-k_s)/k_s] \gtrless 0,$$

$$\partial\dot{h}/\partial h = -z(1-h) < 0.$$

The reader can verify that the stability conditions of the transformed system are identical to those of the original system. The advantage of this transformation is that there are only two possible configurations in the (w_s, h) plane which are consistent with stability. These cases are depicted in figs. 5 and 6. Fig. 5 represents the case where $k_s > k_u$ (although it is also consistent with values of $k_s < k_u$ which still maintain $\partial h/\partial w_s > 0$) while fig. 6 shows the case where k_u is strongly larger than k_s, such that $\partial h/\partial w_s < 0$. In fig. 5 the approach to the steady state must be asympotical and thus it corresponds to the cases of figs. 1 and 4 of the original system, whereas in fig. 6 the approach could be cyclical and this corresponds to the cases of figs. 2 and 3. In both figures, the paths of the skilled wage and the human capital ratio can be followed once their initial values are determined. For example, in fig. 5, the path starting at a shows the path of an economy with a low initial human capital ratio but a high wage for skilled labor, whereas the path starting at b depicts an initial situation with a relatively higher human capital ratio but a low wage for skilled labor.

3. Comparative statics

In this model there are five distinctive parameters which, together with technology, determine the dynamic paths of the economy and the steady-state

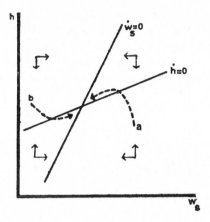

Fig. 5.

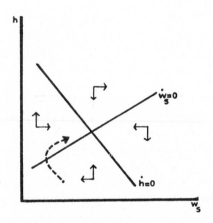

Fig. 6.

solution: the foreign wage for skilled labor (w^*), the savings ratio (s), the migration cost (M), the education cost (e) and the natural rate of population growth (n). In this section we will analyze comparative static changes in stable steady-state solutions due to variations in the above mentioned parameters. The variables whose changes we attempt to explain are the real factor rewards, human capital ratio, capital–labor ratio, actual rate of population growth, per capita income and per capita consumption.

From the necessary condition for a steady state (17), we can derive the changes in the skilled wage w_s, which in turn determines the variations in the other factor rewards from (4)–(6). Given the changes in factor rewards, the response of the human capital ratio can be obtained from the differentiation of (14) equated to zero; similarly, the change in the capital–labor ratio is derived from (9) after substituting for the changes in h and factor rewards and using (4)–(5). Finally, the change in the actual rate of population growth is obtained from (13).

Table 1 summarizes the direction of the changes in the endogenous variables in response to increases in the levels of the exogenous parameters. Changes in per capita income and consumption are described later in this section. It must be remembered that in obtaining the results of table 1 explicit use has been made of the local stability conditions described in (18′).

Table 1

Comparative static effects of changes in various parameters (signs).

Effect on	Increases in				
	w^*	s	M	e	$\bar{n}$
h	$(-)$	$(+)$ if $k_s > k_u$ $(?)$ if $k_s < k_u$	$(+)$	$(-)$	$(?)$
k	$(+)$ if $k_u > k_s$ $(-)$ if $k_u < k_s$	$(+)$ except in fig.3	$(-)$ if $k_u > k_s$ $(+)$ if $k_u < k_s$	$(-)$ if $k_u < k_s$ $(?)$ if $k_u > k_s$	$(?)$
$\bar{n}$	0	$(-)$	0	$(+)$	$(+)$
w_s	0	$(+)$	0	$(-)$	$(-)$
w_u	0	$(+)$	0	$(-)$	$(-)$
r	0	$(-)$	0	$(+)$	$(+)$

An interesting result which follows from this exercise is that all the steady-state factor rewards are independent from the foreign wage w^* and the migration cost M; this, however, will not preclude changes in per capita income and consumption since the human capital ratio, and thus the composition of the labor force, will change in response to variations in w^* and M, as will also the capital–labor ratio. The reason for this result is clear from the inspection of the steady-state condition (17) which determines the skilled wage as a function of n, s and e only; thus changes in w^* or M will not affect the steady-state level of the skilled wage, and in consequence, by (4)–(6), neither will they affect any other factor rewards. This result differs substantially from those of McCulloch–Yellen (1974) where it is changes in the cost of education that do not affect factor rewards whereas changes in w^* or M do affect them. The completely opposite nature of these results clearly points out the differences in assumptions regarding technology, education, saving, and migration functions.[6] Since the implications of either model are far from being trivial, it is clear that further study into the relevance of the assumptions made becomes essential.

[6] It was pointed out to me by Hamada that this result depends critically on my assumption that there are only savings out of profits. If workers also save, per capita savings in eq. (17) will also depend on the distribution of income (or total per capita income if their savings ratio is the same as that of capitalists) and thus on the human capital ratio. It then follows that (17) alone will not suffice to determine all steady-state factor rewards independently of the migration cost.

As shown in table 1, increases in the foreign wage will reduce the capital–labor ratio if the skilled sector is capital intensive, and increase it otherwise. Since changes in the migration cost have exactly the opposite effects of changes in the foreign wage, it follows that an increase in the migration cost will increase the capital–labor ratio if $k_s > k_u$, and reduce it otherwise. Increases in the savings ratio will increase the capital–labor ratio in all cases except in that depicted in fig. 3.

The human capital ratio is shown to decrease with increases in the foreign wage or the education cost and to increase with the migration cost; increases in the savings ratio will raise the human capital ratio provided the skilled sector is capital intensive, otherwise the effect is ambiguous. Finally, the effects of increases in the natural rate of population growth are ambiguous on h and k while they decrease wages and increase the interest rate.

We now proceed to describe the changes in the steady-state levels of per capita income and consumption. Although still far from describing changes in welfare levels, the behavior of these two variables may be more helpful in this direction than the behavior of factor rewards or factor endowments taken independently. Gross per capita income equals the market value of output and also the sum of factor payments,

$$y = hf(k_s) + (1-h)g(k_u)$$

$$= w_s h + w_u(1-h) + rk. \tag{19}$$

Differentiating (19) we obtain

$$dy = (w_s - w_u)dh + r\,dk, \tag{20}$$

where use has been made of the fact that

$$h\,dw_s + (1-h)dw_u + k\,dr = 0,$$

which follows from (4)–(6) and (9).

Thus, gross per capita income increases with both the capital–labor ratio and the human capital ratio (to the extent that $w_s > w_u$). After substituting in (20) for the changes in h and k in response to variations in the different parameters, we obtain:

$$dy/de = \{rz + k\partial k/\partial k[g(k_u) - f(k_s)]\}(1-h)\cdot n\cdot x_2/(h\cdot \det\cdot X)$$

$$< 0 \quad \text{if } f(k_s) > g(k_u),$$

$$dy/ds = [h\partial h/\partial k[f(k_s) - g(k_u)] + rz(1-h)/h]\cdot r/\det\cdot X$$

$$> 0 \quad \text{if } k_s > k_u,$$

$$dy/dM = [g(k_u) - f(k_s)]hz_2/z \gtreqless 0 \quad \text{as } f(k_s) \gtreqless g(k_u),$$

$$dy/dw^* = [g(k_u) - f(k_s)]hz_1/z \gtreqless 0 \quad \text{as } f(k_s) \lesseqgtr g(k_u).$$

Note that since $k_s > k_u$ guarantees that $\partial h / \partial k > 0$ and that $f(k_s) > g(k_u)$ (the skilled sector has a higher wage and a higher capital–labor ratio but the same interest rate) the direction of all the changes in per capita income is unambiguous in this case. If, however, $k_u > k_s$, but output per man is still higher in the skilled sector, only the effects of changes in the savings ratio become ambiguous (because the sign of $\partial h / \partial k$ becomes ambiguous).

We conclude that, with per capita output higher in the skilled sector, per capita income decreases with the education cost and the foreign wage, while it increases with the migration cost and depends ambiguously on the savings ratio (positively if $k_s > k_u$). If, however, per capita output is higher in the unskilled sector, per capita income will increase with the foreign wage, decrease with the migration cost and respond ambiguously to the education cost and the savings rate.

Although per capita income is widely used as an economic indicator of well-being, a much better indicator is certainly per capita consumption. However, since we are making comparisons of steady states, our results should be taken as only indicative, in view of the fact that the transition towards the new equilibrium is ignored.

Steady-state per capita consumption $\bar{c}$ is equal to gross per capita income minus those investment expenditures required to keep the capital–labor ratio and the human capital ratio constant. Steady-state per capita investment in physical capital equals the product of the actual rate of population growth and the capital–labor ratio $\bar{n}k$, while per capita steady-state educational expenditures are

$$e \cdot n[h + x(1-h)] = e(h \cdot \bar{n} + n - \bar{n}),$$

since in the steady state we have $\bar{n} = n(1-x)$. Thus, per capita consumption can be expressed as

$$\bar{c} = h \cdot w_s + (1-h)w_u + r \cdot k - \bar{n} \cdot k - e(h \cdot \bar{n} + n - \bar{n}),$$

and it changes according to

$$\begin{aligned} \mathrm{d}\bar{c} = & \, e\{[(w_s - w_u)/e] - \bar{n}\}\,\mathrm{d}h + (r - \bar{n})\,\mathrm{d}k - (k + eh)\,\mathrm{d}\bar{n} \\ & - e(\mathrm{d}n - \mathrm{d}\bar{n}). \end{aligned} \tag{21}$$

It follows that when the rates of return to education and physical capital are larger than the actual rate of population growth, increases in the capital–labor ratio or in the human capital ratio will increase steady-state per capita consumption. Thus, the well-known result that increases in the capital–labor ratio raise per capita consumption to the extent that the interest rate exceeds the rate of population growth also generalizes to the case of human capital.

The third term in (21) measures the contribution of changes in the actual rate of population growth to per capita consumption; this contribution is negative since a higher rate of actual population growth implies higher steady-state investment requirements in both physical and human capital. The interpretation of the last term in (21) is not straightforward: from (13) it follows that $n - \bar{n}$ is equal to hz which, the reader can verify, is the ratio of migrants to population; thus the term $e(\mathrm{d}n - \mathrm{d}\bar{n})$ equals the education cost times the change in the ratio of migrants to population, and it is substracted from per capita consumption because those migrants who get educated do not contribute later with their labor since they migrate.

Unfortunately, it is not possible to go much further than identifying the sources of the changes in consumption per capita; even granting that the rates of return to physical and human capital are larger than the actual rate of population growth, inspection of table 1 shows that the different sources of changes in $\bar{c}$ usually move in opposite directions such that the net change in $\bar{c}$ is in general ambiguous. The simplest cases to analyze are those of changes in the foreign wage and the migration cost, because for them the actual rate of population growth remains unchanged. Even in these simple cases we can get a definite result only when h and k move in the same direction, which is the case when the skilled sector is capital intensive; in this case, decreases in the foreign wage and increases in the migration cost will unambiguously increase consumption per capita (if the rates of return on both types of capital exceed the actual rate of population growth). If $k_u > k_s$, h and k will move in opposite directions whenever w^* or M change, and thus the net contribution on $\bar{c}$ is unclear unless we assume that the rate of return on one of the two assets falls short of the actual rate of growth in population, a not very realistic assumption in light of the well-established empirical evidence to the contrary.

4. The effects of minimum wages

In this section we discuss the effects of minimum wages above the competitive level in the context of a Harris–Todaro (1970) labor market where laborers in the affected sector do not react to the actual wage but rather to the expected wage. If at every instant the existing jobs are randomly allocated among all the applicants, the probability of getting a job equals the number of job offerings divided by the number of applicants. Since those applicants who do not get employed must remain unemployed during the period, this probability equals unity minus the unemployment rate. The expected wage is then the product of the actual wage times the probability of being employed. As was mentioned in the introduction, Bhagwati and Hamada analyzed this problem in the context of a model similar to this, with the exception that capital is implicitly assumed to be specific to each sector and thus it is directly omitted from their analysis. In this model capital is freely mobile between sectors and thus its rate of return must be equalized in both if there is going to be incomplete specialization. This equalization of the rates of return to capital, together with the linear homogeneity of the production functions, determines a unique relationship between both capital–labor ratios as described in (6). Thus fixing the wage in one sector determines the capital–labor ratio for which the marginal product of labor equals this minimum wage and, indirectly, through the equalization of the marginal productivities of capital, also determines the capital–labor ratio in the other sector and its wage rate. In summary, due to the mobility of capital between sectors, the determination of a minimum (effective) wage in one sector determines a unique wage in the other sector to the extent that both goods continue being produced. This implies that independent minimum wage fixation in each sector is in general incompatible with incomplete specialization.

I will first discuss the effects of a minimum wage in the skilled sector and then in the unskilled sector.

4.1. Minimum wage in skilled sector

Assume that a minimum wage, $\bar{w}$, larger than the competitively determined one is imposed in the skilled sector. Since producers will hire skilled labor until its marginal product equals the minimum wage, this determines the capital–labor ratio in the skilled sector, $\bar{k}_s$, and, as discussed before, also determines the capital–labor ratio in the unskilled sector, $\bar{k}_u$, and the unskilled wage rate, $\bar{w}_u$. Note that under incomplete specialization, $\bar{k}_s$, $\bar{k}_u$ and $\bar{w}_u$ are constants determined only by the minimum wage $\bar{w}$ and technology.

Workers, to the extent that there is unemployment, do not react to the minimum wage but to the expected wage w_s^e, which equals one minus the unemployment rate times $\bar{w}$. Denoting by v the employment ratio in the skilled sector (one minus the unemployment ratio), the expected wage in this sector is

$$w_s^e = v \cdot \bar{w}. \tag{22}$$

The migration and education functions are now assumed to depend on the expected wage in the skilled sector:

$$x = x(w_s^e - \bar{w}_u, e) = x(v), \tag{23}$$

given $\bar{w}$ and e; also, $dx/dv > 0$;

$$z = z(w^* - w_s^e, M) = z(v), \tag{24}$$

given $\bar{w}$, w^* and M; also, $dz/dv < 0$.

Denoting by N_s the skilled population and by L_s those employed in the skilled sector, full employment of capital implies

$$L_s \bar{k}_s + L_u \bar{k}_u = K, \qquad (25)$$

and total population equals

$$N_s + L_u = L. \qquad (26)$$

Denoting the human capital ratio as $h = N_s/L$ and the employment ratio as $v = L_s/N_s$, (25) can be written as

$$h \cdot v \cdot \bar{k}_s + (1-h)\bar{k}_u = k, \qquad (27)$$

from where it follows that

$$dv = \frac{dk - (v\bar{k}_s - \bar{k}_u) \cdot dh}{h \cdot \bar{k}_s}. \qquad (28)$$

Following the lines of the first section, we derive the rates of change in the human capital and capital–labor ratios,

$$\dot{h} = (1-h)[nx(v) - hz(v)], \qquad (29)$$

$$\dot{k} = k[sr(\bar{k}_s) - n + hz(v)]. \qquad (30)$$

The partial derivatives of the system (29)–(30) in the neighborhood of the steady-state solution are:

$$\partial \dot{h}/\partial h = (1-h)\{[n(dx/dv) - h(dz/dv)](dv/dh) - z\},$$

$$\partial \dot{h}/\partial k = (1-h)[n(dx/dv) - h(dz/dv)](dv/dk),$$

$$\partial \dot{k}/\partial h = k[h(dz/dv)(dv/dh) + z],$$

$$\partial \dot{k}/\partial k = k \cdot h \cdot (dz/dv)(dv/dk).$$

It follows from the above expressions that the determinant of the matrix of the partial derivatives describing the linear approximation to (29)–(30) is given by

$$-(1-h) \cdot n \cdot k \cdot z(dx/dv)(dv/dk),$$

which, it is easy to verify, is always negative, implying that any interior steady-state solution to the system of differential equations (29)–(30) is locally unstable. This does not mean that a stable steady-state solution does not exist when there is a minimum wage in the skilled sector but rather that there is no stable solution with both goods being produced and/or with x, z and v lying within their permissible boundaries. Unfortunately, I have thus far not been able to specify the nature of any noninterior steady-state solution towards which the economy may tend following the imposition of the minimum wage in the skilled sector.

4.2. Minimum wage in the unskilled sector

The case of a minimum wage in the unskilled sector is considerably more simple to analyze because, through the determination of the marginal product of labor in the unskilled sector, it also determines the skilled wage and thus also the migration rate z (given w^* and M).

To the extent that unemployment prevails in the unskilled sector, we redefine the employment ratio v as the ratio of those employed in the sector to the total unskilled population. Similarly, the expected unskilled wage equals the product of the employment ratio and the minimum unskilled wage $\bar{w}$,

$$w_u^e = v \cdot \bar{w}. \tag{31}$$

Full employment of capital and the skilled labor force implies

$$h \cdot \bar{k}_s + v \cdot (1-h) \cdot \bar{k}_u = k, \tag{32}$$

where, since all factor rewards are constant, both capital–labor ratios are also given and depend only on the minimum wage. It then follows that the employment ratio depends on the human capital and capital–labor ratios according to

$$dv = \frac{dk + (v\bar{k}_u - \bar{k}_s)dh}{(1-h)\bar{k}_u}. \tag{32'}$$

The migration rate, given w^* and M, depends only on the fixed unskilled wage, while the education ratio x will depend only on the employment ratio v as long as the education cost and the minimum wage remain constant. The dynamic behavior of h and k is described by

$$\dot{h} = (1-h)[nx(v) - h \cdot z], \tag{33}$$

$$\dot{k} = k[sr(\bar{k}_s) - n + h \cdot z], \tag{34}$$

where $\partial x / \partial v < 0$ and v depends on h and k as described in (32'). The partial derivatives of (33)–(34) in the neighborhood of the steady-state solution are:

$$\partial \dot{h}/\partial h = (1-h)[n\cdot\partial x/\partial v\cdot\partial v/\partial h - z] \gtrless 0,$$

$$\partial \dot{h}/\partial k = (1-h)[n\cdot\partial x/\partial v\cdot\partial v/\partial k] < 0,$$

$$\partial \dot{k}/\partial h = k\cdot z > 0,$$

$$\partial \dot{k}/\partial k = 0.$$

From the inspection of these partial derivatives it follows that there is only one stable case when $\partial \dot{h}/\partial h < 0$. This stable case is depicted in fig. 7, where it can be clearly seen that the system will approach the steady-state with h and k moving in opposite directions.

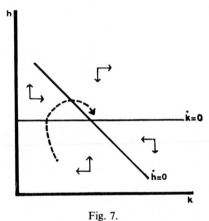

Fig. 7.

Table 2 describes the qualitative effects of changes in various parameters on the steady-state values of k and h. Probably the most surprising conclusion which follows from here is that an increase in the education cost e will lower the capital–labor ratio but leave the human capital ratio unchanged. The reason for this comes from eq. (34) which, once equated to zero (for an unchanged capital–labor ratio), determines the steady-state value of the human capital ratio as a function of the savings rate, the rate of population growth, the interest rate and the migration rate; since all of these variables are, in this minimum wage model, independent of the cost of education, so is the human capital ratio. It also follows easily from (34) that since an increase in the minimum wage increases the wage in the skilled sector and thus also decreases the interest rate and the migration rate, the new human capital ratio will have to be higher in order to preserve an unchanging capital–labor ratio. Thus higher minimum wages in the unskilled sector are associated with higher steady-state values for the human capital ratio. The net effect on the capital–labor ratio is, however, ambiguous, depending on the relative capital intensities in both sectors. As shown in the table, the capital–labor ratio also responds ambiguously to changes in the rate of population growth, the foreign wage and the migration cost, but increases with the savings ratio. The human capital ratio is shown to decrease with increases in the savings ratio and the foreign wage and to respond positively to increases in the rate of population growth and the migration cost. Since factor rewards depend only on the minimum wage, they do not change at all with changes in w^*, s, n, M or e. This independence of factor rewards from most of the parameters of the system (other than the minimum wage) is fundamentally due to the assumptions about the technology, savings and the fixed terms of trade.

Table 2

Comparative static effects with a minimum wage in the unskilled sector.

Effect on	Increases in					
	w^*	$\bar{w}$	s	n	e	M
k	(?)	(?)	(+)	(?)	(−)	(?)
h	(−)	(+)	(−)	(+)	0	(+)

5. Short- and long-run effects of a migration tax

Several studies have been recently concerned with the possibility of implementing a special tax on the incomes of migrants from LDCs by the receiving DCs, the proceeds of which could be allocated to some international agency for redistribution to the LDCs [see Bhagwati and Dellalfar (1973), McCulloch and Yellen (1975)]. The model developed in the later sections is specially suited for both a short- and long-run analysis of the effects of such a tax. In fact, to the extent that a migration tax is fully equivalent to an increase in the migration cost, we have already discussed several of the long-run effects of the tax. In this section we describe some additional long-run results of the migration tax and also analyze the difference between the long-run and short-run effects of the tax on several endogenous variables.

In particular, we will be concerned with the short-run response to a migration tax of the capital–labor ratio, the human capital ratio, factor rewards and the rate of unemployment (when a minimum wage prevails in the unskilled sector).

5.1. Some additional steady-state results

In the flexible wages regime, the migration tax does not affect steady-state factor rewards (see table 1). It then follows that, given the cost of education, the education ratio for those born to unskilled parents, x, will also be independent of the migration tax in the steady state. Also, to the extent that the wage differential remains unchanged, the migration tax will reduce the migration rate z by the full amount of the elasticity of that rate with respect to the migration cost.

When a minimum wage prevails in the unskilled sector, it follows from the steady-state condition for the capital–labor ratio, (30), and the fact that the human capital ratio is increased (table 2), that the migration ratio z will fall with the migration tax in order to keep the term hz equal to the constant term $n - sr(\bar{k}_s)$. But if the product hz is independent of the migration tax, so also will the term nx if the steady-state condition for the human capital ratio, eq. (29), is satisfied. The constancy of nx implies the constancy of x (given the constant n) and, given the minimum wage in the unskilled sector and the educational cost, this implies that the employment ratio in the unskilled sector is also unchanged. Table 3 summarizes the additional long-run effects of the migration tax discussed above.

Table 3
Long-run effects of a migration tax.

	Flexible wages	Minimum unskilled wage
Factor rewards	0	0
Education ratio (x)	0	0
Migration ratio (z)	$(-)$	$(-)$
Employment ratio (v)	0	0
Human capital ratio (h)	$(+)$	$(+)$
Capital–labor ratio (k)	$(\pm)$	$(\pm)$

5.2. Short-run effects of the migration tax

Following the implementation of the migration tax, the short-run response of the variables discussed in table 3 may be the same or different than in the long run. Clearly, the decision on the implementation of the migration tax cannot rest on its long-run effects alone. For example, to the extent that the tax seems to increase both the human capital and capital–labor ratio in the steady state (if $k_u < k_s$) without affecting factor rewards, the tax seems attractive since it increases two variables closely associated with economic development without at least having undesirable effects on income distribution. If, however, during the transition to the new steady state (as will be shown to be the case), an unambiguous income distribution from labor towards capital or an increase in the unemployment rate takes place, the tax may look much less attractive in the eyes of the policy-makers, and some kind of weighting between the short-run costs and the long-run benefits becomes essential.

5.2.1. Short-run effects on factor rewards in the flexible wages regime. From table 1 it follows that factor rewards do not change in the steady-state, while the human capital ratio increases in response to a migration tax. However, from figs. 5 and 6 describing the dynamic behavior of the system in the (h, w_s) plane, this must imply that both the $\dot{w}_s = 0$ and the $\dot{h} = 0$ schedules must shift vertically upwards such that at the new intersection a higher h and the same w_s prevail. If prior to the imposition of the tax the economy was in the steady-state, it follows that the vertical shift in both schedules will leave the economy in a region where $\dot{h}$ is positive and $\dot{w}_s$ is negative. Thus, the short-run effect of the migration tax is to reduce the skilled wage and, by (4)–(6), it also reduces the unskilled wage and increases the rental on capital. The paths of the unskilled wage and the rental of capital will appear as in fig. 8. The path of the unskilled

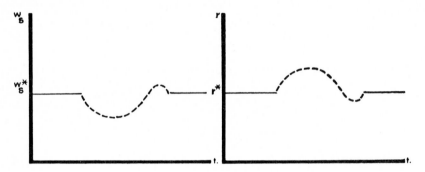

Fig. 8. Paths of the skilled wage and rental on capital.

wage will parallel that of the skilled wage since both wages must move together given our assumptions about technology.

5.2.2. Short-run effects on unemploment in the minimum unskilled wage regime. For this purpose it is better to transform the dynamic system (33)–(34) into an equivalent one in the (h, v) plane using (32'). The transformed system is

$$\dot{v} = \frac{\dot{k} + (v\bar{k}_u - \bar{k}_s)\dot{h}}{(1-h)\bar{k}_u},$$

$$\dot{h} = (1-h)[nx(v) - h\bar{z}].$$

Since in the neighborhood of a steady state $\dot{k}$ depends only on h [see eq. (34)], the above two equations define a system of two differential equations in v and h for values close to the steady state. There are only two possible stable configurations for the $\dot{v} = 0$ and $\dot{h} = 0$ schedules which are shown in figs. 9 and 10.

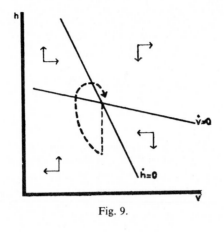

Fig. 9.

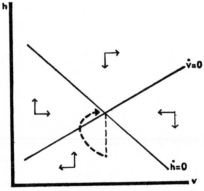

Fig. 10.

Following an increase in the migration tax, the new intersection of the $\dot{v} = 0$ and $\dot{h} = 0$ schedules must be at the same level of v (the employment ratio) and a higher h (human capital ratio); this follows from the steady-state results described in table 3. Thus both schedules must shift vertically upwards by the same proportional amount, leaving in both cases the initial steady-state values of v and h in a region where the rate of change of the employment ratio is negative and that of the human capital ratio is positive. The dynamic behavior of h and v following the increase in the migration tax is described in figs. 9 and 10 by the paths starting at point A. It is clear that in both cases the employment ratio in the unskilled sector must initially *fall* following the implementation of the migration tax, although in the long run it eventually goes back to its initial level.

5.2.3. Short-run effects on the capital–labor ratio and the human capital ratio. The signs of the short-run responses of h and k due to' a change in the migration cost must be equal to the signs of the derivatives $\partial h/\partial M$ and $\partial k/\partial M$ evaluated around the original steady state. In both the flexible wage and minimum wage regimes, the signs of these derivatives are

$$\partial \dot{h}/\partial M = -(1-h)h\partial z/\partial M > 0,$$

$$\partial \dot{k}/\partial M = kh\partial z/\partial M < 0.$$

Thus, in both regimes, the short-run effect of the migration tax is to increase the human capital ratio and decrease the capital–labor ratio. To the extent that the human capital ratio is always increased in the long run, there is no disparity between the direction of the short- and long-run effects of the tax. The capital–labor ratio, however, may rise or fall in the steady state depending on relative factor intensities, and thus the direction of the short-run response may be the same or opposite to the long-run response.

6. Conclusions

The model presented here has attempted to describe the dynamic path and comparative static changes of a modified neoclassical growth model where individuals have three basic behavioral decisions: education, migration and capital accumulation. The simplest possible assumptions were made with respect to the determination of those decisions, despite which many of the responses of the system to changes in exogenous parameters were undetermined, mainly in regard to the behavior of the capital–labor ratio and per capita consumption. Contrary to most of the literature, the model analyzed the effects of minimum wages in the context of a dynamic, growing economy.[7] In this regard it was found that minimum wage fixation in the skilled sector is always inconsistent with a locally stable interior solution. The model proves abundant in comparative static results, some of them in the expected, intuitive direction, others not. Among the latter we can mention the independence of factor rewards from the migration cost and the foreign wage and, in the case of a minimum wage in the unskilled sector, the independence of the human capital ratio from the cost of education.

The difference between the short- and long-run response of factor rewards, unemployment rate and factor endowments to the introduction of a tax on the income of migrants was analyzed in the last section of the paper. It was found that even though the tax does not affect the long-run levels of real factor rewards or the unemployment rate, it unambiguously produces in the short run an income distribution from labor towards capital (in the flexible wages regime) or an

[7]A dynamic Harris–Todaro type model is presented in Robertson and Wellisz (1974). Their model is concerned, however, with the rural–urban migration problem and no allowance is made there for human capital or education.

increase in the unemployment rate (when a minimum wage in the unskilled sector prevails), effects which certainly should be taken into account by weighing them against any long-run desirable consequences of the tax.

References

Berry, R. and R. Soligo, 1969, Some welfare aspects of international migration, Journal of Political Economy 77.

Bhagwati, J. and W. Dellalfar, 1973, The brain drain and income taxation, World Development 1, nos. 1 and 2.

Bhagwati, J. and K. Hamada, 1974, The brain drain, international integration of markets for professionals and unemployment: A theoretical analysis, Journal of Development Economics 1, no. 1.

Corden, W. and R. Findlay, 1975, Urban unemployment, inter-sectoral capital mobility and development policy, Economica, February.

Grubel, H. and A. Scott, 1966, The international flow of human capital, American Economic Review, May.

Harris, J. and M. Todaro, 1970, Migration, unemployment and development: A two sector analysis, American Economic Review, March.

Johnson, H.G. 1967, Some economic aspects of brain drain, Pakistan Development Review 3.

Kenen, P., 1971, Migration, the terms of trade and economic welfare in the source country, in: J. Bhagwati, R. Jones, R. Mundell, and J. Vanek, eds., Trade, balance of payments and growth (North-Holland, Amsterdam).

McCulloch, R. and J. Yellen, 1974, Factor mobility and the steady state distribution of income, Discussion Paper No. 369 (Harvard Institute of Economic Research, Cambridge, MA), June.

*McCulloch, R. and J. Yellen, 1975, Should the brain be taxed? Paper presented at the Bellagio Conference on Brain Drain and Income Taxation, Bellagio, Italy.

Rodriguez, C., 1975, On the welfare aspects of international migration, Journal of Political Economy, forthcoming.

Sjaastad, L., 1962, The costs and returns of human migration, Journal of Political Economy, October (supplement).

Wellisz, S. and P. Robertson, 1974, Steady state growth of an economy with intersectoral migration, Working Paper (Department of Economics, Columbia University, New York).

CHAPTER 10

EFFICIENCY, EQUALITY, INCOME TAXATION AND THE BRAIN DRAIN

A second-best argument

Koichi HAMADA*

Tokyo University, Tokyo, Japan

This note conducts a second-best examination of the effect of the brain drain. If the size distribution of income is a welfare objective, lump-sum taxation is unavailable, and an Atkinson-type optimal income tax is used, it is shown that the opportunity to emigrate will create special difficulties for the LDC policy-maker.

In the absence of domestic distortions, static welfare theory tells us that a 'small' brain drain will not cause harm to the people remaining behind as far as their per capita income is concerned.[1] However, if we consider the size distribution of income as one of the welfare objectives, then the presence of the opportunity of emigration for the highly educated imposes an additional difficulty for the government. This note is designed to illustrate this point in the context of the theory of optimal income taxation.[2]

Suppose that the leisure–income or education–income choice of individuals depends on the marginal rate of income taxation. If a lump-sum tax in its purest form is impossible, we then have the second-best problem of choosing between efficiency and income equality.

Using a particular formulation developed by Atkinson (1973), we assume that the individual's earnings depend on ability n and on the number of years of education received S. While undergoing education the individual has zero income and after education he works for R years, which is common to every individual, earning an annual income of $Z(n, S)$ ($Z_n > 0$, $Z_S > 0$ and $Z_{SS} < 0$). The after-tax income of the individual is given by $\alpha + \beta Z(n, S)$, where

$$(1 - \beta)Z(n, S) = T(Z)$$

---

*I am very much indebted to Jagdish Bhagwati and Asim Dasgupta for their constructive suggestions. A brief statement of similar arguments is also made in Cooper (1974).
[1]Grubel and Scott (1966). See also Johnson (1972).
[2]Mirrlees (1971). See also Sheshinski (1972) and Atkinson (1973).

is the linear tax schedule, with α as a guaranteed minimum income and $(1-\beta)$ the marginal rate of taxation, and he maximizes the present value of his lifetime income,

$$I = \int_S^{S+R} \{\alpha + \beta Z(n, S)\} \, e^{-it} \, dt,$$

where i is the rate of interest. After the maximization, the earning function $Z(n, S)$ can be rewritten as a function of n, α and β, that is,

$$Z(n, S) = z(n, \alpha, \beta), \qquad \frac{\partial z}{\partial n} > 0, \frac{\partial z}{\partial \alpha} < 0, \frac{\partial z}{\partial \beta} > 0.$$

Now, if $f(n)$ is the frequency distribution of people with inert ability of type n, then the revenue constraint of the government, on the assumption that the net revenue to be obtained by taxing and subsidizing all individuals (with ability varying from the infimum to the supremum level of n) is zero, can be written as

$$\int_{\tilde{n}}^{\bar{n}} \{\alpha - (1-\beta) z(n, \alpha, \beta)\} f(n) \, dn = 0. \tag{1}$$

We assume $f(n) > 0$ for $\tilde{n} \le n \le \bar{n}$, where $\tilde{n}(\ge 0)$ and $\bar{n}(> 0)$ are constants indicating the infimum and supremum level of inert ability, respectively.

The usual utilitarian procedure is to plan the tax schedule so that it maximizes, with respect to α and β and subject to (1), the integral

$$\int_{\tilde{n}}^{\bar{n}} U(I) f(n) \, dn, \tag{2}$$

where $U(I)$ is a concave utility function. Since (1) determines the value of α in terms of β, one can write the problem as that of maximizing

$$\int_{\tilde{n}}^{\bar{n}} U(I(n, \beta)) f(n) \, dn$$

with respect to β. The first-order condition for the maximum is

$$\int_{\tilde{n}}^{\bar{n}} \frac{\partial}{\partial \beta} U(I(n, \beta)) f(n) \, dn = 0. \tag{3}$$

It should be noticed that, in this formulation of the problem of optimal linear income taxation, the income of an individual receiving more than the average income is reduced when the marginal tax rate $(1-\beta)$ is increased.[3]

[3]This is because α is a decreasing function of $(1-\beta)$ under the normal circumstances. Cf. Itsumi (1974, pp. 371–381).

Now let us introduce the possibility of emigration. Suppose that the potential income to be earned abroad by an individual with inert ability n is given exogenously. Then, the proportion γ of emigration from the population with inert ability n can be assumed to be a function of the domestic disposable income I. The value of domestic disposable income is a function of n, α and β. But by rewriting the revenue constraint of the government, we have

$$\int_{\tilde{n}}^{\bar{n}} \{\alpha - (1-\beta)z(n, \alpha, \beta)\}\{1 - \gamma(I(n, \alpha, \beta))\}f(n)\,\mathrm{d}n = 0, \tag{1'}$$

so that α can again be expressed as a function of β. Therefore γ can be written now as

$$\gamma = g(I(n, \beta)).$$

Now, one of the features of the brain drain is that emigrants possess high intellectual ability. Thus emigrants are normally from the population earning more than the average income. Because the increase in the marginal tax rate $(1-\beta)$, or the decrease in β, reduces the income of the population earning more than the average income, and accordingly increases incentives for emigration, it is natural to suppose that

$$\frac{\partial g}{\partial \beta} < 0.$$

Now, define the value of n for the individual who is earning the average income as n^*. In this context of linear (negative) income taxation, individuals with ability greater than n^* are receiving more than the average income. Thus we can summarize our assumption as:

$$\gamma \equiv g(n, \beta) = 0 \qquad \text{if } n \leq n^*,$$

$$1 \geq g(n, \beta) \geq 0 \quad \text{and} \quad \frac{\partial g}{\partial \beta} < 0 \qquad \text{if } n > n^*.\,[4]$$

Under this framework, we shall now choose as the welfare criterion the per capita utility (or per capita equivalent income) of those remaining behind,

$$J(\beta) \equiv \int_{\tilde{n}}^{\bar{n}} U(I(n, \beta))\{1 - g(n, \beta)\}f(n)\,\mathrm{d}n \Big/ \int_{\tilde{n}}^{\bar{n}} \{1 - g(n, \beta)\}f(n)\,\mathrm{d}n. \tag{4}$$

---

[4] $\gamma \geq 0$ indicates that $\gamma > 0$ for some value of $\bar{n} > n > n^*$. Generally n^* may vary with the tax schedule. Rigorously, the assumption is that $g(n, \beta)$ is positive only if $n > n^*(\beta)$.

Note that the left-hand side is a function of β alone, because α is eliminated from the tax-revenue constraint (1').

In order to understand the property of the optimal rate of taxation $(1-\beta)$ in the presence of the emigration opportunity, let us now differentiate (4) with respect to β,[5]

$$J'(\beta) = \int \frac{\partial U}{\partial \beta} (1-g) f \, dn \Big/ \int (1-g) f \, dn - \int U \frac{\partial g}{\partial \beta} f \, dn \Big/ \int (1-g) f \, dn$$

$$+ \int U \cdot (1-g) f \, dn \cdot \int \frac{\partial g}{\partial \beta} f \, dn \Big/ \left\{ \int (1-g) f \, dn \right\}^2$$

$$= \int \frac{\partial U}{\partial \beta} (1-g) f \, dn \Big/ \int (1-g) f \, dn - \left[\int U \frac{\partial g}{\partial \beta} f \, dn \Big/ \int \frac{\partial g}{\partial \beta} f \, dn \right.$$

$$\left. - \int U \cdot (1-g) f \, dn \Big/ \int (1-g) f \, dn \right] \int \frac{\partial g}{\partial \beta} f \, dn \Big/ \int (1-g) f \, dn.$$

(5)

Now, $\int U(\partial g/\partial \beta) f \, dn / \int (\partial g/\partial \beta) f \, dn$ is the per capita utility of marginal emigrants before leaving the country; and $\int U(1-f) f \, dn / \int (1-g) f \, dn$ is the per capita utility of the total population $\int (1-g) f \, dn$. Therefore, from our assumption that only people above the average income are eligible for emigration, the expression in the bracket is positive. Noting further that $\partial g/\partial \beta < 0$, and accordingly that $\int (\partial g/\partial \beta) f \, dn < 0$, we then have

$$- \left[\int U \frac{\partial g}{\partial \beta} f \, dn \Big/ \int \frac{\partial g}{\partial \beta} f \, dn - \int U(1-g) f \, dn \Big/ \int (1-g) f \, dn \right]$$

$$\times \int \frac{\partial g}{\partial \beta} f \, dn \Big/ \int (1-g) f \, dn > 0.$$

Let us denote by $(1-\hat{\beta})$ the optimal rate of linear income taxation for a closed economy with the constant population $\int (1-g) f \, dn$. Then the first term of (5) vanishes for such a value of $\hat{\beta}$. Therefore we obtain

$$J'(\hat{\beta}) > 0.$$

(6)

In the normal case, where the second-order conditions are satisfied, equation

---

[5] The range of integrals and the arguments in functions are omitted to simplify the notation.

(6) then indicates that *the optimal marginal rate of income taxation* $(1-\beta)$ *should be lower for an open economy with the possibility (or the threat) of emigration than for a closed economy.* In this comparison between a closed economy composed of the nonemigrants and an open economy inclusive of potential emigrants, we have then shown that the open economy must sacrifice its utilitarian or egalitarian objective to give negative incentives for emigration by lowering the marginal rate of income taxation.[6]

Another, probably more meaningful, comparison, however, is between the situation where there are potential emigrants in a closed economy, and the one where these potential emigrants have the opportunity to emigrate. In other words, we may compare the maximand of an open economy, $J(\beta)$ in (4), with the maximand of the closed economy,

$$\int_{\tilde{n}}^{\bar{n}} U(I(n, \beta)) f(n) \, dn.$$

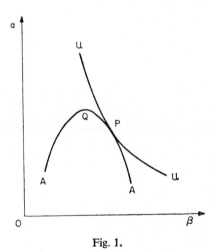

Fig. 1.

In order to carry out this comparison, let us return to the original formulation (1) and (2) of a closed economy, which explicitly takes account of α as well as β. The feasible combination of α and β can be depicted as curve AA in fig. 1. On the other hand, the iso-per-capita utility indifference curve can be drawn as

---

[6]Even in the absence of emigration possibility, *some* sacrifice of per capita income has to be made in order to obtain utilitarian or egalitarian objectives in this second-best formulation. Our analysis shows that *additional* sacrifices must be made in an open economy with the opportunity of emigration. If there is another policy variable, such as an education subsidy, the economy can 'almost' reach the first-best optimum with income equality in a closed economy [cf. Hamada (1974, pp. 145–158)]. However, this mechanism would not work for an open economy with the possibility of emigration, and the economy would have to sacrifice its egalitarian objective to limit the incentives for emigration.

UU. The point of tangency P gives the optimal configuration of α and β.[7] Now let us introduce the possibility of emigration. The society will maximize, subject to (1'), the following expression,

$$J(\alpha, \beta) = \int_{\bar{n}}^{\bar{\bar{n}}} U(I(n, \alpha, \beta))\{1 - \gamma(n, \alpha, \beta)\} f(n) \, dn /$$

$$\int_{\bar{n}}^{\bar{\bar{n}}} \{1 - \gamma(n, \alpha, \beta)\} f(n) \, dn. \tag{2'}$$

Then from our assumption that $\gamma(n, \alpha, \beta) \geq 0$ for $n > n^*$ and zero otherwise, one can deduce from (1') that the same β gives a smaller value of α than in the case of a closed economy (1).[8] Thus the feasibility locus AA shifts downward. Similarly, because only those individuals earning more than average go abroad, it can be shown that the same combination of α and β gives a smaller per capita utility (2') for an open economy.[9] Therefore the iso-per-capita utility curve $J(\alpha, \beta) =$ const. (UU) also shifts upward for the open economy. Accordingly we have shown that *the per capita welfare* (2') *in the open economy with the opportunity for emigration is strictly inferior to the per capita welfare* (2) *in the closed economy.*

It is easy to see that the difficulties presented here stem from the distorting nature of the brain drain, namely that not all the workers but only workers of a highly skilled category are allowed to move. Needless to say, if the income taxation of the emigrants by the home country were possible at all,[10] it would mitigate, by shifting the $\gamma(n, \beta)$ schedule, this additional difficulty for a government that pursues the egalitarian welfare objective.

----

[7] For the property that P lies to the right of Q (the max–min Rawlsian taxation), see Sheshinski (1972).

[8] Let α_0 be the value of α corresponding to β in the closed economy, and α_1 the value of α corresponding to the same value of β in the open economy, both on the feasibility locus AA. That is,

$$\alpha_0 = (1 - \beta) \int z(n, \alpha_0, \beta) f(n) \, dn,$$
$$\alpha_1 \int (1 - \gamma) f(n) \, dn = (1 - \beta) \int z(n, \alpha_1, \beta)(1 - \gamma) f(n) \, dn.$$

We would like to show that $\alpha_1 < \alpha_0$. Assume the contrary, then $\alpha_1 \geq \alpha_0$. On the other hand writing $\gamma \equiv \gamma(n, \alpha_1, \beta)$ and $f \equiv f(n)$, we have

$$\alpha_1 \int (1 - \gamma) f \, dn = (1 - \beta) \int z(n, \alpha_1, \beta)(1 - \gamma) f \, dn$$
$$< (1 - \beta) \int z(n, \alpha_1, \beta) f \, dn \cdot \int (1 - \gamma) f \, dn$$
$$< (1 - \beta) \int z(n, \alpha_0, \beta) f \, dn \cdot \int (1 - \gamma) f \, dn$$
$$= \alpha_0 \int (1 - \gamma) f \, dn.$$

This leads to the contradiction $\alpha_1 < \alpha_0$. The second inequality comes from $z_\alpha < 0$; the first inequality comes from writing $\bar{z} = \int z(n, \alpha, \beta) f \, dn$ and noting that $\gamma \geq 0$ only when $n > n^*$, so that

$$\int_{\bar{n}}^{\bar{\bar{n}}} \{z(n, \alpha, \beta) - \bar{z}\}(1 - \gamma) f \, dn = \int_{\bar{n}}^{\bar{\bar{n}}} \{z(n, \alpha, \beta) - \bar{z}\} f \, dn$$
$$- \int_{n^*}^{\bar{\bar{n}}} \{z(n, \alpha, \beta) - \bar{z}\} \gamma f \, dn < 0. \tag{7}$$

[9] This statement can be derived by a similar reasoning as used for (7) in footnote 8.

[10] Cf. Bhagwati and Dellalfar (1973).

References

Atkinson, A.B. 1973, How progressive should income tax be, in: M. Parkin, ed., Essays in modern economics (Longmans, London) 90–109.

Bhagwati, J. and W. Dellalfar, 1973, The brain drain and income taxation: A proposal, World Development 1, 94–101.

Cooper, R.N., 1974, Economic mobility and national economic policy (Almqvist and Wiksell, Stockholm).

Grubel, H.B. and A.D. Scott, 1966, The international flow of human capital, American Economic Review 56, 268–74.

Hamada, K., 1974, Income taxation and education subsidy, Journal of Public Economics 3, 145–158.

Itsumi, Y., 1974, Distributional effects of linear income tax schedules, Review of Economic Studies 41, 371–381.

Johnson, H.G., 1972, Labor mobility and the brain drain, in: G. Ranis, ed., The gap between rich and poor nations (Macmillan, London).

Mirrlees, J.A., 1971, An exploration in the theory of optimal income taxation, Review of Economic Studies 38, 175–208.

Sheshinski, E., 1972, The optimal linear income tax, Review of Economic Studies 39, 297–302.

PART IV

EMPIRICAL ANALYSIS OF THE BRAIN DRAIN
DCs and LDCs

EDITOR'S NOTE*

Jagdish N. BHAGWATI

1. Introduction

The quantitative estimates of gains and losses resulting from the brain drain must rest on prior conceptualization of these gains and losses. This has already been done in this volume in the introduction (ch. 1) as well as in the theoretical review of Bhagwati and Rodriguez (ch. 5).

There are, in fact, few attempts at making realistic estimates of the *consequences* of the brain drain. Before reviewing these, so as to put the papers by Reubens and Berry–Mendez in this part into perspective, note that quantitative measures of the *magnitudes* of the brain drain are indeed available, though they are inevitably built on data that are subject to the serious limitations noted in ch. 1.

It is nonetheless clear from Reubens' valuable paper (ch. 11) that the magnitudes of these PTK (professional, technical and kindred) flows from LDCs into DCs are *not* large as proportions of DC stock or (annual, incremental) flow of PTK manpower for the three major DC recipients: the U.S., U.K. and Canada.[1] On the other hand, it is equally important to note that small absolute numbers or proportions do *not* necessarily imply that the *consequences* of such migration are also small. Thus, economists recognize, more generally, that a single transaction (or even the possibility, rather than the actuality, of a transaction) can be sufficient to establish the presence of a competitive market, though noneconomists will typically fall into the trap of equating the lack of 'many' transactions with the absence of a working market. Indeed, in the case of the flow of skilled manpower, where issues such as externalities and the effect of migration on domestic distortions (e.g., the Bhagwati–Hamada emulation effect) can be readily invoked, it is entirely reasonable to expect that what

---

*Thanks are due to Ray Hill for research assistance in writing this note.
[1]This is true regardless of whether nonimmigrant PTKs, entering into the U.S., for example, on temporary visas, are included or not. Reubens' inclusion of these is somewhat dubious because, as with the distinction between short-term and long-term loans, one should distinguish between temporary inflow and immigrant inflow: just as short-term loans may be renewed forever and long-term loans may be repaid prior to maturity, the temporary migrant may decide to continue as a migrant for long periods and the immigrant may return home prematurely. Clarity in discussion requires here a convention; and it seems best to consider the two sets of flows as separate entities.

look like small numbers of migrants could cause large effects. Furthermore, large aggregates such as 'physicians' can hide substantial variations by dis-aggregated occupations (e.g., neurosurgeons) so that the inference of smallness from the overall aggregates often does conceal 'large' numbers in some occupa-tions.[2]

Having entered these caveats, however, about simple measures of magnitude of the flows of PTK manpower from LDCs to DCs, we can consider the estimates of the *consequences* of these flows. Recalling the discussion in ch. 1, as also in the Bhagwati–Rodriguez paper in ch. 5, one can then classify the few available estimates as follows. We will consider only the estimates regarding the existing brain drain – as distinct from purely hypothetical estimates or estimates relating to other kinds of immigration.[3] We can also classify the former as those relating to the 'gains to DCs' and those relating to the 'loss of LDCs'.

2. The effect of the brain drain on gains to the DCs

There are basically three different types of measures which have been made in the literature.

(1) The 1974 UNCTAD study (earlier referred to in chs. 1 and 5), works out the gains to DCs as the gain of the immigrants themselves *plus* a simple, hypo-thetical 'externality' effect for the rest of the DC population, the latter being related as a simple set of alternative percentages to the welfare gain of the immigrants.

The study focuses only on the gains of the United States (from immigration of PTK manpower from all LDCs). The component of these gains represented

---

[2]In this connection, the reader should also note the discussion by Reubens of the quality problem, which is raised by the American doctors in particular. It is generally claimed that the foreign doctors who are allowed to immigrate into the U.S. are of inferior quality, the test being frequently the fact that they fail the tests devised by the AMA. This 'evidence' needs to be taken with more than the usual cynicism, as most nondoctor immigrants tend to compare the American medical system unfavourably with their own – frequently citing lack of intuition, trigger-happiness by specialists who like to operate at the first sight of a willing patient, etc. – and the casual testimony of many immigrant doctors, for example, suggests that they have far more experience and ability than American doctors in equivalent age-groups, the major advantage that native American doctors enjoy being, in many cases, access to better equipment and facilities. Also, as every teacher knows, it is always easy to devise tests which work to exclude from success those who have not had the benefit of particular texts and teachers: it is highly probable that U.S. doctors would flunk Indian medical tests in numbers as large as the other way around! I would be inclined therefore to take the AMA complaints of foreign doctors' inadequacies with more than mere skepticism.

[3]Among these latter, there are only two which are worth mentioning, both in papers re-viewed by Bhagwati and Rodriguez in ch. 5. The first is Johnson (1967), where the income loss in a one-product Cobb–Douglas economy by labour migration is estimated. The other is Mishan and Needleman (1968); they estimate the income effect of immigration, using a CES production function (and a dynamic framework so that the time-path of the income impact is also worked out) and also making adjustments for hypothetical terms of trade changes.

by the improved incomes of the immigrants is estimated as simply the *PDV* of the migrants, taking the difference between DC and LDC earnings over their lifetime. Alternative assumptions ('high', 'median' and 'low') are made with regard to the rate of discount chosen for arriving at the *PDV* values, as also for the externality coefficient used to arrive at the second component of the

Table 1

Contributions to the United States net income gain, by developing countries, from skilled immigration into the United States in 1970 under 'median' assumptions.[a]

Country	Total number of immigrants (1)	Net income gain (million U.S. $)		
		Scientists and engineers (2)	Physicians and surgeons (3)	Total (4)
Asia	8,993	1,809.1	1,092.4	2,901.5
Philippines	2,318	383.8	496.8	880.6
India	3,141	718.2	156.3	874.5
Korea (Rep. of)	541	77.5	147.3	224.8
Hong Kong	262	54.8	26.5	81.3
Other	1,797	400.6	116.3	516.9
Near and Middle East	934	174.2	149.2	323.4
Africa	1,212	252.2	121.4	373.6
Latin America	1,031	172.4	214.5	386.9
Cuba	114	15.3	33.6	48.9
Colombia	114	19.2	23.3	42.5
Mexico	92	15.5	18.7	34.2
Argentina	73	10.1	20.7	30.8
Brazil	70	15.5	4.5	20.0
Peru	41	6.9	8.4	15.3
Venezuela	42	7.6	7.1	14.7
Ecuador	32	4.4	9.0	13.4
Chile	33	5.4	7.1	12.5
Bolivia	24	2.2	9.7	11.9
Other	396	70.0	72.4	142.4
Developing countries[b]	11,236	2,233.7	1,428.3	3,662.0

[a] *Source*: Table IX from the UNCTAD study.
[b] The externality factor used was 2 percent.

gain to DCs (i.e., the gains to the nonimmigrant DC population). The net result of this exercise, for 'median' assumptions, is that the UNCTAD estimates the 'net income gained by the United States from skilled immigrants into the United States from developing countries in 1970' to be a figure as large as $3.7 billion (see table 1).

Unfortunately, the bulk of this large number is nothing but the gains to the immigrants themselves, and ch. 1 has already discussed at 'ength why this is a procedure which is dubious, at best, and wrong, at worst.[4] And an insignificant fraction constituting the rest of the sum is nothing but a simple assumption. So we are left really with little that is useful here.

(2) Two other measures, which have been produced by Reubens in his paper and by the U.S. House (1974) are, in fact, not welfare measures at all but are really what I called in ch. 1 the *SIC* measure.

Reubens' careful estimates of *SIC* are readily available in this volume and hence need not be repeated.[5] Note merely that his best estimates refer to the United States, next to the U.K., and the Canadian estimates are already verging on the hypothetical.[6] More importantly, he presents estimates which are 'special' on two grounds: (i) he does not take into account the full costs of education, but only the post-college educational costs, on the ground that everyone gets educated up to college level anyway in the DCs; and (ii) he would like to exclude from his reckoning, quite naturally, the educational attainments reached in the DCs themselves, so that he excludes what he calls the 'student stay-ons' altogether from his preferred calculation. The former procedure is certainly sound, though a logical consequence of it might have been for Reubens to put his *SIC* measure against only the post-college outlays in DCs rather than against total educational expenditures, to convey to the reader a proper sense of how 'large' or 'small' the *SIC* measure of the PTK imm'gration was. The second adjustment, however, is seriously incomplete because it excludes altogether the fact that many LDC students already come with post-college education and that, in many cases, the U.S. professional education is relatively marginal, and often only a method of acquiring the credentials (much like the Arrow–Spence theory of education) or even acquiring the instrument of job competition (much as in the Bhagwati–Srinivasan theory of education) to get suitable job offers, and hence the ability to immigrate under current immigration rules in the DCs. Indeed, one can think, through sheer casual empiricism alone, of countless cases where students have gone from first-rate LDC institutions to second- and third-rate DC institutions, just in order to 'get out and make it'. Insofar therefore as this LDC professional training is ignored in the reckoning by

---

[4]Quite aside from the crippling conceptual basis for the UNCTAD estimate, it is also subject to the problem that it does not adjust the estimates downwards at all for reverse and to-and-fro migration.

[5]Reubens describes his measure as *ACE* (avoided costs of education) in preference to my earlier *SIC* terminology; but the two are the same, if properly computed.

[6]Also his immigration estimates for the U.K. are dramatically below those reported, from an alternative source, by Balacs and Gordon in Bhagwati–Partington (1976). The Reubens estimates relate only to the B-voucher entrants, though he considers the problem of A-voucher entrants as well. The differences in the Balacs–Gordon and Reubens estimates also imply differences in concepts: a problem that does not arise with the well-defined PTK categories in U.S. immigration statistics.

omitting 'student stay-ons', the Reubens *SIC* estimates are again an under-estimate of the *SIC* measure.

The U.S. House report does not state all its assumptions in the same detail as Reubens carefully does, so it is difficult to assess its significance. However, it does explicitly use the official immigration data for the United States, which are naturally 'gross' data that make no adjustments at all for reverse outflows or for the educational level at which the migrants entered the U.S. Its estimates of *SIC* are reproduced, however, in table 2 here, and indicate that these measures were at a level of nearly a billion U.S. dollars per annum during 1971 and 1972.[7]

Recall, however, that, no matter how sophisticated one gets in making up SIC estimates, they are *not* welfare measures and, at best, provide only one of the pieces of information that could be useful in arriving at a welfare measure of the impact of the PTK immigration into the DCs.[8]

(3) Finally, mention might be made of Amuzegar's estimate of the 'worth of the services of these professionals and skilled immigrants to the host country': which is the *flow* counterpart of the *SIC* measure – this correspondence being only approximate as the latter is *not* identical to the capitalized value of the former because of the adjustments (e.g., subtraction for educational expenses incurred in DCs for training the LDC PTK immigrants) in the latter. Amuzegar estimates this worth to be $315 million in 1967, for over 23,000 professional and semi-professionals and 13,000 technicians and operative immigrants, all from LDCs in Asia, Africa and Latin America.[9]

Needless to say, this 'worth' measure is about as lacking in welfare significance as the *SIC* measure, despite its possible interest for other purposes.

3. The effect of the brain drain on losses to LDCs

Here again, we can distinguish among three major types of estimates.

---

[7]See U.S. House (1974, p. 172). In addition to the Reubens and the House report estimates, there are available in the literature stray, but rarely-spelled-out 'estimates' of such *SIC* 'gains' to DCs. Thus, Amuzegar, now of OPEC fame, has stated that:

Professor Richard Titmuss of the London School of Economics, however, puts the number of doctors, scientists, and engineers absorbed by the United States from the outside world between 1949 and 1967 at 100,000 and the 'savings' for the United States by not having to educate and train this enormous number of skilled manpower at $4 billion – a figure considered greater than total American foreign aid during the same period. Still another estimate, based on (1) an average cost figure of $20,000 (suggested by the 1967 U.S. House staff report on brain drain) for the education and training of a scientific professional, and (2) the emigration to the United States of over 38,000 scientists, engineers, and physicians in the five years between 1962 and 1966 alone may put the 'investment loss' by the developing countries at over $7,600 million [Amuzegar (1968, p. 703)].

[8]These issues have been discussed thoroughly in ch. 1, in the subsection on gains to DCs (excluding immigrants).

[9]Amuzegar (1968, p. 703).

Table 2

Total estimated savings to the United States in educational costs of immigrant scientists, engineers, physicians and surgeons entering the United States from LDCs as immigrants, fiscal years 1971 and 1972 (in U.S. $).[a]

Area	Fiscal Year 1971		Fiscal Year 1972		Total (1971 and 1972)	
	Scientists, engineers, physicians, surgeons	Estimated educational savings[b]	Scientists, engineers, physicians, surgeons	Estimated educational savings	Scientists, engineers, physicians, surgeons	Estimated educational savings
All countries	18,850	$952,424,560	18,466	$1,003,667,440	37,316	$1,956,092,000
All LDCs[c]	16,315	835,459,560	16,012	882,820,000	32,327	1,718,279,560
West Europe: Greece	217	10,302,200	190	10,444,254	407	20,746,454
Latin America[d]	1,378	89,574,120	1,279	70,836,680	2,657	160,410,800
Asia	13,803	705,406,440	13,713	757,177,400	27,516	1,462,583,840
Near and Middle East	1,036	57,862,560	1,239	76,860,680	2,275	134,723,240
Far East	12,767	647,543,880	12,474	680,316,720	25,241	1,327,860,600
China	1,104	49,724,160	934	46,686,800	2,038	96,410,960
India	5,283	241,050,280	5,369	278,976,760	10,652	520,027,040
Korea	1,449	99,243,000	1,336	87,038,880	2,805	186,281,880
Pakistan	791	36,136,400	751	39,393,480	1,542	75,529,880
Philippines	2,568	141,755,840	2,371	124,844,200	4,939	266,600,040
Other	1,572	79,551,200	1,693	103,376,600	3,265	182,927,800
Africa	811	39,794,920	692	37,206,240	1,503	77,001,160
Egypt	533	26,158,360	354	18,215,920	877	44,374,280
Other	278	13,363,560	338	18,990,320	616	32,353,880
All other areas	106	4,639,920	138	7,155,760	244	11,795,680

[a]*Source*: U.S. House (1974, table 29). For further details, see the report.

[b]The figure for the estimated educational savings for immigrant scientists, engineers, physicians and surgeons is computed on the basis of $9,070 as representing an approximation of the annual average cost per student and $83,000 per person for medical undergraduate school costs for 4 years of training. The $9,070 figure, relating specifically to estimated real costs of higher education for the year 1971–72, was computed by Bowen and Servelle in a study published by the American Association for Higher Education. In presenting the data, the authors state: 'These estimates are crude and should be used only to indicate rough orders of magnitude. Even so, the table shows how heavily the real costs of higher education bear upon students and their families' [Bowen and Servelle (1972)].

The estimated figure of $83,000 per person for educational costs of a physician was cited in Henderson (1970, p. 132). Henderson cites this figures for surgeons who are, as he says, 'the most expensive'. However, the figure of $83,000 per person is not excessively high as Henderson suggests. According to a recent report by the AAMC (1973, pp. 1–2), the annual cost per medical student in the undergraduate medical educational program leading to the M.D. degree is estimated to range from a low of $16,300 to a high of $26,400. Over 4 years this would amount to $65,200 and $105,600, respectively. The average total annual cost from a selected 12 schools amounts to $21,350 per student, or a 4-year total of $85,400. The estimate, figured in 1972 dollars, was based upon a study of 12 medical schools. The components used in computing costs were instruction, research, clinical activity, other administrative, scholarly, and professional activities. The report indicated that even this figure represents only a part of the total cost of preparing a physician for independent practice.

[c]LDCs are understood to mean the following areas and countries [listed in NSF (1973, table 1)] Greece, North and Central America (excluding Canada), South America, Asia, Africa, and 'all other areas'.

[d]Latin America is understood to mean those areas and countries listed in NSF table 1 as North and Central America (excluding Canada) and South America.

The statistical data in this table relating to the number of immigrants and areas are drawn from NSF (1973, p. 2).

(1) The 1974 UNCTAD study estimates the income impact of LDCs of PTK emigrants, essentially by guesswork, as a certain proportion again of the sum of the incomes of the emigrants themselves and a fraction thereof which is given as the externality component. The conceptual basis for the former component, as an indicator of welfare change, is negligible, at best, and the latter component is built on nothing more than simple 'guesswork'. Hence, the resulting measure of the loss of LDCs that the UNCTAD study comes up with, lying between an average of 45,000 to 10,000 U.S. Dollars in 1970 per PTK immigrant into the U.S., is not of much significance to an economist.[10]

(2) More interesting, but still not of welfare significance, are the LIC estimates of the brain drain. A recent example is in the 1974 U.S. House report, already cited for its *SIC* estimates of DC savings. Its estimate of the lost investment costs for LDCs, arising from the brain drain, are reproduced here in table 3. For 1971 and 1972, they come to an annual sum of nearly $325 million, and are based on the figure of investment costs in LDCs per PTK emigrant of roughly $20,000 per professional.

(3) Finally, the only significant (even if incomplete) attempt at estimating the welfare consequences of the brain drain, in an empirical context, for an LDC appears to be that made by Berry and Mendez in this volume for Colombia (ch. 12). It primarily focuses on the implications of educational subsidization but is notable also for its attempt to include offsetting elements such as remittances. Since the reader can judge the methods for himself, no further commentary is required from the editor. Note however that these losses can be significantly large, despite the inclusion of the offsetting elements in the making of the estimate and the difficulty of including the loss from externalities and 'factor-proportions-change' (which is, of course, the 'finite-emigration-loss' point made by Berry–Soligo originally in qualification of the Grubel–Scott proposition about no impact from infinitesimal emigration, as noted in ch. 5).

In conclusion, note that the literature on the brain drain also contains (at least) three attempts at estimating the *imputed flows of capital* implied by the flows of professionals. They however do not relate to the brain drain from LDCs to DCs: which is the focus of this volume. (i) Thus, Grubel and Scott (1966) estimated the gross 'inflow of human capital' into the U.S. during 1949–1961

---

[10]The averages refer to the simple average of the 'high' and the 'low' estimates in table 5 of the UNCTAD paper. These are *PDV* values of incomes in LDCs (though the data are primarily those of India but extended, with minor adjustment upwards for average salary differences between India and the other LDCs, to the LDCs of origin) as a group. Table 6 also presents these *PDV* values for LDCs as a group, by different skill groups, but without mentioning whether they are based on 'high', 'median' or 'low' assumptions with regard to the discount rate.

Table 3

Estimated educational cost to sending nations of immigrant scientists, engineers, physicians and surgeons entering United States from LDCs as immigrants, fiscal years 1971 and 1972 (in U.S. $).[a]

Area	Fiscal Year 1971		Fiscal Year 1972		Total (1971 and 1972)	
	Scientists, engineers, physicians, surgeons	Educational cost	Scientists, engineers, physicians, surgeons	Educational cost	Scientists, engineers, physicians, surgeons	Educational cost
All countries	18,850	$377,000,000	18,466	$369,320,000	37,316	$746,320,000
All LDCs[b]	16,315	326,300,000	16,012	320,240,000	32,327	646,540,000
West Europe: Greece	217	4,340,000	190	3,800,000	407	8,140,000
Latin America[c]	1,378	27,560,000	1,279	25,580,000	2,657	53,140,000
Asia	13,803	276,060,000	13,713	274,260,000	27,516	550,320,000
Near and Middle East	1,036	20,720,000	1,239	24,780,000	2,275	26,852,000
Far East	12,767	255,340,000	12,474	249,480,000	25,241	504,820,000
China	1,104	22,080,000	934	18,680,000	2,038	40,760,000
India	5,283	105,660,000	5,369	107,380,000	10,652	213,040,000
Korea	1,449	28,980,000	1,356	27,120,000	2,805	56,100,000
Pakistan	791	15,820,000	751	15,020,000	1,542	30,840,000
Philippines	2,568	51,360,000	2,371	47,420,000	4,939	98,780,000
Other	1,572	31,440,000	1,693	33,860,000	3,265	65,300,000
Africa	811	16,220,000	692	13,840,000	1,503	30,060,000
Egypt	533	10,660,000	354	7,080,000	887	17,740,000
Other	378	5,560,000	338	6,760,000	616	12,320,000
All other areas	106	2,120,000	138	2,760,000	244	4,880,000

[a]*Source*: U.S. House (1974, table 29).

[b]LDCs are intended to include the following countries and areas listed in the NSF (1973) report: Greece, North and Central America (excluding Canada), South America, Asia, Africa, and 'all other areas'.

[c]Latin America is intended to include those areas listed in NSF (1973, p. 2) as North and Central America (excluding Canada) and South America.

This table uses the figure of $20,000 as the cost of education per person. This figure was used 7 years ago (in 1967) by Dr. Kidd and the House Government Operations Committee. Some sources say the estimate is high; others say it is conservative. Thus, the estimate ought to be regarded as only an approximation of cost to the sending nations.

The table is based upon 2 assumptions: (1) that the $20,000 of education cost per person is a reasonable estimate; and (2) that those professionals entering as immigrants are remaining and establishing permanent residency.

as $1,055 million, or $23,000 per immigrant for 48,000 'scientists and engineers' immigrants. This human capital was estimated as a replacement cost in the U.S., basing it on direct educational costs *plus* foregone earnings.[11] Note that this estimate is the HC_i measure that was distinguished in ch. 1. (ii) In 1969, these two authors used similar techniques to measure the 'net gain in human capital' by Canada from the bilateral exchange of economists with the United States.[12] This paper therefore inevitably raises many of the conceptual issues distinguished in ch. 1, since the flow goes two ways and hence the distinctions between which country's costs are being considered, even for HC measures, become relevant, for example. The reader, in assessing the precise procedures used in the 1969 Grubel–Scott paper, must therefore keep in mind the issues raised in ch. 1; this is, however, not the occasion to make such an evaluation. (iii) Finally, we have Parai's (1965) calculation of HC_i, the replacement cost, at Canadian values of the net immigration of professional manpower into Canada during 1953–1963; putting the estimate at Canadian $455 million, composed of $240 million in direct educational cost and $215 million in foregone earnings.

[11]Since there was no information on the immigrants' education, each immigrant was assumed to be 23 years old, to have had 12 years of basic training, 4 years of university education, and 1 year of graduate study.
[12]Grubel and Scott (1969).

References

Amuzegar, J, 1968, Brain drain and the irony of foreign aid policy, Economia Internazionale 21.

Association of American Medical Colleges (AAMC), 1973, Undergraduate medical education: Elements, objectives, costs, Report of the committee on the financing of medical education (AAMC, Washington).

Bowen, H.R. and P. Servelle, 1972, Who benefits from higher education – And who should pay? ERIC Clearinghouse on Higher Education, George Washington University (American Association for Higher Education, Washington), 31–33.

Grubel, H. and A. Scott, 1966, The immigration of scientists and engineers to the United States, 1949–1961, Journal of Political Economy, August.

Grubel, H. and A. Scott, 1969, The international movement of human capital: Canadian estimates, Canadian Journal of Economics, 375–388.

Henderson, G, 1970, Emigration of highly skilled manpower from the developing countries (UNITAR, New York).

Johnson, H., 1967, Some economic aspects of brain drain, Pakistan Development Review.

Mishan, E, and L. Needleman, 1968, Immigration: Some long-term economic consequences, Economia Internazionale.

NSF, 1973, Highlights, immigrant scientists and engineers, August.

Parai, L., 1965, Immigration and emigration of professional and skilled manpower during the postwar period, ECC special study no. 1 (Queens Printer, Ottawa), 79–83.

U.S. House of Representatives, Committee of Foreign Affairs, 1974, Brain drain: A study of the persistent issue of international scientific mobility (GPO, Washington).

CHAPTER 11

SOME DIMENSIONS OF PROFESSIONAL IMMIGRATION INTO DEVELOPED COUNTRIES FROM LESS DEVELOPED COUNTRIES, 1960–1973

Edwin P. REUBENS*

City College of The City University of New York, New York, NY 10031, U.S.A.

1. Introduction

This paper presents some empirical dimensions of the immigration of professional, technical and kindred personnel (PTK) from the less developed countries (LDCs) as received by the developed coun·ries (DCs). For the chief receiving DCs, this immigration is measured not only in gross reported flows (which are the most commonly used measure in the brain drain literature), but also in estimates of net flows, accumulated stocks, and net changes in stocks. These gross and net magnitudes are then assessed in manpower terms, relative to the labor market for PTK in the receiving DCs, so as to obtain several measures of 'increments to the labor supply' (abbreviated as *ILS*). Finally, the net professional immigration is evaluated in financial terms, namely the 'avoided costs of education' at home (abbreviated as *ACE*),[1] and weighed against the total educational outlays in the receiving economy. All of these measurements, showing orders of relative magnitude, are intended as realistic guidelines for public policy on immigration control, on manpower programs and on proposals for compensating the LDCs for their contributions of migrants to the DCs.

The measures used in this paper are selected from a wide array of possible approaches, which include the demographic and ecological impact of immigration, the gross output or income of the immigrants, the net social marginal product (SMP) generated by the immigrants, the opportunity cost of the educational resources saved by obtaining trained personnel from abroad, and finally, the net gains from immigration as regards the domestic 'welfare' (including the distribution and incidence of those gains). Of these various approaches, the welfare criterion appeals most strongly to theoretical economists. But economic welfare is like Heaven in the old song: not everyone who talks

*The author wishes to acknowledge typing assistance from the Institute for World Order and editorial rules from the editor of the volume.
[1]The *ACE* measure corresponds to Bhagwati's term *SIC* (saving in investment costs), which appears in his introduction to this volume.

about it is really to going to enter there; and in fact this concept may not be statistically operational without much sacrifice of definitional purity.

Our adopted measures of *ILS* and *ACE* are specific, identifiable, and measurable with available data.[2] They are also close to the common sense of the brain drain problem; and are particularly relevant to the international issue among the nations concerned, namely the unrequited transfer of a capital asset from LDCs to DCs (sometimes described in United Nations debates as 'reverse foreign aid').

In our treatment of increments to the labor supply, we adopt primarily the usage of the Immigration and Naturalization Service (I.N.S.) of the United States – the country receiving the largest numbers of PTK immigrants, and reporting in the greatest detail; the data of other countries is brought into closest feasible conformity with the U.S. classifications. The term 'immigrants' refers to aliens officially reported each year as 'admitted to permanent residence' – but we point out some divergences, and make some adjustments, between those legal admissions and the actual physical entries (notably as regards 'stay-on students', who are included in the immigration statistics of some countries; also as regards 'limited-stay foreign workers', who are usually excluded from the immigration tables; and as regards 'illegal entrants', few of whom are believed to be PTK). In occupational scope, we deal with the whole category of so-called 'PTK' in the usage of the U.S.I.N.S., which extends from Ph.D.s and M.D.s through degree-holding engineers, accountants, architects, teachers, and so forth, to formally-trained (certificate-holding) technicians and nurses. We examine more closely certain important and debated occupations – notably physicians, nurses, scientists and engineers – where the inflow of foreign professionals is commonly supposed to be large and crucial.

In our treatment of educational costs for training PTKs in the DCs, we try as far as possible to count direct professional education (excluding prior education, which might have been undertaken anyway; and also excluding research, public services, and other institutional functions which are not primarily training activities) plus income foregone by students during their professional training. Because of complications in these exclusions and inclusions, we show at some points not only the narrower but also the more inclusive computations.

Beginning with a world-wide perspective on immigration and the PTK (section 2), we then focus on the cases of the U.S. (section 3), Canada (section 4) and the U.K. (section 5). For each of these receiving countries, we show: (1) PTK immigration trends: gross and net flows, stocks, and increments in stocks, of PTK from LDCs, 1960–1973; (2) Increments to the labor supply (*ILS*),

---

[2]Useful measurements along both these lines were made by Watanabe (1969), using data for earlier conditions (ending in 1966), and focussing on the LDCs. The *ACE* type of approach to the DCs receiving the immigration was applied to a limited range of occupations by Grubel and Scott (1966). For application of both the *ILS* and *ACE* measures to the effects of PTK emigration on the LDCs of origin, especially in the Asian countries which since 1966 have generated surpluses of PTK, see Reubens (1975).

from the gross and net immigration of PTK; and (3) Avoided costs of education (*ACE*): the replacement costs of PTK immigrants, and the relative magnitude of these costs in the host economy. Following the text pages are appendixes I–III.

2. Trends in immigration and the PTK share – gross and net

Large-scale international immigration has long been neglected in official circles as in most economic literature. Indeed, most economic theory assumes that national populations are fixed in place, and deal with each other's economies only through exchanges of goods, services, finance, and technology.

The largest scale of international movements of population in this century – other than emergency flights – was seen in the decade before World War I, when 750,000–1,200,000 aliens annually were admitted into the U.S. Thereafter, international migration was severely curtailed by prevailing conditions during World War I, and by restrictive quota legislation during the 1920s; and was reduced to far lower levels during the Great Depression and during World War II. However, in the 1950s immigration began to build up once more, attaining 400,000 admissions into the U.S. alone in 1973. This expansion has involved some new source countries and some new receiving countries, and has generated some apprehension regarding the magnitude, trend and composition of these migrations; in particular, that very large outflows of professional, technical and kindred personnel were moving from LDCs (which needed them), to settle in DCs (which are supposedly better supplied with such personnel).

The actual inflows of these professionals have gone predominantly to three nations: the U.S., Canada and the U.K.[3] Table 1 presents the gross immigration record as extracted and assembled from the immigration statistics of these three DCs.

The tabulation – together with less specific data for earlier years – shows that in the U.K. the inflow was at a peak early in the 1960s, and has subsequently been sharply reduced, largely by restrictive legislation and administration. In the case of Canada, which showed a rising trend, restraints were imposed after 1966. The U.S. has always been the largest recipient; and after the regulations were liberalized in 1965, the reported admissions zoomed far beyond those reported by the other receiving countries. Asians and other LDC professionals accounted for the largest share of the zoom. The three-country total doubled from the early to the later part of the 1960s, and rose by another 25 percent to the 1971–1972 level. In 1973, however, when the U.S. inflow dropped sharply while the Canadian figures rose, the three-country total probably declined.

In order to move from the gross figures of officially reported immigration to an estimate of the net inflow of foreign-trained professionals, several ad-

---

[3]On the much smaller inflows into continental Europe, see appendix I.

Table 1

Gross immigration of professional and technical personnel from less developed countries into the United States, Canada and United Kingdom, 1962–1973.[a]

Year	United States	Canada	United Kingdom	3-country sum
1962	9,024	1,381		
1963	11,029	1,525	4,600	17,154
1964	11,418	1,873	–	
1965	11,001	3,707	3,230	17,938
1966	13,986	5,548	–	
1967	23,361	7,897	2,900	34,158
1968	28,511	6,930	2,420	37,861
1969	27,536	7,585	1,720	36,841
1970	33,796	6,118	1,000	40,914
1971	38,647	5,184	1,270	45,101
1972	39,106	5,360	377	44,843
1973	31,939			

[a]Coverage of 'less developed countries' comprises all countries in Africa, Asia, North America (excluding Canada and the U.S.) and South America. Coverage of 'professional and technical personnel' is based on 'professional, technical, and kindred workers' in the usage of the United States Immigration and Naturalization Service Annual Reports, table 8; data refer to fiscal years (ending June 30 for year shown), and immigrants' country of birth. Data for Canada are taken from the closest corresponding occupational categories as reported by Department of Manpower and Immigration Annual Immigration Statistics, table 11, categories 2–48 inclusive; data refer to calendar years, and country of former residence. Figures for United Kingdom are blown up (at ratio of 100:85) from Commonwealth immigration data, according to country of citizenship, in Rose et al. (1969, pp. 83, 86), for the period 1962–1966, and from Home Office Commonwealth Immigrants Statistics, annual reports for the period 1967–72, table 9 covering arrivals of holders of 'category B-vouchers' (excluding those from Australia, Canada and New Zealand); calendar years.

Listing of persons by occupation is generally based on the immigrant's own declaration, subject to scrutiny by the immigration authorities. Canadian officials report that of all qualified immigrants (all occupations) about 60 percent enter their declared occupation after admission.

justments are necessary. First to be deducted is the annual outflow of foreign-born professionals who, having arrived as immigrants some time earlier, leave for home or other countries; this deduction yields what is commonly called 'net immigration'.

Another item which may be deducted for certain purposes is 'stay-on students': foreign students who arrived on student visas but upon graduation are granted visas for permanent residence. This category has long been included in U.S. immigration reports, and in Canada since 1967. These stay-on students, who have received their professional education largely at the expense of the host country, should be deducted when we estimate the *ACE* for foreign-trained immigrants (ideally, we should also allow for students who first return home, and subsequently immigrate, but the data are lacking). It is also useful to take note of the stay-on students when estimating the professional *ILS* attributable to qualified immigrants – as distinguished from unqualified immigrants who might obtain professional training after arrival in the host country.

Among possible additions to the immigration record are the short-term foreign workers of professional type ('exchange visitors', 'distinguished foreign specialists', etc.), who are counted in the foreign-born stock as of any census date, and who contribute to the host-economy during their period of stay. However, these do not add very much to the national stock or to the annual net inflows of immigrants (being on short-term permits, the visitors' annual inflows are nearly offset by their annual outflows from earlier arrivals, except where their arrivals are on a rising trend).

The magnitudes and net outcome of these various additions to and deductions from official 'immigration' are discussed below under each DC case.

3. The United States of America

The U.S. receives by far the largest numbers of immigrants of all types, as well as the largest numbers of PTK immigrants from all countries and from LDCs. It also presents in many respects the most complete and detailed statistical reports on migration. Accordingly it is the most frequently studied and cited case. However, the U.S. is the only case of a continuing rise in immigrants from the early 1960s through 1972; moreover, its proportion of PTK in the total, of around 10 percent, is substantial but is not the highest in the world (being exceeded by Canada and perhaps other countries). This is to say that the U.S. is not typical of general migration or of 'brain drain' in all countries nowadays.

The U.S. record reflects the shifts in U.S. immigration policy. In 1965, the system of national quotas restricting immigration from the Eastern Hemisphere was replaced by a new system of ceilings (120,000 persons annually from the Western Hemisphere and 170,000 from the Eastern Hemisphere, which in addition is subject to a per country limit of 20,000 persons), plus certification by the U.S. Department of Labor that the immigrant's occupation and skills are in short supply in the U.S. (relatives and dependents, refugees and certain other classes being exempt from the labor certification criterion).

3.1. U.S. immigration trends

The numbers of immigrant professionals coming from LDCs into the U.S. during the past decade, as shown in table 1, have been rising strongly until 1973. The gross inflow soared from an average number of 11,300 a year during 1962–66 to some 39,000 a year in 1971 and 1972; it then dropped to under 32,000 in 1973.

Temporary professional arrivals from the LDCs (estimated from the categories 'exchange visitors' and 'workers of distinguished merit', as shown in appendix II, part I) rose from about 12,000 a year during 1962–66 to 15,600 in

1971. This was a comparatively moderate rise in these categories, which represent on the whole a revolving stock growing rather slowly.

There are in addition large numbers of illegal entrants, whose numbers are of course not officially tabulated but have sometimes been estimated as high as 800,000 a year, with a rising trend in recent years. These are mostly short-stay seasonal workers and other manual labor, with very few PTK among them, as professionals must usually deliver documentation as to their qualifications and careers.

The whole stock of LDC professionals in the U.S. – comprising both LDC professionals on immigrant visas and some temporary-visa LDC professionals, as enumerated at census time – amounted according to our estimates (appendix II, part 2) to 110,000 persons in 1960 and 246,000 persons in 1970. These figures show an increment of 136,000 persons over ten years, or 13,600 per year on the average.

3.2. Increments to the U.S. labor supply (ILS)

The magnitude of the PTK inflows can be assessed by relating them to the PTK labor force in the U.S. along four different lines, as shown in table 2a: stock–stock ratios, flow–stock ratios, flow–flow ratios, and unemployment rates. We apply the first three ratios initially to the aggregate PTK, then to particular occupations; then the unemployment rates are related to surpluses and shortages of PTK in the aggregate and in the outstanding occupations.

3.2.1. The stock–stock ratio for all PTK.

We begin with this measure, shown in line (a) of table 2a, as it is both more reliable than the flow figures and clearer to interpret. The total stock of LDC professionals, which we have estimated at 246,000 persons in the U.S. in 1970, amounted to 2 percent of the nation's whole stock of PTK.

3.2.2. The flow–stock ratio for all PTK.

Line (b) of table 2a shows the gross inflow of immigrant PTK from LDCs in relation to current national stocks of PTK. For the 1962–1966 period, the average annual gross number (11,300) of LDC professionals admitted to the United States as immigrants works out to one-seventh of one percent of the 1960 stock of professionals in this country (7.5 million persons); and less against the 1965 stock. At the much higher rates of inflow during 1967–1969 (averaging 26,500 a year), taken against the then-current stock (11.4 million in 1970), the annual gross flow–stock ratio was about one-fourth of one percent a year. When the inflow rate soared again after 1969 (to a level of about 39,000 a year in 1971 and 1972) the annual flow–stock ratio attained one-third of one percent.

Table 2a

Labor force contribution of professionals (PTK) from LDCs, in the U.S., 1962–1972.[a]

	All PTK			Particular professions		
	1962–66	1967–69	1971–72	Scientists	Engineers	Physicians and surgeons
(a) Resident stock from LDCs as % of host professional stock		2 (1970)		2 (1966) 3 (1970)	2 (1966) 3 (1970)	10 (1970)
(b) Annual average gross immigration as % of host professional stock	0.12	0.25	0.33	0.4 (1970)	0.6 (1970)	0.7 (1970) 1.5 (1971)
(c) Annual average gross immigration as % of host annual professional increase	under 2	3.5	5	7 (1965–69) 11 (1971–72)	16 (1965–69) 26 (1971–72)	27 (1970) 51 (1972)
(d) Unemployment rate of host professional stock as % (excluding the self-employed)	1 (most of 1960s)		over 3 (1970)	1 (1960s) 2.5 (1971)	under 1 (1960s) 3 (1971)	

aSources: Annual gross immigration figures from table 1; host-country data from national censuses, national manpower reports, and special studies, notably: N.S.F. (1972); Stevens and Vermeulen (1972); Atkinson, Barnes and Richardson (1970); Canada Prices and Incomes Commission (1972); Gish (1971); U.K. (1971); and O.E.C.D. (1970).

Projecting ten years of this recent rate of gross admissions – making no deductions for return flows of immigrants, nor for foreign students already in the United States converting to permanent residents – would add $3\frac{1}{3}$ percent to the 1970 stock.

To convert the foregoing gross *ILS* to 'net immigration' *ILS*, we must subtract return flows. These in our estimate come to about 30 percent of the gross inflows (see appendix II, part 2); i.e., the net inflow is 70 percent of the gross inflow. Thus the above-projected PTK inflow for ten years would be reduced from a $3\frac{1}{3}$ percent gross increment in the 1970 stock, to $2\frac{1}{3}$ percent net *ILS*. If we wished to count only LDC immigrants arriving with professional qualifications, we would subtract another 20 percent of the gross inflows (see appendix II, part 3).

3.2.3. The flow–flow ratio for all PTK.

Our third ILS measurement has been constructed for the United States by setting the annual gross immigration of LDC professionals against the annual graduations of professionals from U.S. schools, as shown in line (c) of table 2a. For 1962–1966, the resulting overall ratio comes to less than 2 percent, and reaches $3\frac{1}{2}$ percent for 1967–1969. With the still higher inflows observed in 1971 and 1972, this ratio rises to about 5 percent. If return flows are deducted the ratio for net immigration drops to 3.5 percent in these recent years.

3.2.4. The ILS measures for engineers and scientists.

The stock–stock ratios for LDC engineers and scientists in the U.S., according to the estimates shown in table 2a, are not very different from that ratio for all PTK, as they run at 2 or 3 percent, during 1966–70. The flow–stock ratios for the engineers and scientists around 1970 run considerably higher than the aggregate ratio, reflecting the surge in these categories of immigration. The third measure, flow–flow, shows much higher ratios than the aggregate, reaching up to one-fourth of the annual graduations in the U.S. in the field of engineering, and reflecting the rapid rise in the immigration during 1970–72 against the much smaller rise in U.S. graduations.

3.2.5. The ILS measures for physicians and surgeons.

In the medical field the inflow of LDC personnel has been truly massive. The stock–stock ratio for 1970 stands at 10 percent, or five times the ratio for all PTK. The flow–stock ratio in 1971 was nearly five times the corresponding ratio for all PTK. Above all, the flow–flow ratio not only reached ten times the aggregate ratio in 1972, but it represents a gross inflow proportion of 1:2 against graduations from U.S. medical schools. However, we must recall once more that all these percentages shrink if the stated gross numbers of 'immigrants' are reduced for repatriations of earlier immigrant professionals and perhaps also for nonreturning foreign graduates of U.S. schools. On the other hand, the gross arr vals are augmented by exchange visitors and distinguished workers. These were particularly important among physicians, where the exchange visitors during the early 1960s were over twice the number of annual formal immigrants (during subsequent years the annual inflow of exchange visitor physicians remained approximately constant, while the annual inflow of immigrant physicians expanded, until in 1971 the former was down to 0.8 of the latter); but most of these exchange visitors represent only a continuing circulation (since the annual inflow numbers were not in a rising trend), although the average period of stay was probably lengthening.[4]

3.2.6. Unemployment, surpluses and shortages.

We turn now from the statistical stock and flow ratios of the professional immigration, to the *ILS* contribution in terms of shortages and surpluses. It should be noted first that during most of the 1960s the unemployment rate of professionals in the United States was very low: barely above 1 percent for the whole PTK category, and even below 1 percent for some subcategories, such as engineers. Such low rates probably merely represent job-changing, voluntary leisure, and other nonhardship idleness. It is reported that 'through much of the 1960s, new graduates could barely keep pace with job openings and in a number of fields there were manpower scarcities'.[5] In these circumstances, the inflow of LDC professionals during the late 1960s – adding at most one-fourth of one percent a year to the then-existing stock in the United States, as already noted – surely contributed to relieve the shortages in a small degree without posing any painful competition with native professionals, at least until quite late in the 1960s.

During the early 1970s, however, the picture changed markedly in the direction of hardship unemployment, due to governmental cutbacks in technical programs and also due to general economic recession. Unemployment of professionals rose to a peak of over 3 percent in 1971, then receded slightly in 1972, then climbed again with the recession of 1974[6] – while in these years, a flood of new graduates came pouring out of the schools, and the immigrants came streaming out of the less developed countries: it was perhaps a classic cobweb-type response. Appreciable hostile reaction is now evident as immigrant professionals compete with natives for employment.

Probably the most urgent need filled by LDC professionals in the United

---

[4]Relationships derived from data in Stevens and Vermeulen (1972, appendix tables A2 and A5, and text pp. 56–57).
[5]See the Monthly Labor Review, October 1972, p. 9.
[6]U.S. Department of Labor (1973, p. 19) and subsequent news releases.

States (as also in the U.K., discussed below) is medical service at junior levels. It is generally said that a 'shortage of physicians' exists in the U.S. at present (although there are many different views as to the causes, incidence, and remediability of that shortage). It is evident that foreign medical graduates (FMGs) serve to relieve the shortage not only in the aggregate but particularly in several types of agencies and functions (notably as interns and residents in hospitals, clinics, and geriatric agencies, as general practitioners, and in posts in slums and ghetto areas where many American physicians are unwilling to practice).

As of 1970, the total of FMGs working in the U.S. was nearly one-fifth of the whole stock of physicians and surgeons in this country; in U.S. hospitals alone, FMGs comprised 30 percent of the full-time staff; and LDCs were the source of some 60 percent of these FMGs.[7] Since 1970, these proportions have evidently risen as the inflow of FMGs soared, and the share of Asians expanded. At the present time, many hospitals could not perform their functions without them.

More debatable are the secondary effects of that substantial inflow. Physicians' fees have continued to rise rapidly. Preventive medicine is still not advancing fast compared to curative medicine. Furthermore, there are numerous complaints about the quality of some FMGs, and their ability to communicate in English.[8] In addition, the FMGs have disappointed some of their advocates because few of them move into the smaller towns in the interior, where medical service is disproportionately thin; nor has the FMGs' presence in the cities driven many more American doctors into the towns. Indeed, the FMGs have been attacked as a deterrent to faster expansion of the U.S. medical schools in the aggregate and in opportunities for U.S. native minority groups.

The situation for nurses is in some respects similar to physicians. There is a parallel shortage in most of the same locations and agencies. Immigrant nurses relieve some of these shortages but are also unwilling to go to remote small towns. More than the immigrant physicians, the immigrant nurses' quality is generally approved, and many are highly commended for thorough performance and personal interest despite some language barriers. The chief complaint against foreign nurses seems to be that they impair unionization and the whole drive to elevate nursing salaries.

Another important contribution of immigrants is in the field of 'technicians' – scientific, medical, electronic, repairmen, and some other specialities. Immigrants seem to relieve some of these scarcities, and to moderate the wage levels; but their quality is frequently said to be inadequate, and they avoid small towns.

Scientists and engineers, on a higher professional level than technicians, have shown some sharp fluctuations in availabilities during recent years. During the 1960s, when they were scarce in this country, numerous immigrants came from

[7]Stevens and Vermeulen (1972), appendix tables D4 and D7, and text pp. 16–17).
[8]See New York Times (1974a, b).

Britain and other European countries, and later from India, Taiwan and other Asian countries. Towards the end of the 1960s, however, conditions in the U.S. economy, together with cutbacks in the Federal programs for NASA and other technical work, generated something of a surplus of scientists and engineers, such that the European inflow declined (probably turned into a net outflow) and the Asian inflow weakened; and in 1971 the Labor Department curtailed its certifications for the categories in question. It may therefore be said that foreign scientists and engineers made a noteworthy *ILS* contribution to this country during the last decade; but that more recently their further inflow has been adding to unemployment, which in 1972 was running at about 2.5 percent for engineers and 1.9 percent for physical scientists (both rates more than half again as high as in 1970, although always far below unemployment rates for the whole labor force).

These judgments refer to large groups of immigrants, whose average quality is assumed to be about equivalent to that of the host-country professionals. There are of course some exceptionally gifted and extraordinary productive persons among the immigrants, as also among the host population; just as there are many persons at the low end of the scale in both groups.

3.3. Avoided costs of education (ACE)

While the preceding section assessed the PTK immigration primarily in labor-market terms, we now consider the economic contributions of professional immigration in terms of the avoided costs of educating additional natives to the same professional qualifications. We pursue two separate approaches which should arrive at the same point: (1) evaluating the net increment in manpower stocks, and (2) evaluating the net annual inflows.

(1) We begin with the intercensal gain of 1960–70. Over this period the net increment in PTK manpower stocks from LDC origins – counting both immigrants and temporary-workers as enumerated on the census dates – amounted, as estimated in a previous section, to 136,000 persons, or 13,600 per year. These numbers are to be multiplied by an estimate of relevant costs of professional education, namely $15,000 per professional for the mid-1960s, in the practices and prices of that time (see appendix II, part 4). Multiplying the number of net immigrants by this average replacement cost yields a figure of $2,050 million net *ACE* to the U.S. from immigration over that decade; or $205 million a year.

(2) The alternative approach to this measurement, via net inflow figures for each year, yields broadly similar *ACE* estimates. For 1962–66, when the gross formal immigration averaged 11,300 persons a year, the net qualified immigration – after deducting 20 percent for stay-on students as well as 30 percent for repatriation flows of immigrants – came to 6,320 persons a year; multiplying

by the representative cost figure of $15,000 for that time yields an *ACE* of $95 million a year. A similar calculation for 1971, using the much enlarged immigration volume and the elevated costs of the relevant education, yields an *ACE* of $485 million, in the prices of 1971. If these flow figures are combined in a weighted average, they appear to be consistent with the foregoing stock-increment measure of $205 million of *ACE* value per year for the decade 1960–1970 (in 1965 prices).

The significance of this value figure may be assessed against U.S. educational outlays during the same period. Set against the total expenditures by all levels of government for all levels of education (about $36 billion per year), the $205 million annual estimated replacement cost would come to less than 0.6 percent. Set against total expenditures on higher education alone (both public and private and includ'ng much sponsored research and public services, but excluding all income foregone), which averaged $16 billion per year, the annual replacement cost of immigrants shows up as 1.3 percent.

In terms of the much higher volume of PTK immigration from LDCs during 1970–72, the 1971 *ACE* was just under 2 percent of the higher educational expenditures (since the estimated value of the net immigration, as calculated above, came to nearly $500 million in 1971 prices, while the expenditures on higher education in the U.S., using the same definitions as before, amounted to $27,100 million in 1971).

As the foregoing flow calculations have been made with figures for adjusted immigration flows – with a 20 percent deduction for foreign students who converted to immigrant status and a 30 percent subtraction for repatriation flows – it seems prudent to show the magnitudes of *ACE* if both these subtractions are cancelled and we revert to the gross immigrat'on figures.

In effect, the above measures of *ACE* must then be multiplied by 1.8. Thus the value of the *ACE* in 1971 is lifted from $500 million to $900 million, and the proportion to higher education expenditures becomes 3.3 percent. These figures may be treated as 'outside limits'; since some allowance must be made for converting students and for returning immigrants, the appropriate estimate should lie somewhere between the gross measures and our estimates.

Some commentators would wish to reduce the foreign contribution in view of quality differences. Thus it is frequently alleged in the medical profession that many doctors from LDCs have not been trained up to U.S. standards; similar allegations have been heard regarding foreign engineers and other professionals – these judgments being made for large groups, without denying the high or superior levels of performance of some individual immigrants. To the extent that these assessments are correct, the measured average *ACE* should be reduced below the full costs of educating a substitutable native-born American. In other words, a smaller outlay would have sufficed to train an American to the quality level of the average immigrant professional. Much careful research would be required, however, to determine whether, and to what degree, a quality differential exists, before attempting to put a financial valuation on it.

4. Canada

4.1. Immigration trends

The Canadian record, as shown in table 1, consists of rather small numbers of professional immigrants from LDCs in the first part of the 1960s, followed by a five-fold rise to a peak of nearly 8,000 in 1967, then an irregular decline into the early 1970s.

Policy restrictions, designed largely to limit entry to foreigners possessing skills needed in Canada, produced a moderate reduction of immigration during 1968–72, and will be tightened again according to official declarations in October 1974.

The trend of immigration for the individual professions shows some variance from the trend for the total of professionals over the period 1962–71. There was a rather steady upward trend for scientists, engineers and for 'others'; there was a peak for teachers and doctors in 1969, followed by a decline; and there was a peak for nurses in 1966, followed by a very sharp cutback.

4.2. Increments to the labor supply (ILS)

As with the discussion of the U.S. in the preceding section, we will consider alternative *ILS* measures for Canada.

4.2.1. The stock–stock ratio for all PTK

The net accumulation of LDC professionals in the Canadian labor force is difficult to measure because the 1971 census results have not yet been published in the necessary detail, and even the 1961 census provided an inadequate breakdown of countries of origin. A rough estimate from the data for 1961 indicates that LDC professionals' stock in Canada in that year, as stated in table 2b, line (a), was between one percent and 2 percent of the whole professional stock.

4.2.2. The flow–stock ratio for all PTK

As for the flow rates, the gross immigration of LDC professionals, summarized from table 1 over the eleven years 1962–72 – with no reduction for return outflows, retirements and deaths – came to just over 53,000 persons. These

Table 2b

Labor force contribution of professionals (PTK) from LDCs, in Canada, 1962–1972. [a]

	All PTK	Particular professions		
	1962–71	National scientists	Other scientists	Engineers
(a) Resident stock from LDCs as % of host professional stock	1–2 (1961)	3 (1967)	2 (1967)	2 (1967)
		Physicians scientists, engineers		Nurses
(b) Annual average gross immigration as % of host professional stock	0.8	1.3–1.9 (1962–72 inflows as % of 1961 stock)		1
(c) Annual average gross immigration as % of host annual professional increase	10			
(d) Unemployment rate of host professional stock (excluding the self-employed)	0.9 (University degree holders, 1965–70)			

[a] *Sources*: See table 2a.

constituted a summary *ILS* contribution of 8.5 percent to the stock of just under 630,000 professionals in Canada at the beginning of this period. Accordingly, as shown in table 2b, line (b), the average annual rate of gross inflow of LDC professionals was 0.8 percent of the 1961 stock. These rates would be still lower if we could estimate and subtract return flows, let alone deducting stay-on foreign students.[9] If the Canadian experience parallels the U.S., 30 percent of the PTK gross immigration should be deducted for return flows, yielding 'net immigration' at 70 percent of the gross reported inflows; on the other hand, the net inflow rates should be raised if professional 'visitors' are increasing.

4.2.3. The flow–flow ratio for all PTK

The flow–flow magnitude of LDC professionals' gross immigration, related to Canada's own production of professionals, was quite substantial. As shown in table 2b, line (c), the annual gross inflow amounted to nearly 10 percent of Canada's annual increment in stock of PTK.

Comparisons may be made with the U.S., along all three lines, (a), (b) and (c), of table 2b. Canada shows about the same proportion of LDC professionals accumulated in the national stock as of 1961 and 1967. However, in recent years Canada shows a much heavier proportion of gross inflow to national stock and likewise to current national graduations of PTK. But in both countries the percentages are quite modest and would be substantially smaller in terms of net immigration.

4.2.4. The ILS measures for particular professions

As of 1967, as shown in table 2b, line (a), LDC personnel accounted for a little over 2 percent of Canada's total stock of engineers, 3 percent of her natural scientists, about 2 percent of her social scientists, and a similar proportion of other scientifically trained personnel.

In flow–stock terms (line (b) of table 2b), some particular professions showed *ILS* rates higher than the average for all PTK. Thus the gross inflow of LDC engineers, scientists and doctors during 1962–72 averaged annually between 1.3 and 1.9 percent of the 1961 stock in these professions. On the other hand, lower-than-average rates of annual *ILS* appear for teachers, dentists, and unspecified others. Nurses (including nurses in training), who added about one percent a year to the 1961 stock, were slightly above the all-PTK average *ILS* of 0.8 percent.

---

[9]Canada in 1967 adopted a visa-conversion system whereby non-immigrant 'visitors' may be granted 'landed immigrant' status. Such conversions as reported for 1970 and 1971 amounted to 15 percent and 28.6 percent of all the reported immigration in the respective years; but breakdowns of the conversions are not available by occupations and by country of origin.

4.3. Avoided costs of education (ACE)

We may start with the gross inflow of 53,000 persons over the eleven years 1962–72, or 4,820 per year on the average; data are lacking on return flows to be deducted, in order to measure 'net immigration'. If the U.S. cost-avoidance can be applied to the Canadian situation, at the same $15,000 per average immigrant (in U.S. dollars),[10] the annual ACE comes to $72 million in terms of gross immigration.

For the single year 1971 – which was actually the lowest point of the immigration during recent years – the gross immigration of 5,184 persons may be multiplied by the then-current U.S. cost of $22,500 per average immigrant-replacement, yielding a total gross ACE of $116 million. Setting this amount against Canada's total public expenditures for all levels of education in 1971, which was just under $8,000 million, the ACE ratio was 1.4 percent.

5. United Kingdom

5.1. Immigration trends

From the middle 1950s onward there was a rising inflow into the U.K. of New Commonwealth citizens, reaching a peak rate during January 1961–June 1962. During that eighteen-month period over 200,000 immigrants of all types arrived from the developing countries comprising the New Commonwealth. At that point the British authorities began closing the open door, by imposing an economic screening through vouchers for permanent settlement in the U.K. ('A'-type for persons having a specific job awaiting them in the U.K., and 'B'-type for persons possessing qualifications, mainly professional, deemed needed in the U.K.); while additional persons were admitted for permanent stay as 'dependents' of authorized settlers or as 'special settlers' (e.g., persons coming to marry or to retire in the U.K.), while still other persons were admitted for limited periods as 'long-term visitors', 'working holiday-makers', or as 'students'. Under this system, the occupational immigration for permanent stay from the whole Commonwealth was cut down drastically by the end of the 1960s to some 5,000 persons holding employment vouchers in 1967, and only 3,500 – 4,000 a year in the early 1970s (of whom just under three-fourths came from the New Commonwealth). Arrivals under the B-vouchers – which approximate our concept of PTK – amounted to about one-half of those figures. In 1971, for example, B-voucher admissions from the New Commonwealth countries amounted to 1,080 persons; blown up to include PTK from other LDCs, the figure comes to the 1,270 shown for 1971 under the U.K. column in table 1.

[10]Unpublished studies by the Education Division of Statistics Canada, on higher-education costs in 1971–72, indicate close parallels to the U.S. pattern shown in appendix II, part 4.

Much larger figures for professional immigration from LDCs into the U.K. are sometimes computed along more inclusive lines, which depart still further from our concept of 'PTK immigrants' (see the discussion in appendix III, part 1, below). Most of the statistical uncertainties on migration flows could be resolved by figures on inter-censal stock changes; but regrettably the 1971 census results are not available in the breakdowns required here. We therefore fall back upon the stock position shown in the 1966 sample census, as discussed in the next section.

5.2. Increments to the labor supply (ILS)

5.2.1. The stock–stock ratio for all PTK

As shown in table 2c, line (a), the overall ratio was 3.2 percent in 1966. The calculation uses the 1966 census figure which indicates in the U.K. some 77,400 PTK who originated in LDCs (counting stay-on students as well as professionally qualified entrants).

5.2.2. The flow–stock ratio for all PTK

For the flow–stock measures, we must rely on the gross formal immigration figures, as shown in the B-voucher statistics, blown up for all LDCs in table 1. These figures, which are subsequent to the immigration curtailment of mid-1962, indicate (line (a) of table 2c) a tiny annual increment to Britain's aggregate stock of professionals from 1963 forward; by 1971, the annual increment was down to about 0.05 percent a year for the whole PTK category. As these increments should, strictly speaking, be measured for net inflows, the gross inflow figures lean toward exaggerating the *ILS* contribution.

Leaning still further, we might also add in the A-voucher immigrants who may include some professionals, along with the 'B' types counted in the preceding paragraphs. The effect in 1970 and 1971 would be approximately to triple the *ILS* figures and ratios used. For example, the combined gross inflow of 'A' and 'B' types in 1971 would represent 0.15 percent annual gross addition to Britain's stock of PTK. Over say a ten-year period, even at this inclusive inflow rate – again leaving in the return flows and the British-trained foreign students – the PTK from LDCs would add only 1.5 percent to Britain's 1966 PTK stock.

5.2.3. The flow–flow ratio for all PTK

As the necessary data on the intercensal changes in the British stock of all PTK were not available as this paper was being written, the aggregate flow–flow ratio could not be computed.

5.2.4. The ILS measures for particular professions

The stock–stock ratios for some particular professions are well above the

234   *E.P. Reubens, Professional immigration into DCs from LDCs*

Table 2c

Labor force contribution of professionals (PTK) from LDCs, in the U.K., 1962–1972.[a]

	All PTK		Particular professions		
	1963	1970–71	Engineers and Scientists	Physicians	Nurses
(a) Resident stock from LDCs as % of host professional stock	3.26 (1966)	3.4 (1971)	4.5 (1969–71)	15 (1966)	7 (1971)
(b) Annual average gross immigration as % of host professional stock	0.2	0.05	0.3 (1966) 0.1 (1969–71)	1.5 (1962–69)	0.75 (1970–71)
(c) Annual average gross immigration as % of host annual professional increase			5 (1966) under 1 (1970)	40 (1962–66)	13 (1970–71)
(d) Unemployment rate of host professional stock as % (excluding the self-employed)		5.4 (recent university graduates)	4.5 (recent university graduates)		

[a]*Sources:* See table 2a.

average ratio, as shown in table 2c. One of the highest is shown for LDC physicians, at 15 percent of all physicians in the U.K. in 1966. Indeed, in certain lower grades of doctors' employment, especially in hospitals, the LDC share was as high as 63 percent. In this numerical sense, British hospitals are extremely dependent upon LDC doctors; on the other hand, two-fifths of the LDC doctors were trained in British medical schools, not abroad.

Likewise, the flow–stock ratios were substantial for certain professions. Again, the major instance is the medical profession, where the gross immigration of LDC doctors on B-vouchers in the later 1960s added about 1.7 percent a year to the country's stock. However, by the early 1970s, as a result of the immigration restrictions, the annual gross increment had been reduced to two-thirds of 1 percent. To shift to a net flow–stock basis, these percentages should be reduced by perhaps one-third in each year.[11]

5.2.5. Unemployment, surpluses and shortages

Proceeding beyond the numerical ratios to the functional significance of the LDC professionals in the British labor market, there seems to be little need for the PTK immigrants (except doctors and nurses) in the sense of unfillable vacancies at prevailing salaries and working conditions. Reported unemployment rates for recent university graduates have been in the range of 4–6 percent. Surveys by the Department of Trade and Industry have found that many graduates have been hired to fill vacancies among technicians and technical supporting staff, where real shortages may in fact exist. A recently initiated series by the Department of Employment indicates that among males in professional occupations as a group, the unemployed are about five times the number of vacancies; this suggests surplus, not shortage. The chief exception is in the female list, for the nursing profession, where the unemployed persons are only 20–30 percent of the available notified vacancies, suggesting a real shortage of nurses. Scarcities also persist in the lower ranks of physicians, especially in hospitals and in remote areas, under current conditions.

5.3. Avoided costs of education (ACE)

In accordance with our chosen procedure, the value of the LDC professionals at the time of their arrival in Britain may be estimated as the direct costs of the British equivalent of the education and training brought in by these immigrants. As calculated in appendix III, part 2, the 1966 stock of LDC professionals

---

[11]The inflow and return flow of foreign doctors have been studied by the Royal Medical Society and by the Department of Health [cited Gish (1971, ch. 3)]. Their data – mingling true immigrants with limited-stay visitors – indicate that annual returns amount to some 40–60 percent of the current gross mingled inflow. The return rate for B-voucher immigrant doctors alone might be put at 30–40 percent of the current inflow.

in Britain – selecting from the net accumulation only those who were trained abroad – had a cost value of embodied training perhaps worth as much as £454 million,[12] using British estimates at 1964 prices: the cost of actual training as received in the LDCs abroad would naturally be considerably less than this *ACE*.

As for the flow aspect of the LDC brain gain, the annual gross inflow in 1970 and 1971 – counting only new B-voucher immigrants who had already qualified – was worth in *ACE* terms some £15 million a year, in British prices adjusted to 1971 (appendix III, part 3, again using the estimates of unit costs of education in Britain). This value of annual gross inflow, related to the current GNP of Britain, amounted to about 0.03 percent thereof. Related to the British Government's annual outlay for education at all levels, the aforesaid *ACE* amounted to about 0.6 percent of that outlay. For the early 1960s, when the immigration inflows were much larger, and the real GNP and the real educational outlays were smaller, the foregoing ratios should be multiplied by a factor of about 5. For evaluating the inflows net of returns, as well as net of stay-on foreign students, all the foregoing relative measures should be reduced considerably, perhaps by at least one-fourth.

6. International summary and comparisons

In the three preceding sections we have measured the immigration of PTK from the LDCs into the three chief receiving countries since 1960 by estimating the net magnitude of this immigration and evaluating two of its effects: first its impact on national stocks and flows of personnel (the *ILS* effect), then its financial contribution as a transferred capital asset (the *ACE* effect).

We found that the gross migration trends recorded over the past decade were quite dramatic, and disturbing or gratifying to many persons involved. But we also found that these trends went in different directions in the three countries during this period, as indicated by the timing of the peak inflows: the peak in the U.K. occurred in the early 1960s and was followed by severe reduction; in Canada 1967 was the peak year until the much higher surge in 1973 and 1974; while in the U.S. the trend was strongly upward until a peak was reached in the early 1970s.

When we adjusted from gross inflows to 'net immigration' – by deducting return flows – we obtained for the U.S. a 30 percent cut in the gross immigration figures. Stay-on students accounted for another 20 percent. For the

---

[12]As specified in appendix III, the cost figures for training professionals in Britain include all education subsequent to the minimum school-leaving age (formerly 16 years, now 17 years). This coverage is therefore more inclusive than the U.S. and Canadian figures used in our text sections 3 and 4 above, where only the years of professional-level education were counted. On the other hand, the British data seem to count only student-support costs instead of full incomes-foregone as counted in the U.S. and Canadian cost estimates.

other two receiving countries, the data do not permit similar adjustments but there is reason to believe that somewhat lower percentages prevailed than were calculated for the U.S.

Measuring the effects of the PTK immigration, sometimes using the gross figures for lack of the adjusted estimates in all instances, we found rather small orders of magnitude of these effects in all three receiving countries. In the *ILS* effect, the stock–stock ratios, which are on a net basis, showed the (adjusted) immigrants to be only a few percent of the national personnel stocks of PTK – except in a few professions, notably physicians and nurses. The flow–stock ratios showed the annual gross inflows to be well below one percent of the national stocks – again excepting certain professions. As for the *ACE* effect of PTK immigration, it amounted to only a few percent of national expenditures on higher education, even when gross immigration figures were used. Among the three receiving countries, our estimates of the *ACE* effect for the U.K. are not directly comparable to those for the U.S. and Canada, since the educational cost data for the U.K. include more years of education than do the other two countries, but conversely count maintenance costs of students instead of incomes foregone.

If compensation is to be paid to the countries of origin of the PTK migrants, one criterion might be the magnitude of the *ACE* effect on the receiving countries. Such a payment would clearly exceed the sunk costs of education in the LDCs, as the cost of professional education in many LDCs (although not in Africa) is only a fraction of the avoided costs in the DCs upon which the compensation might be based. Whether to use this criterion of compensation, or some other principle such as estimated welfare gains and losses, will depend upon international negotiations on matters such as foreign aid from DCs to LDCs.

Appendix I: PTK immigration in northern Europe

Professional immigration into the developed economies of Northern Europe – other than the U.K. – is not adequately reported, but almost all indicators suggest small absolute and relative inflows from the LDCs. According to Henderson (1970, pp. 19–40), the chief receiving countries at the end of the 1960s were the U.S., Canada and the U.K.; in second place were Australia, France, West Germany and the Netherlands; for other countries, the immigration was 'not in significant quantity'.

The study done by Education and World Affairs (1970) at about the same time ranks PTK immigration from LDCs into the European receiving countries, as set forth in its ch. 17, putting U.K. first, France second, and West Germany third, and stating that immigration of this kind into the Scandinavian countries was 'negligible', and into Southern Europe was 'very little'. In the same volume, ch. 18 on the Netherlands shows that the gross inflow of physicians from developing countries during 1959–1968 amounted to only 96 persons altogether, and contributed much less than 1 percent to the Netherlands' stock of physicians; indeed, the net *ILS* contribution must have been still smaller because of the heavy return flow (which seems to have been about 40 percent of the gross inflow).

More detailed data for France, specially obtained from the Office national de l'immigration, for the years 1961–71, indicate very low ratios of all foreign professionals to the total stocks and flows of professionals in France – so low that the developing countries' share shrinks to negligible proportions. For example, the flow–stock ratio for all foreign professional inflow works out to 0.1 percent for each of the years 1969, 1970 and 1971; while in turn the professionals who came from developing countries alone amounted to less than one-sixth of all the professional immigrants.[13] Turning to the stock–stock ratio,[14] we find that professionals from all foreign countries together with 'Algériens et français musulmans nés en Algérie', who were residing in France in 1968, amounted to only 2.8 percent of the category 'professions libérales et cadres supérieurs' in the whole population of France. Among those foreigners, PTK from developing countries were only perhaps one-eighth (estimated at some 3,300 persons out of 27,000 foreign PTK in France).

The number of PTK immigrants into France has been kept small by the official regulations which have reserved nearly all posts in the liberal professions to French nationals having a French degree.[15] A special door is kept open for citizens of developing countries which were previously French territories, provided they have acquired a French degree; but the number of these is now dwindling. Another door, provided by the European Economic Community, was actually opened for the first time by resolution in February 1975, probably taking effect in 1976, to permit the free movement of physicians among lal the member countries of the E.E.C.

The small numbers of PTKs entering Northern European countries from the LDCs is further confirmed by data from some of the chief sources of emigration. Thus the national registry information from India[16] implies that only one-fifth of that nation's professional emigrants go to countries other than U.S., Canada and U.K. Reports from the Philippines indicate that 'apart from the U.S., Canada and Australia, there are hardly any other countries of emigration for Filipinos'.[17]

In the perspective of the millions of 'guest workers' who have come into Northern Europe during recent years, the proportion of PTK is tiny and

---

[13]Data from detailed tables of Institut national de la statistique et des études économiques (1971), combined with special tabulations of immigration from the Office national de l'immigration.

[14]Drawn from Institut national (1971, table 20).

[15]See Tapinos (1973).

[16]Council of Scientific and Industrial Research (CSIR) (1972a, b).

[17]Gupta (1973, p. 176).

negligible. For example, data on migration from Turkey – an LDC country, and one of the two largest suppliers of labor to Northern Europe – show the percentage of PTK to be virtually zero (whether we use the reports from the Turkish side or the reports from West Germany, one of the principal receiving countries). At the same time, the 3 percent of Turkish emigrants having higher-education degrees, as shown in a recent Turkish study, evidently represents flows of PTK predominantly to the U.S. and Canada.[18]

Appendix II: Calculations for the United Sates of America

II.1. Gross inflows of 'exchange visitors' and 'workers of distinguished merit'[a]

1965		
Exchange visitors (all occupations)	33,768	
of which 45% PTK	16,000	
of which 62.5% LDCs		10,000
Workers of distinguished merit (all occupations)	8,295	
of which 93% PTK	7,700	
of which 25% LDCs		1,900
Total		11,900
Averaged for 1962–1966		12,000
1971		
Exchange visitors (all occupations)	53,393	
of which PTK	26,955	
of which 45% LDCs		12,000
Workers of distinguished merit (all occupations)	11,990	
of which PTK	11,611	
of which 31% LDCs		3,600
Total		15,600

[a]*Source*: U.S. Department of Justice (1965, 1967, 1971; tables 16, 16a, 16b).

II.2. Stocks, increments in stocks, and return rate of LDC professionals in the U.S.

The annual return rate, estimated at 30 percent of annual immigration, is calculated from stock and flow data for the 1960s. Specifically, the initial stock in 1960 plus the gross immigration 1960–1970, and minus the final stock in

[18]See Paine (1974, pp. 25, 56, 192, 197).

1970, should yield the number of returns and other disappearances, which may then be expressed as a percentage of the number of gross immigrants. The chief difficulties in the calculation are the identification of the immigrants from LDCs in the census data, and the treatment of visitors and other stay-ons in addition to immigrants.

The 1970 U.S. census report (1973) provides a usable approximation of our LDC category in the form of a tabulation of the occupations of the foreign-born residents according to a good many countries of origin: those countries represented by at least 300,000 persons in the U.S. population. This tabulation gives numbers for China, Mexico, Cuba, Other West Indies, Other Central and South America, and All Others. We have taken the category of All Others to consist mainly of LDCs, although it no doubt includes some persons from DCs, and combined it with the enumerated LDCs, to arrive at a total of 246,280 persons representing the stock in question in 1970.

For the corresponding stock in 1960, we have used and adjusted the data from the 1960 Census, which did not provide detail as fine as that of 1970. Specifically, we have taken the 1960 data for Mexico plus the data for All Others minus an adjustment for the considerable number of DCs included there in 1960 (based upon the figures available for 1970, it appears that just over one-fifth of the 1960 All Others should be removed). The result is a figure of 110,000 persons representing the stock in question in 1960.

The stock increment from 1960 to 1970 was therefore 136,280 persons.

The data on gross immigration flows during the 1960s comes from our table 1, by summing the annual figures for fiscal 1961 through fiscal 1970 (we have supplied the 1961 figure at 7,200 persons, based on the 1962 figure in the table and the trends shown for 1961–62 in N.S.F. (1972). This sum comes to 177,000 persons.

The calculation therefore yields the following.

Initial stock, 1960		110,000
Immigration 1960–1970		+177,000
	Sum	287,000
Final stock 1970		−246,280
	Difference	40,720

If we ignore exchange visitors and student stay-ons, (who are included in both stocks), and likewise ignore deaths, retirements, change of occupations, and other disappearances, and thus attribute the above difference of 40,720 persons entirely to returns of the immigrants recorded during 1960–1970, then the indicated return rate would be nearly 23 percent of the immigration.

On the other hand, if we recognize that our stock figures include exchange visitors and former students still staying on in the U.S. at census time – to a greater degree in April 1970 than in the census of 1960 due to the rising trend in their numbers – then the 1970 stock should be reduced to comparability with 1960. If this reduction is as little as 6 percent of the 1970 stock, or 14,777 persons, it raises the inter-censal difference to 55,497; and this indicates a return rate of 31 percent of the recorded immigration. But this calculated difference should be referred to the immigration of *qualified* persons – i.e., the gross numbers less 20 percent for converted students – which amount to 141,600; against this figure, the disappearance of 55,497 persons amounts to a 39 percent rate of return.

On balance of all these considerations, we settle on the figure of 30 percent for the rate of return of qualified immigrants.

This estimate is broadly supported by other evidence. See the U.S. Congress (1967, p. 105) statement by Charles Kidd, estimating a 25 percent rate of return flow of Latin American PTK immigrants during 1961–65. Note also higher return rates for Indian PTK (including temporary visitors) suggested by data in Institute of Applied Manpower Research (1970, pp. 45–47), and still higher rates for LDC doctors leaving the U.K. (see footnote 11). See also recent surveys of migration intentions of LDC professionals and students in the U.S., by the National Science Foundation (1973, especially appendix table B.23), and by UNITAR [see Glaser (1974)].

II.3. LDC students converting to permanent immigrants in the U.S. (data available for 1967–1970).[a]

	1967	1968	1969	1970
Number of LDC Students converted from F visas to immigrant status	6,456	4,889	4,839	6,796
Percentage of LDC total immigrants	27.6	17.2	17.6	20.1

[a]*Sources*: U.S.I.N.S. (1965, 1967, 1971; tables 6c and 8); U.S.I.N.S. (1967–1970; charts 10, 24); NSF (1972).

II.4. Educational cost of U.S. equivalent of PTK immigrants from LDCs, as of 1965

This calculation relies chiefly on data assembled by Cartter in his chapter on 'The economics of higher education' in Chamberlain (1969). We have adapted Cartter's figures on direct educational costs to society and on incomes foregone (assuming no part-time earnings) per student in professional schools, except for medical students whose instructional costs are derived from Department of Health, Education, and Welfare (1974, table 18). The data used here have been found to be broadly consistent with the limited studies available on the average costs of professional education. In all our unit education figures we have sought to exclude the costs of research and social services which are not directly educational activities, and also to exclude capital outlays on plant and equipment while including annual maintenance and depreciation charges; in this sense, our unit costs approximate average variable costs of professional education rather than average total costs. These unit costs are then weighted in correspondence with the mix of professions in the U.S. immigration from LDCs, to yield an average relevant 'social cost' figure for the U.S. equivalent of the professional immigrants.

The basic data are as follows.

Profession	Direct educational costs	Income foregone	Total
Ph.D.s (4 years)	$14,600	$30,000	$44,600
M.D.s (4 years)	22,000	30,000	52,000
Engineering, architecture, accounting, statistics, etc.[19] (2 years)	5,600	10,000	15,600
Other professions[19] (1 year)	2,800	5,000	7,800
Nursing (2 years)	3,600	8,000	11,600

Occupational breakdowns of the immigrants in the I.N.S. reports indicate an average ratio of 1:5 for the 4-year training types versus the 1- and 2-year types. We have accordingly taken the 4-year programs at an average cost of $48,000, with weights of 1; and the other programs at an average cost of $12,000 with weights of 5. The weighted average is $18,000.

This figure comes down to $15,000 by two further adjustments. One is to take account of the indications that Cartter's data do not exclude all the irrelevant outlays on sponsored research and on public services in professional institutions (Cartter's figures come close to but still exceed the professional-level estimates of Grubel and Scott (1966), who sought specifically to eliminate those irrelevant items from their data. A second item to be removed is the actual earnings of graduate students; if these earnings amount to one-fourth of the stated 'income foregone', they would eliminate some 16 percent of the whole educational cost.

Our figure of $15,000 in 1965 is adapted to 1971 by applying the rate of cost inflation at somewhat over 6 percent a year, yielding a 1971 figure of $22,500.

[19]The indicated figures for these professions are moderately and reasonably larger than the annual 'college costs' in 1959 as estimated by Hines et al. (1970) and cited by Psacharopoulos, (1973, table D1).

Appendix III: Calculations for the United Kingdom

III.1. Alternative measures of PTK immigration

The calculations for the U.K. in this paper rely primarily on B-voucher admissions under the Commonwealth Immigration Statistics of the Home Office. In contrast, some scholars choose to include the 'A' vouchers along with the 'B' type. However, most of the 'A' immigrants appear to be subprofessional, and are listed by industry, whereas the 'B' type mostly comprises scientists, engineers, physicians and other professionals listed by occupation. Those professionals who do get counted under 'A' instead of under 'B' are perhaps equalized by those nonprofessionals who get counted under 'B'.

Still larger inflows are shown in some studies by taking the figures of the International Passenger Survey, an annual small sample whose results are published by the Office of Population Censuses and Surveys (O.P.C.S.) annually in the March issue of The Registrar General's Quarterly Return (H.M.S.O., London). In this survey, 'migrants' are defined as 'persons' intending to stay 12 months or more; and the breakdown provides a category of 'professional and managerial' coming from the 'overseas Commonwealth', in the range of 12,000–14,500 persons a year during the period 1967–73; and outflows as well as inflows are tabulated. Unfortunately, these figures appear to be a miscellaneous collection which are unusable for our purposes, as they combine the A- and B-voucher holders together with temporary workers, visitors and extended tourists (a fraction of these stay on indefinitely). They also show outflows running at 66–72 per cent of the gross inflows. In fact, the so-called 'net inflow' of these 'migrants' – i.e., the difference between their annual inflow and out-flow – is only a little larger than the annual arrivals on A- and B-vouchers; this suggests that the others are mostly visitors of a steady circulating kind (corresponding to the 'exchange visitors' and 'temporary workers' in the U.S. statistics). The impression of little accumulation of these visitors in the national manpower stock is reinforced by the fact that neither arrivals nor departures of the relevant categories show any rising trend.

III.2. Educational cost of U.K. equivalent of 1966 stock of PTK from LDCs

	1966 Census	of which trained abroad[20]	
(a) Scientists from developing countries	6,170	80%	5,000
Doctors from developing countries	8,785	60%	5,300
	14,955		10,300
Foreign-trained stock multiplied by average British educational cost[21]			

£15,000 each in 1964 prices:
£154,500,000 aggregate value

(b) All other professionals from developing countries		77,400	total professional and technical stock
	less	15,000	of scientists and doctors above
		62,400	all others
assume 80 percent trained abroad		50,000	foreign-trained stock
		£6,000	each in 1964 prices[22]
			£300,000,000 aggregate value.

(c) Total of (a)+(b)   £454,500,000 in 1964 prices.

III.3. Educational cost of U.K. equivalent of annual inflow of PTK from LDCs

Totals based on immigration in 1970 and 1971 of holders of Commonwealth B-vouchers (all qualified abroad, except for some who studied in Britain then exited, then returned) in gross inflows (returns not deducted here).

(1) Scientists from developing countries (based on 1970–71 average inflow of 195 scientists and technologists, of whom about 40 percent are assumed to be scientists, in accordance with the 1966 census).   80

(1') Doctors from developing countries (based on 1970–71 average inflow, including those on entry certificates).   400

Total   480 persons

  Valued at £15,000 each in 1964 prices (as in part 2 above):   £7,200,000

(2) All other professionals from developing countries.   463 persons
  (by deducting scientists and doctors from average annual inflow 1970–71 of all professionals from developing countries).
  Valued at £6,000 each in 1964 prices (as in part 2 above):   £2,778,000

(3) Total of (a) and (b): approximately £10,000.000 in 1964 prices; equivalent in 1971 prices to just over £13,000,000.

(4) With estimate of nearly one-sixth for professionals from other (non-Commonwealth) developing countries: grand total of £15,000,000.

[20]Estimated percentages derived from data for doctors alone, in Gish (1971).

[21]Based on data for scientists with a B.Sc., or Ph.D., degree, from Working Group on Migration, The Brain Drain (London, HMSO, 1967, Cmnd. 3417), ch. IV; and for doctors, from Royal Commission on Medical Education 1965–68, Report (London, HMSO, 1968, Cmnd. 3569), paras. 409–413, as assembled by Gish (1968, p. 1423). The data for B.Sc. scientists account for six years of schooling (upper secondary plus university), and are said to have excluded research expenditures. The medical data account for three years of upper secondary schooling, two years of university training, and three years of clinical service, along with annual interest and depreciation on the capital value of the schools. Both sources seem to count in the support costs of students, in place of incomes foregone by students. The B.Sc. estimates used here are consistent with estimates by Layard, Sargan, Ager and Jones (1971) as cited by Psacharopoulos (1973, table D1). The postgraduate (professional-level) costs, estimated by Morris and Ziderman in Economic Trends, May 1971 and cited by Psacharopoulos (1973, p. 71), while not fully comparable with those utilized in the present paper, seem consistent with our figures at comparable points.

[22]From Working Group on Migration, The Brain Drain.

(5) Relative magnitudes of the above £15 million: against 1970 GDP of £49.7 and 1971 GDP of £55.0 billion: less than 0.03 of one percent; against 1970 Government educational current expenditure (all levels) of £2.25 billion: less than 0.7 of one percent; or just over 0.5 of one percent of current plus capital expenditures.

References

Atkinson, A., K. Barnes and E. Richardson, 1970, Canada's highly qualified manpower resources (Manpower and Immigration, Ottawa).
Canada, Prices and Incomes Commission, 1972, Inflation, unemployment and incomes policy (Consumer Affairs, Ottawa).
Chamberlain, N.W., 1969, Contemporary economic issues (Irwin, New York).
Council of Scientific and Industrial Research (CSIR), 1972a, National register of scientific and technical personnel (Indians abroad) (CSIR, New Delhi).
CSIR, 1972b, Technical manpower (CSIR, New Delhi).
Education and World Affairs, 1970, International migration of high-level manpower (Praeger, New York), chs. 17, 18.
Gish, O., 1968, The Royal Commission and the immigrant doctors, The Lancet, 29 June.
Gish, O., 1971, Doctor migation and world health (Bell, London).
Glaser, W.A., 1974, Brain drain and study abroad: Findings of a UNITAR research project, mimeo (Columbia University, New York).
Grubel, H.B. and A.D. Scott, 1966, The immigration of scientists and engineers to the U.S., 1949–61, Journal of Political Economy, August.
Gupta, M.L., 1973, Outflow of high-level manpower from the Philippines, International Labour Review, February.
Hines et al., 1970, Social and private rates of return to investment in schooling, Journal of Human Resources, summer.
Henderson, G., 1970, Emigration of highly skilled manpower from the developing countries (UNITAR, New York).
HEW, 1974, Costs of education in health professions, HRA 74–32 (Government Printing Office (GPO), Washington).
Institute of Applied Manpower Research, 1970, The brain drain study, part I (IAMR, New Delhi).
Institut national de la statistique et des études économiques, 1971, Resultats du sondage au 1/20, Recensement général de la population de 1968 (Imprimerie nationale).
Layard et al., 1971, Qualified manpower and economic performance (Penguin, New York).
New York Times, 1974a, Foreign doctors criticized here, 30 October.
New York Times, 1974b, House bill would tie medical school aid, 13 December.
NSF, 1972, Scientists, engineers and physicians from abroad: Trends through 1970, 72–312 (NSF, Washington).
NSF, 1973, Immigrant scientists and engineers in the U.S., 73–302 (GPO, Washington).
Organization of Economic Cooperation and Development (OECD), 1970, The international movement of scientists and engineers, mimeo (OECD, Paris).
Paine, S., 1974, Exporting workers: The Turkish case (Cambridge University Press, Cambridge).
Psacharopoulos, G., 1973, Returns to education (Elsevier, Amsterdam).
Reubens, E.P., 1975, The new brain drain from developing countries, 1960–1972, in: R.D. Leiter, ed., Costs and benefits of education (Twayne, Boston).
Rose, E.J.B., et al., 1969, Colour and citizenship (Oxford University Press, Oxford).
Stevens, R. and J. Vermeulen, 1972, Foreign trained physicians and American medicine (HEW, Washington).
Tapinos, G., 1973, The economic and social consequences of highly skilled migration from developing countries into France (Fondation nationale des sciences politiques, Paris).

U.K., University Grants Committee, 1971, First employment of university graduates, in: New Society, 18 November.
U.S. Congress, House Committee on Government Operations, 1967, The brain drain into the U.S. of scientists, engineers and physicians: A staff study (GPO, Washington).
U.S. Department of Commerce, Bureau of the Census, 1973, National origin and language, PC(2)-1A (GPO, Washington).
U.S. Department of Justice, INS, 1965, 1967, 1971, Annual report (GPO, Washington).
U.S. Department of Justice, INS, 1967–1970, Annual indicators of immigration (GPO, Washington).
U.S. Department of Labor, 1973, Manpower report of the President (GPO, Washington), March.
Watanabe, S., 1969, The brain drain from developing to developed countries, International Labour Review 99, April.

CHAPTER 12

EMIGRATION OF HIGHLY EDUCATED MANPOWER
A problem for Colombian educational policy?

Albert BERRY

University of Toronto, Toronto, Ontario, Canada

Maria MENDEZ

Data Resources, Inc., Canada

1. Introduction

The social payoff from public subsidies to higher education may clearly be lowered if a significant number of the recipients of such subsidies emigrate.[1] This paper considers whether the propensity to emigrate is high enough to worry about, i.e., to take explicitly into account in planning higher education, to evaluate control programs, etc. The issue in question can be raised with respect to specific professions, to all persons with say a university education, or to any other groups of interest. Here our discussion focuses primarily on university trained persons as a group with some limited reference to the specific situations of such groups as doctors and engineers.

Reaching some judgement calls for data on emigration, data on educational subsidies, and an estimated or assumed relationship between the subsidies and the emigration, presumably operating through the stock of educated manpower.

2. Emigration from Colombia

Over the post-WWII period, Colombia has suffered considerable net emigration, much of it to neighbouring Venezuela. The other major destination has been the United States. Most emigrants have been in the lower or middle skill categories, especially those bound for Venezuela. The net outflow over the postwar period appears to have been over one million, with well over half a million living in Venezuela from all indications,[2] probably 100–150 thousand

---

[1] For a discussion see Berry and Soligo (1974). The objective function is assumed to relate only to non-emigrants. When people leave it is assumed that the government feels no further responsibility for them.

[2] The 1961 census of population in Venezuela recorded 88,357 Colombian nationals living in Venezuela and 102,000 persons born in Colombia (including a few thousand born of Venezuelan parents). By 1971 the number of persons born in Colombia had risen to 179,000;

in the U.S.[3] The general nature of the flows is clear enough; they are responses to differentials in economic opportunities and potential income streams. As a result of its oil, Venezuela has become a relatively rich country in comparison with Colombia; the U.S. obviously is.

3. Empirical evidence on migration[4]

Colombian migration statistics, especially those on emigration, under-estimate the phenomenon since a high share of the movement is illegal; most legal migrants probably do show up. Underreporting should be less severe for highly skilled persons since most of them are presumably legal migrants. The series of arrivals and departures of persons planning to change their country of residence[5] are in principle the relevant ones (table 1); total recorded arrivals and departures (table A.1) can also be of interest given the possibility that a fair number of Colombians leave on student or tourist visas and somehow manage to stay abroad.

Defining high-level manpower[6] as persons with university degrees and accept-ing the number of persons on permanent visas as an accurate measure of long term flows,[7] Eusse finds the net (gross) loss of professionals through migration

in 1950 it had been only 46,000. [See Venezuela (1972, p. 19; 1966, pp. 52–61).] The total foreign-born population rose rapidly from 209 thousand in the 1950 census to 542 thousand in the 1961 census, and only marginally to 599 thousand in the 1971 census. The Colombians living illegally in Venezuela are many, so the total population might be 600–800 thousand. Gall (1972, p. 6) reports 'the most common estimate given by Venezuelan officials is that around 500,000 Colombians have entered Venezuela illegally during the 1960s. For the full postwar period the net flow would be substantially higher, even allowing for some return flow to Colombia. Most of these indocumentados (without the appropriate legal entry permit) are engaged in low paying (by Venezuelan standards) jobs in agriculture, domestic service and other jobs which Venezuelans and legalized immigrants tend to scorn.

[3]As of 1970, the U.S. population census recorded about 63,500 residents who had been born in Colombia. For 1975 the figure would be somewhat higher, perhaps 80,000. The number of illegal immigrants appears to be sizeable. A scattering of Colombians reside in Europe, Canada and other Latin countries. During 1964–6, 200 Colombians immigrated to Canada, of whom 41 were professional and technical workers. Over 1962–66 18 new working licences were issued by the French government to engineers and natural scientists from Colombia. (See Henderson (1970, pp. 172–174).

[4]Many useful statistics on flow of high level manpower and students abroad are presented in Eusse (1970). The study also undertakes various types of analysis into aspects of migration. It is summarized in UNITAR (1971, ch. 2). Also of particular interest is Chaparro and Arias (1970).

[5]That is, to stay in the country of destination for a year or more.

[6]We henceforth use this term interchangeably with professionals, technicians and kindred workers, or usually just 'professionals'.

[7]This is, of course, only an approximation. Some persons leave on 'permanent visas' and later return. These moves eventually cancel out for each individual, but at any point in time some people are abroad (in Colombia) who will later return (leave); depending on how many people are in those situations (more precisely on the difference between the size of the group of emigrants which will return and the group of immigrants which will leave again), the approxi-mation used will be more or less accurate. When the time period is fairly long and emigration is not increasing rapidly, it is likely to be a fairly good proxy.

Table 1

Flows of permanent migrants.*a

	Official DANE statistics							U.S. Immigration Service statistics	
	Colombians[b]			Foreigners			Total net emigration[c] (7) = (3)+(6)	Colombian immigrants to the U.S. (8)	Immigrants whose last permanent residence was in Colombia (9)
Year	Emigration (1)	Immigration (2)	Net emigration (3)	Emigration (4)	Immigration (5)	Net emigration[c] (6)			
1953							12,331		
1954							3,299		
1955	3,996	(40)d	3,956	16,212	10,797	5,415	9,371		
1956	4,019	(40)d	3,979	9,691	11,649	-1,958	2,061		
1957	4,086	43	4,043	6,028	5,588	440	4,483	2,891	
1958	5,439	65	5,374	7,062	4,297	2,765	8,139	2,524	
1959	7,084	20	7,064	9,018	2,117	6,901	13,965	2,989	
1960	8,057	227	7,830	11,270	6,303	4,967	12,797	3,559	
1961	7,851	220	7,651	10,982	6,135	4,847	12,478	4,678	
1962	9,822	6,194	3,628	11,693	4,741	6,952	10,580	5,733	
1963	12,654	6,181	6,473	9,071	4,338	4,733	11,206	10,446	
1964	11,028	1,140	9,888	3,021	4,234	-1,213	8,675	10,885	
1965	11,167	939	10,228	3,799	3,124	675	10,903	9,504	
1966	4,018	513	3,505	995	2,182	-1,187	2,318	4,556	
1967	3,049	1,180	1,869	849	3,233	-2,384	-515	6,902	4,679
1968	3,360	621	2,639	1,279	2,011	-732	1,907	7,627	6,999
1969	797	132	665	423	692	-269	486	6,724	7,658
1970									6,738
1971									6,463
1972									5,225
1955-68			78,772			29,952			
1958-68			66,794			26,055			

*Since about 1964 the official DANE statistics are not fully credible; they appear to be underestimated. See the discussion in the appendix.
aPersons on permanent or long term visas.
bBy nationality.
cMinus sign indicates net emigration.
d( ) Estimates; data not available.
Sources: Columns (1), (2), (4), and (5): for 1955-1967, DANE (1955-1967); fc. 1968-1969, DANE (1974); for 1970, unpublished figures made available by DANE. Column (8): U.S. Immigration and Naturalization Service, Annual report, various years.

Table 2

Migration of professionals.

| | Estimates by Eusse based on Colombian statistics: Colombians and foreigners | | | Ratio of: Colombian permanent emigrants to all permanent emigrants[a] | Estimated Colombian[b] permanent emigrants | | Immigration to U.S. of professionals whose last permanent residence was Colombia |
	Permanent emigrants (1)	Permanent immigrants (2)	Net permanent emigrants (3) = (1)−(2)	(4)	Est.A[c] (5) = (1)(4)	Est.B[c] (6)	(7)
1955	4,674	949	3,727	0.198	925		
1956	2,937	1,079	1,858	0.293	861		
1957	1,784	787	997	0.404	721		
1958	1,939	692	1,247	0.435	843	487	
1959	2,538	357	2,181	0.440	1,117	668	
1960	4,226	1,278	2,948	0.417	1,762	1,328	
1961	4,125	1,230	2,895	0.417	1,720	1,119	376
1962	4,035	1,778	2,257	0.457	1,844	1,080	511
1963	3,071	1,821	1,250	0.582	1,787	1,089	691
1964	1,377	1,483	−106	0.785	1,081	909	973
1965	1,810	989	821	0.746	1,350	1,263	868
1966	3,117	1,205	1,912	0.802	2,500	1,591	777
1967	1,315	1,306	9	0.782	1,028	1,136	404
1968	1,450	1,976	−526	0.724	1,050	1,227	764
1969							669
1970							395
1971							436
1972							374
1955–68	38,398	16,928	21,470		18,589	16,555[d]	

[a]Professionals and others.
[b]By place of birth.

[c]See sources and methodology.
[d]Assuming same flows over 1955–57 as in estimate A.

Sources and methodology: Cols. (1) and (2) are from Eusse (1970, pp. 44–45). Col. (4) is based on table A.1. Col. (7) is from Chaparro and Arias (1970, p. 12). Estimate A of the outflow of Colombian professionals on a long term basis ('permanent', to use the terminology of the statistics) assumes the same percentage of professionals who emigrate permanently (Eusse series) are Colombians as for all permanent emigrants, the latter percentage based on table A.1. This should give an upper limit both because the assumption would seem likely to be upward biasing and because the Eusse series is higher than the one we estimated directly from DANE figures. Estimate B uses the authors' calculations of recorded professional migration as well as making some allowance for apparent changes in the inclusiveness of the category 'permanent' in the migration data. As noted in the appendix (table A.1) there was in 1964 a sharp drop in the share of departing foreigners, excluding tourists, who were defined as permanent emigrants; subsequently a higher share were classified as departing nonresidents ('nonresident foreigners returning at the end of their visit'). Over most of the period 1958–1969 the proportion of professionals in this category of 'nonresident foreigners returning at the end of their visit' was higher than in the caregory of departing 'resident nationals and foreigners' (i.e., permanent emigrants), primarily because the former had a lower share of economically inactive. Switching from the latter to the former category a group of foreigners with the professional–total ratio characterizing the group of all departing foreigners except tourists, would lower the professional–total proportion within the (reduced) category of permanent emigrants. The decline would not imply that the share of professionals in Colombian permanent emigrants had fallen. Estimate B (Col. 6) assumes that the ratio 'foreign professional permanent emigrants–all foreign permanent emigrants' was half way between the ratios of professionals–total for 'nonresident foreigners returning at the end of their stay' and for departing 'resident nationals and foreigners'. The estimate of professional emigrants shown in table A.3 is used except over 1966–68; a figure of 1,800 is arbitrarily chosen in 1966, and the Eusse estimates are used in 1967 and 1968.

over the period 1955–1968 to be about 21.5 (38.4) thousand (see table 2). But there is strong evidence that these are overestimates. On the one hand, the official figures suggest a net outflow of Colombian professionals of more like 11.2–15.5 thousand.[8] Meanwhile the net flow of foreigners seems to have been inward to the tune of say 2–5 thousand.[9] The net outflow of Colombians and foreigners would appear to be only about 9–12 thousand, possibly less; 15 thousand would seem to be an upper limit. (The range within which total net outflow is likely to fall reflects the presumption that the degree of under-reporting of net emigration of Colombians is positively related to the degree of

[8] Over 1958–1968, estimate A of table 2 shows 16,082 Colombian professional emigrants and estimate B 11,897. Over 1955–68 the figures would be 18,589 and about 14,404, respectively (using the estimate A figures for 1955–57 in the estimate B calculation). With an estimate of 3,151 Colombian permanent immigrants to Colombia who were professionals (table A.3), the net emigration would be around 11,200–15,400. Underreporting could be of some import-ance but a bias toward overstatement about occupation could work the other way. The net effect of these two possible biases is unclear.

[9] The population census of 1964 suggests an increase in foreign born professionals working in Colombia, vis-a-vis the census of 1951, of about this magnitude. (See the statistical appendix.) Meanwhile, Eusse (1970, table XIV) lists 4,728 foreign professionals under the title 'Foreign professionals working in Colombia; Period 1959–1968' and cites as his source the Colombian Immigration Office. It is not clear whether this was an estimate of the 1968 stock, a flow over the years cited, or what. Given the source, it is probably the gross inflow over those years; some of these persons would leave again within the period.

Table 3

Stock of Colombian high-level manpower in relation to net emigration of professionals.

Field	Stock of titled professionals: 1964 population census			Migration, 1955–64: Eusse data			Net emigration 1955–68 (7)	Authors' estimates		
	Total (1)	Practicing profession (2)	Available stock 1964 (3)	Emigration (4)	Immigration (5)	Net emigration (6)		Net emigration of Colombians (8)	Net emigration 1955–68 as a percent of available stock, 1964 (9)	Net emigration as a percent of graduates 1960–68 (10)
(1) Agriculture and related fields	2,271	1,630	2,157	827	423	404	236	330	10.9	5.4–6.3
(2) Natural and exact sciences	1,695	1,076	1,610	1,910	877	1,033	603	844	37.5	30.5–35.2
(3) Law	11,199	3,446	10,639	1,645	637	1,008	590	864	5.6	8.2–9.5
(4) Humanities, social sciences (except economics), education university teachers and other[a]										
(5) Engineering and related fields (including architecture)	6,952	4,654	6,604	11,326	6,420	4,906	2,870	4,010	43.5	33.0–38.0
(6) Doctors, dentists and surgeons	10,256	8,139	9,743	11,196	4,529	6,667	3,900	5,445	40.0	27.7–31.9
(7) Administration and economics	12,132	11,025	11,525	3,807	1,316	2,491	1,457	2,035	12.6	16.6–19.2
	7,565	3,893	7,187	7,587	2,726	4,861	2,843	3,971	39.6[b]	37.8–43.7[b]
Total	52,070	33,863	49,467	38,298	16,928	21,370	12,500	17,500	25.3	21.9–25.3

[a] These categories were perforce lumped together due to different types of disaggregation among the different types of information used jointly in this table.
[b] Possibly misleading as the migration figures may include a broader range or activities than the stock of flow figures.

Sources and methodology: Cols. (1) and (2) come from the 1964 population census [DANE (1967, p. 106)]. The data on new graduates are from table A.5; Cols. (4)–(6) on migration flows are from Eusse (1970, pp. 44–45). Cols. (7) and (8) are calculated simply as col. (6) × 0.588 and 0.819, respectively, i.e., it is assumed that the total net emigration was 12,500 and it was distributed in the same way by professions as was Eusse's estimate, and that net emigration of Colombians was 17,500 and so distributed (See table 2 and appendix for discussion).

Of considerable importance is the methodological question of how to deal with professionals not exercising their profession; according to the 1964 census only 65 percent of the titled professionals were; if law is excluded the figure rises to 74 percent. Among those not exercising 'their profession' it is useful to distinguish (a) nonparticipants, e.g., retired persons, (b) persons who although in a different profession were doing jobs of more or less comparable complexity, and (c) persons doing substantially simpler and less remunerative jobs. In considering the loss of high talent mapower in general, there may be no particular concern for which type of high level work a person does; a certain percent of any given group will cross occupational lines. In the calculations undertaken here we employ the concept of available stock of a given profession; this includes those actually doing it plus group (b) above; it excludes groups (a) and (c). In practice we abstract from group (c). The estimate of available stock for 1964 (col. 3) assumes that in each field 5 percent of the persons with a title were not working. In highly specialized fields like dentistry and petroleum engineers about 90 percent were working in 'their' profession, suggesting that nonparticipants would not be much more than 5 percent.

For the period 1955–68, we have estimated that Eusse's figure for net emigration may be too high by about 70 percent. For 1960–68, including some years of apparent underreporting of gross emigration, we assume this ratio might be only 30–50 percent. This assumption underlies col. (10).

underreporting of net immigration of foreigners). Net outflow for all occupations was perhaps in the range of 600–700 thousand.[10]

Table 3 places the estimates of migration of professionals in the perspective of the stocks of such manpower and the recent output of graduates in Colombia. It suggests that over 1955–58 net emigration of professionals averaged around 2 percent of the existing available stock; over 1960–68 it averaged about 20–25 percent of the new flow of graduates in Colòmbia. When only Colombians are considered, both ratios are greater still. Evidently then, emigration has been a phenomenon of considerable proportions. Relative to stock or to new flow, the most emigration-prone categories were natural and exact sciences, engineering (including architecture), administration/economics, and a hodge-podge group including humanities, teaching, social sciences and 'other'. The low emigration groups were law, agricultural sciences and (relatively speaking, in any case) medicine. In absolute terms, emigration of engineers accounted for nearly a third of the total loss.

In the early sixties (1961–63) the ratio net emigration–new graduates in Colombia was possibly as high as 40–50 percent.[11] By 1968–70, the same ratio

[10]Over 1955–1968, recorded permanent emigrants were 196,600; and recorded immigrants were 107,464. Figures since about 1963 are almost certainly underestimated (relative to the criterion of the earlier years); out best estimate of legal net emigration is 112 thousand (see the appendix). But the major flows of migrants, quantitatively speaking, are the essentially one-way illegal ones – especially to Venezuela. Counting these, the total gross (net) emigration over the period in question was probably something like 900 (650) thousand.

[11]The ICETEX figures taken literally imply a ratio of 75 percent. Our best estimate, however, is 40–45 percent and it is unlikely the true figure could lie above 50 percent.

was perhaps 15–30 percent,[12] not because emigration had clearly declined in absolute terms (though it may have) but because the flow of graduates had risen sharply, more than doubling over this period (see table A.5). Unfortunately, evidence is very spotty since the mid-1960s, so one can only speculate as to whether a systematic trend has developed. Legal immigration into the U.S. of professionals with last permanent residence in Colombia has declined in the early seventies (see table 2); it seems probable that total net emigration of professionals has done the same,[13] although if so this could be due in part to the boom conditions in Colombia since the mid 1960s, and therefore reversible if those conditions were to change (à la Venezuelan oil boom coupled with Colombian recession as at present).

In any case it is worth while to consider whether, at the relatively high level of net emigration prevailing in the early sixties, or the possibly somewhat lower level of the late sixties, the phenomenon constitutes a problem which warrants consideration in the formulation of educational or other policies.

4. Measures of loss (gain) from migration

Depending on the nature of one's concern with migration loss (gain), conceptually different measures will be appropriate. One may ask any of the following questions:

(1) How does current (international) migration affect current income levels of non-migrants?
(2) How do current and past migration affect current income levels of non-migrants?
(3) How does current migration affect the present value of future income streams?
(4) How do current and past migration affect the present value of future income streams?

Question 3 is the appropriate one for most policy questions related to migration (e.g., should it be curtailed or encouraged; should educational policy take account of possible losses (gains) from migration?). Question 4 is of more academic interest, for example in understanding how migration may effect non-migrants over the development process. The same goes for questions 1 and

---

[12]For specific short periods it is not possible to be at all precise about the net emigration figures since our basic consistency checks come from the population censuses in Colombia, Venezuela, and the U.S.

[13]It is well known that there have been many illegal entrants to the U.S. in recent years, and that Colombians are among these. Presumably most come on tourist visas and then 'drop out of sight'. Illegal emigrants to Venezuela use tourist cards or frontier passes, or simply slip across the border [Gall (1972, p. 6)]. But it seems unlikely that many professionals can operate in such a tenuous situation. Such professionals as evade normal immigration to another country presumably do so on the basis of falsified visas and other such devices, so they would normally be recorded in the statistics.

2, but since they can in some cases be answered more accurately than 3, it is useful to bear them in mind. The discussion which follows focuses mainly on question 3 but also alludes to the others.

4.1. Sources of possible loss from emigration of highly skilled persons

Entirely apart from the conceptual questions in which one may be interested, the appropriate way to measure the loss from emigration of professional talent is open to debate due to our lack of knowledge about its effects. In the estimates made here we try to effect a reasonable amount of sensitivity analysis around some of the assumptions which are particularly arbitrary. High and low estimates of loss are designed to bracket the true loss with a fair level of confidence. Calculations are made for the groups of years 1961–63 and 1966–68, a choice dictated in part by data availability and in part by the hypothesis that the significance of the brain drain was reduced between the two periods.

The simplest set of assumptions used, designed to capture the more obvious and more easily measurable components of gain and loss, is:

(1) Non-emigrants (hereafter referred to as 'Colombia') receive as benefits from the education of emigrants the remittances sent back by the emigrants, but nothing else.

(2) Emigrants are typical of all graduates in their professional category as concerns the public subsidy they receive.[14]

(3) Had the emigrants stayed in the country, their income (as a group) in each future period would have been equal to their marginal social product, an assumption only plausible when the outflow is small relative to the remaining and future stocks (not always true for some high-talent categories).

Under this set of assumptions, the only source of loss from the migration is the educational subsidy going to the emigrants, and question 3 is particularly straightforward. Some of the conceptual problems which arise with respect to other sources of loss (gain) are not present in this case.[15] On the basis of 1962 public expenditure figures by level of education, we estimate that the average subsidy received by a person completing a university degree was in the range 25,000–31,000 current pesos.[16] Most of the subsidy occurs at the university

---

[14]The public subsidy is that part of the cost of their education which is borne by the government. We do not include the intrafamily transfers to the student nor transfers through such private institutions as the Roman Catholic Church.

[15]But note that the group of people called the non-emigrants, whose welfare constitutes the objective function of this analysis, is a changing group as emigration occurs over time. Thus the non-emigrant group (losers from transfers to emigrants) of an early period will include people who later emigrate themselves. Various conceptual complexities in the measurement of educational subsidy loss to non-emigrants are discussed in Berry and Soligo (1974).

[16]This is assuming 4.5 years of university training.

level. With an annual net emigration of 1,250–1,700 (1961–63)[17] the annual loss would be in the range of 31–53 millions of pesos, or 22–30 percent of public expenditures on higher education. (The latter ratio has a narrower range than its numerator, since estimates of numerator and denominator are positively related – see the appendix.) Meanwhile remittances from professionals working abroad averaged perhaps 10–35 million pesos, indicating in that event a loss of current income flows due to past and present migration (or most of the remittance income is of course associated with past emigration). To appraise the welfare effect of current emigration (i.e., to answer question 3 above), the discounted value of future remittances from the persons currently emigrating is the relevant magnitude. Our calculation suggests a value in the range of 7–29 million pesos. The remittances are not sufficient to offset the educational subsidy loss, and a net loss of about 17–38 million pesos, or 13–22 percent of higher educational expenditures, therefore from the emigration.[18]

With a net outflow averaging perhaps 500–1,000 persons during 1966–68,[19] and a 1967 subsidy figure of 31–40 thousand pesos per student, the annual loss would be 16–40 million pesos, or 5–9 percent of public expenditures on higher education. Remittances probably averaged 44–112 million pesos,[20] suggesting a net gain in terms of current income from present and past migration. Discounted future remittances of the annual net emigrants are, in this case, estimated at 6–44 million pesos; the lower and upper limits for the net loss from the two variables were 5 and 18 million, respectively, a more modest 3–9 percent of higher education cost.

A more refined measure of net loss through high talent emigration would also take account of the following factors.

(1) Factors implying additional loss:
  (a) Any positive externalities of the presence of additional highly skilled manpower in the country.
  (b) 'Factor proportions loss' if the total flow significantly alters the ratio of skilled manpower to other factors.[21]

---

[17]Eusse's data, which we conclude to have overestimated net emigration by 70 percent over 1955–68, imply an average of 2,134: if this is 70 percent overestimated, the true value is 1,255. But it appears that the overestimation may have been less during these years than later ones. With our higher estimate of net emigration of Colombians during these years, an average of 1,783 (table 2) and low levels of Colombian immigration and net foreign immigration, the figure could reach 1,700.

[18]See the appendix for calculation of the subsidies and table 4 for the way in which the lower and upper limit for the combined effect of the two variables is calculated.

[19]This is based on an average net outflow of Colombians of about 800–1,000 per year and a possible net inflow of foreigners of 0–300 per year.

[20]See the appendix.

[21]This effect was discussed in Berry and Soligo (1969). We disregard here any effect associated with atypically high or low savings ratios the emigrants might have.

(2) Factors implying gain (or reduced loss):
   (a) Increased welfare of non-emigrants (e.g., family) from seeing the emigrants better off than they would be in Colombia.
   (b) Any cases in which the income of the last emigrant is above marginal social product – as a result, for example, of monopoly power exerted by the professional groups in question, fee setting by governments at scales unrelated to (and above) social product, or possibly in imitation of developed country levels.[22]

None of these effects can be satisfactorily measured at present. Here we attempt estimates of the range for the first two, but not the last two.

4.2. Externalities of skilled emigrants

A variety of arguments could be adduced to the effect that persons like doctors, engineers and teachers do generate positive externalities,[23] so that their wage earnings are below their social product, but no solid evidence can be brought to bear. For our 'high loss' estimate we assume arbitrarily that social product is 15 percent above earnings; for the low estimate we assume that the two are equal.

A rough estimate of the income foregone annually in Colombia by the highly skilled net emigrants of 1961–63 is 54–74 million pesos;[24] 15 percent of the upper estimate future income stream for this group over 35 years and discounted at 8 percent would be 133 million pesos.[25] The comparable figure for the annual net emigration flow over 1966–68 (in 1967 pesos) would be 171 million.

4.3. Factor proportions loss

Even if each emigrant would have been paid his marginal product in Colombia there would, under neoclassical conditions (or some approximation thereto), be a loss to non-emigrants when the amount of migration leads to a discrete change in the remunerations of the skills in question. For a short period of

---

[22]These assumptions are prominent in the position taken by Bhagwati and Dellalfar (1973).

[23]E.g., if with more doctors medical care reaches more people, with some of the additional ones receiving a consumer's surplus from the purchase of medical services. For some other groups, perhaps especially lawyers, it could be as readily argued that there are negative externalities. And it is not clear without detailed analysis how the pricing of the services of professionals (such as doctors and engineers) responds to demand and supply. There may be some monopolistic price setting and/or some degree of monopolistic competition. In either case marginal social product could be below income.

[24]We refer to the average annual net emigration over the period. For details of the calculations see the appendix.

[25]The assumptions of 35 years and of full employment are upward biasing; that of no income increases over time is downward biasing.

time, and therefore a small emigration flow, this effect would be small or negligible. But since it is an increasing function of the amount of emigration (more directly, of the degree to which that emigration has affected the relative stock of any skill), the loss in present income due to past migration could be large. Being the result of an alteration in factor proportions, the welfare loss depends on whether the loss of a given skill through emigration is partially made up by more rapid production of the skill, and on the length of any lag between the emigration and the subsequent supply reaction.

Given the current state of our knowledge, the shape of the marginal productivity curve of given professions, or of highly skilled personnel as a whole, is very much guesswork; so is the supply response of students to the higher earnings resulting from emigration. We assume at the one extreme that the elasticity of the skilled wage in relation to the stock of professionals is -1 in the relevant range and that the supply response is such that 25 percent of the emigration loss is made up by additional domestic production of the skills in question, with no time lag.[26] At the other extreme we assume an elasticity of -2 and a supply response such as to offset 75 percent of the emigration.

The factor proportion loss attributable to the migration of a single year tends to be small, as noted above. But this loss over a period is greater than the sums of the loss attributable to the individual years. Hence, some way must be found to get a feel for the 'typical' annual loss if a migration flow continues over some period. If the 1961–63 net emigration loss (as a share of the stock) were maintained for 20 years, and one twentieth of the total loss in present value were 'charged' to the current year, this loss would fall between 2 and 66 million pesos.[27] At the net emigration rate estimated for 1966–68, it would be in the range of 6–187 million pesos. Since this form of loss can clearly be substantial if the elasticity of earnings to stock is high,[28] total loss estimates become quite sensitive to the length of the period over which emigration is assumed to occur, as well as to the assumptions made about elasticities.

---

[26]Both these assumed values (-1 and -2) are low compared to many guesstimates. For example, Dougherty (1971) in his work on the Colombian education system assumed alternative elasticities of substitution among seven different skill (i.e., education) categories of -4, -6, and -8. The highest category was 'persons with three or more years of higher education'. We disregard here the difference between (1) the elasticity of substitution and (2) the relationship between quantity and price of professionals, since the change in quantity and price of other educational categories would presumably be quite small for reasonable changes in the stock and price of professionals. The assumption that 75 percent of the loss of professionals through emigration is recouped by their expanded output may well be too high, partially offsetting any downward bias in the estimate of -2 for the elasticity of substitution.

[27]The choice of a 20-year discounting period was arbitrary. Unfortunately, the discounted factor proportions loss increases at an increasing rate with the length of the period considered. As with remittances, it was not obvious that relevant conditions would remain unchanged indefinitely. In any case, this loss would eventually dominate unless the discount rate was very high.

[28]But not too high. If loss is low it seems more likely that this would be due to a high elasticity of substitution between high level manpower and other factors rather than a low one.

4.4. Summary of quantifications for professionals

The previous discussion, summarized in the figures of table 4, suggests that emigration of high-talent manpower has not caused a large percentage change in the incomes of non-emigrants. Our high estimate of annual loss in present

Table 4

Summary of estimated annual loss from net emigration of 'high level' manpower.[a]

	1961–63 average (value in millions of 1962 pesos)		1966–68 average (values in millions of 1967 pesos)	
Component	Low estimate	High estimate	Low estimate	High estimate
(1) Educational subsidy	31	53	16	40
(2) Discounted future remittances	−14	−15	−11	−22
Subtotal (1)+(2)	17	38	5	18
(3) Discounted future externalities	0	133	0	171
(4) Discounted future factor proportions loss	2	66	6	187
Total (1)+(2)+(3)+(4)	19	237	11	376
As a percent of national income	0.07	0.82	0.002	0.55
As a percent of public expenditures on higher education	10.8–13.9	135–173	2.4–3.3	72–112

[a]For all components of loss or gain, except discounted future factor proportions loss, the values are related to the net outflow of the specific years in question and nothing else. But for factor proportions loss, as indicated in the text, no interest attaches to that calculation so the value reflects what would happen if the current rate of loss of stock through emigration were to prevail for another 20 years, with the total resulting loss divided equally among the 20 years.

Sources and methodology: The estimates are those presented elsewhere in the paper except in the case of remittances. For that variable the figure appearing under the low (high) estimate is the result of choosing that set of assumptions which generates the highest negative result but is consistent with the set which generated the low estimates for the other variables. Thus, for example, the low estimate of the educational subsidy for 1961–63 involved an annual net emigration of 1,250, so the figure for remittances must use the same assumption; given that, it is based on the set of assumptions (related specifically to the remittance flows) which gives the maximum figure. The converse applies in the case of the figure in the high-estimate column. As a result the two figures are not the two noted in the text as lower and upper limits.

value of the future income stream during 1961–63 is about 240 million pesos of 1962; the low estimate was only about 20 million. Comparable figures for 1966–68 (in 1967 pesos) would be about 375 million and 10 million, respectively.

More detailed knowledge about the various sources of loss is a prerequisite to a satisfactory understanding of the issue as a whole; one reflection of this is the very wide gap between our high and low estimates. In view of the number of arbitrary assumptions made, the present discussion must be considered exploratory, and in some respects illustrative. Looking ahead, the possibly important externalities and factor proportions losses, as well as remittances, will at best be difficult to estimate, so that the range within which the true net loss lies will be hard to narrow down. Apart from better estimates of certain variables of obvious relevance, serious attention must be given to the following possibilities:

(1) Marginal social product of at least some professions may be below earnings.
(2) The tax-payers who indirectly finance the emigrants receive nonmonetary benefits from their children's successes abroad.
(3) Gross emigration and gross immigration are sufficiently independent to make it meaningful to consider their effects separately.[29]
(4) Emigrants are atypical in the extent to which they have taken advantage of public subsidies to education.

5. Educational policy and emigration loss

Although even the higher estimates of loss through emigration do not loom large in relation to national income, they do when compared to public spending on higher education. Only if a high share of the emigrants had been educated in private institutions could the loss be a small share of those expenditures. Correspondingly, the emigration has probably had a major effect on the social rate of return to investment in higher education,[30] possibly pushing it to a point where a substantial reallocation of resources (e.g., towards physical capital) would be needed to equalize marginal social rates of return.[31] On the

[29]If no emigration occurred, immigration would probably be less as well. In any case, it is relevant to note that total permanent emigration in the professional categories considered above was over twice as high during 1955–68 as net emigration. If immigration responded to different factors than emigration, then the prevention of the latter could have a substantially higher payoff than implied by the discussion presented here.

[30]Recent studies of the rate of return of Colombia's education system have arrived at a consensus on the low social payoff to higher education, at least as measured by the income differentials associated with different education levels in the current state of the Colombian economy. (Although they differ to some extent on rate of return calculations for other levels of education, the two major studies to date agree on this. See Selowsky (1969) and Schultz (1968). Schultz calculated a private internal rate of return to university over secondary of between 4 and 5 percent (for persons working in Bogota); Selowsky's most relevant estimate referring to the nation as a whole was 6 percent. Schultz's calculation of the social rate of return was 3 percent. These estimates disregard emigration and are therefore biased upwards, probably substantially.

[31]Optimally, educational decisions would be based on a good feel for the marginal social productivity of additions to the stock of given professions *and* estimates of the share of the additions which would be lost via emigration. For Colombia, both of the estimates of the rate of return to university education put it so low (6 percent or less) as to imply overinvestment, even with no allowance for emigration loss. But no estimates are available for specific professions where rates might of course be much higher. Estimates of 'emigration/new graduates' are available by profession but behave erratically over the period considered, making it rather difficult to use them in such a decision process.

other hand, current emigration may be substantially less, relatively speaking, than that of the 1960s. The lag in availability of data is a serious constraint in the evaluation of the present situation.

An appropriate perspective on the brain drain in Colombia would be to view it as an important issue for attention (research attention before policy attention, however), but not as a national crisis. If a quarter of the public expenditures on higher education is being lost through emigration, prevention of that loss would have to rank as a priority issue in educational policy, but not necessarily in national policy. The training of engineers and doctors warrants particular attention as both are relatively expensive and characterized by large absolute levels of emigration. Since the propensity to emigrate has been much greater for engineers, it may be that the traditional concern over the outflow of doctors should be more appropriately placed on that of engineers.

Appendix

A.1. Migration statistics for Colombia

Each person arriving in or departing from Colombia is required to fill in a card with data on origin, destination, nationality, occupation, type of visa, and a few other pieces of information. These cards are tabulated by DANE, the Central Statistical Office, and they are the basis for the Colombian migration data used in this study. Most international travellers enter and leave by air, facilitating this reporting procedure. The data on nationality, visa, origin, etc., should be reasonably accurate since it can be checked by the government personnel to whom the cards are presented. Data on occupation cannot be so easily checked but is of no real concern to the control personnel; problems of definition arise through the open-ended nature of the question.

Table A.1 shows the historical series on total entries and departures, and those of persons listed as planning to stay for one year or more in the country of destination. Table A.2, meanwhile, presents data from the U.S. Immigration and Naturalization Service on arrivals of persons born in Colombia, by visa status. The Colombian figures on permanent (i.e., a planned stay of one year or longer abroad) departures and arrivals (cols. 1 and 5 of table A.1) are plausible for the decade 1953–63; in 1964 a definitional change occurred which affected only nonresident foreigners. A sudden drop in the figures for both Colombians and foreigners in 1966, and the subsequent virtual disappearance of this category, indicate that there was another change in the way travellers interpreted its definition.[32]

---

[32]Factors like the tightening up of U.S. immigration laws, the rapid economic growth in Colombia of the late 1960s and early 1970s, and the slower expansion in the U.S. might work to reduce the migration, but they would hardly wipe it out. It is interesting that a sharp drop in recorded emigration and immigration occurred in 1966, just after one of the changes in U.S. legislation designed to curtail immigration, especially of lower-skill workers. But the same abrupt decline occurred for the number of foreigners leaving and entering as for the number of Colombians.

The inconsistencies in definitions over time can most easily be demonstrated for Colombians alone (i.e., excluding foreigners). From 1966 on, the number of Colombians immigrating to the U.S. (table A.2, col. 4) actually exceeded the number reported as leaving their country on permanent visas (table A.1, col. 1a). A comparison of the two columns suggests that permanent departures of Colombians began to be understated around 1964, and were seriously so by 1966. Interestingly, a decrease comparable to that observed for permanent departures also characterizes the figures on permanent arrivals (table A.1, col. 5). A best guess would perhaps be that a typical observed ratio of 'recorded Colombian immigrants to U.S.[33] to recorded Colombian emigrants from Colombia', during 1968–1963, of around one half or less was plausible.[34] Meanwhile, between the 1950 and 1961 Venezuelan population censuses, the number of persons (residents or non-residents) reporting Colombia as their place of birth rose by 5.1 thousand per year; over 1961–1971 it rose by 7.7 thousand per year. Most of these persons were probably registered as permanent emigrants on their departure from Colombia; this would be consistent with the proposition that less than half were U.S. bound. Thus, Venezuela was probably receiving more duly recorded permanent immigrants from Colombia over this period than was the U.S. The share of such emigrants going to the U.S. may have been a little higher from 1964–71, when 63,084 persons born in Colombia immigrated to the U.S. The number entering Venezuela legally was perhaps 55–60 thousand.[35] Given these data, the DANE statistics on emigration of Colombians for 1964 on must be increasingly underestimated over time. If departures to United States and Venezuela accounted for 90 percent of Colombians legally immigrating to some other country, the total for 1964–71 might have been about 135 thousand, or nearly 17 thousand per year. During this period, and through 1973, the flow of immigrants to the U.S. trended downward. No information is available to permit a judgement as to whether this was true for Venezuela; we have not tried to build up series on Colombian immigration to other countries. Accordingly, it remains unclear whether or not the total outflow from Colombia has fallen since the mid-1960s.

[33]Persons whose last permanent residence was Colombia were 2 or 3 percent more.

[34]For 1964–68 the ratio was 1.3, which is clearly impossible. Over 1958–1968, the Colombians leaving Colombia on permanent visas were 83,529, or 7,594 per year; Colombians immigrating to the U.S. were 64,687, or 5,881 per year, which averaged 3,724 per year (assuming the 1962 figure was 4,698).

[35]Between the 1961 and 1971 population censuses in Venezuela, the number of persons giving Colombia as their birth place rose by 77 thousand, implying a net inflow over the period of perhaps 80,000, approximately equal to the gross inflow. Allowing for the only partial overlap with the 1964–71 period under discussion and for the fact that not all the persons recorded in the census would be permanent emigrants from Colombia (we assume 85–95 percent – given the high participation rate of foreign born persons in Venezuela, it seems that relatively few would be on tourist visas, student visas, etc.), a reasonable guess would be 55–60 thousand. The major source of uncertainty with this estimate is whether the same Colombians who are without immigration papers in Venezuela (indocumentados) are also not captured in the Colombian permanent emigration figures. We assume here that the two groups are identical.

The data on immigration and emigration of foreigners present similar difficulties. The main check on the DANE statistics is the Colombian census information. The 1951 and 1964 population census recorded, respectively, 27,133 and 33,129 foreigners in the Colombian labor force,[36] for an increase of 5,996 over that period. A net emigration of 33,849 foreigners during 1955–1964 is indicated by the migration statistics. If the participation rate of foreigners leaving (entering) Colombia was the same as for all persons leaving (entering), this net emigration (made up of a gross emigration of 91,048 and a gross immigration of 60,199) would imply a decrease of 17,937 in the number of foreigners working in Colombia. Only if there was a heavy immigration during 1951–54 could the two sources be consistent; the figures on total entries and departures (table A.1) argue against this. In short, it is clear that the net flow of foreigners who reside in Colombia on a permanent basis cannot be estimated from the migration statistics. Perhaps the most plausible explanation for this fact is that many foreigners who on their arrival were appropriately not classified as permanent immigrants, because they did not plan an extended stay in Colombia, are later defined as permanent emigrants because they are leaving the country permanently. To make the figures parallel, persons would only be classified as permanent emigrants if they had been previously classified as permanent immigrants.

With the rough assumption that the foreign labor force in Colombia grew over 1955–68 at the same rate (1.55 percent per year) observed between the 1951 and 1964 population censuses, the absolute increase would be from 29,714 to 35,229, or 5,515 persons. Accepting the DANE figures for immigration of Colombians and for emigration over 1955–63, and assuming over 1964–68 that 60 percent went to the U.S., the net emigration of Colombians is estimated as 117 thousand. Implied in these figures is an overall legal net emigration of 112 thousand persons. Illegal emigration is very large but hopefully of limited concern to us here, if it may be assumed that a substantial majority of professionals migrate legally.

Statistics on the high-skill categories

Of more direct concern to us here are the statistics on the higher-skill groups. Assuming that primary interest is attached to the flows of Colombians,[37] a major problem in interpreting the Colombian data by occupations is that the travellers recorded as being on permanent visas are not distinguished by nationality. A high share of these were non-Colombians, until the mid-1960s when the share went down sharply (see table A.1). It is useful, once again, to compare figures on total immigration of Colombians and professionals to the

---

[36]See Dane (undated (a); 1967).
[37]This is actually on persons who have, at one time or another, had long-run plans to reside in Colombia; but the data do not permit the isolation of this category.

U.S. with those of emigration from Colombia. Table A.3 compares Eusse's (1970) series for professionals[38] with those we derived from DANE data. As with the aggregate statistics, there is evidence of underreporting in the late sixties; reported immigration of professionals to the U.S. exceeds the DANE based estimate of professional Colombian permanent emigrants from Colombia in 1969. A presumption of underreporting for professionals is created by the evidence of severe overall underreporting of permanent emigration; over 1966–69 Colombians immigrating to the U.S. (28,589) were over twice the number of Colombians reported as emigrating from Colombia, regardless of destination (11,224). It is true that from 1966 on the share of all recorded permanent emigrants classified as professionals rose sharply. This could suggest less serious or even no underreporting of departing professionals (at least through 1968), or it could be the result of a sharp real increase in the share of emigrants who were professionals – perhaps due to the changed immigration laws in the U.S. – and thus consistent with the same degree of underreporting of professionals as others. Such an increase in the professional/total ratio for emigrants is not at all suggested by the data on Colombian immigrants to the U.S., rather the contrary (table A.3). One possibility is that in the face of the increasing preference in countries of immigration for professionals, there was an (increased) upward bias in the reporting of occupation. But it is not clear why persons coming to Colombia would also do this, and the profession/total share rose for them as well. The most likely reason is a change in the DANE classification of permanent emigrants (immigrants), resulting in an elimination of a disproportionate number of the nonprofessionals previously so classified. Eusse's estimates for 1966–68 were evidently not based on the DANE data, suggesting the belief that the data were not accurate.

In 1964–65, by which time most persons listed as permanent emigrants (professional or otherwise) were Colombians, the number of permanent professional emigrants reported gives a good indication of the number of Colombians so characterized; the ratio 'Colombian professional immigrants to U.S. to recorded Colombian professional emigrants' averaged 0.76 or 0.85 – depending on which estimate of Colombian professional emigrants is chosen from table 2; over 1966–68 it averaged 0.42 or 0.49. Earlier, over 1961–1963, it had averaged 0.29 or 0.48; and over 1961–68, the averages were 0.43 and 0.57.

Over the whole of the period under consideration, it seems clear that the official data have underreported total permanent emigration, but it is also probable that the reporting of occupation has been biased toward the higher prestige categories like professionals. As a result the number of professionals emigrating could be either overreported or underreported.

With respect to foreign born professionals working in Colombia, some hints are provided by the Colombian population censuses. In 1951 and 1964, foreign

---

[38]This includes technicians and kindred workers.

born persons working in Colombia numbered 27,133 and 33,129, respectively. Foreigners were not disaggregated by occupation, only by sector. They were found disproportionately in the sector where most professionals are concentrated, i.e., services. If one applies the observed sectoral 'professional–total labor force' ratio to the sectoral distribution of the foreign labor force, and assumes that no foreigners were working as maids, the implicit estimates of foreign professionals are 1,860 for 1951 and 4,384 for 1964. However, this 'professional–total labor force' ratio in a given sector may be higher for foreigners than for nationals. If, for example, it were twice as high, the figures would be 3,720 for 1951 and 8,768 for 1964, and these are probably closer to the truth. Note that if one accepted the figures of col. 3 of table 2 as net emigration of professionals over 1955–64, col. 5 of table 2 and col. 7 of table A.3 as, respectively, emigration and immigration of Colombian professionals, then by implication the movement of foreign professionals over that period would have been a net outflow of 11,173, inconsistent with the population census figures.

A.2. Data on education

Magnitude of educational subsidies to emigrants

The average public subsidy per student going through the educational system is estimated in table A.4. The major problem in estimating the amount per emigrant is the lack of information on whether emigrants tend to have utilized public educational facilities (especially universities) more or less than the average student.

University graduates

Data for the period 1960–1973, by the categories used elsewhere in this study, are presented in table A.5.

A.3. Remittances of Colombians working abroad

This variable, unfortunately, is one of the hardest to estimate for Colombia, since no detailed studies have been done on it. The IMF presents figures for 1970–72,[39] but these are so low (an average of 7.3 million dollars per year) as to imply an implausibly low per worker remittance of about 10 dollars per year. Emigrants from Greece and Spain, for example, where the remittance phenomenon has been studied in some detail, sent back in the neighborhood of half a billion dollars per year, according to the IMF Balance of Payments Yearbook. In each case the remittance per emigrant worker is in the hundreds of

---

[39]See International Monetary Fund (1972).

dollars. In the case of Colombia, of course, this figure would be much lower, since many of the emigrants work at relatively low paying jobs in Venezuela and since a higher share of workers are permanently settled in the country of current residence, leaving their ties with the home country less strong. Still, it would seem reasonable to place the average in the range of 50–100 dollars as of 1971. Gall (1972, p. 3) emphasizes the considerable remittances of the 'indocumentados' in Venezuela; in his view these appear to run into the tens of millions of dollars.

In the early seventies it would appear that, say, 600–700 thousand Colombians may have been working abroad. The participation ratio of emigrants is above average because the age structure is tilted towards the working years; thus while the overall participation rate in Colombia was 0.294 in 1964, the rate for persons recorded in the 1961 Venezuela population census as having been born abroad, about one fifth of them from Colombia, was 0.627. Illegal residents might have a lower participation rate but probably not dramatically so. For earlier years we employed the following assumptions to calculate dollar remittances: (1) a remitting population growing at 7 percent per year, and (2) real remittances per person growing at 2 percent per year. Nominal dollar remittances allowed also for the U.S. inflation: they were converted to pesos at the principal selling rate plus 15 percent in 1961–63, and the principal selling rate plus 5 percent for 1966–68. (A good share of remittances are converted in the black market.) Assuming 650 thousand such workers, remittances would have been 22–66 million dollars. Under these assumptions total annual remittances would be about 17–35 million dollars in 1961–63 and 24–48 million dollars in 1966–68.

The share of professionals among all Colombians working abroad is of course small. As a share of recent immigrants to the U.S. it has usually been less than 10 percent. In the 1960s the share of working Colombians abroad falling in this category would perhaps be 4–6 percent. If we assume their per capita remittances were 1.5–2.5 those of nonprofessionals, their annual contributions during 1961–63 would have been 10–35 million pesos, and during 1966–68 44–112 million pesos.

For the net emigrants of these two periods, assuming an annual increase of 2 percent in the real remittance of a person of given age and preparation, and applying a discount rate of 10 percent (8 percent) to future remittances over 20 years, the present value of future remittances would be 7–29 million and 6–44 million for the groups emigrating in 1961–63 and in 1966–68, respectively. The wide range between the two limits reflects the number of coefficients used in the estimate about which our knowledge is very partial.

Table A.1

Colombia: Emigration by category.

Year	Residents planning to stay abroad more than one year (Colombians or foreigners)			Nonresident foreigners leaving	Residents planning to remain abroad less than one year	Total
	Total (1)	Colombians[a] (1a)	Others (1b)	(2)	(3)	(4)
1936						9,898
1937						10,738
1938						13,788
1939						12,712
1940						12,515
1941						18,087
1942						14,547
1943						(16,653)
1944						(19,613)
1945						(22,333)
1946						(34,708)
1947						(33,964)
1948						
1949						(29,933)
1950						(34,641)
1951						(36,141)
1952						(41,819)
1953	23,990			21,864		45,854
1954	12,459			38,266		50,725
1955	20,208	3,996	16,212	30,469		50,677
1956	13,710	4,019	9,691	39,136		52,846
1957	10,114	4,086	6,028	36,549		46,663
1958	12,501	5,439	7,062	29,501	21,199	63,201
1959	16,102	7,084	9,018	28,746	34,737	79,585
1960	19,327	8,057	11,270	36,100	41,594	97,021
1961	18,833	7,851	10,982	32,643	43,055	94,541
1962	21,515	9,822	11,693	40,985	41,531	104,031
1963	21,725	12,654	9,071	40,450	54,781	116,956
1964	14,049[d]	11,028	3,021	60,650	66,328	141,027
1965	14,966[d]	11,167	3,799	68,607	53,043	136,616
1966	5,013[d]	4,018	995	82,482	58,217	145,712
1967	3,898[d]	3,049	849	100,528	61,683	166,109
1968	4,639[d]	3,360	1,279	118,114	70,594	193,347
1969[c]	1,220[d]	797	423	93,268	80,363	174,851
1970	498[d]	na	na	120,176	87,598	208,272
1971	na					288,921

Table A.1 (continued)

Colombia: Immigration by category; net emigration.

	Immigration								
	Nonresidents planning to stay more than one year			Returning residents		Visitors (nonresidents) (8)	Total (9)	Net emigration (10) = (4) − (9)	Net emigration of permanent migrants (11) = (1) − (5)
Year	Total (5)	Colombians[a] (5a)	Others (5b)	Colombians (6)	Foreigners (7)				
1936	(11,659)	(40)[b]	11,619				11,172	−1,274	12,371
1937	(9,200)	(40)	9,160				11,855	−1,117	3,299
1938	(10,837)	(40)	10,797				14,703	−913	9,371
1939	(11,689)	(40)	11,649				12,884	−712	2,061
1940	5,631	43	5,588				15,648	−3,133	4,483
1941	4,362	65	4,297				14,749	3,338	8,139
1942	2,137	20	2,117				14,525	22	13,965
1943	6,530	227	6,303				(16,745)	92	12,797
1944	6,335	220	6,135				(18,901)	712	12,498
1945	10,935	6,194	4,741				(24,575)	−2,242	10,580
1946	10,519	6,181	4,338				(38,043)	−3,335	11,206
1947							(35,411)	−1,447	
1948							(29,583)	350	
1949							(33,021)	1,620	
1950							(36,597)	456	
1951							(38,766)	3,053	
1952							45,815	39	
1953							49,399	−1,326	
1954				34,156			52,261	−1,584	
1955				40,199			54,959	−2,113	
1956				22,032			45,518	−1,145	
1957				19,014		24,256	61,776	−1,423	
1958				20,207		19,680	75,883	3,702	
1959				22,480	7,135	27,799	95,100	1,921	
1960				24,866	9,564	39,316	91,810	2,731	
1961				33,624	3,313	51,633	99,451	4,580	
1962				29,986	5,649	49,840	105,471	11,481	
1963				23,942	7,039	57,535	130,679	10,348	
1964	5,374[d]	1,140	4,234	35,348	8,731	50,793	122,065	14,551	(8,675)
1965	4,063[d]	939	3,124	52,472	11,342	61,491	140,461	5,251	(10,903)
1966	2,695[d]	513	2,182	36,163	12,870	68,969	161,096	5,013	(2,318)
1967	4,413[d]	1,180	3,233	41,030	13,850	82,886	178,266	15,081	(−515)
1968	2,632[d]	621	2,011	43,089	12,739	100,855	175,712	861	(2,007)
1969[c]	824[d]	132	692	40,967	7,744	126,935	205,450	2,822	(396)
1970	14[d]	na	na	54,814	5,108	114,966			(484)
1971	na			61,289	10,607	133,540			

[a]By nationality.

[b]( ) Estimates; data not available for Colombians but the figure would presumably be small, given those of subsequent years.

[c]Almost all (if not all) the demographic statistics were lower in 1969 than in 1968 (e.g., births, deaths, etc.). It seems possible, but not certain, that these migration figures are also underreported.

[d]Figures for these years (1964 and on) are not fully credible (see the discussion in the text). In 1964 the category labelled 'nonresident foreigners returning at the end of their visit' would appear to have been redefined. Evidently some of the persons subsequently included in that category (a large one) had previously been included in the category labelled 'resident nationals and foreigners'. In any case the sudden drop in foreigners listed as permanent departures was not matched by any significant decline for nationals.

Sources: DANE (1955–1967). For 1969–71, data are from tabulations supplied by DANE.

Table A.2

Arrivals of persons born in Colombia or having last permanent residence in Colombia to the U.S.[a]

		Arrivals by permanence of visit		Persons born in Colombia	Arrivals by visa status: nonimmigrants				Persons whose last permanent residence was in Colombia
Year	Total arrivals (1)	Persons in transit or returning resident aliens (2)	Others (3)	Immigrants born in Colombia (4)	Temporary workers and trainees (5)	Tourists (temporary visitors for pleasure) (6)	Students (7)	Other nonimmigrants (8)	Immigrants (9)
1951									
1952									
1953									18,048
1954									
1955									
1956									
1957									
1958	13,953	1,523	12,430	2,891	22	7,480	698	2,862	
1959	15,595	3,268	12,327	2,524	21	7,891	655	4,504	
1960	19,058	3,385	15,673	2,989	11	10,855	581	4,622	
1961	17,465	3,476	13,989	3,559	21	8,793	438	4,654	
1962				(4,698)[b]					
1963	33,678	4,936	28,742	5,733	18	19,897	801	7,229	25,047
1964	47,999	5,067	42,932	10,446	30	28,997	1,012	7,514	
1965	46,614	3,863	42,751	10,885	14	27,863	1,090	6,762	11,171
1966	41,414	3,915	37,499	9,504	26	23,825	1,203	6,856	9,736
1967	36,753	4,044	32,709	4,556	39	23,396	1,479	7,283	4,679
1968	53,022	6,588	46,434	6,902	98	34,051	1,669	10,302	6,999
1969	63,402	9,139	54,263	7,627	79	40,079	2,116	13,501	7,658
1970	65,755	10,865	54,890	6,724	158	40,503	2,762	15,608	6,738
1971	73,747	15,440	58,307	6,440	225	43,620	2,532	20,930	6,463
1972	89,587	24,468	65,119	5,173	202	50,307	2,976	30,929	5,225
1973	100,485	27,850	72,635	5,230	224	56,715	2,910	35,406	

[a] Persons in transit are included as are returning resident aliens.

[b] Estimate based on the number of immigrants whose last permanent residence was in Colombia; the latter was, over 1965–7, 1.025 times the number of immigrants born in Colombia.

Source: U.S. Immigration and Naturalization Service, Annual report.

Table A.3

Statistics on the migration of professionals into and out of Colombia.

Year	Professionals emigrating from Colombia				Professionals emigrating to Colombia				Colombian professionals immigrating to the United States (9)	Share (percent) of professionals in total Colombian immigrants into the United States (10)
	Eusse series (1)	Total (2)	Authors' series		Eusse series (5)	Total (6)	Authors' series			
			Colombians (3)	Foreigners (4)			Colombians (7)	Foreigners (8)		
1955	4,674	3,757			947		5			
1956	2,937	2,055			1,079		6			
1957	1,784	1,462			987		6			
1958	1,939	1,691	487	1,204	692	798	10	788		
1959	2,538	2,228	668	1,560	357	312	2	310		
1960	4,226	3,717	1,328	2,389	1,278	1,313	39	1,274		
1961	4,125	4,046	1,119	2,927	1,230	1,417	40	1,377	376	10.6
1962	4,035	3,956	1,080	2,876	1,778	1,749	929	820	511	10.9
1963	3,071	3,166	1,089	2,077	1,821	1,927	1,065	862	691	12.1
1964	1,377	1,475	909	566	1,483	1,421	262	1,159	973	9.3
1965	1,810	2,008	1,263	745	989	966	188	778	868	8.0
1966	3,117	837	627	210	1,205	879	133	746	777	8.2
1967	1,315	700	521	179	1,306	1,363	295	1,068	404	8.9
1968	1,450	721	498	223	1,976	866	161	705	764	11.1
1969		159							669	8.8
1970									395	5.9

Sources: Cols. (1) and (5) are from Eusse (1970). Cols. (2)–(4) and (6)–(8) are the authors' calculations based on the DANE data cited in table A.1. The separate estimates of emigration for Colombians and foreigners utilized the methodology described in table 2, estimate B, with no adjustments. A similar methodology was used for the immigration estimates. Col. (9) is from U.S. Immigration and Naturalization Service, Immigration into the United States of aliens in professions and related occupations, annual indicator.

Table A.4

Per student government subsidies to education, 1962 and 1967.

	1962		1967	
	Low estimate	High estimate	Low estimate	High estimate
Post-secondary	20,300	25,900	25,550	34,631
Secondary	702	4,725	4,741	4,643
Primary	500	735	706	1,017
Total	25,502	31,360	30,997	40,291

Sources and Methodology: The data come from DANE (1964; 1972 undated (b)). Several arbitrary guesses had to be made as to the distribution of certain expenditures by level of education, and as to the appropriate assumptions about capital costs (which fortunately are not the bulk of public expenditures on education). But the informal confidence level implicit in the limits shown is high.

Table A.5

Professionals graduating from Colombian universities by field, long and short courses, 1960–1973.[a]

Areas	1960	1961	1962	1963	1964	1965	1966	1967	1968	1969	1970	1971	1972	1973	Accumulated total 1960–1973
Total long duration[b]	2025	2541	2819	3269	3950	4283	4803	5277	5892	7111	8209	7832	10329	10925	79,263
Business administration, economics, accounting and similar	75	178	227	205	340	527	613	787	816	1,144	1,403	1,386	2,098	2,229	12,028
Agricultural sciences and similar	107	149	176	231	318	348	430	470	573	647	608	512	687	918	6,174
Architecture and fine arts	157	142	148	148	124	236	234	248	329	425	440	446	530	470	4,077
Exact sciences, natural sciences	100	102	50	105	118	100	142	125	77	126	191	240	302	318	2,096
Health	643	760	706	763	857	723	791	754	747	938	975	952	1,192	1,163	11,964
Social sciences	56	85	80	82	140	205	217	284	307	368	579	498	619	729	4,249
Law	387	410	491	646	723	869	821	814	711	933	1,010	1,054	1,248	1,273	11,390
Education	133	411	218	285	436	475	634	815	942	1,087	1,309	1,127	1,528	1,834	10,694
Humanities	60	93	99	95	98	96	96	109	194	177	293	290	413	343	2,456
Engineering and related	307	481	624	709	796	704	825	871	1196	1,266	1,401	1,327	1,710	1,648	13,865

[a]Data differs slightly from those presented in ICFES, Estadisticas Universitarias, 1960–70 and 1971, 1972, 1973 due to corrections made as a result of visits by ICFES personnel to some of the educational institutions.
[b]Lead to a professional degree; 4 years or more of study.
Source Instituto Colombiano para el Fomento de la Educacion Superior (ICFES), oficina de planeacion, seccion de estadistica.

References

Berry, A. and R. Soligo, 1974, Optimal wage and education policies in light of the 'brain drain', mimeo (Rice University, Houston).

Berry, A. and R. Soligo, 1969, Some welfare aspects of international migration, Journal of Political Economy 77, no. 5.

Bhagwati, J. and W. Dellalfar, 1973, The brain drain and income taxation, World Development 1, nos. 1–2, 94–101.

Chaparro, F.O. and E.O. Arias, 1970, La emigracion de profesionales y tecnicos Colombianos y Latino Americanos 1960–1970, Fondo Colombiano de Investigaciones cientificas y proyectos especiales 'Francisco Jose de Caldas' (COLCIENCIAS, Bogota).

DANE, undated (a), Censo de población de Colombia 1951: Resúmen (DANE, Bogota).

DANE, undated (b), Anuario de estadisticas fiscales y financieras 1966–1967 (DANE, Bogota).

DANE, 1955–1967, Anuario general de estadistica (DANE, Bogota).

DANE, 1964, Estadisticas fiscales 1960–1962 (DANE, Bogota).

DANE, 1967, XIII Censo nacional de población (15/7/74): Resúmen general (DANE, Bogota).

DANE, 1972, Boletin mensual de estadisticas no. 249 (DANE, Bogota).

DANE, 1974, Anuario demografico 1968–1969 (DANE, Bogota).

Dougherty, C., 1971, El futuro de la educacion Colombiano: Proyecciones y prioridades, Revista de Planeación y Desarrollo 1, no. 1.

Eusse, G.H., 1970, The outflow of professional manpower from Colombia (Instituto Colombiano de Credito Tecnico y Estudios Tecnicos en el Exterior (ICETEX), Carácas).

Gall, N., 1972, Los indocumentados Colombianos, American Universities Field Staff Reports, East Coast South America Series 16, no. 2.

Henderson, G., 1970, Emigration of highly skilled manpower from the developing countries (UNITAR, New York).

IMF, 1972, Balance of payments yearbook, 1972 (IMF, Washington).

Schultz, T.F., 1968, Returns to education in Bogota, Colombia, Rand Corporation memo RM 5645–RC/AID, September.

Selowsky, M., 1960, El efecto del desempleo y el crecimiento sobre la rentabilidad de la inversión educational, Revista de Planeación y Desarrollo 1, no. 2, 5–68.

UNITAR, 1971, The brain drain from five developing countries (UNITAR, New York).

Venezuela, 1966, Noveno censo general de pablación (26/2/61): Resúmen general de la república, parte A(DGE, Carácas).

Venezuela, Dirección General de Estadistica (DGE) y Censos Nacionales, 1972, X censo general de población (2/11/71): Tomo 1: Resultados generales del país y de las entidades federales (DGE, Carácas).

PART V

ALTERNATIVE TYPES OF SKILLED MIGRATION

EDITOR'S NOTE

Jagdish N. BHAGWATI

While the focus of the customary economic analysis of the migration of skilled manpower from the LDCs is on the 'brain drain' where the migration is under 'normal' conditions, there are two other major 'types' of such emigration which need to be distinguished: (1) the expulsion of professionals, as in Uganda and (2) the flight of the bourgeoisie from a socialist transition, as in Allende's Chile.

Interestingly, in East Africa, all three of the skilled migrations we are distinguishing are to be found in cross-sectional coexistence: Uganda has the expulsion phenomenon; Tanzania is subject to the flight from a socialist economy; and Kenya has its brain drain (which, in turn, illustrates the difference between net and gross flows as Kenya receives the brain drain from Tanzania and loses to DCs outside East Africa).

While the skilled emigration of these three varieties is, in principle, modelled in essence in the same fashion as indeed is demonstrated in his paper in part V by Tobin's (1974) elegant and independent discovery of the loss of surplus to those left behind when aliens were expelled, there are fundamental asymmetries as well which await theoretical analysis and policy attention. Tobin touches on some of these asymmetries for the expulsion phenomenon. To these, one can add yet others. For example, while the problem of to-and-fro migration is important for the analysis of the brain drain, it is not for the expulsion situation. Again, for expulsion, remittances are most unlikely to be significant: not so for the brain drain.

The 'flight of the bourgeoisie' offers yet other contrasts. The phenomenon arises as a transition to a socialist economy implies redistribution of incomes, with a squeeze on the earnings and (possibly) wealth of the bourgeoisie, although the loss of a traditional 'life-style' must play a role in inducing the flight as well. The 'open-door' policy of Allende's Chile and Nyrere's Tanzania, putting up with the consequences of the resulting loss of skilled manpower, stands in contrast with the closed-door policy of the communist countries such as China, where the attractions of the outside world to the local elites enmeshed in the egalitarian policies of narrowed wage differentials have been neutralised by ruling out emigration. The emigration of skilled manpower during the transition to socialism is likely to be disruptive on a substantially larger scale than 'normal' brain drain, militating against the egalitarian policies[1] or against economic performance (and almost certainly resulting in the latter).[2] Unfortunately no systematic analyses of these open-door socialist economies are available to date and readers will have to address themselves to the issues without the aid of a suitable paper on the topic in this volume.

[1]This option is a possible response. Thus Pryor (1968) has noted that East German salary differentials tend to be among the widest for the East European countries, probably reflecting the relatively moderate difficulty with which disaffected professionals could escape the closed-door into West Germany.

[2]For a simulation analysis of the consequences of such and foreign-induced disruption in an economy seeking to transit to socialism, see Bhagwati and Grinols (1975).

References

Bhagwati, J. and E. Grinols, 1975, Foreign capital, dependence, destabilisation and feasibility of transition to socialism, Journal of Development Economics 2, no. 2, 85–98.
Pryor, F., 1968, Public expenditures in communist and capitalist nations (Allen and Unwin, London).
Tobin, J., 1974, Notes on the economic theory of expulsion and expropriation, Journal of Development Economics 1, no. 1; reprinted in this volume.

CHAPTER 13

NOTES ON THE ECONOMIC THEORY OF EXPULSION AND EXPROPRIATION*

James TOBIN

Yale University, New Haven, CT 06520, U.S.A.

1. Introduction

When aliens are expelled from a nation, what is the effect on the economic welfare of the remaining residents? The question is suggested in General Amin's expulsion of Asians and Europeans from Uganda.[1] A quieter, slower, and more humane policy of Africanization continues in Kenya, as non-citizens are gradually denied renewal of trade licenses and work permits. These policies are explicitly premised, at least in part, on the expectation that the economic welfare of African citizens will be improved, certainly in the long run if not immediately. Against this official premise stand the dire predictions of some observers and commentators, mostly foreigners, that these countries will suffer great economic loss by forcing productive members of their economies to depart.

What can economic theory say about this conflict of analysis and prediction? It is too much to expect to answer empirical questions without empirical research, which will not be able to provide conclusive answers for some time to come if ever. But theory should at least be able to offer some guidance for such research, delineating the facts on which the answers depend.

To avoid misunderstanding at the outset I stress two points. First, I am not concerned here with the ethics of policies of Africanization, either their objectives or the means by which they are pursued. The paper concerns only the efficacy

*The paper was written at the Institute of Development Studies, University of Nairobi, Kenya, where the author was a Visiting Professor 1972–73. I am grateful to the Rockefeller Foundation, the University, and the Institute for making the visit possible. To say the needless, they are in no way responsible for anything in the paper. The paper was originally written, and presented at an I.D.S. seminar, to provoke some *economic* discussion of the most striking and widely discussed current events in East Africa.

[1]I am aware that Amin expelled Ugandan citizens of non-African descent as well as aliens proper. Throughout the paper I use the terms 'aliens' and 'citizens', but I do not mean them in a literal juridical sense. In East Africa some citizens have more citizenship than others, and it is to describe the true sons and daughters of the land that the term *wananchi* has become current.

of the policies with respect to their stated objectives. Second, I am concerned only with the economic objectives and motivations of the policies. I recognize that the policies could have, doubtless do have, important political and social goals as well. Conceivably the majority of East Africans and their leaders would find the gains of 'controlling our own economy' worth some loss of per capita income and consumption, should that price have to be paid. Conceivably improvements in the positions of certain native elites might have decisive weight in political evaluation of the merits of expulsion, for national as well as self-interested reasons. I confine myself to the narrower question, the effect on the average per capita income of citizens.

The loss of human capital by expulsion is in many ways analogous to its loss via voluntary emigration, the 'brain drain' which has already been extensively analyzed by economists.[2] In both cases the basic theoretical presumption is the same. If just one worker who has been receiving his marginal product goes, voluntarily or involuntarily, the output available for those left behind is unchanged. This is true for any withdrawal which can be regarded as infinitesimal. But if a finite withdrawal occurs, the country loses some of the 'surplus' formerly obtained from productive inputs complementary to those of the remaining residents. The dominance of the complementary effects follows from the customary assumption that production sets are convex.

There are, however, some differences between 'brain drain' and expulsion. Expulsion without expropriation leaves the economy with a foreign debt burden. Expelled aliens have typically accumulated considerable property. Some of it they will manage to export in one form or another, and for immovable properties left behind they may be entitled to compensation. Young professional emigrants are likely to be less well endowed with non-human capital and will probably remit to the home country some of their earnings abroad. On this score, expulsion (without expropriation) is more damaging to the economy than brain drain.

A second difference that works the other way may be important. It is sometimes argued that brains are paid less than their marginal social product in poor developing countries. If there are real external benefits to the presence of natives of high education and professional skill, the standard argument understates the loss from their emigration. Such externalities seem less likely in the case of aliens, even those who are highly trained professionals. Just because they form a tightly knit community apart from the general culture, they have little spill-over as models or teachers for the native population. To the extent they have succeeded in erecting barriers to entry to certain occupations – a possibility analyzed below – their private product exceeds their social product.

---

[2] I am indebted to Jagdish Bhagwati (1973) for illuminating the similarities and differences. On 'brain drain', see his article with Hamada in this issue, and the literature there cited.

2. The standard argument

I will begin by rehearsing the standard argument. The first approximation it provides is a useful point of reference for further considerations. The proposition is that expulsion without expropriation cannot increase but may well decrease the average income of the remaining residents. This answer depends on certain assumptions which it is well to put on the table right away; some consequences of possible failure of these assumptions will be discussed in later sections. The assumptions are:

(a) As already stated, there is no expropriation of the non-human properties of the expelled aliens. They are paid full value for properties they leave behind, though they are not compensated for the loss of their incomes from personal labor and skill, 'human capital'.

(b) Before and after expulsion the economy is in competitive equilibrium, in which factors of production are paid their marginal private and social products.

(c) Production is subject to constant returns to scale in the economy, and production sets are convex. [That is, if x_1 and x_2 are any two feasible vectors of inputs and outputs, then any linear combination of them $bx_1 + (1-b)x_2$ $(0 \leq b \leq 1)$ is also feasible.]

(d) The output of the economy can be regarded as a single homogeneous commodity produced by a large number of inputs. This is a convenient, and I think innocuous, simplification. It enables me to define income unambiguously and to avoid welfare calculations in terms of utilities.

There is no need to prove the theorem here. Instead, I shall sketch the result, using a linear activity model of production. This will be convenient later for discussing some qualifications to the argument, but of course the basic proposition does not depend on this specialization of the production model.

The homogeneous output is produced by n inputs. The quantity of the ith input initially owned by citizens is c_i; the quantity initially owned by aliens is a_i; of this a_i' remains in the country after expulsion, while the remainder departs with the aliens $(0 \leq a_i' \leq a_i)$. The price of the ith factor, measured in terms of output, is p_i before expulsion and p_i' after expulsion. In each case the price of the factor is its marginal product. Initially, before expulsion, total output Y is $\Sigma p_i(c_i + a_i)$; this equality is assured by the assumption of constant returns to scale, which implies that payment of marginal products to all inputs just exhausts output. Of this total Y citizens receive $\Sigma p_i c_i$, which I will denote as y. After expulsion, total output Y' is $\Sigma p_i'(c_i + a_i)$. The income of citizens is $\Sigma p_i'(c_i + a_i') - \Sigma p_i a_i'$, y' for short. The second term in y' is the compensation annually paid to aliens, in the case of no expropriation, for the productive properties they left in the country. Note that this compensation is paid at the initial prices p_i, the earnings of these factors of production prior to expulsion. The 'first approximation' proposition is that y' is at most equal to y.

A further word about compensation is in order. We do not have to imagine a literal annual payment to the former alien owners. More likely they will have sold the properties outright and obtained in exchange foreign assets previously owned by the citizens or government of the country they left. Or that economy will have borrowed abroad the sums needed to pay the aliens full capital value. Either way there is an increase in the net annual interest burden on the economy payable abroad, equal to $\Sigma p_i a_i'$.

In summary:

$$y = Y - \Sigma p_i a_i = Y - \Sigma p_i a_i' - \Sigma p_i (a_i - a_i'), \tag{1}$$

$$y' = Y' - \Sigma p_i a_i', \tag{2}$$

$$y = y' = [Y - \Sigma p_i(a_i - a_i')] - Y'. \tag{3}$$

The question at issue is the value of $y - y'$ as given in eq. (3).

Production is a set of linear activities or processes. Each process is subject to constant returns to scale and is characterized by fixed requirements of various inputs per unit of output. Production of the homogeneous output can be carried out by any number of the m available processes, each one using some or all of the n factors of production. A competitive equilibrium is the solution of a linear programming problem, maximizing output subject to the constraints imposed by the n factor supplies. In the equilibrium some s processes are operated, where s cannot exceed either m or n. Correspondingly, s of the factor supply constraints – obviously never more than n or m – will be binding, while the remaining $n - s$ factors will be in excess supply. In linear programming jargon the selection of s operating processes and s fully employed factors is a *basis*, and the programming problem is to find that basis which maximizes total output, given the factor supply constraints.

Factor prices are marginal productivities. The prices of all the surplus factors are zero. The prices of the other s factors are found by imputing the value of the production of each operating process to the s non-surplus inputs used in its operation. They may be found by solving s simultaneous break-even equations, one for each process in the basis, for the prices of the s factors in the basis. At these factor prices, any process not in the solution basis, i.e., any process that is inefficient to use, would cost more to operate than it could produce.

How does the competitive equilibrium, the solution of the linear programming problem, change when factor supplies are altered by expulsion? There are two possibilities. One is that the solution basis is unchanged. This will certainly be the case if expulsion simply scales down all inputs proportionately. Constant returns to scale are built into the model. In this case, expulsion simply reduces the scale of the economy. Prices are unchanged, and so are the incomes of residents. If 5% of factor inputs are lost, production declines by 5%, but there are 5% fewer mouths to feed.

It is also possible that the basis is unchanged even if the relative supplies of inputs are changed. Geometrically, the production function consists of plane facets. Each facet corresponds to a different basis, as do the boundary lines and points between facets. The tangent or 'supporting' plane, instead of touching the production surface only along one line, the ray from the origin, may coincide with a whole facet. The change in factor supplies may not be so great as to move out of this facet. In this case, since the basis is unchanged, factor prices are

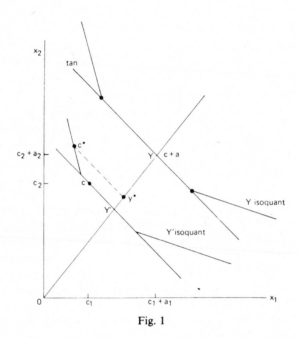

Fig. 1

unaffected and $y = y'$. A two-factor example is diagrammed in fig. 1. Here x_1 and x_2 are the two factors, owned in amounts c_1, c_2 by citizens and a_1, a_2 by aliens. For simplicity I take the a_i', alien-owned properties left behind, to be zero. Broken-line isoquants for outputs Y, obtainable with inputs $c_i + a_i$ and Y', obtainable with inputs c_i, are shown. Input prices before expulsion are represented by the slope of the isoquant through point $c + a$; citizen income before expulsion is indicated by a parallel line through point c. The output equivalent of citizen income before expulsion can be gauged by observing where this line intersects the ray from the origin to point $c + a$. In the case shown the value of citizen income is Y', which is also the value of output and citizen income after expulsion. This equality will be true so long as c is located anywhere on the middle segment of the y' isoquant. Suppose, however, it had been located on one of the other segments, say at c^*. Then initial citizen income would exceed y', and citizens would lose by expulsion. In the diagram this would be indicated by the fact that a line through c^* parallel to the original price line ('tan') would intersect the ray OY above Y'.

This illustrates the second and more interesting possibility, namely that the equilibrium basis is altered. Some processes formerly in operation may drop out, while others previously unused become efficient. Some factors initially surplus may become binding constraints, while others become unemployed for lack of cooperating factors. The dimension of the basis s may rise or fall. In any event the following is true: Let the prices p_i correspond to the initial basis B for factor supplies $c_i + a_i$, and the prices p_i' correspond to the post-expulsion basis B' for factor supplies $c_i + a_i'$. Then if B' is different from B, $\Sigma p_i(c_i + a_i')$ exceeds $\Sigma p_i'(c_i + a_i')$. Therefore $\Sigma p_i c_i$ exceeds $\Sigma p_i'(c_i + a_i') - \Sigma p_i a_i'$. That is, y exceeds y'.

The general proposition is the duality theorem of linear programming. The minimum valuation of given factor supplies occurs with the prices of that basis which maximizes the objective function (here total output) with those factor supplies. The prices of some other basis, one which would be the maximizing solution for a different set of factor supplies but not for this set, will give a larger valuation of the actually given factor supplies.[3]

There is another interesting and intuitively reasonable implication. The inputs withdrawn by the aliens are in aggregate more valuable, anyway not less, at the factor prices that prevail *after* their expulsion. It is not surprising; the factors most heavily reduced in supply would be expected to become relatively scarce and high-priced. To see this, use in reverse the theorem discussed and employed above: $\Sigma p_i'(c_i + a_i) \geq \Sigma p_i(c_i + a_i)$, that is:

$$\Sigma p_i'(c_i + a_i) + \Sigma p_i'(a_i - a_i') \geq \Sigma p_i(c_i + a_i') + \Sigma p_i(a_i - a_i').$$

But

$$\Sigma p_i'(c_i + a_i) \leq \Sigma p_i(c_i + a_i').$$

Therefore

$$\Sigma p_i'(a_i - a_i') \geq \Sigma p_i(a_i - a_i').$$

Before discussing below the limitations of the first approximation, I should emphasize what it does *not* mean. Let us assume, realistically I think, that the loss of inputs due to expulsion is uneven rather than proportionate, that aliens were not providing the same mixture of inputs as citizens. Let us assume indeed that the changes of relative factor supplies are drastic enough to alter the basis. So the first approximation conclusion is the stronger one that aggregate citizen

---

[3]Ties are of course possible. Two or more bases may be solutions for a given set of factor supplies. Prices will be indeterminate between them, but total output and factor income will be the same whichever basis and price system is used. I assume that if the basis and prices that prevailed before expulsion continue to be one of the possible solutions, even though not the only one, after expulsion they will continue to prevail.

income is lower after expulsion. This does not imply that *every* marginal product, every factor price, declines. Some citizens, those who can supply factors formerly provided substantially by aliens, will enjoy increases in their incomes. Others, those who supply factors complementary to aliens' productive inputs, will suffer losses. Convexity implies that in aggregate the complementary effects dominate, so the gains are smaller than the losses. But substantial shifts of income distribution can certainly occur.

If the East African stereotype of aliens as shopkeepers, traders, independent professionals or semi-professionals, and small business managers is accurate, citizens with these capacities will be in scarce supply after expulsion. Their marginal products and earnings will rise. On the other hand, citizens whose jobs and productivity depend on having shopkeepers, traders, professionals, and managers to assist will suffer.

I have distinguished between those alien inputs which are physically withdrawn from the country and those which remain after compensation of former alien owners. What difference does it make how alien inputs are divided between these two categories? At one extreme, if all alien inputs remained in the country – as would happen if all aliens were simply rentiers and absentee landlords – the argument implies that expulsion does not alter citizen income: $y = y'$. Indeed it does not even alter the distribution of citizen income. It doesn't matter whether the aliens are resident capitalists or non-resident capitalists.

We have no way to compare intermediate cases with each other or with the other extreme, where all alien factors are physically withdrawn. But realistically it is quite conceivable that citizen losses are especially acute when alien inputs are partly immobile and partly mobile. The immobile inputs may well be especially complementary to the mobile ones, so that the prices of the immobile inputs are especially depressed by expulsion. Yet the citizen economy is saddled with a debt for these immobile properties, calculated at the pre-expulsion prices. High complementarity of this kind seems likely between shops, workshops, and professional equipment and the self-employed proprietors and professionals who formerly owned and operated them. In other words, if the citizen economy had the option of destroying the immobile properties without compensating their alien owners rather than preserving and operating them while paying full compensation, the former alternative might well be chosen.

3. Alternative compensation and expropriation

It is time to recognize the third alternative, to keep the properties without full compensation at pre-expulsion values. Clearly citizens can gain by full or partial expropriation of aliens, or of non-residents for that matter. In the algebra, $\Sigma p_i'(c_i + a_i')$, with little or no deduction for debt to former owners of the a_i', may easily exceed $\Sigma p_i c_i$, even if the p_i are on balance better prices for citizen inputs than the p_i'. No one ever doubted that expropriation pays, at least in the short run before repercussions on foreign investment are felt. The basic first approximation proposition is that expropriation is the only aspect of expulsion that promises gains.

I have used 'expropriation' to refer to compensation less than the initial market values of the properties, the pre-expulsion prices p_i. But an alternative principle of compensation is to use the new prices p_i', and perhaps this does not merit the pejorative term 'expropriation'. In effect, the expelled aliens retain equity in the

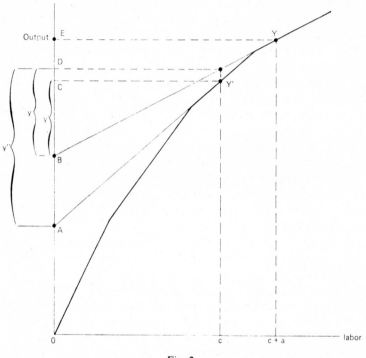

Fig. 2

properties they leave behind, and their earnings depend on the marginal productivities of these properties in the post-expulsion economy.

With this form of compensation, it is conceivable that citizens gain in aggregate. They will gain if their inputs are highly substitutable for the withdrawn alien inputs but complementary to the retained alien inputs. Imagine, for example, a two-factor economy, in which the ratio of alien-owned capital to alien labor is much higher than the ratio of citizen-owned capital to citizen labor. Expulsion of alien labor raises the overall capital–labor ratio and raises wages. The marginal product of capital declines, and with respect to alien-owned capital the decline is absorbed by alien owners rather than by citizens. The country is not burdened with the obligation to pay the aliens the pre-expulsion earnings of their properties.[4]

This case is illustrated in fig. 2, where the broken line $OY'Y$ represents the relationship of output to labor input, on a given capital stock, assumed for convenience to belong wholly to aliens. Before expulsion total labor input is $c + a$, of which c is provided by citizens. Expulsion reduces output from Y to Y'. Initially the wage rate is the slope of the line BY. Total labor income is BE, but only y of it (BD) is earned by citizens. Capital income is OB. On the first principle of compensation, capital will continue to earn OB, and citizen income after paying the compensation will be only y' (BC). The competitive wage rate after expulsion is the slope of AY', and the competitive earnings of capital are reduced to OA. On the second principle of compensation, citizens as workers earn and retain y'' (AC).

Two questions arise, one ethical and one empirical. The ethical question is difficult. On the one hand, aliens could argue that the decline in the value of their property is not a normal risk of ownership, but a consequence of their own expulsion, injury added to injury. In response, citizens could complain that aliens never had the right to believe their capital would be immune to the residential and citizenship policies of the nation.

The empirical question is whether citizens would in fact gain by expulsion even with the second method of remuneration. The example just described is only a possibility, and it depends on a high and perhaps unrealistic degree of substitutability between citizen and alien labor.

4. Occupational barriers

The argument so far was based on the assumption that factor incomes are competitively determined, equal to the marginal products of available factor supplies. But, it will be asked, what if the aliens had some monopolistic market power?

The first answer is merely an extension of previous arguments. If the monopolies were attached to particular immobile properties and sites owned by aliens, and if the compensation paid them fully capitalized the monopoly incomes, transfer of these properties and sites to citizen ownership and operation cannot increase aggregate citizen income. Of course the new owners and managers may not shoulder any or all of the debt burden, so that they personally benefit. But other citizens, taxpayers or consumers, will suffer correspondingly. Once again the gain, if any, can only come from expropriation.

If expulsion were the occasion for eliminating the monopolies associated with these properties, the citizen economy could gain whatever deadweight loss had been due to the previous distortion and misallocation. But this could presumably

---

[4]I am indebted to Richard C. Porter for insistently calling my attention to this possibility.

have been accomplished without expulsion. Indeed one may suspect that monopolistic power will be reinforced by the loss of potential competitors.

Other monopolies may have been attached to the mobile human capital or
labor skills of the expelled aliens. Suppose that there had been artificial restrictions on entry into occupations where aliens were heavily represented but
qualified citizens were excluded. Excluded citizens were forced into lower-
paying occupations below their capacities, occupations where their marginal
products were further depressed by the artificially swollen supplies. When the
aliens leave, citizens take their slots. Here there is a potential gain in citizen
income. The loss of alien inputs is at least partially compensated by an upgrading
of marketable citizen factor supplies.

An extreme example will make the point. Suppose that all aliens benefited,
so far as their mobile inputs are concerned, from restrictions on entry to their
occupations. Suppose that exclusion of qualified citizens from these high-paid
occupations resulted, via a chain of bumpings down the ladder, in an actual
surplus of general unskilled citizen labor. (The linear production model allows
for the possibility of surpluses of some factors.) The marginal product and price
of this labor is then zero. Suppose that this unemployment was no larger than
the number of privileged skilled aliens expelled. After expulsion the citizen labor
force shuffles up the skill ladder. At every rung qualified recruits replace departing aliens or replace other citizens who move up to fill higher-level vacancies.
There is a new set of citizen factor supplies c_i', identical to the old factor supplies
$c_i + a_i - a_i'$, which were distorted by monopolistic restrictions before expulsion.
Therefore the total output of the economy will be unchanged, but now all of it,
except the compensation for aliens' immobile inputs $\Sigma p_i a_i'$, belongs to citizens.
Citizen income gains by $\Sigma p_i(a_i - a_i')$.

The analysis is the same in principle but more complex in detail if the
restrictions took the form of excluding potentially qualified citizens from education and training. For example, maybe citizen children capable of acquiring
the same human capital as aliens were prevented from doing so by allocation of
school slots to alien children. Presumably then the returns on investment in
citizen human capital, especially in view of the low opportunity cost of diverting
young citizens from labor force to schooling, exceeded the social interest rate.
In the long run the human capital of the departing aliens is replaced, and the
returns on it all accrue to the citizen economy. And these returns, thanks to the
sub-optimal level of education and training in the first place, exceed the interest
costs of the investment.

Others can judge better than I the realism of these scenarios, or of less extreme
scenarios with the same qualitative results. They cannot be either excluded or
accepted a priori. Were aliens in East Africa in fact able to restrict citizen entry
and competition in their professions and lines of business? Were they in fact able
to keep citizens out of scarce school slots or to prevent the expansion of educational opportunities for citizens? If so, an economist is bound to observe that

anti-monopoly pro-competitive measures were an alternative to expulsion. Indeed the argument above suggests that these measures would add more to citizen income than expulsion could. Better to retain the aliens and their skills, but to pay them only their true competitive marginal products, the prices they would command in competition with all qualified citizens.

5. Other possible qualifications

The assumption of constant returns to scale may not be justified. How would the first approximation conclusions have to be modified? On the one hand, it might be argued that there are diminishing returns to scale in the inputs of labor and reproducible capital because of limited supplies of natural resources, for example unimproved land. On these grounds diminution in population, even accompanied by a proportionate curtailment of capital inputs, could be welcomed because it would raise output per unit of input. I doubt the applicability, or at least the importance, of this consideration in East Africa, where population density is not high and much land and space are unused.

On the other hand, the national markets may be so small that many economies of scale have yet to be fully exploited. Even though the countries engage in international trade, the size of their domestic markets is relevant, given the natural obstacles and costs of distance as well as tariffs and other governmental barriers to free trade. On this score, reduction in the size of the domestic market by expulsion is, other things equal, bad for per capita income. Expelled aliens in England and India are not a substitute, so far as the size of the market is concerned, for aliens in Nairobi and Mombasa and Kampala – a fact reinforced by the likelihood that their marginal productivities are lower in their new and strange locales.

Another assumption that might be challenged is the aggregation of output into a single homogeneous good in the models analyzed above. Departure of aliens probably changes the mix of output, since their tastes are not the same as those of citizens. Some may wonder whether aliens' high incomes were due to the fact that their inputs were especially well adapted to the pre-expulsion final bill of goods and would not be so valuable in producing the goods and services favored in a citizen economy. The question almost refutes itself. In the extreme, the aliens might have been a separate economy, producing for themselves to satisfy their own tastes. If so, their departure – regardless of how rich they were – could neither help nor harm the separate citizen economy. To the extent that their incomes were due to their own tastes, their influence on the rest of the economy was neutral. If they earned incomes by selling to citizens, it is because their inputs were in some degree adapted to citizen tastes, and their withdrawal has the kind of effects already described.

One could indeed apply a two-country international trade model to the alien and citizen communities and obtain the standard conclusion that normally each side gains from trade, or at worst does not lose. The extreme possibility that aliens manipulate the terms of trade so as to capture all the gains for themselves means that citizens would not lose by the termination of the trade when the aliens depart. It does not mean that they would gain. Anyway this suspicion is just the question of alien monopolies in another guise, a subject already discussed in the previous section.

6. Concluding remarks

Sometimes official economic rationales of policies of Africanization, implicit and explicit, seem to be based on an image of the economic process quite different from the models discussed above. The image is an economy whose aggregate wealth and income are naturally and exogenously determined, independently of the effort, skill and saving of the inhabitants. Jobs and shops and businesses are just tickets that allow the holders to claim shares of these exogenously fixed, though it is hoped growing, amounts of wealth and output. The tickets can be reassigned without danger to the total, so obviously the lot of citizens can be improved by giving them tickets formerly held by aliens. Maybe such an economy is approximated by an oil-rich sheikdom or by a country whose land effortlessly yields crops for export or home consumption or displays scenic beauties greatly prized by foreigners. But it is a dangerous model for almost all real countries, and a possibly serious consequence of expulsion policies may be that these rationales will be believed by the governments that espouse them and the people the policies are supposed to benefit.

Economics and economic theory cannot evaluate that danger, and they are equally helpless to appraise an intangible effect of great potential importance in the opposite direction. This is the response of the populace to national challenge, evoked by the political appeal of economic independence and self-sufficiency and even accentuated by the initial hardships and disruptions incident to expulsion. (Let us show the world and ourselves that we can do it on our own, just as the Egyptians confounded skeptical prophecies and operated the Suez Canal.) The example of communist China shows that nationalistic and patriotic motivations, tinged until fairly recently with xenophobia, can support indigenous economic progress. Whether the example can be copied in Africa or elsewhere, with or without communism, only the future can tell. But the Chinese case suggests one more lesson, namely that economic progress occurs after 'wars' of economic independence stop and are supplanted by hard work and careful administration, sustained by appropriate shift in the party line. In some ways the Great Cultural Revolution of the 1960's in China was the moral and political equivalent of the policies of expulsion and Africanization in East Africa. It did considerable economic damage, but the Chinese leadership knew when to declare peace and to shift the emphasis of policy and propaganda from blaming economic ills on enemies to extolling hard work and self-reliance.

INDEX